Contents

6 ■ Management and leadership

7 ■ Structure in organisations

8 ■ Organisational power, politics and conflict

9 ■ Organisational culture

10 ■ The impact of national culture on organisational behaviour

Case studies

Contributors

Ian Brooks is Head of School of Business and Management at University College Northampton. His research interests include the study of organisational culture and sub-culture, new managerialism and the NHS.

Hugh Davenport is a Senior Lecturer in Organisational Behaviour and Occupational Psychology in the School of Business and Management at University College Northampton. He co-edits *Occupational Psychologist*.

Jon Stephens is a Senior Lecturer in International Business in the School of Business and Management at University College Northampton, with research interests in international and comparative management.

Stephen Swailes is a Principal Lecturer and Strategic Management Subject Group Leader in the School of Business and Management at University College Northampton. His research interests include the study of organisational commitment, particularly among professional employees, and psychometric evaluation.

Preface

This book provides an introduction to organisational behaviour. It is intended for students on a range of courses including:

- Business Studies/Business Administration or similar business and management undergraduate degrees at level 1 or 2.
- a half or full module in Organisational Behaviour on a variety of different undergraduate programmes.
- post experience/postgraduate courses, part of which comprise Organisational Behaviour as an introduction or underpinning of HRM, management of change, crosscultural management, or business strategy.
- a general reader as a focused and lively introduction to the subject.

The book is shorter and, arguably, more accessible than the market leaders in the field. It provides a more succinct and focused, yet robust, coverage of the subject. In my experience many undergraduate students find a larger text, particularly those of North American origin, inaccessible and rather daunting. Considerable research was undertaken prior to the design of the text to ascertain the needs of students and tutors in this regard. Their responses and advice have directly influenced the design objectives and content of the book.

Every effort has been made to trace and acknowledge ownership of copyright. The publishers will be pleased to make suitable arrangements with any copyright holders whom it has not been possible to contact.

I should also like to acknowledge the contribution of Chris Blundell and Billie Osborne in providing administrative and academic support and guidance, and various student groups at University College Northampton for offering constructive feedback on the material.

Ian Brooks

1

Introduction

LEARNING OUTCOMES

On completion of this chapter you should be able to:

- appreciate the nature and scope of Organisational Behaviour (OB);
- recognise the value of a behavioural approach to management;
- appreciate the complex nature of individual and group behaviour within organisations;
- comprehend and appreciate the structure of this book;
- understand the importance of the three themes of change, conflict and communications to the study of organisational behaviour.

KEY CONCEPTS

- *individual behaviour*
- *group behaviour*
- *organisational behaviour*
- *multidisciplinary study*
- *theory to practice*
- *change*
- *conflict*
- *communications*

Introduction

Organisational Behaviour (OB) is the study of human behaviour in organisations, with a focus on individual and group processes and actions. Hence, it involves an exploration of organisational and managerial processes in the dynamic context of the organisation and is primarily concerned with the human implications of such activity.

Studying organisational behaviour

Organisational Behaviour (OB) is the study of human behaviour in organisations with a focus on individual and group processes and actions. Hence, it involves an exploration of organisational and managerial processes in the dynamic context of the organisation and is primarily concerned with the human implications of such activity. The subject is rooted in the behavioural sciences, notably sociology and psychology, and is similar in many respects to the study of management. It is an applied behavioural science which seeks to draw on a broad and extensive theoretical and practical knowledge base to advance our understanding of the complexities of human behaviour in organisations and to inform management thinking and activity. Both OB and management are social sciences partly informed by research and partly by debate in the traditional subject disciplines of psychology, sociology and, to an extent, anthropology, political science and economics. Psychologists are generally concerned with the study of individual human behaviour and the personality system, whereas a branch of that subject, social psychology, looks at group, including organisational, behaviour. Sociologists focus on social behaviour and are particularly concerned about societal structures and control. Anthropologists explore culture, that is, the symbolic, attitudinal and behavioural factors which unite various social groups. In so far as it relates to OB, political science is the study of power and control between individuals and groups whereas economics attempts to provide a rational explanatory framework for individual and organisational activity. As organisational behaviour has roots in many traditional academic fields, it is considered to be a multidisciplinary subject.

A knowledge of OB should enable you to explain and predict human behaviour in organisations and even control it if appropriate. Additionally, OB is both informed by and contributes to organisational theory and management theory and, as a consequence, it forms an integral part of most Masters and undergraduate programmes and sub-degrees in business studies and management.

The structure and rationale of this book

Many of the theories and arguments presented in this book have value to the work of managers and other employees in organisations. Even for students with little or no formal organisational work experience, the ability to apply OB to other 'organisational' contexts should prove possible and valuable. Your family, your circle of friends, sports or other clubs and the university or college in which you study are all organisations. Organisational behaviour is relevant to the work, and play, that takes place within these entities.

As a result of studying this subject it is quite possible that you may alter your 'management philosophy' including, perhaps, long-harboured beliefs, and you may obtain the answers to outstanding questions about issues such as: how people are motivated or led, how groups or teams function, why the structure of an organisation influences the behaviour of people who work in it, and how both the culture and power relationships in organisations affect human behaviour at work. The study of OB should also enable you to diagnose organisational problems with some insight and expertise. Following that diagnosis you may be able to develop solutions to problems, ways of dealing with difficult 'human' issues or, perhaps crucially, ways of avoiding certain problems in the first place. In short, there is something very practical about many of the theories presented in this book: you, the scholar and the 'manager', will however need to interpret and apply them to the particular context in which you operate. That, if achieved, would represent a highly worthwhile, constructive and meaningful learning experience and should make you a more effective manager.

Human behaviour in organisations is complex as it is affected by, and in turn influences, an array of factors, including managerial action, changing competitive circumstances and new technologies. People in organisations interact with their environment, with stakeholders and with others in the organisation. There are significant differences in personality between individuals, many people behave differently in groups than when working alone and most are influenced by the norms and values of the organisation and of the society in which they live and work. These influences and interconnections make the study of OB inherently interesting and enlightening, especially for those concerned with human or people issues in organisations.

Overview of the book

In order to make the study of OB manageable, we have subdivided the broad subject into ten chapters. We begin, following this introduction, with consideration of the individual. Each person has a unique set of attitudes, perceptions and values which influence their personality and behaviour. This personality set affects the way people work, how they communicate with others and their propensity to co-operate in teams and be motivated and managed. Hence Chapter 2 looks at personality and perception, values and attitudes, learning and decision making. Remaining largely, but not exclusively, at the level of the individual, we look, in Chapter 3, at motivation. This is a critically important aspect of OB and of management theory and practice. The chapter explores some of the extensive and wide-ranging theoretical work and empirical research findings which inform our understanding of how people are motivated, and indeed demotivated, in the workplace.

Chapter 4 develops the level of analysis from the individual to the group. However, it begins this process by focusing on the various personality types that are thought to comprise a successful team. We explore the process of group formation and the nature, causes and consequences of inter- and intra-group conflict, in addition to the characteristics of successful group work.

The book then focuses on the organisation or macro-level of analysis, and Chapter 5 introduces this by outlining the development of thinking about organisations and management. It recognises that the way we work, think and behave in organisations is, in part, a product of organisational norms and accepted ways of organising. Knowledge of organisation and management theory gives you a particular insight into the development of modern organisations. We explore contemporary views and research in this regard and take a look at organisations through many different 'lenses' and from various perspectives. This enables you to appreciate the complexity of organisations and of people's behaviour.

Chapter 6 explores the nature of management and of leadership, discusses some of the principal schools of thought in this regard and examines contemporary thinking, particularly about leadership. The chapter also seeks to determine the qualities of successful leadership and explore the intrinsically behavioural nature of both leadership and followership. Chapter 7 explores how organisations are structured and how they consider issues of formal control. The chapter examines contemporary and possible future developments towards flexibility, and flexible organisations, drawing on a burgeoning research base.

There is a constant struggle for control in all organisations. Power and political activity are omnipresent. Chapter 8 explores these issues, in addition to powerlessness. Chapter 9 focuses on the anthropologist's concept of culture applied at the level of the organisation. Organisational culture, as a field of study, has become of great significance in the past two decades. It is widely believed that the culture of a company may have a major bearing on its attempts to change, on both the process and outcome of managerial decision making, on its competitiveness and upon its performance.

Chapter 10 broadens the subject of OB to consider the global context in which organisations operate and people work. It explores the nature and influence of national culture and cultural differences on managerial and workplace activity. This chapter seeks to draw together the topics and themes addressed in a global, dynamic, context.

In the interests of focus and brevity this text does not cover all the topics that are often considered within the 'territory' or remit of organisational behaviour, or at least, does not provide detailed coverage of them. These include aspects of personnel and human resource management (HRM). Certainly OB underpins and informs these functional areas and a knowledge of OB is a useful, if not essential, prerequisite for any personnel manager and all managers who, as part of their line responsibilities, work with people. It is, however, not essential for an OB book to discuss the various HR considerations which are adequately covered elsewhere. We have also avoided focusing on Organisational Development (OD) and other 'people issues', such as stress, organisational learning and the impact of technology. These topics are important yet would, if covered in appropriate detail, necessitate a far more weighty tome than this. The contents of this book represent the areas of focal importance in the subject and its design is, largely, derived from research conducted among academic tutors of organisational behaviour in over thirty universities and higher education organisations.

Case studies

Each chapter in the book contains a small number of mini-cases which serve to illustrate a particular aspect of the material covered. They aim to provide an insight into a 'real-life' scenario and are worthy of further analysis and debate. Some of the scenarios can be critically analysed or explored from a number of perspectives. Some encourage a management problem-solving approach whereas others invite fresh insights in order to better understand organisational behaviour.

A number of medium-sized case studies grouped at the end of the book illustrate the subject of OB. They aim to further develop your understanding of OB by encouraging you to apply many of the theoretical ideas covered in the book and explore explanations for observed behaviour. It is hoped that you will attempt to demonstrate your capacity for critical thinking when tackling the cases and make efforts to get beneath the surface in your analysis. It is also hoped that the cases will assist you to appreciate that organisational life is complex and rich and will help you to develop the capacity to engage in rigorous analysis of behavioural scenarios in organisations.

Three themes: change, conflict and communications

Three themes inform and influence a number of the topics covered in the book. These themes, organisational change, communications and conflict, often form separate chapters in OB texts. However, in an attempt to illustrate the interconnectedness of organisations and the all-embracing significance of these three themes they are integrated into each key chapter. To a large extent behaviour in organisations is influenced by and in turn influences the nature of change, communications and conflict. All three are omnipresent in organisations. They are part of the fabric and reality of organisational life. The degree of success in the management of change, the management of communications and the management of conflict influence the competitiveness of the organisation and its ability to meet its objectives.

The three themes closely relate to the main topics covered in this book, such as motivation, teamwork, structure, politics and culture. For example, organisational culture is often seen as 'an intangible glue' (Morgan, 1986) which binds people together. As such, it is argued, culture reduces potential conflict in organisations which have a strongly held value and belief system. Organisational change often goes hand in glove with cultural change; an appreciation of the former involves knowledge of the latter, whereas communication, in its broadest sense, is the mechanism whereby culture is learned and changed. Hence, these three themes improve our understanding of and enrich the concept of culture and the other topics covered. This approach should enable you to understand better the complexity of organisational reality.

Figure 1.1 illustrates the structure of this book. It indicates the main topic of each chapter, plus the three themes that are integrated throughout and the three levels of analysis; individual, group and organisation. The whole is enclosed in a circle, illustrating the global context in which organisations operate, reminding you of the significance of context in the study and appreciation of OB. The relentless trend

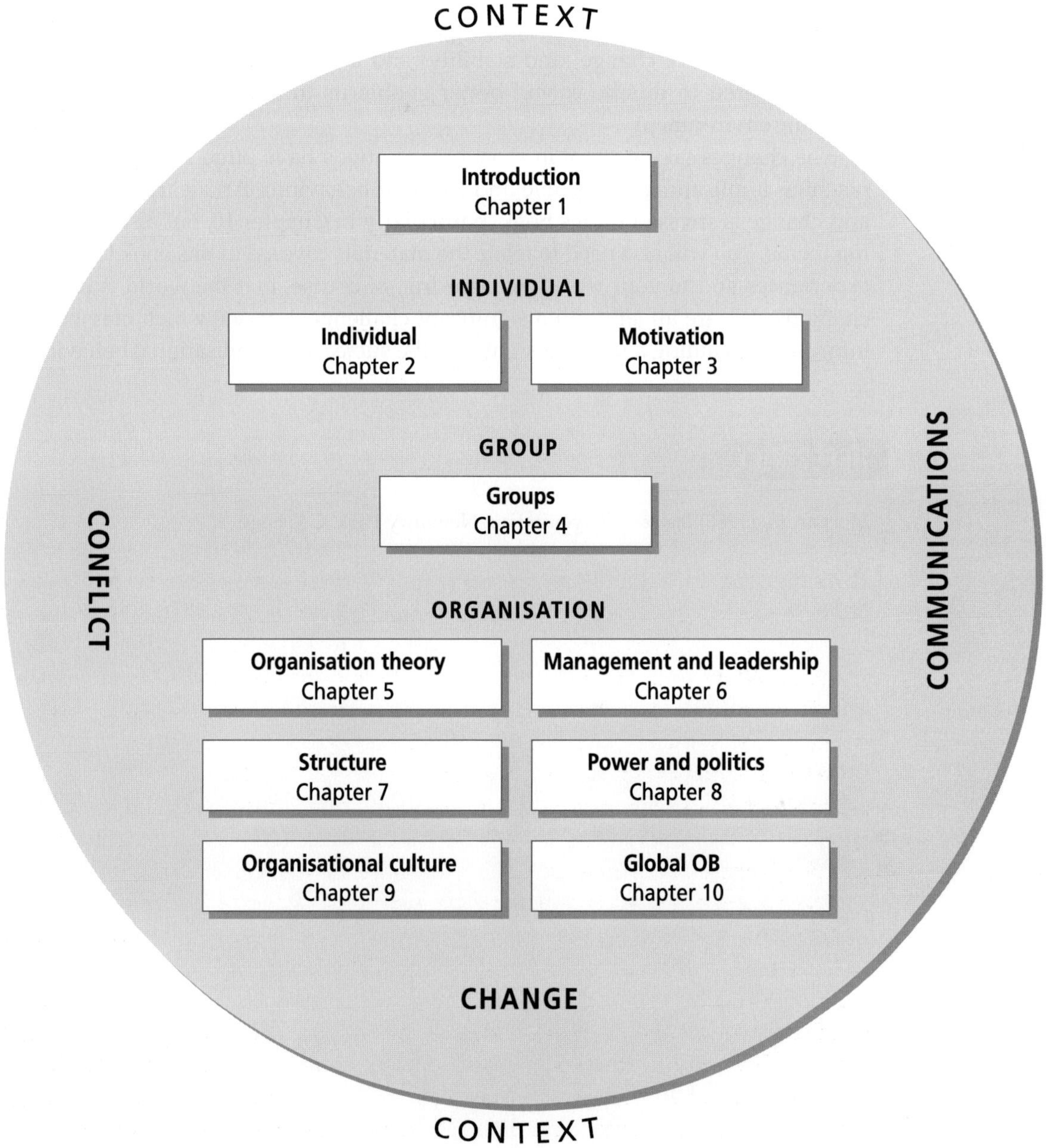

Fig 1.1 The structure of this book

towards globalisation, driven by technology in the fields of communication and information dissemination, together with the rapid pace of sociopolitical changes, are creating the highly dynamic global environment within which organisations now have to operate. Change in organisations can be said to be omnipresent and discontinuous, that is, it is not always predictable in its direction, its nature or its pace.

Ironically, and often not particularly usefully, most OB theories are not themselves dynamic. Nevertheless, the study of organisational culture is intrinsically linked to the appreciation of change (and stability) and a knowledge of many of the other topics covered in this book will better enable us to appreciate, and work in, a dynamic environment.

The changes taking place in most organisations have often immediate and far-reaching implications for people and for their behaviour. An awareness of context and change is stressed in this book, particularly in Chapter 10, but also as an ongoing theme. You will also need to relate the materials covered in this book to your own experiences and to your world, recognising, of course, that the world is itself ever changing. We are all left with a significant challenge, but one which may be better informed by gaining a useful insight into the subject of organisational behaviour.

REFERENCE

Morgan, G. (1986) *Images of Organization*. Newbury Park, CA: Sage.

2

Perspectives on individual behaviour

JON STEPHENS

LEARNING OUTCOMES

On completion of this chapter you should be able to:

- understand different theories about how personality is formed;
- appreciate how the organisation can use personality testing as a recruitment device;
- define and understand the process of how perception may influence the working of an organisation and the relative status of individuals in that organisation;
- understand how attitudes are formed in an organisation and identify the problem of attitudinal change;
- evaluate the process of incorporating values into an organisation at an individual level and assess the dangers of value conflict;
- appreciate how learning takes place at an individual level and how this can be influenced by the organisation;
- appreciate the importance of effective decision making and the significance of cognitive style;
- understand all of the above within the context of change, conflict and communication with particular reference to the Johari Window and psychological contracts.

KEY CONCEPTS

- *individual personality and behaviour*
- *personality in the organisation*
- *personality testing*
- *perceptual processes*
- *attribution theory*
- *attitudes and values*
- *individual learning*
- *learning styles*
- *individual decision making*
- *the Johari Window*
- *psychological contracts*

Perspectives on individual behaviour

An organisation comprises the individuals who make up its membership and it is the behaviour and interaction of these individuals which influence all other areas of organisational behaviour, whether group behaviour, leadership or the corporate culture of the organisation itself. Thus an understanding of individual behaviour is an essential tool to help us understand the way people behave and how they interact with each other and perhaps, even, to understand our own behaviour in an organisational context.

Introduction

An organisation, by its very nature, is composed of individuals who are 'organised' in some way or form in order to achieve certain objectives. Thus, individuals are the basic building material around which an organisation functions and an understanding of individual behaviour is an essential prerequisite to the exploration of how individuals work in groups and how the organisation itself behaves. Organisations sometimes forget this point in the struggle for corporate survival. However, it could be argued that the radical changes being forced on organisations as a result of increasingly turbulent environments are forcing them to reassess the role of individuals in terms of their capacity for individual and collective development and the potential which this has for revitalising the organisation. It is interesting that one of the most significant developments in recent years has been the concept of the Learning Organisation (Senge, 1990; Burgoyne, 1995) which seeks to develop people so that the organisation can constantly learn from good practice and continually adapt itself in a fast-moving environment.

Emphasis is being placed increasingly upon individuals in terms of assessing the significance of the personality of the key players in the organisation, how learning occurs in an organisation, how decisions are made, how values and attitudes are determined and how they can be changed and how perception influences all of these. This chapter examines some of these issues in the light of relevant theories and recent trends. The context of change and conflict in the organisation and the importance of communication as the effective cement which holds the organisation together are also considered.

Individual behaviour and personality

The starting point for an examination of individual behaviour in the organisation is personality. Personality theory overlaps strongly with other disciplines, most notably psychology, and there are a large number of personality theories (Ewen, 1988), each taking a different perspective. There is a similarly wide range of definitions of personality which can make the concept more complex. For our purposes we will define personality as: *specific characteristics of individuals which may be open or hidden and which may determine either commonality or differences in behaviour in an organisation.*

The definition given above suggests that personality affects other people in an organisation through interaction but also that it affects how individuals see themselves and thus the extent to which individuals are a positive or a negative force in the organisation. For example, personality differences can lead to hostility between individuals which could hinder the development of effective teams, although the right mix of different personalities can lead to the formation of efficient teams (Belbin,

1996). Attitudes and motivation are influenced by personality in terms of how individuals respond to motivational stimuli or, more negatively, how a negative concept of self can lead to attitudes which might hamper attempts to motivate individuals at an organisational level. Leadership styles are also affected and the ability to create commonality of purpose may be significant in relation to the process of developing a strong organisational culture.

Furthermore, it could be argued that personality may have a major bearing on the way people behave in an organisation. An issue often debated is the *extent* of this interaction, as it is argued that behaviour is determined by a number of innate factors, based around personal attributes, and also by a number of environmental factors outside the control of the individual. Some of these factors can be seen in Table 2.1.

Table 2.1 Variables affecting individual behaviour

Innate factors	Environmental factors
Personality	Organisation/work factors
Perception	Family
Values	Peer group pressures
Abilities	Personal life experiences
	National culture

The concept of factors affecting behaviour was developed by Lewin (1951) with the model:

$$B = f\,(P, E)$$

where: B = Behaviour
P = Person (innate) and
E = Environment

Lewin's theory suggests several ideas which have been developed by interactional psychology and which argue that people are influenced by both innate and environmental factors and that behaviour results from the continuous interaction between these factors. Furthermore, it suggests that environmental factors can be changed by situations in the organisation but also that they have the capacity to change the organisation. The person aspect indicates that people are influenced by many innate factors. The theory proposes that individual behaviour should be examined both from the organisational perspective (objective) and from the individual's perspective (subjective). In this chapter we focus primarily on innate individual characteristics, although we also look at organisational factors that influence, or are influenced by, different aspects of behaviour.

Personality theories

If we accept that personality is the driving factor influencing a range of innate characteristics of the individual, then we have to look at how personality is formed and to explore some of the typologies which relate to personality. However, just as with behaviour, there is a debate concerning the extent to which personality is innate or is determined by environmental factors such as those identified in Table 2.1. These two perspectives have been called a nomothetic perspective and an idiographic perspective (*see* Hicks, 1996). The nomothetic approach strongly supports the view that personalities are fixed and determined by heredity and cannot be significantly influenced by environmental factors. This approach would suggest that there are a number of clear personality types that can be identified and which it is possible to measure. This approach suggests that it might be possible to predict behaviour in the organisation.

The idiographic approach takes the opposite perspective and, while recognising that individuals do have unique innate characteristics, it also suggests that personality can be moulded and that both personality and behaviour are influenced by specific environmental experiences. On this basis supporters of this approach are less willing to accept the belief that personality can easily be identified by testing.

It is clear that the debate about whether personality is influenced by nomothetic or idiographic factors has implications for education and crime issues but in this chapter we look at personality theories from an organisational perspective.

Trait theories

Trait theories clearly fit the nomothetic approach in the sense that it is suggested that *people have certain inherent traits which determine their personality* and thus their behaviour (*see* Chapter 3 for a discussion of trait theories of motivation). These theories have been popular since the days of Hippocrates, who identified four main types of personality – phlegmatic, sanguine, melancholic and choleric – which were often incorporated into medical examinations in ancient times with often bizarre medical remedies being used to treat or temper these 'conditions'. The concept was developed further by Allport (1961) and Eysenck (1973), among others.

Eysenck (1973) identified a range of personality characteristics along scales from extrovert to introvert and neurotic to stable. Thus, phlegmatic could be seen as stable introvert, sanguine as stable neurotic, melancholic as neurotic introvert and choleric as neurotic extrovert. From this Eysenck suggested that if the relevant traits of an individual can be identified then that person's behaviour can be predicted. Although Eysenck's theory can be criticised for its relatively simple approach to a complex issue, it has attracted considerable attention from managers who saw the appeal of trait identification as a means of selection in the organisation. This idea was further developed by Cattell and Kline (1977) who devised a much more sophisticated range

Table 2.2 Cattell and Kline's 16 personality factors

Factor	Low score description*	High score description*
A	Reserved	Outgoing
B	Less intelligent	More intelligent
C	Affected by feelings	Emotionally stable
E	Humble	Assertive
F	Sober	Happy go lucky
G	Expedient	Conscientious
H	Sly	Venturesome
I	Tough-minded	Tender minded
L	Trusting	Suspicious
M	Practical	Imaginative
N	Forthright	Shrewd
O	Self assured	Apprehensive
Q1	Conservative	Experimenting
Q2	Group-dependent	Self-sufficient
Q3	Undisciplined	Controlled
Q4	Relaxed	Tense

*On scale of 1 to 10.

Source: Cattell, R. B. and Kline, P. (1977) *The Scientific Analysis of Personality and Motivation*, Academic Press, Table 4.1, pp. 44–5.

of traits which could be used as the framework for personality testing. These are shown in Table 2.2.

Trait theorists have argued (*see* Weiss, 1996) the existence of five main personality traits which are the most significant for determining behaviour. These key traits are:

- *agreeableness* – an individual can be seen as very agreeable or very uncooperative;
- *openness to experience* – the range is from very open minded to closed and narrow minded;
- *extrovert or introvert* – the range is from very sociable and outgoing to more reserved and cautious;
- *conscientiousness* – the range is from responsible to irresponsible;
- *emotionally stable* – the range is from an ability to control emotions to a more unstable emotional pattern.

Such theories continue to be the subject of criticism however, on the grounds that so close a focus on innate personality traits can mean that the influence of other factors is diminished or sidelined. It could therefore be argued that it is too simplistic an approach to yield meaningful insights into a very complex issue.

Humanistic approach

The humanistic approach, developed by Rogers (1970), also focuses on the individual and is nomothetic in parts. A central part of Rogers' view is that individuals experience a need for personal growth and fulfilment ('self-actualisation'). This approach is very much focused on the development of the individual but also explores the concept of 'self' and the self-concept, that is, how people perceive themselves. The potential fulfilment for the individual will depend upon the self-concept as much as, if not more than, on any objective measures of fulfilment or development.

Psychodynamic theory

Psychodynamic theory relates to the work of Freud and certainly possesses an idiographic (environmental) perspective in that Freud saw personality as being developed by a number of environmental factors, most notably parental relationships and the effects of various types of trauma. One significant aspect of Freud's work in the present context is the theory that behaviour can be driven by unconscious or hidden personality factors and that these influences can sometimes be used to explain various types of irrational behaviour. For Freud, behaviour and personality were determined by a constant battle between the id (which is the basic drive in the personality which can often act irrationally and on impulse), the superego (which imposes a whole range of environmental influences such as parental and societal factors on to the mind or conscience) and the ego (which seeks to balance the often conflicting directions of the id and superego).

It is suggested that it is this compromise by the ego which leads to certain behavioural characteristics. Some of these may be significant for the organisation, such as 'denial' – where the individual refuses to recognise a change which can be harmful and so ignores it. 'Compensation' is another behavioural characteristic – where an individual compensates for weaknesses in one area by doing too much in another, for example, avoiding making important strategic decisions by making numerous small operational ones which still avoid the main problem.

Although Freud's work has led to the development of psychoanalysis, it has been criticised in an organisational context as many of the suggestions have not been proven. Nevertheless, the concept of the subconscious and some of the behavioural patterns identified by Freud are useful for understanding personality.

Jung's personality theory

The personality theory developed by Jung is linked to some aspects of psychodynamic theory but also has more practicable implications in that it has led to the design of different types of personality testing. Also idiographic in nature, Jung's theory looked at four dimensions of personality. He started from personality types

Table 2.3 Myers–Briggs type indicators

Personality type	
Extrovert	**Introvert**
Outgoing	Quiet
Publicly expressive	Reserved
Interacting	Concentrating
Speaks then thinks	Thinks then speaks
Gregarious	Reflective
Perception	
Sensing	**Intuitive**
Practical	General
Specific	Abstract
Feet on the ground	Head in the clouds
Details	Possibilities
Concrete	Theoretical
Judgement	
Thinking	**Feeling**
Analytical	Subjective
Clarity	Harmony
Head	Heart
Justice	Mercy
Rules	Circumstances
Relating to environment	
Judging	**Perceiving**
Structured	Flexible
Time orientated	Open ended
Decisive	Exploring
Organised	Spontaneous

Source: Adapted from Nelson and Quick (1996) *Organisational Behaviour: The Essentials*. Copyright West Publishing Corporation, St Paul, Minneapolis, p 86.

also identified by Eysenck, namely 'extrovert' or 'introvert', and then went on to pick out two types of perception which he called 'sensing' and 'intuiting' and which referred to the way in which people get their information. The third dimension of this theory concerned judgement, which he differentiated into two types which he called thinking and feeling, terms which also refer to decision-making styles. The fourth dimension is that of judging or perceiving, which reflects how we relate to the environment. The significance of Jung's analysis, apart from its place in the development of psychology as a discipline, was that his concepts were used by Myers and Briggs (1987) to develop the Myers–Briggs Type Indicator (MBTI) which can be seen in Table 2.3.

Questionnaires, informed by the criteria illustrated in Table 2.3, are used to evaluate personality and develop profiles based on combinations of characteristics identified in the table. These are used extensively in organisations as a tool in staff selection, development, promotion and even redundancy, although the validity of personality testing has been questioned.

Personality in the organisation

There are a number of organisational situations in which personality has an impact but, equally, there are certain personality characteristics which might be more important for understanding people who work in organisations and which can be used to explain the behaviour of individuals in organisations.

One area of significance is that of locus of control, which is *the amount of control that individuals feel they have over a situation*. If an individual feels that he or she has a high degree of control over what happens to him or her then that person is said to have an internal locus of control, whereas an individual who feels that he or she is primarily influenced by other people, or the organisation, is said to have an external locus of control. Those with an internal locus of control tend to be more motivated and committed as they believe that they can influence outcomes in terms of their career progression, whereas those with an external locus of control are less likely to take this view. The motivational aspect can be linked to expectancy theory (*refer to* Chapter 3), which states that where individuals feel that they can influence the environment in which they operate, they will generally exert more effort to achieve, and may work more independently: the individual with an external locus of control is more likely to need a more structured environment such as is found in bureaucratic organisations.

A key factor in this regard is how individuals perceive themselves within the organisation. This is particularly pertinent in the areas of self-esteem and self-efficacy. The concepts of self-esteem and self-fulfilment relate back to Rogers' humanistic theory. Self-esteem is seen as *an individual's evaluation of self-worth*; basically, this relates to how good the individual feels about him or herself in the organisation. Obviously, if a person has high self-esteem this person will be more confident, although there is always a danger of overconfidence in that the individual's perception of his or her self-worth may not be matched by the organisation's perception. However, positive self-esteem can lead to an individual adopting a positive attitude in the organisation and this will affect that person's motivation, attendance record and ability to handle stress. The more serious issue for the organisation is that of low self-esteem, which may lead to a more negative outlook towards issues relating to the organisation and an individual's worth to the organisation.

This concept of organisational-based self-esteem (OBSE) is being increasingly recognised by managers as a mechanism whereby self-esteem can be built up in organisations. It has implications in terms of the extent to which managers should seek to encourage or control it. Self-efficacy is linked to self-esteem in that it relates to *an individual's perception of his or her ability to complete a task*. Given the complexity of many tasks in the modern organisation it is important to help individuals develop their self-efficacy and to encourage them to believe that they can complete tasks effectively, perhaps through training in time management and other techniques. If an individual has low self-efficacy then it may affect that person's behaviour and ability to complete tasks. In a task-based culture, failure in this respect could be detrimental to the individual concerned and the organisation's development. It should also be noted that the concept of 'self' may vary between one national culture and another. Factors that may cause high self-esteem and self-efficacy in one culture may not transfer so readily to another (*refer to* Chapter 10).

A further area which could be of significance is how individuals in an organisation handle stress. A number of approaches have been developed to evaluate stress and an individual's ability to handle stress. One such approach attempts to categorise people into personality types, type A or type B, in relation to how they deal with stress. The type A personality profile is of an individual who is always moving, who talks rapidly, is impatient, feels continuously under time pressure, is competitive, is obsessed by numbers and is often aggressive. The type B personality is more patient, less concerned about time and tends to be more relaxed in his or her approach to work. As one may surmise, the type A personality is more likely to suffer from stress, although possibly is more successful in career terms. In addition, type As are also more prone to heart diseases and other stress-related illnesses.

One of the organisational areas where personality issues are most significant is personality testing. Such testing can inform decisions in relation to selection and advancement and even be used to facilitate downsizing. We have already seen two

Testing times for personality tests

Personality testing is something which many of us will undergo during our careers, with an interview being preceded by a bank of questionnaires which are meant to give our current, or prospective, employer an idea of our personality, personal characteristics and potential. However, recent developments are suggesting that personality testing may not be as effective as it was intended to be.

One problem has been that some candidates manage to 'second-guess' the tests and give answers that they believe would please the employer rather than give their true response. This is particularly true with some well-known types of tests about which candidates can find out before the interview. As a result the Halifax Bank, worried about the manipulation of traditional tests, has turned away from traditional psychometric tests towards more work-related aptitude tests.

A second area of concern has been the fear of legal action by individuals who feel that the tests have discriminated against them, especially on a racial basis. A series of race-bias cases has led to a sharp decline in the use of personality testing in the USA. In the UK Asian guards at Paddington station feared that their career prospects would be diminished after they achieved poor test scores. It was shown by the Council for Racial Equality that cultural differences would affect the candidates' responses to tests. This case was settled without going to court and the procedures were amended.

The issue of Western cultural bias in personality testing has also surfaced, especially when multinational organisations have used personality testing on a global basis (Cronbach, 1995). Some of the problems that have been encountered are familiarity with the types of questions encountered, language awareness, the speed at which responses are expected and different social and cultural norms. Thus a UK-derived questionnaire may lead to distorted results if applied in English to a group of Indonesian managers.

Fig 2.1 Criticisms of personality testing

examples of personality tests – Cattell's Trait Analysis and the Myers–Briggs Type Indicators based on Jung's analysis. Although other forms of testing are used in organisations, such as graphology, which is favoured in France, personality tests are still used widely. In the UK, for example, some 51 per cent of companies use tests to recruit executives and 40 per cent use them for non-executive appointments (Willis, 1997). However, there are a number of reasons why personality testing is being increasingly questioned, as can be seen in the mini-case presented in Figure 2.1.

Perception and the perceptual process

Perception is an essential factor in determining individual behaviour both inside and outside an organisation. We all look at events that happen to us, or situations that occur, in different ways. Imagine your favourite football team losing a match. As a supporter you might perceive that this has been caused by the team having poor players; a fellow supporter may see the outcome as a result of poor management and yet another supporter may see it as a significant improvement on previous defeats! We are all looking at the same situation (the football match) but from a different perspective and thus our reactions to the situation may differ considerably. Within an organisation a continual stream of things may take place and yet these can be perceived very differently by individuals. Imagine an organisation announcing an impending reorganisation. This may be perceived by some in the organisation as an opportunity for advancement through new job opportunities, whereas others might see it as a threat to their existing job; thus some may welcome the change and others may seek to resist it.

So what is perception? In simple terms it is *how we view and interpret the events and situations in the world about us*. It can be looked upon as a cognitive process and a social information process whereby we go through the process of:

- picking up some external stimuli, such as some event or perhaps some personal interaction;
- screening, when we only acknowledge the stimuli we choose to acknowledge;
- some interpretation and categorisation of these stimuli, possibly based on previous experience or on our upbringing.

Thus, in the previously-mentioned example, perhaps the external stimulus is hearing that my football team has lost yet again. I may screen this information in a negative manner, assuming that something is wrong with the team rather than that it has just had a bad day. Finally, I may interpret this information on the basis of previous experience of supporting the team, and decide that it is a further example of bad management.

Within organisations, perception has a major impact on such matters as selection interviews but it can apply to a range of situations, one of which we use to illustrate the basic model of social perception – *see* Figure 2.2.

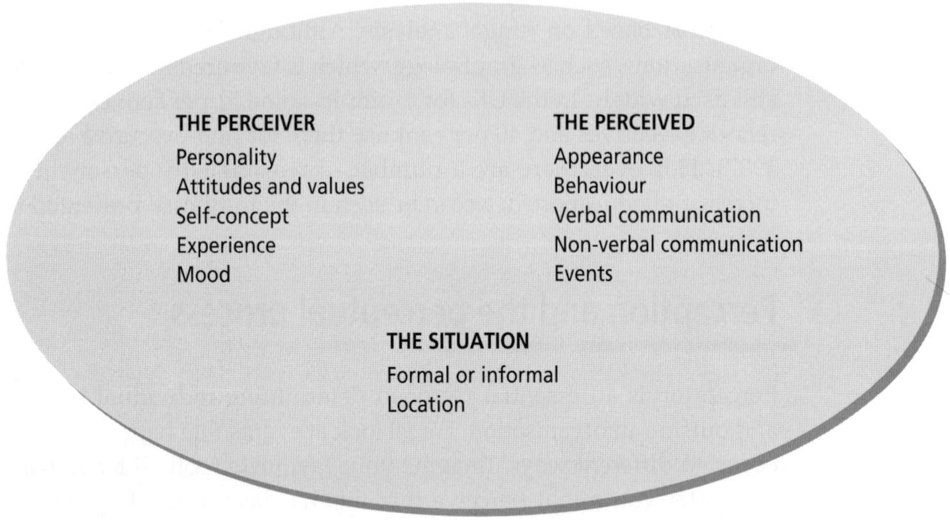

Fig 2.2 The perceptual process

Imagine a situation where a new leader has arrived in an organisation and he or she is perhaps seeking to bring about a cultural change by addressing some middle managers on the need to adopt new objectives or to create a new vision for the company. In other words, this is a change situation. Much of the success of the change process will depend on the nature of the perceivers (the middle managers), who may initially be suspicious of the new leader because of their experience of other leaders, or because they have low self-esteem or because they may associate change with job losses. Much will therefore depend on the abilities of the perceived (the new leader) to overcome their fear and suspicion and thus change their perception of him or her. The new leader will need good presentational skills – using positive verbal and non-verbal communication – backed by a reassuring appearance and the ability to convince them of the value of the change. The situation may also be significant, that is, whether the presentation is made in an office at work during their lunch break or on an away day, where the middle managers can focus on the change issues under consideration and mix both formally and informally. Ultimately, this interaction and the perception of the new leader by the middle managers may have a crucial bearing on whether the change process is successful.

However, one must be aware of a number of factors that can distort this whole process. One of the most common of these is perceptual stereotyping, *where generalisations are made about certain groups of people*. What will happen if the new leader is a young woman and the middle managers all older men? There is of course the danger that the middle managers hold stereotypes of younger women which will interfere with her ability to get her message over to them. There are many areas where the ethos of male managers dominates despite the lack of any apparent rational reason for this (Hansard, 1990), and where women have trouble reaching the top of the organisation. This tendency can be very pronounced in male-dominated national cultures such as that of Japan, where Hofstede (1984) has indicated that the high masculinity index found in that country makes it very difficult for women managers to progress in organisations (*see* Chapter 10).

Selective perception is a further development of stereotyping, in that *the perceivers may already be conditioned as to how they perceive the perceived.* In the example quoted above, the new leader may have brought from a previous organisation to the new organisation a reputation as a 'job cutter'. Thus, given the initial suspicion of the group, it may prove almost impossible to change their attitudes if they only perceive the new leader as someone who has come there to cut jobs (probably their jobs) in the organisation. It is probable that other 'messages' that do not conform with the expected stereotype are screened out or ignored. The result of a meeting between the middle managers and the new leader can be fairly easily predicted.

On the other hand the 'halo effect' may apply, where *the perceivers pick upon a particular attribute of the perceived and it is this which determines their overall perception.* It may be that the perceived communicates well, or has a good sense of humour, or is seen as 'one of the gang' in a social setting and this may influence perceptions irrespective of the new leader's ability. Sometimes a new leader arrives with a high reputation which leads to an initial positive perception and, consequently, the newcomer may enjoy a 'honeymoon' period.

Another possible distortion can arise from self-fulfilling prophecies – *the expectation that others will act in certain ways no matter what they actually do or say.* Returning to our example, the new leader may be trying to explain a much wider strategic change in the company but the middle managers may only pick up on any comment or issue which could be seen to affect jobs. Thus, whereas the overall theme of the talk by the new leader may be strategic and positive, it will be perceived by the middle managers as operational (that is, dealing with the possibility of job losses) and negative, that is, it is fulfilling their prophecy.

Attribution theory

The concept of attribution is related to perception in that it seeks to evaluate the way we perceive our own behaviour and the behaviour of others; that is, we seek causes or attributes of our own behaviour and that of people with whom we come into contact inside the organisation. The original work on attribution (Heider, 1958) was developed by Kelley (1973) with his attributional theory.

Attributions, that is, *the perceived causes for our behaviour or the behaviour of others,* can be seen to be internal, that is, being derived from our own personal attributes. Thus, we have some control over them: in other words, we enjoy a high locus of control. External attribution, on the other hand, suggests that external forces, such as factors in the organisation, are the cause of our attributes. Obviously we all have different patterns of attribution. Achievement-orientated individuals may well see their attributions as being based primarily on internal factors and their own ability to achieve success. Kelley developed this concept by looking at whether we attribute other people's behaviour as being a product of either internal or external causes. He based this analysis on three key factors:

- *Consensus*: do other people in the same situation behave in the same way?
- *Distinctiveness*: was the observed behaviour distinctive or does the person behave in the same way in other situations?
- *Consistency*: has the person always behaved in this way over a period of time?

The answers to the above questions depend on the judgement of the perceiver. Imagine that you (as a senior manager) receive a complaint about the behaviour of one of your middle managers towards a client. If on investigation you find that no other client has complained about any other manager, this would imply low consensus, whereas if there were a number of complaints about a number of managers it would imply high consensus. If there had been complaints about the same manager in a different context it would imply low distinctiveness, but if there had not been any previous complaints about this manager in different areas of the organisation it would suggest that the manager's action was very distinctive and thus had high distinctiveness. Finally, if there have been complaints about this manager over a period of time it would suggest high consistency, whereas if there was no history of complaints about the manager it would suggest low consistency.

If, following this analysis, you ascertain that the attributional characteristics of the manager are low consensus, low distinctiveness and high consistency, this would imply that the behaviour of the manager arose from internal characteristics rather than being the result of external forces. This is a case of internal attribution and you may consider that there was something about the behaviour of this manager that needed further investigation. If, however, a pattern of high consensus, high distinctiveness and low consistency emerged, it might suggest that the action of the manager was primarily determined by external factors, that is, it was a case of external attribution. As a result you may consider that this was a unique event which may reflect more on the nature of the complaint than on the specific behaviour of the manager concerned.

It was previously stated that attribution is to a large extent based on perception and there is still therefore the danger of bias or distortion of perception, as mentioned earlier. One type of distorted perception is known as fundamental attribution error, whereby we tend to look at other people's behaviour from an internal attribution bias. We assume that aspects of their attribution are determined by their own personality, intelligence, moods and so on rather than accept that external factors may have had some impact on their behaviour. For example, we may observe a colleague who is forgetting things or snapping at other people and attribute this to their personality, whereas in reality it may be a stress reaction caused by external factors over which the individual has no control. The second distortion can come from a self-serving bias by which *any successes we have we attribute to our internal factors* (intelligence, skill and so forth) and any problems or lack of success that we encounter, we attribute to external factors (usually linked to some aspect of the

The perception of older workers

Although perceptual bias and distortion are frequently linked to racial and sexual discrimination in the organisation, an area which is becoming of increasing importance is how older people are perceived within the organisation. This issue has acquired greater significance as the number of older people in the population has seen a substantial increase and, furthermore, these people are increasingly fitter and more active than at any time in the past. At the same time, organisations undergoing restructuring and shifting towards more flexible types of operations have tended to 'downsize' by removing many of this age range from the workforce. According to Casey (1990) and Lyon and Pollard (1997) common stereotypes of older people are that they are slow, are physically unfit, cannot cope with new technology, have trouble grasping new ideas, adapt less well to change and learn less quickly. The positive perceptions are that they are more loyal to their employer, are more reliable, are more customer conscious and that they work harder. Although older workers who are 'known' in an organisation are often considered effective, the problem arises when they leave an organisation for whatever reason and are seeking new employment: invariably their perceived characteristics as older workers can militate against them in competition with younger workers. Lyon and Pollard carried out a survey with MBA students (the managers of the future), from which emerged a much less positive view of older workers than currently exists among personnel managers. This suggests that the negative perceptions are being reinforced, although it is fair to surmise that as some of the MBA students become older in positions of responsibility, their perceptions may change – especially their self-perception as they themselves age.

The extent to which perception fits with reality can be debated. There are cases of older workers struggling with new information technology, for example, but in many other respects the perception can be seen to be a false one, yet one which disadvantages a large number of people. A different perspective can be seen in the study by Hogarth and Barth (1991) who studied the experiment by the B & Q store group which recruited 55 people in its Macclesfield store, recruited exclusively from those aged over 50.

The outcome was that the store outperformed other local outlets competing in the same sector, in terms of profitability, low staff turnover, good product knowledge and high productivity; even absenteeism through illness was lower than that in some of the store's rivals. These results probably changed the perception of B & Q which now sees older people as a valuable alternative source of employees. The firm has since designated more stores as employers of the over 50s. It should be stated, however, that many of these workers aged over 50 had previously been employed in higher-status jobs and been made redundant. Their skills were, therefore, higher than those of workers who normally applied for jobs at that level.

One could also widen this discussion to the level of national culture. Age is much respected in some cultures, such as in Asia, where the perceptions of older people differ accordingly.

Fig 2.3 Perceptual bias

organisation). For example, you may receive a poor mark for an essay, and argue that this is because the question was phrased badly or too little time was given for its completion. Finally, we have to be aware of cultural differences. In some cultures, behaviour and outcomes are viewed as a product of fate rather than as something that can be determined by our own actions. In such cultures behaviour would be seen as having an external rather than an internal attribution. The mini-case presented in Figure 2.3 illustrates this.

Attitudes and values

Attitudes

Attitudes, especially personal attitudes, have a key bearing on how an individual functions within the organisation, particularly as these attitudes may be reflected in positive or negative behaviour. Sometimes attitudes may be influenced by the organisation itself, and one of the challenges facing the modern manager may be how to effect an attitude change in the organisation within the broad context of cultural or strategic change.

An individual's attitude may result from a number of factors acting together. An attitude may have an emotional element, reflecting feelings or moods about an individual or an event, a cognitive component, based more on beliefs, opinions and knowledge held by an individual and, finally, a behavioural aspect, based on an individual's behavioural pattern. For example, if an employee is asked to undertake some weekend work when he or she is conditioned to the Monday to Friday pattern, the response may vary. The attitudinal response may depend upon the employee's emotional response to working a weekend, the effect on his or her behavioural pattern (e.g., whether it disrupts a regular commitment on the Saturday morning) and what this person thinks about the policy of weekend work (e.g., whether it is seen as an opportunity to earn more overtime or an undesirable and inevitable trend in the particular industry). If the individual is unhappy about changing from the current employment pattern and feels it would disrupt the normal weekend behavioural pattern and, further, disagrees with the concept of weekend working, there is a strong likelihood of a negative attitude. On the other hand, if the individual would quite like a change, does not feel it would greatly disrupt the weekend behavioural pattern and agrees with the logic of weekend working (and, possibly, higher pay rates), the attitudinal response is likely to be more positive.

Attitude formation is partly a reflection of personality formation. Attitudes are formed from the reaction of a mixture of external events with the individual's own personality. Sometimes direct experience is a powerful moulder of attitudes. If you had an unhappy time studying physics and did not get on with your teacher, this may prejudice your attitude towards the subject for the foreseeable future. Attitudes based on direct experiences can be very strong and very hard to break. For example, if the workforce feel that they have been seriously let down by their managers over a particular issue, this direct experience can lead to the formation of attitudes which current, or any future, managers may find it very difficult to change. The other source of attitude formation lies with social learning, which reflects attitudes picked up from our peer groups, from our families or other social influences in our life. The peer group factor can be especially strong and can be seen in group behaviour. Once a group behavioural norm is set, it becomes very hard for members of the group to go against the group attitude (*see* Chapter 4 for a discussion of cognitive dissonance and the phenomenon of groupthink). Very often any dissenting action may lead to their isolation from the group so they prefer to adapt their attitudes to those of the group.

Also of significance in this context is the concept of modelling where an individual 'models' him or herself on another and seeks to follow and reproduce that person's behaviour. Role models often, but not always, can have a benign influence inside and outside the organisation.

One of the central issues about attitude is the extent to which knowledge about an individual's attitudinal set can be used as a predictor of that person's behaviour inside the organisation. There has been considerable debate around this issue, but no clear conclusion has emerged. One can, however, postulate certain tendencies; for example, if an individual has a very strong attitude on a particular issue (possibly based on strongly held beliefs) it might affect that person's behaviour more directly; that is, strongly held religious or political beliefs might trigger an immediate behavioural response in certain situations. If an issue is very threatening (for example, if there is a proposed job reorganisation directly affecting an individual's job), attitudes will be very focused, so triggering a strong behavioural response. Obviously personality factors influence attitudinal responses but it must also be remembered that there are a number of strong social constraints in any organisation which might dampen an attitudinal response. For example, an individual may disagree strongly with a viewpoint taken by a line manager but is unlikely to respond too aggressively because (a) aggressive attacks on colleagues may go against the prevalent social norm or culture and (b) antagonising the line manager may weaken the individual's position in the organisation. Thus, a restrained attitudinal response is called for.

One factor that influences attitudes in the organisation is cognitive dissonance. This results from *a conflict between the behavioural and cognitive aspects of attitude*. An example of this might be a middle manager who is promoted and is put in charge of a group of middle managers who were previously his or her colleagues. The immediate reaction may be a behavioural one, in that he or she strives to keep on good terms with their previous friends and behaves in a casual, relaxed manner as they may have done previously. However, the demands of the new job, which will be cognitive in nature, may put the senior manager in the position of disciplining one of these old friends or even of making one of them redundant. Thus the behavioural aspect comes into conflict with the cognitive needs of the new job and the result is cognitive dissonance. This may cause confusion which may have to be resolved by:

- the changing of his or her attitude to the old friends and distancing him or herself from them; or
- getting someone else to make the decision, to avoid being put in this quandary; or
- quitting the job if the tensions are too great.

A topical application of this might be that of a football player who is promoted to manage the team at short notice and who may have to make immediate decisions about changing the team formation or team personnel.

Managers in organisations are obviously concerned about attitudes to work in their organisations as they may have a significant bearing on achieving high productivity and developing innovation in the organisation. For example, it may be difficult to achieve these when there is latent hostility between the management and the workforce or between the managers themselves (the 'them and us' phenomenon). This can be contrasted with the experience of Japanese companies where there is a strong commitment to work, so much so that the danger of overwork has been a problem (Japan is one of the few countries that has a word – *karoshi* – which means *death through overwork*). Many surveys are carried out to measure individuals' attitudes to work and especially their level of job satisfaction. It is argued that, if problems in attitudes to work can be identified, they can be corrected by organisational changes. However, although one would anticipate that a high level of job satisfaction would lead to high performance, the evidence is that there is little correlation, as the issue of job performance is a very complex one.

Changing attitudes

We have seen that it is hard to measure attitudes clearly and that it is difficult to establish simple links between attitude and behaviour and job performance. This is an area of great concern to managers. The issue of changing attitudes may be highly significant for a manager who is seeking some form of change in the organisation. Many of the previously state-owned industries, British Rail and British Gas for example, had to make significant changes in their operations when they changed from being state-run industries with no competition, to being part of a much more competitive privatised sector. Suddenly they had to become 'leaner', had to respond more quickly to the marketplace and, thus, had to change attitudes in the organisation, for example by becoming more customer focused. How, as a senior manager, can you effect a change in attitude in the organisation? Much will depend upon issues already covered such as personality and perception, although the issue of communication is vital here too, as can be seen in Figure 2.4.

As already indicated, much depends on the nature of the person carrying out the change or 'the source'. The issue of perception is crucial in this context. The better the communication skills and 'charisma' of the source, the stronger will be the source's chances of changing attitudes and perceptions. It is no surprise that politicians are coached in performing in front of cameras as their performance may have a major influence on people's perception of them and, thus, on their ability to lead change. It seems a modern trend for political leaders to have to be telegenic in order to change attitudes, although such a need is perhaps less evident in the business world. The nature of the target audience affects the process of changing attitudes. If we return to the change scenario previously considered, we can appreciate that the

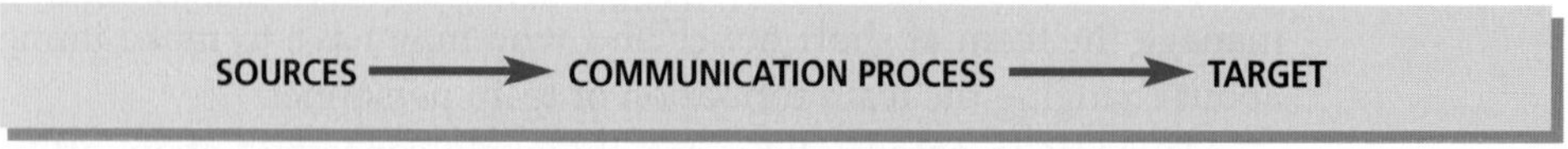

Fig 2.4 Aspects of changing attitudes in organisations

senior manager may have to address and convince people at different levels in the organisation for the change to succeed and thus will have to think very carefully about whether the same approach should be used with different groups of people. All groups may need reassuring, though what may be a reassuring message by one group might be perceived as a threat by another and thus might engender a different attitudinal response: one group might welcome the change, another resist it.

A further factor is how the message is presented: whether it is in simple or complex language, whether both negative and positive aspects of the change are discussed or only the positive aspects. Paradoxically, the identification of negative factors may lead to a more realistic response from the target audience than if only the good points were to be emphasised.

Values

Another factor that influences individual behaviour is values. Many people would suggest that attitudes and values are fairly closely related, yet it may be strongly argued that values are deeper than attitudes and more embedded in our character. It is also suggested that values are longer lasting and that they give us a sense of what is right and wrong and what is good and bad. Values are developed over time and may be strongly linked to societal factors like family or peer group or strongly held beliefs emanating from membership of organisations or deriving from particular creeds. Organisations have become increasingly interested in both the individual and collectively held values which permeate the organisation. Of particular significance is the issue of ethics in the organisation. The organisation may seek to portray a strong ethical stance in its operations, reflecting commonly held ethical values inside the organisation. The Co-operative Bank is a good example of this, particularly in relation to its ethical investments. The other reason that an organisation may be interested in values is that if it can develop a set of commonly held values among its workforce then it is, in effect, creating a specific corporate culture which might differentiate it from its competitors, thus giving it competitive advantage.

The question, then, is how to identify values. Rockeach and Ball-Rockeach (1989) divided values into terminal values and instrumental values. Terminal values can be seen as desired outcomes, for example, peace, harmony, security, happiness, partnership, love and so forth, and instrumental values can be seen as means of behaviour to achieve these terminal values. The most significant values found in the survey carried out by Rockeach and Ball-Rockeach were honesty, ambition, responsibility, a forgiving nature and open-mindedness. It should be noted, however, that this was essentially an American study of an area in which there might be distinctive national differences as to what constitutes values. From Rockeach and Ball-Rockeach's American values survey, you can see why the issue of ethics is quite strong in many American companies. A different set of national values, however, could put a totally different complexion on issues like, for example, the receiving of gifts. What might be seen as corrupt behaviour in one country would be seen as essential politeness in another. This is why the ethical stance of multinational companies may have to be more complex than those of organisations which operate only in their home country.

When terminal values are transferred to an organisation, they may comprise the achievement of excellence or high quality, becoming innovative or, perhaps, becoming an ethical organisation. When an organisation tries to inculcate terminal values such as these among its workforce, it may seek to promote or develop instrumental values that will lead to these objectives. These could be attempts to develop attitudes to work or ways of communicating in the organisation. Ideally the instrumental values can be developed to create some terminal value or values which will help determine the new culture of the organisation. They may even be enshrined in the organisation's mission statement. For example, Mercury Communications, in its 'Mercury 97 imagine' programme, proclaimed its values as:

- we always put the customer first;
- we are innovative and creative;
- we are true to our word;
- we communicate openly, honestly and with responsibility;
- we all make a difference;
- we value teamwork;
- we produce results.

However, with values as with attitudes, there is a danger of value conflicts occurring between individuals and groups within the organisation. Therefore it can be difficult to reconcile these values with organisational values.

Individual learning in the organisation

The issue of learning has become an increasingly important one, both for the individual in his or her own right and also in terms of the role of individual learning in the organisation. One reason for this is that restructuring into 'flatter' organisations (i.e., having fewer levels between senior managers and the lowest level of worker – *see* Chapter 7) is leading to more 'empowerment', with decisions having to be made lower down the organisation. Increased use of teamwork is requiring individuals to learn within a group context. Furthermore, as we move into the twenty-first century, the increased complexity of the nature of work has meant that there is an added need for people to be able to adapt and to develop in the organisation. There is a large group of workers seen as 'knowledge workers', whose importance in the organisation lies as much in their skills and ability to learn, as in their adaptability to new technology. It is probable that this category of worker will increase in the future at the expense of traditional, manual trades. Thus the issue of individual learning and of how individuals can learn within the organisation has gained prominence. We can even talk of the 'Learning Organisation' – one which seeks to learn through its experiences in order to adapt to rapidly changing environments.

Studies of individual learning often have their roots in the field of psychology. One of the most significant schools is that of the behaviourists which includes the work of people such as Pavlov and Skinner. Pavlov (1927) is famous for his work with dogs and, in particular, for the experiment in which a plate of food was put in front of the dog, making it salivate. If a bell was rung when the plate of food arrived, there would eventually come a time when the dog would salivate on hearing the bell, regardless of whether food was there. This indicated that the dog had 'learned', or had been conditioned, to react to the sound of the bell. Its behaviour had been modified. This is called the stimulus-response model as it implies *a behavioural response to some sort of stimulus*. This approach was further explored by Skinner (1974), who developed the concept of operant conditioning – which suggested that the vast majority of learning is due to what happens *after* we carry out a certain action. That is, learning is driven by the behavioural consequences. A dramatic example might be if you are travelling on the Underground and a warning is issued for people to be vigilant for pickpockets. Would this change your behaviour when you are in a crowded carriage with people pressing close to you? Your behavioural response may have been affected by this stimulus (the announcement). Linked to operant conditioning is the concept of reinforcement theory, which suggests that behaviour can be changed, or we can 'learn', by encountering specific responses to our actions. Reinforcement can be of two types. Positive reinforcement can suggest that your behaviour has been condoned and even appreciated by other people in the organisation; therefore you are more likely to repeat this behaviour. For example, if I have put in extra time to finish a report and my boss seeks me out to thank me and compliment me on the report then I am going to be much more motivated to carry out this action again. Negative reinforcement is the opposite; for example, if one is singled out for criticism for some prior action, one will probably not repeat that action.

There has been criticism of reinforcement theory as a means of behaviour modification as it is argued that self-reinforcement is the vital factor, that is, the individual's decision to change his or her behaviour through self-motivation, rather than through the negative or positive responses of other people. There is also the risk that a person could appear to change his or her behaviour in order to achieve some short-term reward but may revert to type later on. The behaviourist school has also been criticised for oversimplifying human behaviour and for the fact that too much of the theory is based purely on laboratory tests.

The cognitive school derives from the work of Tolman (1932) and sees learning as more complex than just a response to a stimulus. It sees learning as a cognitive process which is based on *expectations and on the connection in the mind between two or more stimuli, that is, it is a thinking process rather than a purely reaction-based response*. Learning depends, according to this theory, more on values and beliefs and on whether expectations based on values and beliefs are confirmed as behaviour takes place. Hence this school suggests that if an individual believes that his or her friendly behaviour towards other people will tend to be followed by a friendly response and this then happens, this person is likely to repeat this behaviour. Similarly, if a person discovers over time that there are certain times when humour can help a situation and other times when it cannot, then that person starts to develop a 'cognitive map' which will help guide him or her in future situations.

Learning styles

What might be of more significance to the organisation than the cognitive process or the behavioural responses is an awareness of learning styles and the ways in which people learn. One of the most significant styles of learning is illustrated by Kolb's learning cycle. Kolb (1976) sees learning as a continuous process which is based on experiences we encounter and depends on how we interpret and respond to these. Figure 2.5 illustrates this.

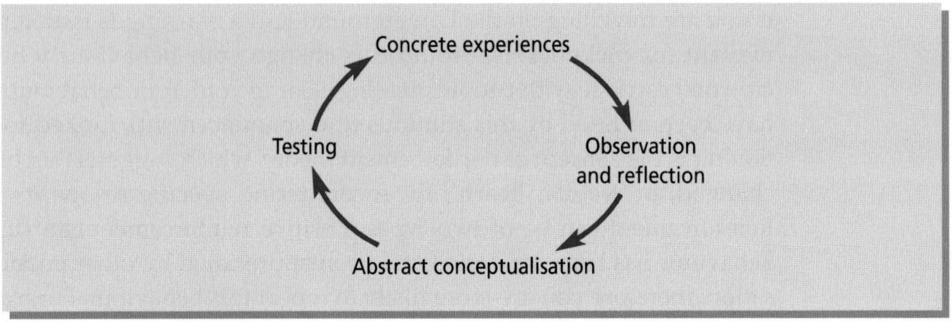

Fig 2.5 Kolb's learning cycle

In a sense, Kolb's model can be seen as experiential learning, constructed on the belief that *we learn by our experiences*. Let us assume that my goal is to speed up communications with another part of the organisation. I might have e-mail installed as a means of contacting other people electronically rather than by written memos. Thus my concrete experience is attempting to send messages via e-mail. I may then observe that I appear to be taking less time to deal with issues than I did when I was using traditional memos. Following this observation, and having reflected on it, I may then start to draw the conclusion that e-mail is a much more efficient method of sending information around the organisation than methods I had used previously (the abstract conceptualisation phase). Having made this conclusion I may then seek to test it out a little more, for example, by transferring files via e-mail. If this confirms my conclusion that e-mail is more efficient then I will probably change my behaviour and use it much more. In essence I have learned through experience, reflection and action. In fact the process might not stop there: Kolb's model suggests the idea of continuous learning through experiences. In the example just discussed, the success of my use of e-mail may encourage me to experiment with other forms of electronic information interchange, such as the Internet or web pages.

It is clearly attractive to the organisation to have an element of continuous learning taking place as this will improve the skills and flexibility of the workforce. Given the trend towards an increased dependence on knowledge workers and more complex business environments, this could give the organisation some form of competitive advantage over its rivals. An example of this is EDAP (Employee Development and Assistance Programme), implemented by Ford UK, which sets up a whole range of courses within and outside the organisation (e.g. learning how to use e-mail) with the objective of developing their employees as individuals. The firm sees this programme as being clearly linked with the well-being of the company. Kolb's cycle is, therefore, a useful model that can be used in an organisation, but the challenge is to ensure that, in order to achieve learning within the organisation, individuals must have clear goals, otherwise they might not seek new experiences. We should also remember that concepts such as reflection, and the development of abstract concepts, may well create different results in different cultures and thus may potentially affect learning within the organisation.

Kolb's model also led to the development of studies on cognitive styles – that is, *the way we organise and process information*, which may or may not be linked to cognitive ability (Sadler-Smith, 1998). This was explored by Honey and Mumford (1982) who based their model on Kolb's cycle and related it to management in the UK. They identified four cognitive styles linked to the phases of Kolb's cycle: the activist (linked to concrete experimentation), the reflector (reflective observation), the theorist (abstract conceptualisation) and, finally, the pragmatist (active experimentation/testing). Their work led to the development of a learning styles questionnaire which could be used in organisations for selection and evaluation. This model, in turn, was tested by Allison and Hayes (1988) who felt there were two broad cognitive styles which they identified as the 'analytic' style, which is reflective and theoretical, and the 'action' style, which is more activist and impulsive in nature. In later work Allison and Hayes (1996) suggest that these two approaches might reflect different parts of the brain (intuition and immediate action from the right side of the brain and analysis and reflection from the left side of the brain). In turn they have developed a cognitive style index which seeks to measure this in individuals.

If one accepts that clearly different cognitive styles are used by different people and that these can be measured, this differentiation can be useful in terms of analysing and developing learning in the organisation. This applies both for the individual, in terms of developing a more effective way of dealing with information, and also for the organisation, in placing people with a cognitive style in the right role, congruent with the needs of the organisation and the environment. The concept of single and double-loop learning (Argyris and Schon, 1978) can also be applied to both the individual and the organisation, especially in terms of how the organisation can learn from changes in its environment and move towards becoming a Learning Organisation. (These concepts are discussed in Chapter 9.)

Decision making

The final area of individual behaviour covered in this chapter is that of how individuals formulate decisions. One of the biggest challenges facing organisations is to ensure that people achieve effective decisions, both in terms of speed of the decision making and the quality of the decisions made. Decision making is obviously important for managers, but, as decision making is increasingly being devolved as we move to 'flatter' organisations, people throughout the organisation are required to be able to make effective decisions. Recent research (Nutt, 1997) suggests that the quality of management decision making is often poor, primarily because managers rush into decisions or become fixated on aspects of a particular solution, even if it has been shown not to work. Poor decision making is often the result of short-term target setting, which is a particular feature of the decision processes of chief executives who are on fixed-term contracts.

Therefore, we need to look at the process of decision making by individuals and ascertain whether this process can be distorted by factors which might diminish the effectiveness of the decisions made. Our starting point is what is known as the *rational model* of decision making which views the making of a decision as a rational, linear process which will produce rational outcomes. This model is used to explain microeconomic behaviour, such as how an increase in price is likely to lead to an individual deciding to reduce his or her demand for a product or service, all other factors remaining equal. It implies that when faced with a decision, people first identify some problem which will need a decision to be taken; second, they gather information and materials which will help them to solve the problem; third, they generate some potential solutions to the problem and fourth, they make a rational choice and select the best solution, which is then implemented. It suggests that a person will always make a rational decision based on the ability to evaluate all the alternatives and effectively calculate the potential success of each alternative. It also suggests a situation where the environment within which the decision is being made is stable and slow moving, that is, the decision maker has plenty of time to gather information, reflect on all the alternatives and reach the rational solution. Most people who have worked in environments where decisions are made under considerable pressure, and are needed quickly, would probably soon begin to question the effectiveness of the rational model as a practical tool.

The potential weakness of this model was first identified by Herbert Simon (1960). He introduced the concept of bounded rationality which accepted that, in practice, decision makers in organisations are under pressure and thus are likely to reach a decision 'that will do' or, to use Simon's phraseology, will 'satisfice'. This often means that they choose the first solution they come across that will satisfice or achieve some sort of satisfactory solution. Finding a solution quickly makes life more comfortable for the manager, so he or she may be keen to make quick decisions on issues. Managers therefore often develop 'short-cuts' (sometimes called heuristics) to solve problems and reach quick decisions. This suggestion was supported in the recent study by Nutt (1997) which showed that in practice this was how many managers do reach their decisions. One factor that is relevant in this context is that people tend to be risk averse and so seek an immediate, expedient solution, rather than explore all the options – an exercise in which more risky solutions might present themselves for evaluation. Such an approach might in turn reflect the corporate structure and culture of the organisation (*see* Chapters 7 and 9).

Another question we have to examine is how some organisations seem to have an erratic and somewhat unpredictable approach to decision making. This may be significant in organisations operating in very volatile business environments where even a satisficing approach may be difficult to implement. This is where the 'garbage can model' (Cohen, March and Olsen, 1972) may be useful. It suggests a scenario where decisions have a random element to them. Within an organisation there are a number of individuals, a number of problems floating about, potential solutions to these problems that can be found and finally (and critically) a number of opportunities for choices to be made by the individuals. For an effective decision to be reached, the problems and solutions must come together. Bringing them together may be seen as a challenge for managers. They have to develop the ability to identify relevant problems and to seek radical solutions by bringing the right people together at the right time in order for them to reach the sometimes radical decisions that will be needed in often turbulent environments.

The rationality and objectivity of decision making may also be compromised by the existence of cognitive biases. As already discussed, an individual's cognitive structure develops over time and is influenced by beliefs, attitudes, values and the person's own personality. The individual's cognitive mindset inevitably has some bearing on the quality of decisions made. The issue of cognitive dissonance has already been discussed in the context of attitudes, where it was explained that this refers to the situation where a clash exists between a person's beliefs and actions. For example, the evaluation of various options for solving a problem may produce a logical solution, but this may still go against the decision maker's beliefs or attitudes and thus the rational solution to the problem may be resisted.

Other cognitive biases which could influence decision making include the illusion of control which means that *an individual believes he or she can handle a complex problem but does not have the capability to do so*. For example, the person may feel confident of being in control of everything and have the need to maintain this illusion no matter how difficult the problem becomes. This can lead to poor decision making for both the individual and the organisation, particularly in a complex and fast-moving business environment. This bias could be linked to that of escalation of commitment. An example of the latter could involve a manager who is in difficulty through the illusion of control. Perhaps she or he has made a deal on forward foreign exchange for the company which is in fact more complex than had been imagined and as a result the company is potentially exposed to some losses. The rational decision to make would be to abandon the deal and take the loss before setting up a better deal. However, it appears that managers who have made mistakes such as these tend to continue in their course of action and often increase, or escalate, their commitment. That is, they increase their foreign exchange exposure, hoping for some turnaround which will offset their initial losses, often running the risk of even further disasters for the company. The classic case of this would have to be that of Nick Leeson, who was working in the global derivatives trading market for Barings Bank Plc and who, by February 1995, had managed to lose $1.3 billion for the company with the result that Barings collapsed and was finally sold for £1 to the Dutch group ING (Hill, 1997). There is clear evidence that Leeson, despite realising that he had made horrendous losses, kept on speculating in an attempt to recoup his losses, incurring still further deficit and ultimately bankrupting his employers. Perhaps he did not want to admit that he had made mistakes as a result of an illusion of control or ego-defensiveness, by which he interpreted what was happening in a positive way – that he could 'correct' his mistakes – so hiding from himself the gravity of the situation. No matter what the cause, the poor quality of decision making in this case was a disaster for the organisation, and for Leeson himself.

Communication, change and conflict

We have seen in this chapter a number of factors that can influence individual behaviour in the organisation, including individual personality, perception, values, learning and decision making. It is clear that these in turn are affected by communication, change and conflict. Examples of areas where this applies are discussed below. First, we examine how communication can change perception by means of the concept of the Johari Window, and second, we look at how change affects the psychological contract and the potential for conflict that this creates inside the organisation.

The Johari Window

One of the most significant ways in which communication can influence individual behaviour is through its ability to change individual perceptions and perceptual bias. We have already seen that people in an organisation have a range of personalities and that they are likely to have differing perceptions of other people within the organisation. Very often their perceptions are conditioned by the structure of the organisation wherein people are pigeon-holed in a specific part of the organisation and thus have little contact with people outside their particular area (*see* the discussion of traditional functionalist structures in Chapter 7). Indeed, they may well have negative perceptual stereotypes about people in different parts of and at different levels in the organisation. With the move towards flatter, more flexible types of organisations there has been a move towards greater teamwork involving people across the organisation. This brings individuals increasingly into contact with people with whom they may have existing negative perceptual stereotypes. If this occurs within a teambuilding context (*see* Chapter 4), the development of new task teams in the organisation, based on drawing together people from different parts of the organisation, may be hindered.

Thus the challenge facing organisations is to change the perceptions that people in one part of the organisation may have about people from another part, in order that they can work more effectively together. The key to success in this process is effective communication because it is through this that perceptual stereotypes or biases can be changed. It is not uncommon, therefore, for organisations to undertake training weekends or days, when they bring together people from different parts of the organisation, in order to tackle these problems and to seek to improve communications throughout the whole organisation. One of the techniques which could be used here is the Johari Window (Luft, 1970).

As Figure 2.6 shows, there are four areas of awareness about an individual. The top left-hand box represents the 'public' open area, *that which is known about the individual by others and which the individual knows about him or herself*; for example, 'Mr Scholes is quite young and works in the Marketing Department.' This area may, initially, be limited in scope, comprises only a minute part of the square and is probably conditioned by perceptual stereotyping and bias (someone working in the production department may, for example, have a negative perception of people who work in the marketing section). The 'blind' section refers to *aspects of an individual's behaviour which may be known to other people but of which the individual is unaware*; for example, an annoying personal habit or trait. The 'hidden' section refers to *facets of an individual that are known to the individual but which are unknown to other people.* The 'unknown' area *may lie in the subconscious* and it may be dangerous to allow untrained people to explore this area.

When new groups of individuals are working together, the aim is for individuals to communicate more information about themselves to other members of the group (widening the 'hidden' area) and for the group to identify aspects of an individual's behaviour about which that person is unaware (widening the 'blind' area), preferably without straying into the 'unknown' area. In practice, most of the progress is usually made on widening the 'hidden' area and as this happens, perceptual stereotyping and biases are broken down. If this can be achieved, more positive perceptions can be

	Known to self	Unknown to self
Known to others	Open	Blind
Unknown to others	Hidden	Unknown

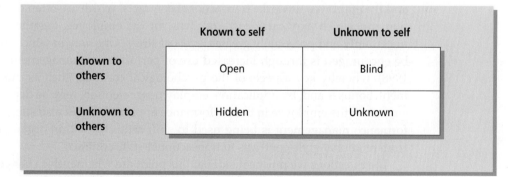

Fig 2.6 The Johari Window

developed between people from the different parts of the organisation, improving communications and the flexibility of the organisation.

This concept could also be applied in other situations, such as integrating the managers of two companies which have merged or in the context of joint ventures and strategic alliances. As will be seen in Chapter 10, perceptual problems may also occur at international level and the process of breaking down national perceptual stereotypes may well determine the success of international alliances or projects.

Psychological contracts

The concept of psychological contracts was developed by Rousseau and others (*see* Rousseau and Anton, 1991) to describe *the reciprocal sets of expectations that individual employees, and the organisation in which they work, have of each other*. These are 'psychological' in the sense that they are not written contracts but represent expectations and beliefs, particularly of employees. For example, in return for loyalty and commitment to the organisation, employees are given the security of long-term employment together with suitable opportunities for career progression within the organisation. This has traditionally been the case in many public and private sector organisations where employees had 'a job for life'.

Psychological contracts have come to the fore in recent years because of rapid organisational change where previously there was a minimal rate of change. This may have been the result of privatisation and deregulation (as in the public utilities) or merely because of a rapid increase in competition, both domestically and internationally. Consequently many organisations have undergone radical changes, including 'downsizing' or 'delayering'. Flatter organisational structures have been created, enabling organisations to respond more quickly to rapid environmental changes. A good example is that of the UK banking sector which shed 65 000 jobs between 1991 and 1994, with many of the losses being middle managers.

These changes have led to a re-evaluation of the psychological contract, especially from the perspective of employees who see change as being imposed in a top-down way, without much consultation. Employees are increasingly seeing a shift from 'relational contracts' based on a long-term relationship between the organisation and the employee towards 'transactional contracts' which are often of shorter duration and which may carry extra burdens for the employee, together with greater uncertainty and potentially greater levels of stress. One way in which this shift may be encouraged is through increased use of performance management (Styles *et al.*, 1998), whereby key aspects of the psychological contract, such as career development, bonuses and, by implication, employment retention, may be dependent on the success of the employee in the performance appraisal. Styles also suggests that performance management is being used to shift attitudes within organisations away from relational-style contracts to transactional-style contracts.

The questions we must consider at this point are whether this change in the psychological contract will alter the individual's relationship with the organisation and whether it could lead to conflict in the organisation. Hendry and Jenkins (1998) have suggested that changes in the psychological contract, especially if linked to longer hours, less security and greater stress, will almost certainly lead to changes in attitudes among employees. If employees perceive that the organisation has changed the old psychological (relational-style) contract, these authors suggest it will lead to an increased sense of powerlessness, a loss of trust in the organisation and consequently less loyalty towards the organisation. Whether there will be greater conflict in the organisation may depend upon individual behavioural characteristics and how individuals respond to the perceived change in the psychological contract. Sparrow (1997) suggests that some individuals will be more flexible and see the changing nature of work towards transactional contracts in a positive light and possibly as a means of advancement. However, it is equally certain that many individuals, who may by nature be resistant to change, will view the change in a negative manner. Some may choose to respond by 'getting out' by means of early retirement, whereas others may seek to respond by 'getting even' with an organisation they feel has let them down; and it is in this area that the potential for conflict in the organisation will arise.

Managerial implications

A series of implications for managers arise from a knowledge of organisational behaviour at the level of the individual. These include:

1 A manager needs to realise that the organisation is built up of individuals who will have a range of different personalities and behavioural patterns. The results of actions taken by managers may, therefore, differ according to the individuals concerned.

2 Personality testing can be used to identify behavioural characteristics in individuals but care should be taken in using such tests and in interpreting their results.

3 Managers should be aware of how perception may influence an individual's behavioural pattern in relation to other people in the organisation. The perceptual process can be distorted by perceptual bias and stereotyping but effective use of communication, including use of the Johari Window technique, can significantly change these perceptual distortions.

4 It is useful for managers to have an awareness of how values and attitudes develop in the individual and how these may relate to the organisation. Managers may need to change attitudes in an organisation if faced with a change situation or if they are seeking to change the corporate culture.

5 It is advantageous for the manager to have some awareness of how learning occurs both at individual level and overall in the organisation. With an increasing number of organisations being dependent on 'knowledge workers', managers will benefit from having knowledge of cognitive styles.

6 Effective decision making is crucial to the well-being of the organisation, especially when an increasing number of decisions are being taken further down the organisation. An understanding of the process of decision making and of how it gets distorted is of value.

Summary of main points

This chapter should have provided an understanding of:

- the complex nature of the factors that influence personal behaviour;
- how personality may be explained through trait, humanistic and psychodynamic theories;
- the way in which the perceptual process takes place and how this is affected by perceptual stereotyping, selective perception, the halo effect and self-fulfilling prophecies;
- the significance of attribution theory in developing our understanding of how we perceive our own behaviour and the behaviour of others;
- how values and attitudes are formed by individuals and how this may lead to cognitive dissonance;
- the process of individual learning and the differences between the behaviourist and cognitive schools of thought on this topic and how learning may be influenced by cognitive styles;
- the process of decision making, how this can be explained in terms of the rational model, the bounded rational model and the garbage can model, and how it can be influenced by cognitive biases;
- the ways in which communication, change and conflict can influence, or be influenced by, aspects of individual behaviour, especially in terms of the Johari Window and psychological contracts.

Conclusions

This chapter has sought to give an overview of some of the main theories which can help us to understand aspects of individual behaviour in an organisation. An organisation represents the coming together of individuals to achieve some common purpose and yet we need to acknowledge the diversity of individual behaviour that is likely to occur when individuals 'organise' themselves together. Thus the danger of assuming that organisations are going to be governed by rational and logical actions and behaviour should not be underestimated. These issues are becoming more important as we move fully into the era of 'post-Fordism', with the shift towards organisations becoming increasingly flexible in business environments that are becoming ever more complex. These flatter and more flexible organisations are putting greater pressures on the people who work in them. The development of behaviour, values, beliefs, learning and decision making is being carried on against a backdrop that is constantly changing. One of the dangers posed to individuals by rapid change is the potential for increased conflict, as we saw in our discussion of the implications of psychological contracts, together with increased stress and insecurity. These will place an ever heavier emphasis on the role of communications in the organisation because it is through effective communication that perceptions, attitudes and beliefs about change can be altered and individuals can learn about the potential benefits of change. Without effective communication, existing values, perceptions and beliefs can harden and ultimately individuals may seek to resist change, again engendering more conflict within the organisation.

QUESTIONS

1 Identify some leading personalities from business and other fields and assess the factors which could explain their behavioural characteristics, making use of theories outlined in this chapter.

2 Critically assess the effectiveness of personality testing for the organisation.

3 It is often suggested that, in a job interview, decisions are made in the first two minutes, although the selection process may go on much longer. To what extent might the perceptual process help explain this?

4 When Gianluca Vialli took over as manager of Chelsea FC in 1998 he moved from being just a player in the club to becoming a player-manager who would have to take important decisions about the future of his fellow players and friends. Evaluate this situation from the perspective of cognitive dissonance and identify some situational problems that Vialli might encounter as a result of this.

5 Think of the number of decisions that you have made today and relate these to theories on decision making discussed in the text. To what extent are you a rational decision maker and are there ways in which you could improve the quality of your decisions?

6 The Prime Minister, Tony Blair, in 1998 faced something of a quandary. He was generally in favour of the UK joining the European Monetary Union (EMU) process and had promised that there would be a full referendum on this issue before any final decision was made by the Government. Despite the Government's generally being in favour, opinion polls suggested that there was still a high degree of scepticism and antagonism against EMU in the country. Thus, Mr Blair had to face the problem of needing to create attitudinal change in the country. How might the theories covered in this chapter help him to create such change?

7 Evaluate the learning that you have undertaken during the last week from both a stimulus-response perspective and a cognitive learning perspective. Which of these has been the more effective and why?

REFERENCES

Allison, C. and Hayes, J. (1988) 'The learning styles questionnaire: an alternative to Kolb's inventory?', *Journal of Management Studies*, Vol. 25, pp 269–81.

Allison, C. and Hayes, J. (1996) 'The cognitive styles index: A measure of intuition-analysis for organisational research', *Journal of Management Studies*, 33(1), pp 119–35.

Allport, G. (1961) *Pattern and Growth in Personality*. New York: Holt, Rinehart.

Argyris, C. and Schon, D. A. (1978) *Organisational Learning: A Theory of Action Perspective*. Reading, MA: Addison-Wesley.

Belbin, M. (1996) *Management Teams: Why they Succeed or Fail*. Oxford: Butterworth-Heinemann.

Burgoyne, J. (1995) 'Feeding minds to grow the business', *People Management*, 21 September.

Casey, B. (1990) *Firm Policy, State Policy and the Recruitment and Retention of Older Workers*. London, Policy Studies Institute.

Cattell, R. and Kline, P. (1977) *The Scientific Analysis of Personality and Motivation*. London: Academic Press.

Cohen, M., March, J. and Olsen, J. (1972) 'A garbage can model of organisational choice', *Administrative Science Quarterly*, Vol. 17, pp 1–25.

Cronbach, L. (1995) *Essentials of Psychological Testing*, 5th edn. London: HarperCollins.

Ewen, R. (1988) *An Introduction to Theories of Personality*, 3rd edn. Hove, East Sussex: Lawrence Erlbaum Associates.

Eysenck, H. (1973) *Eysenck on Extroversion*. London: Crosby, Lockwood & Staples.

Hansard Society Commission Report (1990) *Women at the Top*. London: The Hansard Society.

Heider, F. (1958) *The Psychology of Interpersonal Relations*. New York: Wiley.

Hendry, C. and Jenkins, R. (1998) 'Psychological contracts and new deals', *Human Resource Management Journal*, 7(1), pp 38–43.

Hicks, L. (1996) 'Individual differences' in Mullins, L. (ed.) *Management and Organisational Behaviour*, 4th edn. London: Financial Times Pitman Publishing.

Hill, C. (1997) *International Business*, 2nd edn. New York: Irwin. *See* especially pp 342–8.

Hofstede, G. (1984) *Culture's Consequences: International Differences in Work-Related Values* (abridged edn). Beverly Hills: Sage.

Hogarth, T. and Barth, M. (1991) *Age Works: A Case Study of B & Q's Use of Older Workers*. University of Warwick: Institute for Employment Research.

Honey, P. and Mumford, A. (1982) *The Manual of Learning Styles*. Maidenhead: Peter Honey.

Kelley, H. (1973) 'The Process of causal attribution', *American Psychologist*, February, pp 102–27.

Kolb, D. (1976) *The Learning Styles Inventory*. Boston: McBer & Co.

Lewin, K. (1951) 'Formalisation and progress in psychology' in Cartwright, D. (ed.) *Field Research in Social Science*. New York: Harper.

Luft, J. (1970) *Group Processes: An Introduction to Group Dynamics*. New York: National Press.

Lyon, P. and Pollard, D. (1997) 'Perception of the older employee – is anything changing?', *Personnel Review*, 6(4), pp 245–57.

Myers, M. (1987) *Introduction to Type.* Oxford: Oxford Psychologists Press.

Nutt, P. (1997) 'Better decision-making: A field study', *Business Strategy Review*, 8(4), pp 45–52.

Pavlov, I. (1927) *Conditioned Reflexes*. Oxford: Oxford University Press.

Rogers, C. (1970) *On Becoming a Person: A Therapist's View of Psychotherapy*. Boston: Houghton Mifflin.

Rockeach, M. and Ball-Rockeach, S.S. (1989) 'Stability and change in American value priorities 1968–81', *American Psychologist*, Vol. 44, pp 775–84.

Rousseau, D. and Anton, R. (1991) 'Fairness and implied contract obligations in job terminations: The role of contributions, promises and performance', *Journal of Organisational Behaviour*, 12(4).

Sadler-Smith, E. (1998) 'Cognitive style: Some human resource implications for managers', *International Journal of Human Resource Management*, 9(1), pp 185–200.

Senge, P. (1990) *The Fifth Discipline: The Art and Practice of the Learning Organisation*. New York: Doubleday.

Simon, H. A. (1960) *The New Science of Management Decision*. New York: Harper & Row.

Skinner, B.F. (1974) *About Behaviouralism*. London: Jonathan Cape.

Sparrow, P. (1997) 'Transitions in the psychological contract: Some evidence from the banking sector', *Human Resource Management Journal*, 6(4), pp 75–92.

Styles, P., Gratton, L., Truss, C., Hope-Hailey, V. and McGovern, P. (1998) 'Performance management and the psychological contract', *Human Resource Management Journal*, 7(1), pp 57–65.

Tolman, E. (1932) *Purposive Behaviour in Animals and Men*. Berkeley, CA: University of California Press.

Weiss, J. (1996) *Organisational Behaviour and Change*. St Paul, MN: West.

Willis, P. (1997) 'Testing Times', *Personnel Today*, 30 October, pp 26–7.

FURTHER READING

Most textbooks on OB have good sections on individual behaviour, but those particularly recommended are:

Mullins, L. (1999) *Management and Organisational Behaviour*, 5th edn. London: Financial Times Pitman Publishing, Chapters 9 and 11.

Nelson, D. and Quick, J. (1996) *Organisational Behaviour: The Essentials*. St Paul, MN: West.

Robbins, S. (1989) *Organisational Behaviour*, 4th edn. Englewood Cliffs, NJ: Prentice-Hall International.

Weiss, J. (1996) *Organisational Behaviour and Change*. St Paul, MN: West.

3

Motivation at work

LEARNING OUTCOMES

On completion of this chapter you should be able to:

- define motivation;
- know the main schools of thought and prime contributors to the theory of workplace motivation;
- understand the nature of expectancy theory and assess its value as a frame for analysing motivation theories and for understanding individual motivation;
- understand the often complementary nature of different theories and their ability, collectively, to add richness and insight to our understanding of workplace motivation;
- appreciate the relationship between motivation and interpersonal conflict;
- assess the effects of organisational change on the psychological contract and on motivation;
- understand the relationship between motivation and job design;
- appreciate management's role in enhancing workplace motivation.

KEY CONCEPTS

- *motivation and satisfaction*
- *cognitive and behavioural theories*
- *contents and process theories*
- *expectancy model*
- *goal theory*
- *needs and self-actualisation*
- *extrinsic and intrinsic rewards*
- *equity*
- *psychological contract*
- *type-environment*
- *job design*

Motivation at work

Possibly one of the most contentious, important and frequently debated issues in organisational behaviour and workplace practice is 'how do we motivate our staff?' Whether we are a manager or someone being managed, motivation is a prime concern and of considerable social and economic significance. Intuitively, we recognise that poorly motivated staff tend to underperform whereas in all activities well-motivated individuals and teams are an important ingredient of success. Motivated individuals tend to work with enhanced effort and confidence and enjoy high productivity. Additionally, motivated employees are more satisfied with their work and their environment. In reality the relationship between satisfaction and motivation and between motivation and performance is debatable and complex and will be explored in this chapter.

Introduction

Although motivation is a critical factor in individual, group and organisational success there is some debate concerning its definition. In broad terms *motivation can be considered to comprise an individual's effort, persistence and the direction of that effort*. In simpler terms, *motivation is the will to perform*. It is, perhaps, of more value to identify the characteristics frequently associated with well-motivated individuals. Such people are commonly thought to consistently achieve at work and to exhibit energy and enthusiasm in the process. They often work with people to overcome organisational problems, or obstacles to progress, and frequently demand and accept additional responsibility. They may also be more willing to accept organisational change. In contrast, employees who are demotivated may appear apathetic and may tend to consider problems and issues as insurmountable obstacles to progress. Those who lack motivation might have poor attendance and time-keeping records and might appear uncooperative and resistant to change. Clearly, other things being equal, organisations that can motivate their employees are more likely to achieve their organisational objectives.

This chapter focuses primarily on motivation of the individual in the workplace. It explores the influence of organisational change and conflict on personal motivation and is supported by a number of the case studies presented later in the book, notably Case study 2, 'Organisational Change: multi-skilling in the health-care sector'. The chapter explores expectancy theory, as a useful analytical frame, and as the vehicle by which to examine, in some detail, the likely nature and sources of motivation. Additionally, concepts such as intrinsic and extrinsic rewards, personal needs and environmental stimulation are discussed where they add to our understanding of how people in the workplace are motivated. We argue that the range of different approaches tend, often, to complement one another and add richness to our understanding of this complex topic. The chapter also explores how job design and role characteristics can be enhanced to better ensure a motivated workforce.

Schools of thought

Content and process theories, behavioural and cognitive traditions

Motivation theory has been developed, mainly in the USA, following empirical research activities. It has progressed considerably from the traditional or classical approaches which assumed that people in the workplace acted rationally in an attempt to maximise the economic return to their labour. This rational economic concept assumed that work was inherently unpleasant and that wages compensated workers for their efforts. Indeed the money they earned was considered to be of greater importance to individuals than the nature of the job they performed. People

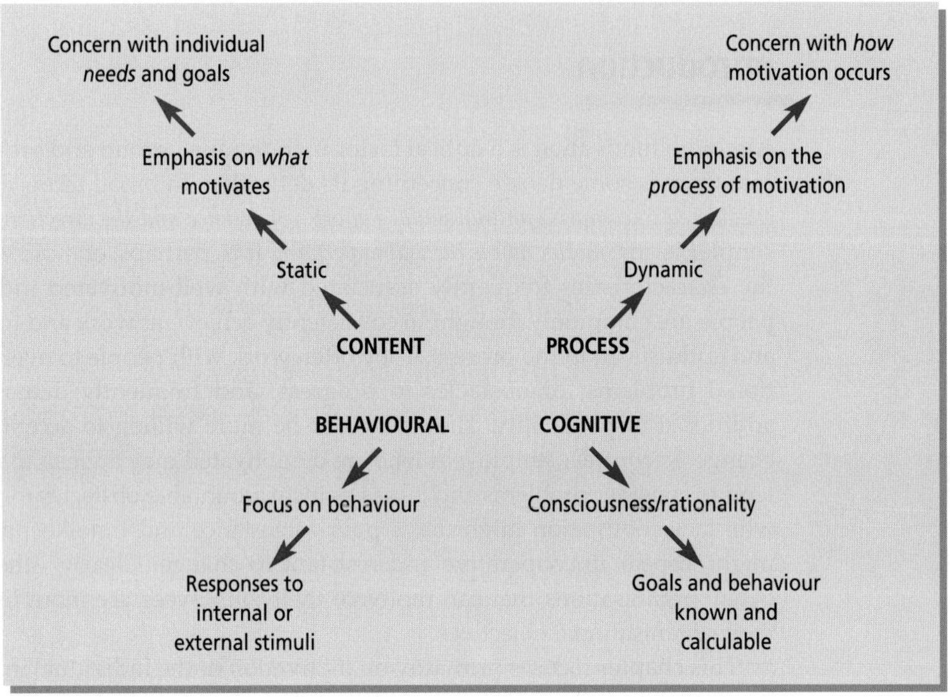

Fig 3.1 Distinction between process/content and cognitive/behavioural traditions

could, it was believed, be expected to tolerate any kind of work if they were paid enough. We will see in Chapter 5 how Frederick Taylor and others in the Scientific School of Management developed this concept.

Broadly, most models and approaches to motivation can be categorised as either content or process theories. Content theories attempt to identify and explain the factors which energise or motivate people whereas process theories focus on how a variety of personal factors interact and influence human behaviour. Quite often the two sets of theories are compatible, in fact, when combined they provide considerable insight into motivation in the workplace.

Additionally, motivation theories derive from either a behaviouralist tradition, where human behaviour is considered to be reflexive and instinctive, a response to certain environmental positive or negative stimuli, or a cognitive tradition. In the latter case it is assumed that people are conscious of their goals and their behaviour and they act rationally and with purpose. Behaviour modification theory and reinforcement theory are located firmly in the behaviouralist tradition. They ignore the inner state of the individual, this being the territory of the cognitive school, and focus instead on the consequences of people's actions. Figure 3.1 graphically illustrates the simple differences between these traditions.

Behaviour modification theory is often associated with both motivation and learning. Broadly, it suggests that behaviour is a function of its consequences, that is, the outcome of a particular behaviour will influence the nature of future behaviour. Both positive and negative reinforcement can increase the strength of a behaviour as people often respond positively to encouraging feedback and/or consider changing their behaviour if it leads to negative feedback. Negative feedback should not, however, be confused with punishment, the former generally being constructive. Punishment, especially if used indiscriminately, may have unintended consequences. However, it can reduce a particular behaviour if it is quick, fair, private, informative, focused and not followed by rewards. Additionally, by their failure to reinforce particular desirable behaviours, managers may encourage that behaviour to be exhibited less. Critiques of behaviourial modification or shaping in the workplace suggest that it dehumanises employees.

In this chapter we explore a number of the more significant models within the framework provided by expectancy theory, which itself is a process theory incorporating elements from both the behaviourial and cognitive traditions.

Table 3.1 illustrates a simple classification of motivation theories.

Table 3.1 A simple classification of motivation theories

Content theories	Process theories
■ Two-factor theory (Herzberg)	■ Expectancy theory (Vroom; Porter & Lawler)
■ Needs hierarchy (Maslow; Alderfer)	■ Equity theory (Adams)
■ Achievement needs theory (McClelland)	■ Goal theory (Locke)
	■ Attribution theory (Heider; Kelley)

Expectancy theory: a framework for the analysis of workplace motivation

This section outlines the nature of expectancy theory and explores other process and content theories which add insight to the nature of workplace motivation.

Expectancy theory has developed since the 1930s as an alternative to the behaviouralist approaches to motivation. It argues that humans act according to their conscious expectations that a particular behaviour will lead to specific desirable goals. The theory, with all its consequent refinements, provides a popular explanatory framework for a range of employee behaviours, including levels of motivation, performance, employee turnover and absenteeism, in addition to leadership effectiveness and career choice.

Expectancy theory: an illustration

A few years ago a colleague considered that she was about 80 per cent (probability +0.8) sure that she would achieve promotion within five years if she (a) published research, (b) developed new courses, (c) managed budgets effectively and (d) indicated a willingness to change and take the organisation forward. That was her subjective probability or expectation (*E*).

At the time she valued the prospect of promotion rather highly and believed that it would enable her to manage the changes that she perceived as important, to more fully utilise her skills and abilities, to develop herself and achieve new outcomes and to earn a little more money. On a scale between –1.0 and +1.0 she would place her valence as +0.9 (*V*).

Hence, at the time she believed it quite probable that by behaving in a particular way, which involved a great deal of hard and thoughtful work, she would quite likely (say four times out of five) achieve an outcome (promotion) that was desired rather highly. Her motivation was:

$$M = E \times V \text{ or Motivation} = 0.8 \times 0.9 = 0.72$$

The maximum score possible is +1.0 whereas the minimum is –1.0. If the score is positive it is likely that the individual would behave in the manner which s/he hopes would lead to the desired outcome.

In this case, a score of +0.72 is rather high and positive, suggesting that she would be strongly motivated to work as indicated above (*see* points (a), (b), (c) and (d)). That she did and she has received the desired promotion. Expectancy theory would suggest that she took a subjective but rational decision, others might argue it was a calculated gamble.

It is worthy of note, however, that despite extensive knowledge of expectancy theory, she did not actually make such a calculation as expressed above. It did not prove a useful tool or source of guidance, although it was never intended as such. Expectancy theory is based on the observation of human behaviour and attempts to depict the cognitive process which individuals are likely to go through. She can now reflect on the theory and suggest that in this case it holds some validity.

Fig 3.2 An illustration of expectancy theory

Vroom (1964), an American psychologist, further developed expectancy theory from the original work of Tolman and Honzik (1930), producing a systematic explanatory theory of workplace motivation. It argued that the motivation to behave in a particular way is determined by an individual's *expectation* that behaviour will lead to a particular outcome, multiplied by the preference or *valence* that person has for that outcome. For example, if by working diligently and for long hours an employee expects to receive promotion at some future date and if that worker values promotion highly (valence) then, rationally, we might expect that employee to show that behaviour. Vroom argues that human behaviour is directed by *subjective probability*, that is, the individual's expectation that his or her behaviour will lead to a particular outcome. The simple expectancy equation is:

$$\text{Motivation } (M) = \text{Expectation } (E) \times \text{Valence } (V)$$

It is assumed that the level of motivation an individual displays results from his/her conscious decision-making process: a rational estimate of the likely result of their behaviour. The theory also considers the value that each individual places on the estimated outcome. The basic theory recognises that individuals differ: that we are unlikely to all value the same outcomes equally. The theory also attempts to measure, via a simple calculation, the strength of motivation by multiplying the individual's estimated probability ($E \times V$, above) of an expected outcome by the value or valence that individual places on that outcome. A simple personal example will illustrate this (*see* Figure 3.2).

Locke (1968) proposed a simple and intuitively appealing cognitive theory of motivation that has certain similarities with the expectancy approach. *Goal theory proposes that both motivation and performance will be high if individuals are set specific goals which are challenging, but accepted, and where feedback is given on performance.* Organisational bureaucracies often make such goal setting difficult and, hence, dissipate the potential motivational benefits from processes such as management by objectives (MBO). It can also be argued that in dynamic environments annual objectives or individual goals often fail to embrace the need for change and flexibility. Additionally, with increasing emphasis being placed on the role of teamwork in organisations, individual goals and rewards can be seen as divisive or even counter-productive.

Porter and Lawler's expectancy model

The basic expectancy model has been further developed, notably by Porter and Lawler (1968). Porter and Lawler's model (Figure 3.3) includes further, hopefully realistic, variables and highlights certain potential managerial implications. In particular it sheds light on the nature of the relationship between employee satisfaction and performance. Figure 3.3 illustrates the more complex expectancy model. At the beginning of the motivational cycle this extended model suggests, as in basic expectancy theory, that effort is a function of the perceived value of potential rewards (valence) and the likelihood of achieving that reward (expectancy). Porter and Lawler's model then adds to existing theory by suggesting that performance is a product not only of effort but also of the individual's abilities and characteristics together with his or her role perceptions. This adds a certain intuitive realism.

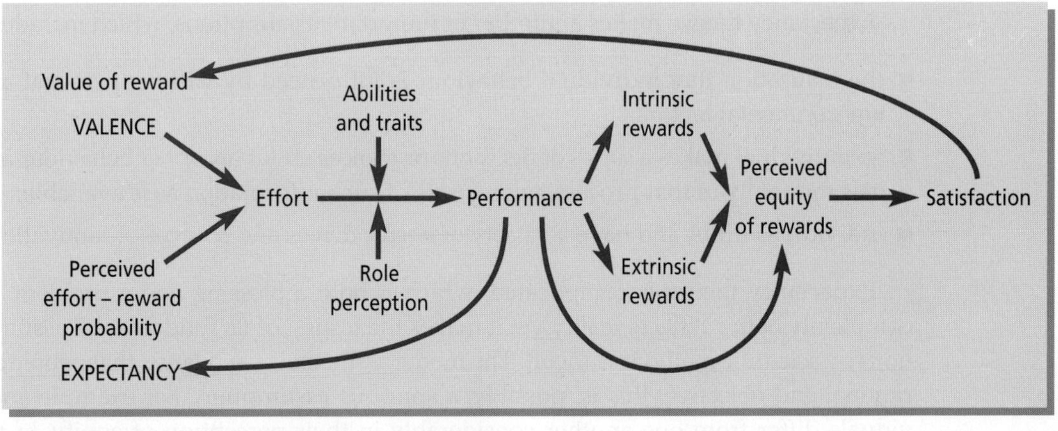

Fig 3.3 Porter and Lawler's expectancy model

Source: Adapted from Porter, I. W. and Lawler, E. E., *Managerial Attitudes and Performance*. Copyright © Richard D. Irwin Inc. (1968), p. 165.

Performance leads to two types of reward. *Intrinsic rewards are intangible and include a sense of achievement, or advancement, of recognition and enhanced responsibility*, whereas *extrinsic rewards are more tangible and include pay and working conditions*. It can be argued that the relationship between intrinsic rewards and performance is both more direct and immediate than that between performance and extrinsic rewards. As a consequence, Lawler (1973) argues that intrinsic rewards are more important influences on motivation than pay or promotion, whereupon, similarly, Herzberg (1968) suggests that intrinsic rewards have a more direct and powerful influence on workplace satisfaction than do extrinsic rewards. Herzberg's two-factor theory, outlined below, sheds light on the motivational effects of these two sets of rewards and makes a useful contribution to our understanding of workplace motivation.

Following receipt of rewards the individual assesses, via social comparison, the equity of the rewards received. Adam's equity theory is discussed below (*see* pp 60–1). If the individual perceives that the rewards received are equitable, that is, *fair or just in comparison with those received by others in similar positions in or outside the organisation*, then that individual feels satisfied. This perceived level of satisfaction then influences the valence of rewards: if an employee is dissatisfied, the valence or value of those rewards is likely to be low. Hence, if rewards are perceived as adequate and equitable, this gives a fillip to performance and hence satisfaction. A positive or virtuous cycle of motivation may occur.

If we refer to the case, discussed above in Figure 3.2, of the woman who achieved promotion, and consider the consequences of her not being promoted, it is possible to illustrate how inequity in the workplace may prove an issue. She was 80 per cent certain that promotion, a desired outcome, would be achieved if she showed effort in a number of specific ways. If a colleague had received promotion ahead of her, she might have felt aggrieved, if she had perceived that the successful colleague had failed to demonstrate greater talents in the key areas of achievement than she herself had displayed. As a consequence she might have become demotivated due to a feeling of inequity.

Expectancy theory makes a number of important assumptions, which include:

- the realisation that individual behaviour is influenced by various personal and environmental factors;
- an individual makes a series of decisions or choices about his or her behaviour and acts rationally in that process, taking note of such information as is available;
- individuals differ and have a variety of needs, drives and sources of motivation.

Expectancy theory is complicated, which is both a blessing and a problem. Its complexity better reflects reality yet it makes the testing of its fundamental assumptions by scientific methods difficult. The model assumes, by and large, that people are rational and objective; this is, possibly, a spurious assumption. For example, individuals differ from one another considerably in their perception of equity, in the value they place on particular rewards (valence) and in their own needs from, and expectations of, work. Nevertheless, research has supported various parts of the model. Pinder (1984) found that both valence and expectancy were related to both effort and performance in the workplace, whereas Campbell and Pritchard (1976) confirmed that an individual's motivation is influenced by the value this person places on expected rewards. Additionally, their research indicates that people need to believe that their efforts will lead to enhanced performance and that their performance will result in the desired outcomes in terms of rewards. Additionally, for many routine activities at work, habit or group norms may be a more typical basis for motivated behaviour. This means workers will not always go through the expectancy theory process before displaying motivated behaviour.

The valence of rewards: needs theories

The extent to which certain outcomes will be valued by individuals in the workplace is dependent upon their particular needs. It has been argued that people share a series of hierarchically related needs which will act as a source of motivation. Other 'needs theories' suggest that people's fundamental requirements or needs differ from one person to another and that, as a consequence, their sources of satisfaction and motivation will also vary. The valence of a particular outcome will, in the latter case, vary between individuals. Perhaps the most frequently cited needs theory is Maslow's needs hierarchy. Unfortunately, it also warrants criticism: empirical evidence has not supported its main contentions and it is highly ethnocentric. Hence, we will only briefly discuss it here before looking at more recent modifications, and in a little more detail, at the work of McClelland.

Needs hierarchy

Maslow, a sociologist writing in 1943, suggested that individuals are motivated to satisfy a set of needs which are hierarchically ranked according to their salience. Hence, man's most basic requirements for food and drink are pursued at all costs until that need has been satisfied. When these basic physiological needs are met he will switch his attention to seeking a higher-order need, that of security. Further fulfilment is then achieved via affiliation with others. Individuals who enjoy sufficient physiological, security and social affiliation may then be motivated to seek the esteem of others and self-respect or self-esteem. Finally, man will attempt to self-actualise, to realise his potential and to achieve something beyond the immediate needs of the body and his social circle. Maslow also suggested that freedom of enquiry and expression and the need for knowing and understanding are essential prerequisites for the satisfaction of other needs.

Implicit in this hierarchy is the belief that individuals will strive to seek a higher need when lower needs are fulfilled, that is, the valence of self-actualisation, for example, becomes stronger when esteem needs are satisfied but is weak or non-existent until these lower-level needs are satisfied. The model also suggests that once lower-level needs are satisfied they no longer serve as potential or actual sources of motivation. In order to be motivated, individuals need to be given the opportunity to satisfy the need at the next level in the hierarchy.

Maslow recognised that this was not a fixed hierarchy and that for some, for example, self-esteem might prove a more powerful motivator than affiliation or the love of others. Similarly, for some, particularly creative people, the need for self-actualisation might even displace their motivation to satisfy certain basic physiological requirements. In contrast, some people who might never be motivated to seek to satisfy higher-level needs instead would be satisfied with sound physiological and social fulfilment. He also suggested that a lower-level need would not necessarily require to be fully satisfied before an individual could be motivated to seek to satisfy other needs: these lower-level needs would still carry some, but limited, valence. It is not an absolute requirement that one must be fed and socially fulfilled before one seeks any measure of self-esteem. However, the lower level needs would take precedence, he argued, if they were not fulfilled. He also argued that the theory was more or less universally applicable, that it was not ethnocentric or influenced by culture.

Applying this theory to the workplace is fraught with difficulties, although it must be said that Maslow did not intend this theory as a managerial or organisational tool. Additionally, it has not enjoyed unquestioned empirical support (Hall and Nougaim, 1968; Lawler and Suttle, 1972). A number of problems and deficiencies have been noted. People often achieve higher-level needs via non-work-related activities. Individuals differ and, as a result, some place more value on certain needs than others. Research has indicated that as managers advance within organisations their need for security and safety tends to decrease, whereas social, esteem and self-actualisation needs increase (Lawler and Suttle, 1972). This same research also suggests that individuals rarely satisfy their higher-order needs and continue to strive for status and autonomy even after experiencing considerable success in these areas. Satisfaction does not necessarily equate to motivation nor does it always lead to improved work performance. Although a commonly held view is that 'a satisfied worker is a more productive worker', numerous studies have shown that a simple link between job attitudes and job performance often does not exist (Iaffaldano and Muchinsky, 1985). There is, however, a link between job satisfaction and absenteeism, staff turnover and the incidence of both physical and mental health problems (Schneider, 1985). Furthermore, the model is highly ethnocentric. It applies primarily to American individuals and might not represent the prime motivational drivers for those of Chinese origin, for example, where social needs, the need for affiliation and belonging, could prove a more fundamental source of motivation than personal physiological needs (*refer to* Chapter 10).

Lawler and Suttle (1972) suggest, following research in two companies, that the needs hierarchy can be reduced to just two levels: the research indicated that physiological needs existed separately and the second level included all other needs.

Alderfer (1972), who adapted Maslow's approach to the workplace, proposed three categories of needs:

- existence (basic survival needs);
- relatedness (including social interaction, respect of, and recognition from, others);
- growth (self-fulfilment, autonomy and success).

Alderfer's model suggests that needs may be activated simultaneously, as opposed to the strict, hierarchical sequence of Maslow. For example, an individual may be motivated by a desire for money (an existence need), by friendship (a relatedness need) and the opportunity to learn new skills (a growth need) at the same time, in parallel. Alderfer also suggested that if higher needs are not satisfied an individual will regress in pursuit of lower-level needs. This is referred to as the frustration-regression effect. Although better received than Maslow, this model's vagueness makes it difficult to verify.

McClelland's achievement needs theory

Perhaps of more significance and potential value to managers and academics attempting to understand motivation in the workplace is the work of McClelland. McClelland's (1961) need achievement theory identifies three basic needs that people develop and acquire from their life experiences. These are the needs for:

- achievement;
- affiliation; and
- power.

Individuals develop a dominant bias or emphasis towards one of the three needs. For example, those with a high achievement need tend to seek situations where they have personal responsibility for solving problems, managing projects and for overall performance, where feedback is often clear and rapid, where tasks are moderately challenging and where innovation is required. These people can be more concerned with their own achievement than they are with broader organisational needs.

Figure 3.4 illustrates the needs profile of a number of hypothetical individuals. If we assume that each individual's combined achievement, affiliation and power needs total 1.0 we are left with considerable scope for individual variation based on the strength or salience of a particular need and/or the weakness of others. This provides a relative measure which might enable us to enhance our understanding of ourselves and others in the workplace. We can construct three quite different and extreme scenarios. For example, individual A has a high need for achievement (0.6), a moderate need for power (0.3) and a low need for affiliation (0.1), whereas B has a high need for affiliation (0.8) and low power and achievement needs (0.1 and 0.1). Individual C is driven or motivated by the need for power (0.7) and less so by achievement alone (0.2), whereas his/her need for affiliation is low (0.1). Clearly, these are extreme cases. Such individuals will, most likely, forge quite different

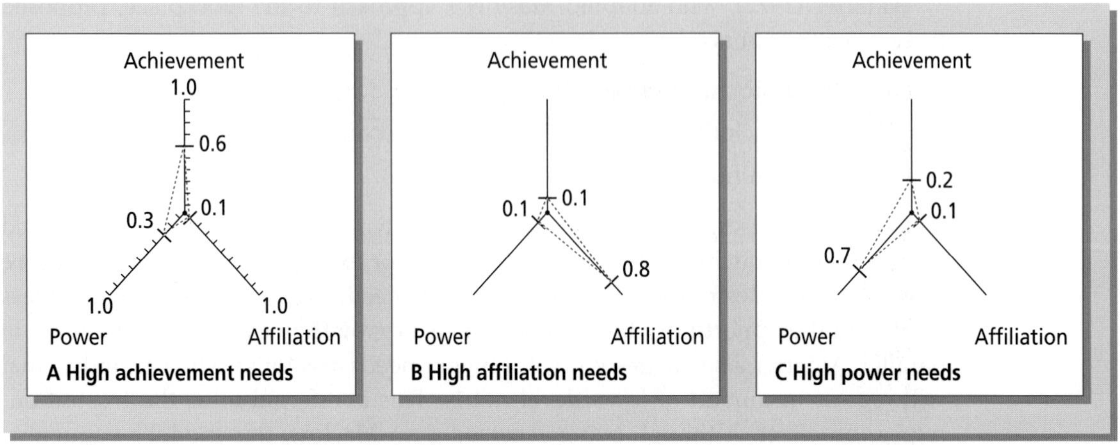

Fig 3.4 Achievement, affiliation and power needs

careers from one another by seeking different ways of meeting their needs. If these three individuals were managed similarly, as is often the case in traditional bureaucracies, then it is unlikely that all would satisfy their needs in the workplace.

In a study in the USA (McClelland and Boyatzis, 1984) it was found that successful managers had high power needs and lower achievement needs. Power appears to be the main determinant of success, particularly when success is measured in terms of status and promotion to senior posts. McClelland distinguished between socialised power and personalised power, the former being useful in assisting managers and leaders in their attempts to achieve organisational and group goals whereas the latter often merely serves the individual in seeking his or her need for domination. The need to achieve is linked to entrepreneurial activity and is viewed as an essential ingredient of organisational and national economic success. Managers tend to have higher achievement needs and lower affiliation needs than non-managers. We are all, perhaps, aware of people who appear, at least, to demonstrate a high need for one of the three drivers identified by McClelland. However, for the achievement of organisational success, those with high achievement needs are generally considered most essential. For these people, money is often considered a measure or indication of success, a method of feedback, but is not a particularly strong motivator in its own right.

McClelland's motives correspond, to an extent, with Maslow's self-actualisation (achievement), esteem needs (affiliation) and love/social needs (power). However, this theory recognises that the relative extent or influence of these needs varies considerably between individuals. McClelland's work emphasises the importance of context, the social environment outside work, for the development of needs or motives, whereas Maslow and others suggest that needs are instinctive.

Of particular interest to managers attempting to instil higher achievement needs in staff is McClelland's (1962) argument that this need can be strengthened by a

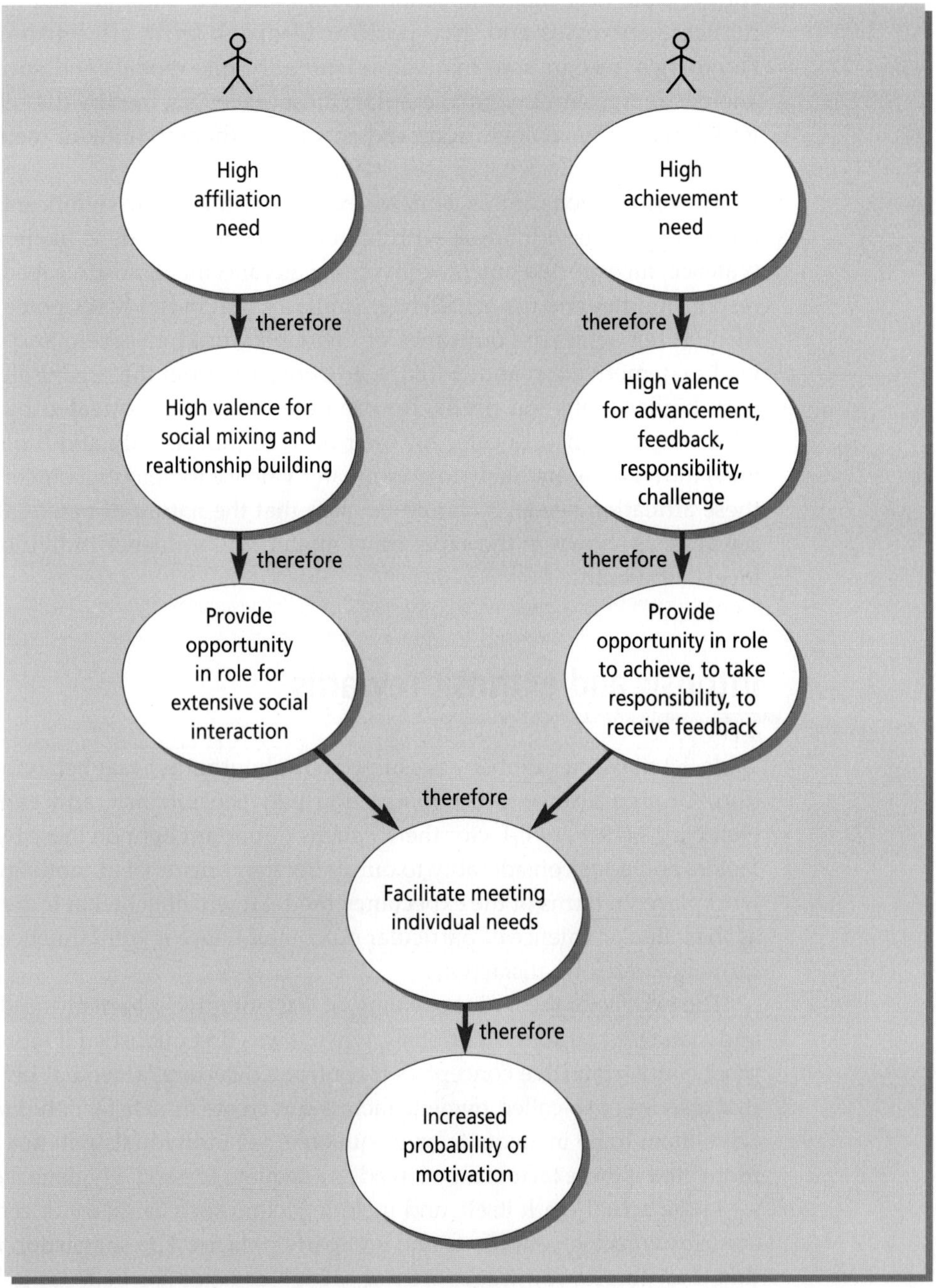

Fig 3.5 Expectancy and needs theory: relationship

combination of managerial action and training. He suggests that managers should reinforce successes and give positive feedback (with effects similar to those of Herzberg's 'recognition' motivators), identify role models and successful mentors and encourage employees to emulate these achievers, modify the self-image of staff with lower achievement needs and encourage them to think of themselves in more positive terms.

The implications of this work for expectancy theory are significant (*see* Figure 3.5). For example, an individual with high achievement needs is likely to value highly (valence) an expected outcome involving advancement, positive feedback, enhanced responsibilities and new challenge. Similarly, that individual's potential disappointment at not achieving outcomes of this kind would be severe and would possibly lead to demotivation and, perhaps, to departure from the organisation. Individuals with higher affiliation needs, for example, might be motivated by tasks and jobs which are designed to cater for their need to mix socially and build relationships. Such individuals are likely to give greater valence to potential outcomes which fulfil these affiliation needs. It should be clear that the nature of potential outcomes and rewards, as shown in the expectancy model, will influence individuals' motivation levels differently.

Intrinsic and extrinsic rewards

Table 3.2 makes a number of assumptions about individual behaviour and motivation. Of significance is the distinction between intrinsic and extrinsic rewards. Herzberg's (1968) two-factor theory sheds important light on these two motivational factors and adds considerably to our understanding of what motivates people in the workplace. In terms of the expectancy model it will affect what individuals perceive as the value or valence of particular outcomes; hence it will influence both their performance and job satisfaction.

The two-factor theory is appealing, at least intuitively, to many academics, students and managers, although, curiously, when it was first published it represented a somewhat counterintuitive concept as it confronted certain 'accepted' beliefs. It suggests that a series of so-called hygiene factors can create dissatisfaction if individuals perceive them to be inadequate or inequitable, yet individuals will not be significantly motivated if these factors are viewed as adequate or good. Hygiene factors are extrinsic to the actual work itself, and include factors such as salary or remuneration, job security, working conditions and company policies. The suggestion is, for example, that if an employee's wages are not as high as he or she believes to be appropriate, then this might lead to dissatisfaction. However, if the employee's wages are thought to be good, that alone will not particularly motivate, or even fully satisfy, him or her. These contextual factors cannot sustain motivation, although they may lead to a state of personal satisfaction. This is in contrast to the traditional belief that pay is the prime, or in some cases only, source of motivation. That traditional understanding was reinforced by the work of Frederick Taylor and the Scientific School of Management in the early part of the twentieth century.

Taylorism advocated the application of 'scientific' principles to job design and work management. It was founded on the belief that if jobs were designed to achieve maximum productivity, and if workers were selected with the necessary physical, as opposed to cerebral, capabilities, then wages could be increased: this, Taylor argued, would provide the necessary incentive for workers. Although productivity did increase significantly as a result of carefully, albeit mechanically, planned tasks and careful worker selection, considerable disenchantment and demotivation often resulted, because of the physically highly demanding and repetitive nature of the resultant jobs. Nevertheless, the common assumption, which became engrained in organisational belief systems, was that pay was a major, if not the sole, source of motivation: this view prevailed, and still exists to an extent today, despite the widespread criticism of the work of the Scientific School of Management.

Herzberg also identified a series of factors which, he suggested, lead to satisfaction and, he at least implicitly suggested, increased motivation. These intrinsic factors are those directly related to the work itself and include a sense of achievement, recognition from superiors and colleagues, responsibility and opportunity for personal growth and advancement. Hence, the implication is that managers should attempt to enable employees to access intrinsic satisfiers, while simultaneously avoiding the dissatisfaction resulting from the perceived inadequacy of extrinsic rewards. The intrinsic rewards, or motivators, equate, to an extent, to Maslow's higher-level needs, whereas the hygiene or extrinsic factors are similar to his lower-level physiological and security needs. The two factors, satisfiers and dissatisfiers, are illustrated in Table 3.2.

Table 3.2 Herzberg's satisfiers and dissatisfiers

Hygiene – Context factors Extrinsic rewards	Motivators – Content factors Intrinsic rewards
■ Company policy and administration	■ Sense of achievement
■ Supervision/relationship with supervisor	■ Recognition
■ Working conditions	■ The work itself
■ Remuneration: pay, salary	■ Responsibility
■ Relationship with peers and with subordinates	■ Advancement
■ Status/promotion	■ Personal growth
■ Job security	

The two-factor theory suggests that the prospect of receiving intrinsic rewards (expectancy) will be more likely to motivate individuals than the possibility of, for example, improved working conditions, job security or salary improvements. Salary enhancements and other hygiene factors might be viewed in the short term as advantageous but, Herzberg suggested, they have only a small effect on sustained motivation in the workplace. The opportunity for personal advancement, recognition for one's contribution, enhanced responsibility for the outcome of an individual's or group's effort and the nature of the actual work itself (possibly stimulating, interesting, involving variety) will serve to motivate on an ongoing and sustainable basis.

Kerr (1975) has noted that the reward systems in many organisations serve to 'reward' undesirable behaviours while, simultaneously, ignoring or even punishing more positive ones. The feedback and reinforcement processes appear to be essential to achieve and sustain a motivated workforce, yet many company practices and policies, usually unknowingly, serve to depress employee motivation. As a consequence, when individuals feel they are not being rewarded for a job well done they become dissatisfied and, potentially, undermotivated.

By and large, prior to Herzberg's work, job satisfaction and performance were thought to result largely, if not exclusively, from extrinsic stimulants, such as pay. He raised the very real spectre of complexity and the likelihood that the factors contributing to workplace satisfaction, motivation and performance undoubtedly include intrinsic rewards. Few academics and practitioners now believe that hygiene factors alone will ensure that organisations have motivated, productive, involved and creative employees and most recognise the need to consider the quality of work life as part of the motivation equation and managerial process. Nevertheless, the issue of pay and status frequently emerges within organisations and is particularly relevant during some organisational change processes. The mini-case presented in Figure 3.6, entitled 'Pay and status differentials', illustrates one such thorny problem faced by a largely well-meaning management team. The potential for conflict and demotivation is apparent in this real-life scenario, as is the scope for enhanced motivation: a thin line exists between the two.

Despite the intuitive appeal of the two-factor theory criticisms can be levelled at its premises and, particularly, at its validity. The original research conducted by Herzberg utilised a relatively small sample size (210) of professional people (accountants and engineers). Therefore, its applicability to other groups has been questioned. Nevertheless, research conducted by Blackburn and Mann (1979) (sample size, 1000) among low to medium-skilled employees found a wide range of orientations and suggested that individuals are often motivated by factors other than, for example, pay. Many of the respondents in this research were found to have a primary and strong orientation towards many of the intrinsic motivators referred to by Herzberg, such as concern for autonomy and for worthwhileness of the work. It also concluded that blue collar workers differ from one another regarding their prime orientation and likely source of workplace motivation. What it did not find was that pay and other hygiene factors totally dominated their considerations. Numerous other studies, using

Pay and status differentials

This mini-case study explores the motivational issues concerning pay and status differentials in the context of the management of change.

In a medium-sized NHS Trust hospital in the UK it is proposed that all cleaning staff, porters, nursing assistants and ward clerks are to form a flexible, multi-skilled, ward-based team of care assistants. Existing formal status and pay differentials between employees would be reduced as a consequence. As a result, many staff would be upgraded and many would receive a basic pay rise but about a third of personnel would not benefit financially or in status terms by these changes; for some the change would signal a reduction in pay. The simple grade and pay spines, which would apply to all care assistants, would reduce status differentials and simplify the highly complex bonus schemes that had evolved. Some staff would be required to change their shift pattern and the total hours they worked within any one week. Managers felt it would improve worker motivation as all would 'feel part of a team'. This would, they believed, particularly apply to the porters and domestics who are often unaffiliated to a ward and consequently are remote from patients and from care assistant colleagues.

Pay issue

One of the major issues discussed at the change project meeting was the proposed pay scales for these new roles. All staff would be classified as either Health Care Assistant 1 (HCA1 – the lower scale) or HCA2 (the higher pay scale) and jobs would be assessed to see into which category they fell. It is likely, for example, that many Care Assistant: Nursing jobs would be graded HCA2 whereas most Care Assistant: Housekeeping jobs would be in HCA1. All employees would have protected pay for a year, that is, even if they were placed on a scale and job rate which is below their existing pay, their income would not immediately fall.

At a recent meeting the Director of HRM argued, 'What I'm interested in is whether the underlying principles are right, that is, are all the jobs, nursing (assistant), housekeeping and administration rated equally, allowing for two grades of these personnel?' The Chief Executive, who is ultimately responsible to the Board of Directors for the Trust budget, suggested that he had 'some difficulties with the concept of thinking that these are all valued the same. I intuitively would have put housekeeping at a lower level than administration and nursing. What I'm worried about is that in order to recruit for the administration and nursing we're going to end up with the highest paid domestic workforce in the locality.' The Director of Nursing interjected, 'It's too easy to drop back into "old speak". Why should people, just because they clean the toilet, be any different from those who make beds?'

Discussion question

Should cleaners be paid on the same scale as porters, administrators and nursing assistants? Discuss the motivational implications of these changes, drawing on theories and models presented in this chapter.

Fig 3.6 Mini-case: pay, status and motivation

workers from a variety of sectors, such as nurses, food industry employees, technicians and assembly staff have, broadly, replicated the original findings.

Herzberg used a method of research known as the critical incident technique which requires respondents to consider their work experiences retrospectively. It can be argued that such historical contemplation may distort 'reality' when respondents consider factors which led to either satisfaction or dissatisfaction. Other writers, notably Vroom (1964) and House and Wigdor (1967) have criticised the theory, the latter suggesting that the two-factor approach is an oversimplification of the potential sources of both satisfaction and dissatisfaction.

In summary, the three most common criticisms of the theory are that it has limited application for non-professional or non-manual workers, that it represents an oversimplification of sources of satisfaction and dissatisfaction and that it is methodologically flawed. It should be noted that, despite the often well-considered criticisms, the theory is not invalidated but merely questioned and refined. One could suggest that it is a measure of the appeal of this theory that so much critical attention has been paid to it.

Motivation and equitable treatment

The content theories discussed above shed further light on the expectancy model and enhance our understanding of the complexity of workplace motivation. Equity theory, developed by Adams (1963, 1965), gives us a particularly useful, if simple, insight into the relationship between rewards and the likely satisfaction individuals gain from them. It qualifies our understanding of the expectancy model. The level of satisfaction and potential motivation resulting from an individual's receiving a reward cannot be considered entirely in isolation. The rewards and treatment of others also influences an individual's level of satisfaction. Additionally, people appear to be motivated to receive what they consider a fair or equitable return for their efforts. For example, where expectancy is high, perhaps unrealistically so, if the desired outcome is not achieved then individuals may feel frustrated or even cheated by this experience. This sense of unfairness or inequity may result in dissatisfaction and demotivation.

Adams's model contains three crucial components: inputs (qualities 'invested' by the individual); outputs (intrinsic and extrinsic rewards from the organisation) and comparison with others. Clearly, the weighting or value placed on both inputs and outputs is a matter of individual perception and consequent judgement. These two factors equate to 'effort' and 'rewards' in the expectancy model (*see* Figure 3.3). How this significantly differs from expectancy theory, another process model of motivation, is its recognition that individuals make comparisons between themselves and others when assessing the scale or worthiness of rewards received. Recognition of this critical contextual variable adds important insight and, hence it is incorporated into Figure 3.3.

If an individual perceives that the overall outputs he or she receives from the organisation (e.g. pay, fringe benefits, recognition) in return for their particular inputs (e.g. hours of work, achievements, qualifications) are equal to, or exceed, those received by colleagues in the company or peers elsewhere, then they will view the situation as equitable or even favourable. The opposite effect leads to under-reward inequity where individuals are motivated to reduce such inequality. This may result in their reducing their input. Such real or perceived inequality can also cause conflict between individuals and groups within and across organisations. It may lead to relationship difficulties between, for example, management and employees if the latter group perceive that they are being treated inequitably. This perception, often held by large numbers of employees simultaneously, is frequently a root cause of union/management strife, worker discontent, or demotivation, and low morale. Equity theory has been shown to hold validity in practice (Goodman and Friedman, 1971). As a consequence the theory underpins the work of managers and, in particular, industrial relations and compensation specialists in HR/financial roles in organisations.

Change, motivation and the psychological contract

Underlying most theories of motivation or satisfaction in the workplace is an assumption that key variables, such as role expectations and operational norms, are fixed or static. They tend to be non-dynamic models, that is, aspects of the individual, the organisation and the business environment are considered either unimportant or unchanging. In reality the individual, and particularly the relationship he or she enjoys with an organisation, is a dynamic phenomenon. The nature of individual, group and organisational roles and objectives continually change. Change can be a source of frustration, fear and anxiety or a challenge and renewed source of motivation: perhaps even both. Organisational change, and the manner in which it is managed, and, if appropriate, communicated, can have a lasting impact on the motivation of those involved.

When people join an organisation they metaphorically 'sign' a psychological contract. In other words, they enter into an understanding with their employer concerning expected and legitimate behaviours and outputs. This joint agreement usually includes an understanding about the level of commitment expected of employees and of support offered from the employer. In general terms, most individuals would expect equitable treatment, some form of involvement in decision making (especially in a managerial position), a certain level of job security and so forth. Employers would expect employees to accept the organisational ideology and its goals, to uphold the image of the company and to show diligence and, for example, trustworthiness. At any time different individuals in an organisation might hold different psychological contracts with their employer. Major organisational change might, therefore, not only violate that contract, but also affect different people in a variety of ways. Similarly, major conflict between individuals and groups and between the organisation and individuals can violate the psychological contract. Such violation can cause bitterness and resentment which might in turn lead to demotivation.

The relentless pressure on organisations to embrace greater flexibility has resulted in the emergence of the flexible organisation. Organisations are adopting flatter structures by delayering and downsizing, they are outsourcing more and employing a smaller core workforce. There is, as a result, a burgeoning peripheral group of employees, some only loosely connected to the organisation. These changes have far-reaching effects on individuals within and around the flexible organisation. Roles are becoming broader and more dynamic, individuals are increasingly required to develop multiskill capabilities and job security is waning. These changes have far-reaching consequences for motivation and pose crucial questions for management and employee groups. Ironically, multiskilling, teamwork and change generally demand greater levels of individual motivation on the part of employees, yet all can lead to stress and a feeling of anxiety and insecurity. The motivation equation is most certainly assailed by these developments.

Motivation and conflict

The management of conflict in organisations affects the motivation of individuals and groups. Contrary to intuitive understanding, conflict can have positive effects. Research has indicated that conflict can arouse enthusiasm in some individuals, whereas intergroup rivalry may act as a source of cohesion and encourage *esprit de corps* within groups. Schmidt (1974), following empirical research conducted among management executives in the USA, revealed both positive and negative effects of conflict. Many of these 'outcomes' can directly influence job satisfaction and affect motivation and performance in the workplace. He found that conflict can stimulate creative thinking and can inspire people to confront longstanding problems and explore new approaches. It may encourage reflection and help people clarify their views, and heighten their interest in the task at hand. It also tests people's abilities.

Clearly, many of these positive outcomes appear to stimulate thinking and action: they energise or motivate people. However, negative effects of conflict can lead to dissatisfaction, demotivation and, potentially, a reduction in performance. Schmidt (1974) found that certain people felt defeated by conflict and, as a result, reduced contact with others and harboured distrust and suspicion. In general, parties that needed to co-operate in the interests of the organisation tended to pursue self-interest. Some executives in the study left their organisation in order to escape conflict. Continued and severe conflict can have a major and sometimes lasting impact on an individual's psychological well-being. Blake and Mouton (1984) suggested that tension, anxiety and resentment result from conflictual situations which threaten individuals' personal goals and beliefs, rendering trusting relationships impossible to maintain. Kohn (1986) suggested that there is a direct link between conflict and resultant motivation. The stress which results from conflict leads to a rigidity in behaviour and thought and a reduction in motivation.

In conclusion, whereas it is thought conflict has its advantages in the workplace, the potential problems, not least to levels of motivation, are potentially severe. Hence, the careful management and control of conflict falls within the remit of all competent and responsible managers.

Contemporary motivation theories

Considerable criticism has been levelled at many of the assumptions implicit in certain motivation theories. Additionally, the practicality of these models as managerial tools is questionable. Nevertheless, there is a relative dearth of rigorous contemporary motivation theory. More recent research in the field has tended to move away from providing all-embracing general solutions to motivation problems towards consideration of narrow and valid issues. Furthermore, another trend, as indicated in this chapter, is towards a consolidated perspective on the main motivation theories, one that aims to identify and work with the relationships between different theories. Finally, emphasis has shifted away from the development of new motivation theories to related areas such as concern with leadership and organisational culture. Research and writing has dwelt on issues of commitment of personnel and of involvement and participation in decision making. Hence from best-selling books, such as *In Search of Excellence* (Peters and Waterman, 1982), to more focused and rigorous research, concern has shifted in recent decades to the human aspects of the workplace, to teamworking and to value added through human endeavour.

It is recognised that the workplace environment is changing rapidly in many cases and that people themselves reflect changes in their national cultures and subcultures. Maccoby (1988) suggests that there are five social character types, each of which differs in terms of their prime drivers. One type he argues, the self-developer, is more prevalent in the modern age. They are well suited to the demands of modern organisations: they are likely to have higher levels of education and are well imbued with problem solving, information processing and diagnostic abilities. Such people, he argues, are motivated by opportunities for expression, by challenge and development. They require management commitment on responsibilities and rewards and need to be involved in business affairs and have access to information. Clearly, this 'type-environment' fit model rejects the rather simplistic claims of Maslow and others that needs are similar for all individuals and that they are hierarchically accessed.

Whereas most traditional motivation theories suggest that individuals largely respond to organisational and other external stimuli, an alternative approach or perspective in the field of psychology suggests that we are not passive receivers and responders (Staw, 1977). Individuals may actively attempt to control factors which influence the rewards they receive. For example, they may employ ingratiation, *the process whereby people manipulate their superiors' opinion of them*, to improve their chances of being awarded desired rewards. This may explain why some employees are more successful in being granted promotion or other rewards.

Work on intrinsic motivation and commitment has shown that individuals who expect to influence or even control performance and reward outcomes for themselves devalue those outcomes if they are imposed or chosen by another. Reactance theory suggests that when freedom and control are threatened individuals are motivated to regain or reassert that freedom or control. Of concern is that if their attempts to regain freedom and control are thwarted, as they so often are in the workplace, individuals who recognise or perceive that they cannot control their rewards experience learned helplessness, a process of giving up and reducing effort. For example, in the competition for promotion that often occurs in organisations, many cannot identify the basis on which others receive promotion. This may lead the 'unsuccessful' to feel disempowered and helpless, a state of mind which may in turn prove demotivating.

Similarly, people construct or attribute explanations, often fictitious, for events such as an individual's promotion or the award of a bonus. Heider (1958) and Kelley (1971) have made a major contribution to attribution theory. The four prime explanations given for success are effort, ability, luck or the degree of task difficulty. If an individual attributes his or her success to luck, this person is unlikely to increase motivation to ensure success continues, whereas if the individual believes effort was the root cause then a high level of motivation is likely to continue. Those with a strong internal locus of control tend to believe that events are within their personal control, whereas others attribute external causes to events. The latter may well suggest that receipt of their recent bonus was a matter of luck, the former individuals would suggest that they had earned it by effort and ability. Clearly, this work suggests that individuals differ and that the ability to motivate employees might, in part, depend on their perceived or real locus of control.

Motivation and job design

It is now appropriate to move on from a theoretical and, at times, abstract consideration of how people are motivated to focus upon how knowledge of motivation theories can influence management and, in particular, job design. Early concern with job design focused on attempts to improve individual motivation by paying attention to job rotaion, job enlargement and job enrichment. Job enlargement involves *increasing the scope of the job, often by increasing the number of tasks to be performed*. Job enrichment is an attempt to build upon Herzberg's two-factor theory by *designing jobs which enrich individuals by giving them opportunity to increase their responsibility and involvement and which allow greater opportunity for advancement, achievement and recognition.*

Existing motivation theory has contributed significantly to job design. For example, expectancy theory predicts that jobs which emphasise the relationship between effort, performance and reward will motivate people, especially those who value an interesting and challenging work experience. Herzberg sought to apply his two-factor theory to the workplace. He argued that in order to enrich jobs, as a mechanism for ensuring satisfaction and enhanced motivation, measures would need to be taken which would enable individuals to benefit from intrinsic rewards and to avoid the potential dissatisfiers. As a consequence he suggested seven vertical loading factors. These are shown in Table 3.3 which relates the factors to various intrinsic and extrinsic rewards that might ensue and suggests potential managerial actions which might serve to achieve each loading category.

The Hackman and Oldham job characteristic model

Hackman and Oldham (1980), perhaps the most significant contributors to work design theory, argued that a well-designed job may enhance employee motivation. Their work drew heavily on the theoretical arguments summarised above, particularly the contributions of Herzberg and some needs theorists, such as McClelland.

Table 3.3 Herzberg's vertical loading factors

Vertical loading factors	Potential managerial actions
Increase individual accountability	Enhance sense of responsibility and personal challenge, hence allowing scope for growth and advancement.
Remove controls	Remove sources of dissatisfaction resulting from a controlling style of supervision. Allow greater freedom of action and give scope for personal growth and recognition via trust.
Allocate special assignments	Delegate responsibility and interesting work, hence giving an opportunity for achievement and growth.
Introduce new tasks	Enhance the desirability of the work itself by introducing variety and challenge and, potentially, greater responsibility.
Create natural work units	Allow for enhanced recognition from one's colleagues by forming groups whose members enjoy each other's company and are otherwise compatible.
Grant additional authority	Enhanced responsibility is a form of recognition. It allows for growth and advancement and may reduce the potential dissatisfaction of having to comply with all manner of company procedures and policies.
Provide direct feedback	This provides potential for recognition and scope for coaching to facilitate growth.

The reader may note the many similarities and logical consistencies between this theory and the 'mainstream' motivation theories.

Motivation increases, they suggested, when individuals achieve three critical psychological states (*see* Figure 3.7):

- experienced meaningfulness;
- experienced responsibility;
- knowledge of results.

There are five job characteristics which should encourage the three psychological states to be achieved and, hence, lead to motivated employees:

- skill variety;
- task identity;
- task significance;
- autonomy;
- feedback from the job.

This theory provides a model to guide job design.

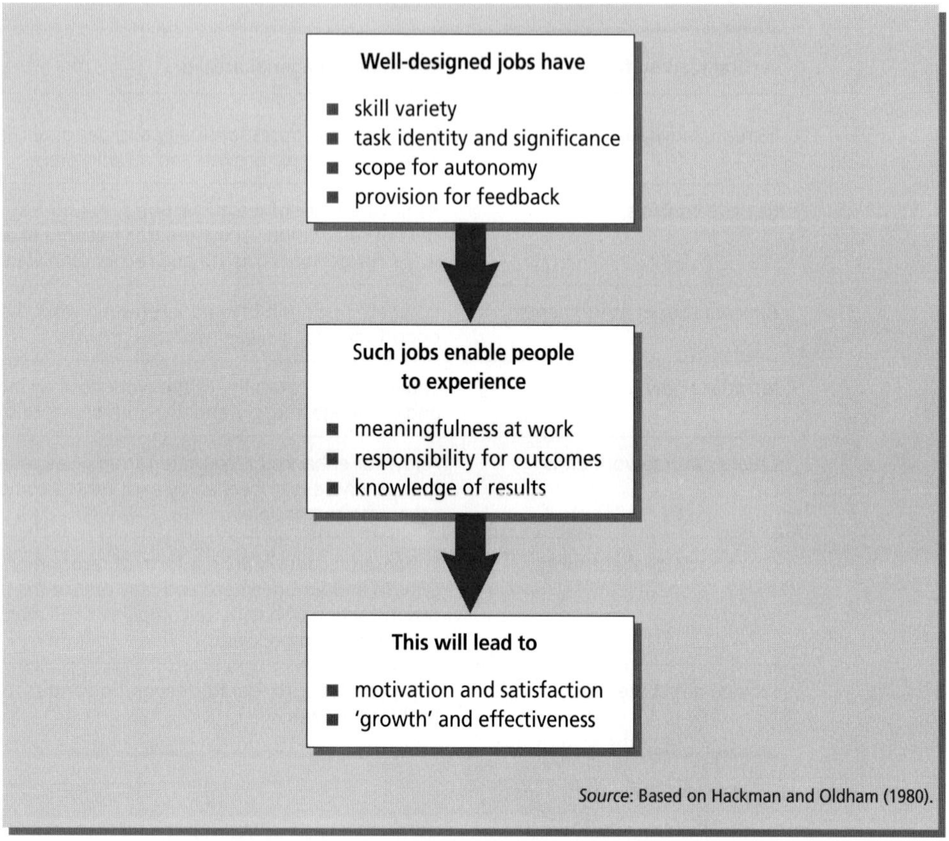
Well-designed jobs have
skill variety
task identity and significance
scope for autonomy
provision for feedback
Such jobs enable people to experience
meaningfulness at work
responsibility for outcomes
knowledge of results
This will lead to
motivation and satisfaction
'growth' and effectiveness
Source: Based on Hackman and Oldham (1980).

Fig 3.7 Hackman and Oldham's work design model

The outcomes from a well-designed job, which considers and incorporates the aspects listed above, include high internal work motivation, growth, general satisfaction and work effectiveness. Hence, the model considers the intrinsic aspects of motivation in addition to job characteristics and individual differences. The model can be used, especially when accompanied by the Hackman and Oldham job diagnostic survey (JDS), to calculate the overall 'motivating potential score' (MPS) for any job.

Managerial implications

Motivation is a complex subject. For managers and aspiring managers with a willingness and desire to learn how to motivate subordinates the plethora of theoretical material can appear confusing. This chapter has attempted to indicate that many of the theories do not in fact significantly contradict one another but, rather, complement each other. Collectively, they shed considerable light on the nature of workplace motivation. In very broad terms, managers need to do the following to motivate others.

1 Managers should identify the needs, drives and ambitions of each individual, the outcomes each employee wants.

2 Managers should relate these characteristics to the nature of the tasks expected of those individuals and the roles they are to perform and give opportunities, for example, for them to seek both intrinsic rewards, such as achievement, affiliation, recognition, responsibility and advancement, and extrinsic rewards.

3 Managers should clarify for individuals the potential outcomes they might achieve for their efforts, especially if these are positive, desirable, realistic and possible to achieve.

4 Managers should carefully examine their reward systems, company policies, supervision styles and so forth, to avoid potential sources of demotivation.

5 Managers should make sure that the reward system is equitable.

6 Managers should bear in mind that although this is a contentious issue, expectancy theory implies that rewards, such as pay increases, will have little motivational effect if awarded to all; rather, they need to be focused on individuals or teams and based on their performance. It may even prove valuable if the selective granting of rewards is made public so all can see the link between performance and reward.

7 Managers should attempt to forge a balance between encouraging an appropriate level and type of conflict, which might stimulate employees, and avoiding the negative aspects of rivalry.

8 Managers should recognise the motivational implications of change programmes and utilise skills of communication to moderate the adverse effects of changes to each individual's psychological contract.

9 Managers should consider motivation theory, and the work of those who have applied this to job design, when creating or changing individual or team tasks and roles.

Summary of main points

This chapter has examined the complex issue of workplace motivation and drawn upon a range of established and contemporary theory and empirical research. The main points made are:

- motivation theories can be subdivided between process and content theories and between those from the cognitive school and those underpinned by behaviouralist principles;
- expectancy theory is a useful explanatory model of motivation which enables us to consider other process theories, such as equity theory, and content models, such as needs and two-factor theories;
- the management of change, its communication and the involvement of people in the change process, together with the management of conflict, all have potentially profound effects on individual motivation;

- motivation theories underpin and direct efforts to enrich jobs and design tasks and roles to maximise potential motivation and/or avoid demotivation;
- there are a series of implications for management that derive from the work of motivation and job design theorists.

Conclusions

There does not appear to be one universally applicable theory of motivation. However, those presented in this chapter increase our understanding of workplace motivation considerably. Motivation is a complex, dynamic and culture-bound concept and the reader should beware of giving too much credence to simple 'solutions' which might claim to provide *the* answer. If motivation were a simple managerial task then most workplaces would be full of well-motivated employees. The extent to which they are motivated is dependent not merely on the quality of management but on many other personal and environmental factors. Clearly, what motivates people differs between individuals, is related to and influenced by, context and is both culturally dependent and ever changing.

QUESTIONS

1 Does pay motivate? Refer to appropriate motivation theories in your attempt to address this crucial question.

2 Explain how various needs theories or Herzberg's two-factor theory contribute to our understanding of expectancy theory.

3 What effect will a major organisational change, for example the creation of a more flexible organisation, have on workplace motivation?

4 What lessons from motivation theory underpin contemporary developments in job design?

REFERENCES

Adams, J. S. (1963) 'Towards an understanding of inequity', *Journal of Abnormal Social Psychology*, 67, pp 422–36.

Adams, J. S. (1965) 'Inequity in social exchange' in Berkowitz, L. (ed.) *Advances in Experimental Social Psychology*, Vol. 2. New York: Academic Press.

Alderfer, C. P. (1972) *Existence, Relatedness and Growth.* New York: Collier Macmillan.

Blackburn, R. M. and Mann, M. (1979) *The Working Class in the Labour Market*. London: Macmillan.

Blake, R. R. and Mouton, J. S. (1984) *Solving Costly Organisational Conflicts*. San Francisco: Jossey-Bass.

Campbell, J. P. and Pritchard, D. (1976) 'Motivation theory in industrial and organisational psychology' in Dunnette, M. D. (ed.) *Handbook of Industrial and Organisational Psychology*. Chicago: Rand McNally, pp 63–130.

Goodman, P. A. and Friedman, A. (1971) 'An examination of Adams' theory of equity', *Administrative Science Quarterly*, 16.

Hackman, J. R. and Oldham, G. R. (1980) *Work Redesign*. Reading, MA: Addison-Wesley.

Hall, D. T. and Nougaim, K. E. (1968) 'An examination of Maslow's need hierarchy in an organizational setting', *Organizational Behaviour and Human Performance*, Vol. 3, pp 12–35.

Heider, F. (1958) *The Psychology of Interpersonal Relations*. New York: Wiley.

Herzberg, F. (1968) 'One more time: How do you motivate employees?', *Harvard Business Review*, 46(1), pp 53–62.

House, R. J. and Wigdor, L. A. (1967) 'Herzberg's dual-factor theory of job satisfaction and motivation: a review of the evidence and a criticism', *Personnel Psychology*, 20 (Winter), pp 369–90.

Iaffaldano, M. T. and Muchinsky, P. M. (1985) 'Job satisfaction and job performance: a meta-analysis', *Psychological Bulletin*, 97, pp 251–73.

Kelley, H. H. (1971) *Attribution in Social Interaction*. Morristown, NJ: General Learning Press.

Kerr, S. (1975) 'On the folly of rewarding A, while hoping for B', *Academy of Management Journal*, Vol. 18, pp 769–83.

Kohn, A. (1986) *No Contest: The Case Against Competition*. Boston: Houghton Mifflin.

Lawler, E. E. (1973) *Motivation in Work Organizations*. New York: Brooks-Cole Publishing.

Lawler, E. E. and Suttle, J. L. (1972) 'A causal correlation test of the need hierarchy concept', *Organisational Behaviour and Human Performance*, Vol. 7, pp 265–87.

Locke, E. A. (1968) 'Towards a theory of task motivation and incentives', *Organizational Behaviour and Human Performance*, Vol. 3, pp 157–89.

Maccoby, M. (1988) *Why work: motivating and leading the new generation*. New York: Simon and Schuster.

Maslow, A. H. (1943) 'A theory of human motivation', *Psychological Review*, Vol. 50(4), pp 370–96.

McClelland, D. C. (1961) *The Achieving Society*. New York: Van Nostrand Reinhold.

McClelland, D. C. (1962) 'Business drive and national achievement', *Harvard Business Review*, 40 (July–August), pp 99–112.

McClelland, D. C. and Boyatzis, R. E. (1984) 'The need for close relationships and the manager's job' in Kolb, D. M., Rubin, I. M. and Macintyre, J. M. (eds) *Organizational Psychology: Readings on Human Behaviour in Organizations*. New York: Prentice-Hall.

Peters, T. J. and Waterman, R. H. (1982) *In Search of Excellence*. New York: Harper & Row.

Pinder, C. (1984) *Work Motivation*. Glenview, IL: Scott, Foresman.

Porter, L. W. and Lawler, E. E. (1968) *Managerial Attitudes and Performance*. Homewood, IL: Irwin.

Schmidt, W. H. (1974) 'A powerful force for (good or bad) change', *Management Review*, December, pp 4–10.

Schneider, B. (1985) 'Organizational behaviour', *Annual Review of Psychology*, 36.

Staw, B. M. (1977) 'Motivation in organisations: towards synthesis and redirection' in Staw, B. M. and Salancik, G. R. (eds) *New Directions in Organisational Behaviour*. Chicago: St Clair Press.

Tolman, E. and Honzik, C. (1930) 'Introduction and removal of reward and maze performance of rats', *University of California Publications in Psychology*, Vol. 4, pp 257–75.

Vroom, V. H. (1964) *Work and Motivation*. New York: Wiley.

FURTHER READING

Herzberg, F. (1968) 'One more time: How do you motivate employees?' *Harvard Business Review*, 46(1), pp 53–62.

Huczynski, A. and Buchanan, D. (1991) *Organizational Behaviour*. Englewood Cliffs, NJ: Prentice-Hall, Chapter 4.

Lawler, E. E., III (1971) *Pay and Organizational Effectiveness*. New York: McGraw-Hill.

Maccoby, M. (1988) *Why work: motivating and leading the new generation*. New York: Simon and Schuster.

Outlines the changing nature of the workplace and categorises people into five types. It outlines the characteristics and sources of motivation and demotivation of each.

Maslow, A. H. (1987) *Motivation and Personality*, 3rd edn. New York: Harper & Row.

Moorhead, G. and Griffin, R. W. (1995) *Organizational Behaviour*, 4th edn. Boston: Houghton Mifflin, Chapters 4–6.

Mullins, L. J. (1999) *Management and Organisational Behaviour*, 5th edn. London: Financial Times Pitman Publishing, Chapters 12 and 18.

4

Groups and teams

HUGH DAVENPORT

LEARNING OUTCOMES

On completion of this chapter you should be able to:

- understand 'our' need for groups;
- differentiate between formal and informal groups;
- explain how groups develop, grow and are maintained and disbanded;
- discuss the dynamics of group performance and effectiveness;
- differentiate between inter- and intra-group conflict and behaviour;
- understand the role technological communication plays within teams;
- appreciate some of the problems inherent with working in groups;
- appreciate the impact of global, cross-cultural and virtual teams.

KEY CONCEPTS

- *groups and teams*
- *formal and informal groups*
- *psychological groups*
- *team development*
- *self-directed and self-managed teams*
- *team roles*
- *group norms*
- *team and group effectiveness and cohesion*
- *conformity and groupthink*
- *technology, communication and change*
- *networks and virtual teams*
- *global and cross-cultural teams*

Groups and teams

Most activities that take place in an organisation require some degree of co-ordination through the operation of group working. Many organisational goals cannot be achieved by members working alone; thus most individuals spend an increasing amount of time working with others in groups. The classical approach to organisation ignored the importance of groups and the social factors at work but the writings of Elton Mayo soon created a cult of the group and this continues unabated today, albeit in the guise of teams and teamworking. Within this scenario, it is an essential requirement that managers and organisations should understand the nature of groups, their processes and behaviour. If managers are to lead and influence the behaviour of a team, they need to be aware of factors which influence their performance and effectiveness.

Introduction

A popular and important aspect of work is that it is increasingly conducted in groups or teams. Some of the reasons for this increased interest in work groups and teams stems from the rapidly changing conditions facing today's organisations. Organisational restructuring is leading to flatter structures, wider spans of control and a general reduction in layers of management. Following on from this comes the inevitable complementary increase in the empowerment of employees. All of these aspects lead to a greater emphasis on the importance of group- and teamworking. Additionally, the impact of global economic competition, increasing diversity within the workforce and the expanding role played by technology suggest that new ways of working are required. Within this increasingly volatile scenario Parker (1990) has identified that the use of teams has led to greater productivity, more effective uses of resources, better decisions and problem solving, better quality products and services and increased innovation and creativity. Within this heightened team culture philosophy the failures of teams can be both dramatic and visible, making the need to understand group and team effectiveness a crucial aspect for organisations wanting to thrive in these new conditions. This chapter will investigate the concepts of groups, psychological groups and teams. We will also explore some of the factors which affect their functioning and performance.

Why gather in groups?

Before identifying and exploring what a group is, it is important to identify why people feel the need to gather in groups and why organisations promote their importance. Having looked into these general areas we will start to focus on the different types of groups and the needs those different groups are attempting to satisfy. Aronson (1992) wrote a book about it and the singing group, The Television Personalities, named a song after it. We congregate in social gatherings to satiate our need for it. 'It' is what might be termed a *sense of belonging*. Gathering in groups has always been a characteristic of human behaviour. We are, in Aronson's words, 'social animals' and need the input from and interaction with others to function effectively as individuals.

However alluring and seductive the above sentiments are, they do not give the whole picture as to why groups are formed and people join them. People do not join groups simply to flock around others, although that may appear to be the case sometimes. Most people belong to a whole variety of groups, both in and out of work, each providing different benefits to their members and satisfying various needs.

Security and protection

'There's strength in numbers', goes a familiar cliché. The mere presence of another person as we watch a horror movie can give us a greater feeling of security. By joining an environmental protest group we can reduce the insecurity (and futility?) of standing alone and we are, as a collective, more resistant to threats. In organisations the situation is no different. Employees who feel their jobs are under threat from new technology may well turn to their particular trade union to reduce their levels of insecurity.

'A problem shared is a problem halved' is another cliché relevant in this context. The members of a new product design team may well feel more secure in their decisions because the responsibility for a bad decision is shared with, and spread among, others. A group, without being aware of it, can dissipate the risk.

Affiliation and status

A recent newspaper headline read, '£1m Lottery winner still goes to work'. Upon further exploration it becomes clear that the headline is not as bizarre as might first appear: the winner still works to satisfy not a monetary need but a social need – 'I really like the people I work with and would miss them'. Regular interactions with a set of people with whom we are familiar can act to fulfil the needs for affiliation and social contact (*see* Chapter 3 for a discussion of needs theories in organisations). At a deeper level, needs for friendship and self-worth are met.

The statement, 'I am a member of the British Psychological Society and sit on the committee of the Section of Occupational Psychology', not only conveys one's status to those outside the group but gives increased feelings of self-worth to the group member. Being asked to join a highly valued and respected group can be even more meaningful in terms of fulfilling one's needs for competence and growth, as well as for status. Public recognition of one's worth and value is a powerful motivator for some. Groups can give us prestige, recognition and status among our peers.

Power

The phrase 'the whole is greater than the sum of its parts' highlights a seductive property of groups, that they represent power. The unachievable becomes possible through group action. As we will see below, informal groups and networks can often provide a mechanism for people to exercise power, an avenue which would not be open to them under the formal structure (*see also* Chapter 8 on power).

Groups and teams

What exactly is meant by a group? Consider the following groups:

- the pop group Oasis performing to a gathering of 70 000 ecstatic people at Wembley Stadium;

- the newly-formed European sales team who have not yet met each other but communicate and interconnect on a daily basis using a whole range of new technology;
- the comprehensively beaten, but informally run, pub quiz team;
- delayed passengers on the 8.15 from Euston who together, while sitting in their compartment, brainstorm a letter of complaint and form a commuters action group;
- the folk singer Clive Gregson strumming away, in his garden, to a dozen friends;
- the victorious village football team.

Which of these 'groups' are merely groups as a collection of people, which of them are something more meaningful, a psychological group, and which of the examples may be categorised as teams?

Groups

There are many ways of defining what is meant by a group. Charles Handy (1993: 150) defines a group as *'any collection of people who perceive themselves to be a group'*. The concept of a group is familiar to most people who socialise, live, work and play in groups. However, in deciding which of the above are merely aggregates of individuals, or something more than simply people doing roughly the same thing, we are forced to hone, sharpen and refocus our definitions. More often than not we will refer to persons standing at a bus stop, or in a queue, as a group. It could be argued though that the essential feature of a group is that its members regard themselves as belonging to the group, that is, they have a common sense of belonging.

A more meaningful definition comes from Schein (1988), who frames the group in psychological terms. That is, a group is any number of people:

- who interact with one another;
- who are psychologically aware of one another; and
- who perceive themselves to be a group.

So the Oasis concert spectators in the list above are not a group, because they do not fulfil all of Schein's criteria. When we use the words groups or group relationship we are, more than likely, referring to the existence of a psychological relationship. As Brown (1971: 32) states, the term group *'is reserved for those aggregates of people which have psychological effects on, and implications for, the individuals composing the group'*. She stresses that becoming a group member *'implies a psychological process of affiliating to others and interaction with others'*.

Teams

Social psychology may still talk about groups and group work but organisations are primarily interested in teams and effective teamworking. The focus on teams in organisations represents a move away from a Taylorist view of employees as costs, to

Defining a team

- Definable membership
- Shared communication network
- Shared sense of collective identity and purpose
- Shared goals
- Group consciousness
- Interdependence
- Interaction
- Group structure and roles
- Ability to act in a unitary manner.

Source: Based on Huczynski and Buchanan (1991) and Adair (1986).

Fig 4.1 Defining a team

a more dynamic approach of viewing people as resources (*see* Chapter 5). With an increasing concentration on working across functional divides, and an emphasis on flexibility, empowerment and innovation, the organisations of the twenty-first century will foster collaborative teamworking cultures and self-directed and self-managed teams.

That teamworking is popular cannot be doubted. A survey by the Industrial Society (1995) of 500 personnel managers found that 40 per cent worked in organisations with self-managed teams. The average team had around eight people and the main reasons cited for their use were improved customer service, increased staff motivation and the quality of output. A 1996 survey by Dale Carnegie Training identified that 90 per cent of American workers spent at least part of their work day in a team scenario, even though only about half received any teamwork training.

Of the many definitions of what a team actually is, one of the more useful is from Katzenbach and Smith (1993: 15) who suggest that '*a team is a small number of people with complementary skills who are committed to a common purpose, performance goals, and approach for which they hold themselves mutually accountable*'. This is a useful definition because it starts to distinguish between real teams and groups of people, who may often be called teams but are anything but teams. Figure 4.1 extends Schein's definition of a psychological group further to include more specific teamworking elements.

Drawing on Figure 4.1 it is possible to consider an effective team as one where:

- there is a clear understanding of the team's objectives;
- there is among the team members the range of skills and know-how needed to deal effectively with the team's tasks;
- a range of team types exists within the team;
- team members have respect and trust for each other, both as individuals and for the contribution each makes to the team's performance;
- some form of team rewards and group bonus system exists.

Self-directed and self-managed teams

The notion of self-directed teams has grown out of the work conducted in the Swedish car manufacturing industry (Norstedt and Aguren, 1973; Valery, 1974; Thomas, 1974). One of the best known experiments was that conducted in the engine factory of the Saab-Scania Group at Sodertalje. From earlier experiments, the company decided to redesign the factory layout. The new layout consisted of a conveyor loop which moved the engine blocks to seven assembly groups, each with three members. Each group assembled a complete engine and decided for themselves how their work was to be distributed and scheduled. The whole assembly process was not mechanically driven; each group was simply given 30 minutes to complete each engine and they decided how that time was spent. Needless to say, productivity increased and labour turnover dropped, product quality improved and absenteeism fell. The assembly workers developed into a more cohesive group who had real ownership of and pride in their output. In time, through 'natural' job rotation, they each developed all, or most, of the skills required to do any part of the engine assembly.

This style of work organisation became known as 'autonomous work groups' and the success of these groups led to the 'high performance teams approach' used by Digital Equipment (Perry, 1984). This in turn has led to the growing acceptance of self-directed teams. A number of definitions are used to describe self-managed teams. Buchanan (1987: 41) developed one of the earlier descriptions: '*A work group allocated an overall task and given discretion over how the work is to be done. These groups are self-regulating and work without direct supervision.*' They might be viewed as a small group of employees responsible for an *entire* work process or segment. To varying degrees, team members work together to improve their operations or products, plan and control their work and handle day-to-day problems. They often become involved in company-wide issues, such as quality and business planning. Salem, Lazarus and Cullen (1994) identified some typical 'pitfalls' and 'benefits'.

The pitfalls included:

- the difficulty of rescinding the system, once it is established and experienced by the workers;
- varying levels and degrees of resistance by elements in the organisation;
- increasing peer pressure and its consequences.

The benefits included:

- reduced absenteeism;
- increased productivity;
- increased employee satisfaction, morale and cohesiveness;
- multiskilled workforce;
- increased flexibility in work practices;
- decreased need for managers.

Clearly, many of the potential benefits listed above were identified some years previously in the Saab-Scania research of the 1970s involving autonomous work groups. A criticism one could level is that the self-directed and managed teams of the 1990s are simply the autonomous work groups of the 1970s under a different name. This criticism may be justified; however, self-directed teams have tended to take responsibility and empowerment a stage further from that enjoyed by the work groups of the 1970s. A further point to make here in defence of current thinking, which may sometimes appear to add very little to what has gone before, is that we all 'stand on the shoulders of others' when it comes to research and experimentation. Someone has probably visited the findings before and we may simply be adding another piece to the jigsaw. Research and development is often about adding small steps together; we cannot (and do not) all land on the moon every day.

The types of organisation which promote and develop the use of self-directed teams undoubtedly differ from the more traditional organisation in a variety of ways:

- fewer layers of managers and supervisors;
- reward systems are often skill or team based, rather than seniority based;
- leaders may be elected by the team;
- the leader is more of a coach and facilitator than a director or authority figure;
- information is shared with all employees;
- employees learn all the jobs and tasks required of the team.

Self-directed teams certainly appear to be a blueprint for how the organisation of the future will function, orientated around learning, shared ownership, trust, autonomy and flexibility.

Groups within groups

One can view groups and teams as a series of concentric circles. The outer circle defines all groups and includes psychological groups and teams. The middle circle, in turn, includes all teams. Not all groups are teams, but all teams are psychological groups. In order to be effective, a team must possess all of the criteria for being a psychological group and a group. This is illustrated in Figure 4.2.

In concluding our discussion of groups and teams perhaps all we need say is that teams differ from groups in the extent to which their members are interdependent (there is more interdependence in teams) and that the team as a whole, rather than the individual members, has performance and reward goals. Clearly, the boundaries between the two are blurred, but the important issue is to recognise that there are some general and significant differences between the two. In summary, external circumstances (e.g. a delayed train) can change a small group of people (the passengers) into a fully functioning psychological group (with the objective of producing a letter of complaint) or even a team (the commuters action group).

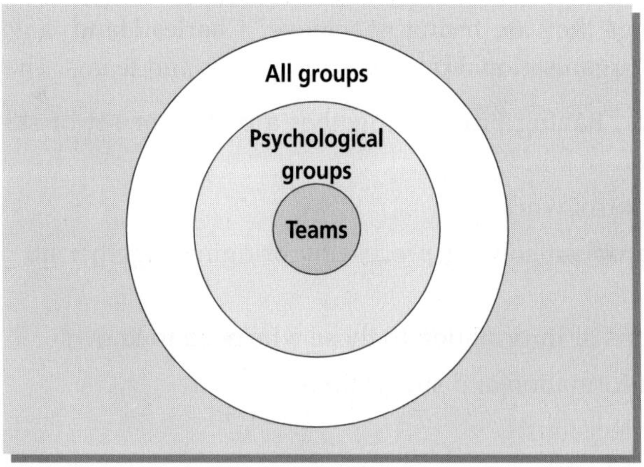

Fig 4.2 Groups within groups

Formal and informal groups and teams

Formal groups

Organisations are constantly organising and reorganising their processes and structures. This may involve disbanding various groups and creating others which are formally constructed, usually by middle or senior managers. Formal groups are, therefore, consciously created to accomplish the organisation's collective mission and to achieve specific organisational and departmental objectives. They are primarily concerned with the co-ordination of work activities and are task orientated. They are embedded and entrapped in the fabric, hierarchy and structure of the organisation: people are brought together on the basis of defined roles. The nature of the tasks undertaken is a predominant feature of the formal group. Goals are identified and developed by management, and rules, relationships and norms of behaviour are established. They have been consciously created and organised, recruited for and put together by somebody for a reason. Formal groups are an important element of the organisational structure (*see* Chapter 7).

Because the individuals in formal groups share some commonality of objectives, goals and (occasionally) rewards, they are more akin to teams – formal teams. They assist people to:

- accomplish goals much less haphazardly than they would in informal groups;
- co-ordinate the activities of the functions of the organisation;
- establish logical authority relationships among people and between positions;
- apply the concepts of specialisation and division of labour;
- create more group cohesion as a result of a common set of goals.

If the above list reflects how formal groups assist people to achieve in certain ways, what are the things they are trying to achieve? Charles Handy (1993) identified a number of major organisational purposes for groups and teams. They are to:

- distribute work, having brought together a particular set of skills, talents and responsibilities;
- manage and control work;
- facilitate the problem-solving process by bringing together all of the available capabilities;
- pass on decisions or information to those who need to know;
- gather ideas, information and suggestions;
- test and ratify decisions;
- co-ordinate and facilitate necessary liaison;
- increase commitment and involvement;
- resolve arguments and disputes between different functions, levels and divisions.

Informal groups

Alongside, within, cutting across and around these formal groups and teams there exist a number of informal groups, such as:

- the office quiz or bowls team;
- the theatre-going group or the Friday lunchtime people;
- the Monday morning 'let's talk about the weekend' group or the folk who regularly swap the latest music CDs;
- the 'let's moan about the organisation' people.

The list is endless.

We can define an informal group as *a collection of individuals who become a group when members develop certain interdependencies, influence one another's behaviour and contribute to mutual need satisfaction.* Informal groups are based more on personal relationships and agreement of group members than on any defined role relationships. They simply emerge in the organisation, from the informal interaction of the members of the organisation. They may be born out of shared interests, friendship or some other social aspect. What informal groups satisfy, in a way that the formal group may not, is that sense of belonging mentioned at the very beginning of this chapter, the idea that we can be wanted, needed and included for what we are and not because the organisation has put us to work with these other people. These informal groups can also satisfy a range of other needs. They can:

- reduce feelings of insecurity and anxiety and provide each other with social support;
- fulfil affiliation needs for friendship, love and support;

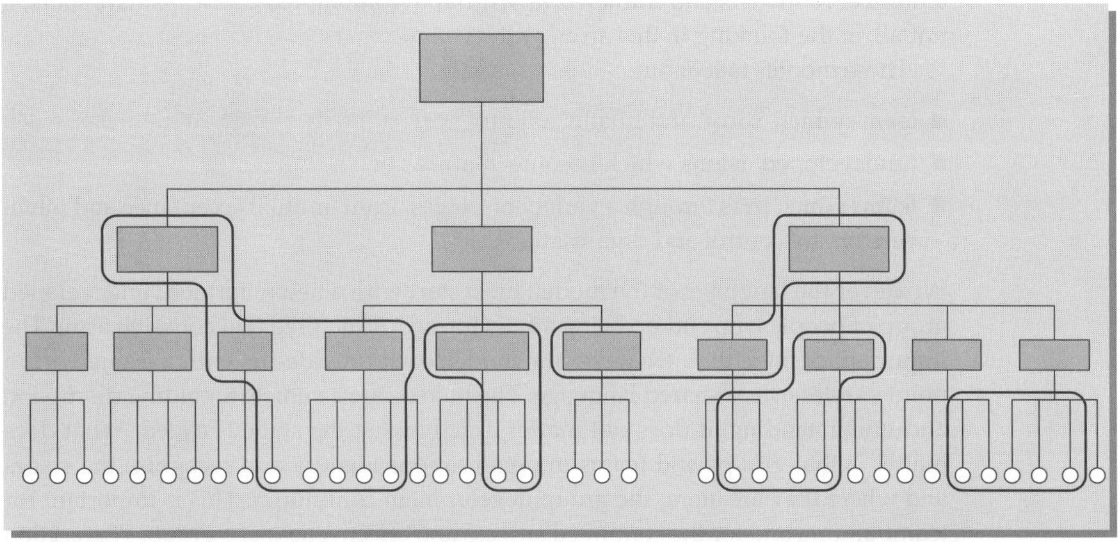

Fig 4.3 Informal groups within the formal structure

- help to define our sense of identity and maintain our self-esteem;
- pander to our social nature, as 'social animals': they are a means of entertainment, alleviating boredom and fatigue, boosting morale and personal satisfaction;
- provide guidelines on generally acceptable behaviour: they help shape group and organisational norms;
- cater for those often ill-defined tasks which can only be performed through the combined efforts of a number of individuals working together.

As can be seen from the list at the beginning of this section, membership of a group can cut across the boundaries created by the formal structure. Individuals from different parts and levels of the organisation may all belong to the same informal group. Informal groups tend to have a more fluid, flexible and variable membership than formal groups, which tend to be fairly 'permanent'. Figure 4.3 illustrates the way informal groups can exist within the formal structure of an organisation.

Formal and informal groups are not separate entities which function independently. Both formal and informal groups can satisfy our own individual needs, such as security, affiliation and self-esteem but formal groups tend to be specifically created to satisfy a number of the organisation's needs as well.

Stages of group and team development

With the increasing focus in organisations on groups and teams, there is a growing need to understand how groups form, grow, develop, mature and change. There are a number of models and frameworks which have attempted to encapsulate some, if not all, of the thinking in this area.

These models talk about:

- teams which 'form' and finally 'adjourn'; or
- 'undeveloped' teams which become 'mature'; or
- teams which pass through a variety of 'stages' from 'mutual acceptance and membership' to 'control and organisation'.

Whatever the language of the model, most start with a newly formed, undeveloped group of people who end up being a fully formed, structured and cohesive team. The important point is that, whatever the model, each provides us with a framework, a point of reference, a shared language. The models are a vehicle for aiding discussion and understanding: it does not matter exactly what the stage is called. What does matter is that groups and teams in organisations identify and recognise the stages and where they are along the group development continuum. This is important for teambuilding and for the continued success and effectiveness of a group. This section now examines three models of group formation and development.

Bass and Ryterband

Within their model Bass and Ryterband (1979) identify four stages in group development.

1. *First stage* – developing mutual trust. Through initial mistrust and fear, group members remain defensive and limit their behaviour through conformity and ritual.
2. *Second stage* – communication and decision making. Members, having learned to accept each other, begin to express conflicts and feelings – in other words, emotions. Norms start to be established and members develop a sense of caring for each other. Open communications develop, along with more constructive problem-solving and decision-making strategies.
3. *Third stage* – motivation and productivity. Members are involved with the work of the group, co-operating with each other instead of competing. They are now more readily motivated by intrinsic rewards, such as a high level of productivity.
4. *Fourth stage* – control and organisation. Work is allocated by agreement and abilities. Members can work independently and the organisation of the group is flexible and can adapt to new challenges.

Woodcock

Woodcock (1979) also views the pattern of team development as having four stages.

1. *Stage 1 – The Undeveloped Team.* This stage is dominated by feelings not being dealt with, or even not being allowed. Although there are unclear objectives at this

stage, any established policy prevails. The group is epitomised by a lack of shared understanding about what needs to be done, the leader often having a different view to the led. Personal weaknesses are covered up because the group lacks the skill to support or eliminate them. Mistakes are used as 'evidence' to convict people rather than as opportunities to learn.

2 *Stage 2 – The Experimenting Team*. The team begins to be willing to experiment and thus risky issues are raised. There are higher levels of listening than in the previous stage and members start to raise their more personal issues and feelings. The group, almost inevitably, becomes more inward looking and may even reject other groups and individuals.

3 *Stage 3 – The Consolidating Team*. More often than not the team decides to adopt a more systematic approach, leading to a more methodical way of working. Rules and procedures are now the agreed operating rules of the team, rather than the edicts from on high, as they were in an earlier stage. The improved relationships and more exciting methods experienced in Stage 2 are maintained but they are used to build the ground rules and working procedures which the team will use.

4 *Stage 4 – The Mature Team*. The openness and improved relationships of Stage 2 and the systematic approach of Stage 3 are now used to complete the task of building a really mature team. High levels of flexibility become paramount. Appropriate leadership is established for different situations. There is optimum use of energy and ability. Development increasingly becomes a priority because continued success depends on continued development. Trust, openness, honesty, co-operation and confrontation, and a continual review of results, become part of the way of the team's life – is this team nirvana?

Tuckman

The final model presented (Tuckman, 1965) is probably the one most often quoted, in no small part because of the rhythm of its sequence, which makes it easy to remember: forming, storming, norming, performing and adjourning.

Forming – initially, this stage is involved with the bringing together of a number of people who may be somewhat anxious, wary and unsure. Clearly in this scenario there are few, if any, ground rules. Ambiguity and confusion reign over the group. Everybody is busy finding out who the other people are, seeking to know one another's attitudes and backgrounds. Members are keen to establish their personal identities in the group and make a personal impression and it is for this reason that considerable anxiety, and even fear, may be generated. Adding to this anxiety is the potential lack of focus and clarity around the purpose of the group and uncertainty about the task ahead and its terms of reference. This anxiety reveals itself in hesitant behaviour, defensiveness and 'scapegoating' aimed at factors outside the group. Examples are complaints about office accommodation, support services or 'them up there'.

Storming – having traversed the slippery slope of 'forming', the group now tackles the choppy waters of 'storming'. This is a period of disagreement, frustration and potential confrontation but every group must go through it. Out of conflict can come good and the group needs to cling to this sentiment at this time. The potential conflict is there because members now feel more confident to challenge each other, and to express their views more openly and forcefully. Some may reject earlier ground rules. There will be some jockeying for positions of power and frustration at apparent lack of progress. The storming stage is important as it raises the energy (and activity) level of the group and can lead on to significant changes in creativity and innovation. One is reminded of the film, *Jerry Maguire*. Embroiled in an argument with a hot-headed football client, sports agent and manager Jerry turns and says, 'You think we're arguing, I think we're finally communicating.'

Norming – at this stage there is a clear sense of group identity, and guidelines, standards, procedures, roles and structure become formally established. Emotions are now expressed constructively and listened to! In organisational settings, it is at this stage that management should intervene if they are looking to influence the group because it is at this stage that those all-important group norms (the rules for all sorts of behaviour within the group) are developed and established. Intervention is required because it shouldn't be taken for granted that what is put in place by the group will automatically lead to effectiveness in management terms. If the Hawthorne Studies of the 1920s and 1930s (*see* Chapter 5) showed us anything, it was that group norms can certainly influence, and often impose limits and restrictions on, all sorts of key areas like productivity and quality. If dysfunctional groups become fully developed, with an entrenched culture and norms, it is much more difficult to alter, or influence, their members' attitudes and behaviour.

Performing – having progressed through the earlier stages, a team will have created some structure and cohesiveness to work effectively. With these 'mechanics' in place, the team can now concentrate on the achievement of its objectives. It is in this stage that task performance is at its most effective. The group should now be close and supportive, open and trusting, resourceful and effective.

As most teams have a limited life, Tuckman and Jensen (1977) added a further stage to the model which they referred to as *adjourning*. The group may disband, either because the task and objectives have been achieved to a satisfactory level or because the members have left. However, before disbanding, it is important for the group to reflect upon their time together – what went well, what didn't go so well and what might they do differently next time and how? Such reflection may be a great source of learning for both the individuals concerned and the organisation.

Figure 4.4 summarises the different models discussed above, and the stages which they propose. All of these models certainly look very straightforward. A group moves from Stage 1 to Stage 2 and onwards to Stage 3 and so on, but is the process as simple and straightforward as this statement implies? Unfortunately, where people are concerned, events do not occur in linear fashion, and teams do not move in straight and predictable lines. In the 'storming' phase groups can generate a general reaction against all prior arrangements and this may well throw the group back into the 'forming' stage. On the surface this may appear a retrograde step but it

Bass and Ryterband (1979)	Woodcock (1979)	Tuckman (1965)	Glass (1996)
Developing mutual trust	Undeveloped team	Forming	Birth
Communication and decision making	Experimenting team	Storming	Childhood
Motivation and productivity	Consolidating team	Norming	Adolescence
Control and organisation	Mature	Performing	Maturity
		Adjourning	

Fig 4.4 Stages in group development

could lead to far more meaningful and creative solutions and ways forward. In other situations some groups may never develop to the stage of performing, becoming bogged down in an earlier stage. Yet other groups may skip about, backwards and forwards, from one stage to another, sometimes missing out or leaping over stages. Teams composed of people who are accustomed to working in that way may jump straight to the norming stage. In the real, more complex world, the journey of team development is not a precise path. Every team is different and different groups may process information differently and proceed at different speeds through the stages. As a result, an understanding of the general principles involved in these models is more important than a detailed appreciation of any one particular approach, and it may often be more realistic and profitable to use a mixture of these approaches. This understanding can help us either to shorten the process or at least to make it a better, more effective one. Moreover, a team whose members understand the dynamics of group formation are less likely to get caught up at one of the intermediate stages.

Roles and routines

Group norms

Groups tend to develop routine ways of behaving and doing things in a very natural and almost unspoken way, a development over time which becomes a shared, 'taken for granted' group psyche. Groups develop habits and rituals the origins of which they cannot explain. A common response might be, 'It's the way we do it around here'. Of course, work groups have some of these rituals and routines spelled out for them and made explicit in the form of procedures, laid down rules and regulations and well accepted (and documented) working practices. However, as the Hawthorne

Studies (*see* Chapter 5) demonstrated, work groups can evolve unwritten and more 'informal' rules of behaviour or 'norms'. Norms may act positively or negatively from an organisational point of view. Any violations of the group norms are not conducive to the harmony of the group and offenders run the risk of punishment, social isolation or expulsion from the group. New members are quickly socialised into the norms and are expected to fit in and comply. Norms can give a group its identity, and can help to differentiate it from others.

Group roles

Within the framework of norms that groups have developed, there also exists a pattern of roles which members develop and demonstrate in that particular group. The roles that individuals perform in a group have an important effect on its development and cohesiveness. Within a typical group activity, such as a team meeting or a seminar discussion, people will indeed show a consistent preference for certain behaviours and not for others. In helping us to study this group and role behaviour a basic, but useful, exercise is to divide a team's activities, and hence roles, into 'task' and 'maintenance'. *Task activities* are aimed at problem solving and achieving the team's concrete goals, such as developing a new product. *Maintenance activities* involve managing how the team works together, its emotional life and the quality of members' interactions. These are focused on areas such as resolving conflict and giving individuals encouragement and support. As an example, a team may contain a number of technical experts who perform well on the task side but are poor at handling the human interaction elements. One outcome might be that the rest of the group rejects the technical solution because some team members were insufficiently involved in its development.

In further work on the distinction between task and maintenance, Benne and Sheats (1948) developed a popular system for the classification of member roles. Roles performed in well-functioning groups are classified under three broad headings: group task roles, group building and maintenance roles and individual roles. Each is outlined below, and specific examples of each are identified.

Group task roles

Group task roles *assume that the task of the group is to select, define and solve problems.* The roles include:

- *initiator-contributor*, who suggests to group new ideas, new group goals, or a new definition of a problem; proposes new procedures, ways of handling some difficulty or forms of organisation;
- *elaborator*, who spells out suggestions in terms of examples or developed meanings; offers reasons for suggestions and tries to deduce consequences of following them;
- *recorder*, who writes down suggestions, makes a record of group decisions; acts as 'group memory';

- *information seeker*, opinion seeker;
- *information giver*, opinion giver;
- *co-ordinator*, orienter;
- *evaluator-critic*, energiser, procedural technician.

Group building and maintenance roles

Group building and maintenance roles *focus towards activities which build group-centred attitudes, or maintain group-centred behaviour*. The roles include:

- *harmoniser*, who mediates the difference between other members; attempts to reconcile disagreements, relieves tension in conflict situations through humour, pouring oil on troubled waters;
- *gatekeeper-expediter*, who attempts to keep communication channels open by encouraging or facilitating the participation of others; proposes regulating the flow of information, imposing limits on the length of contributions so all can have a say;
- *encourager*, compromiser, standard setter;
- *group observer-commentator*, follower.

Individual roles

Individual roles *are directed towards the satisfaction of personal needs*. The roles include:

- *aggressor*, who deflates status of others; expresses disapproval of the values, acts or feelings of others; attacks group or the problem it is working on; jokes aggressively;
- *self-confessor*, who uses the audience opportunity which the group setting provides to express personal non-group oriented ideas, feelings and insights;
- *help-seeker*, who attempts to call forth 'sympathy' response from other members or the whole group through expressions of insecurity, personal confusion or depreciation of him/herself beyond reason;
- *blocker*, recognition-seeker;
- *dominator*, special interest pleader, playboy!

Many other classification systems exist for teasing out and identifying group roles, some employing a shorter and somewhat more simplistic list than that of Benne and Sheats. For example, Obeng (1994) lists only five roles:

- *doers* – who concentrate on the task at hand;
- *knowers* – who provide specialist knowledge;
- *solvers* – who solve problems as they arise;
- *checkers* – who make sure that all is going as well as it can and that the whole team is contributing fully;
- *carers* – who make sure that the team is operating as a cohesive social unit.

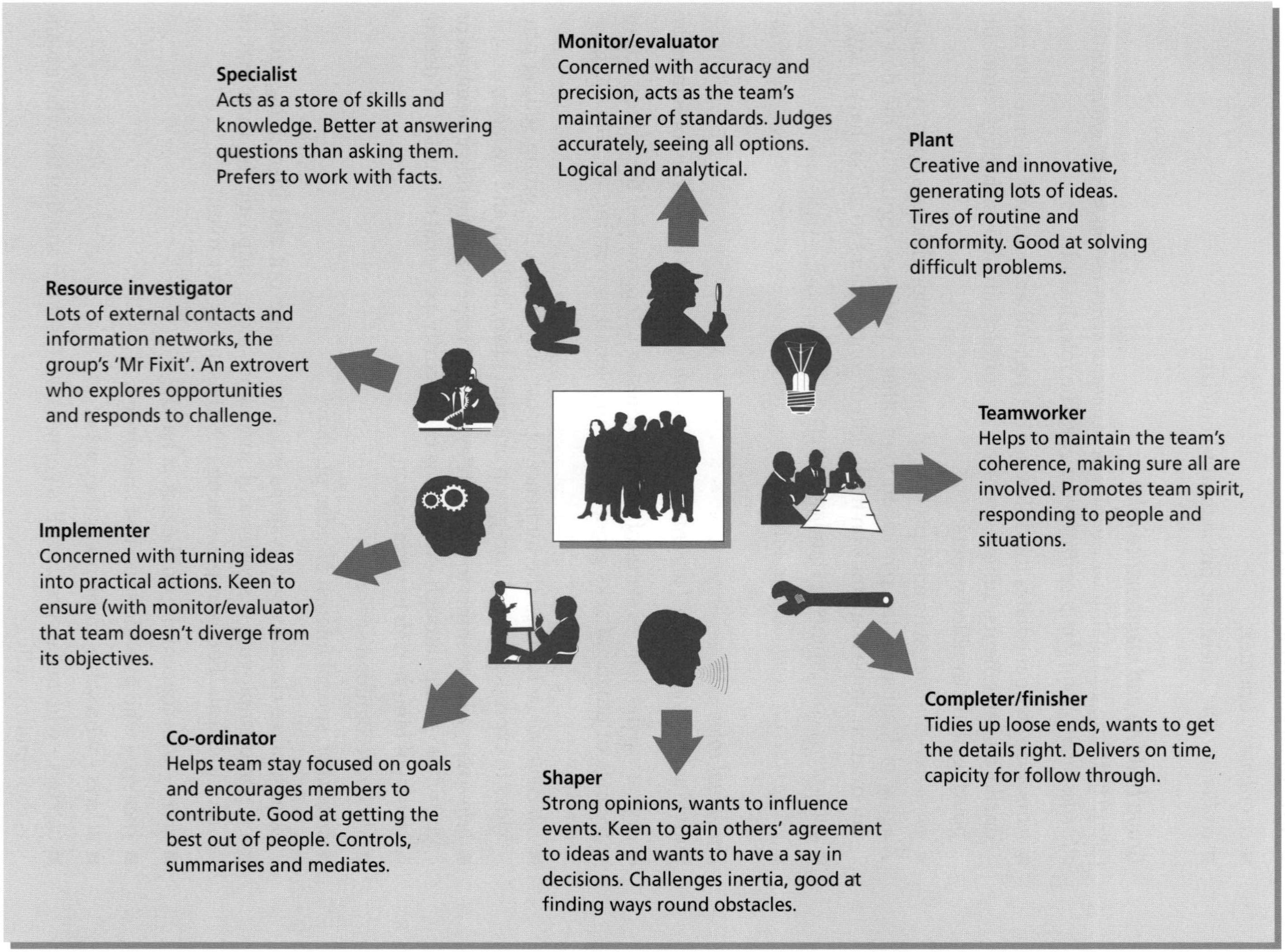

Specialist
Acts as a store of skills and knowledge. Better at answering questions than asking them. Prefers to work with facts.
Monitor/evaluator
Concerned with accuracy and precision, acts as the team's maintainer of standards. Judges accurately, seeing all options. Logical and analytical.
Plant
Creative and innovative, generating lots of ideas. Tires of routine and conformity. Good at solving difficult problems.
Resource investigator
Lots of external contacts and information networks, the group's 'Mr Fixit'. An extrovert who explores opportunities and responds to challenge.
Teamworker
Helps to maintain the team's coherence, making sure all are involved. Promotes team spirit, responding to people and situations.
Implementer
Concerned with turning ideas into practical actions. Keen to ensure (with monitor/evaluator) that team doesn't diverge from its objectives.
Completer/finisher
Tidies up loose ends, wants to get the details right. Delivers on time, capicity for follow through.
Co-ordinator
Helps team stay focused on goals and encourages members to contribute. Good at getting the best out of people. Controls, summarises and mediates.
Shaper
Strong opinions, wants to influence events. Keen to gain others' agreement to ideas and wants to have a say in decisions. Challenges inertia, good at finding ways round obstacles.

Fig 4.5 Belbin's team roles

Source: Adapted from Belbin, R. M., *Team Roles at Work*, Butterworth-Heinemann (1993) p. 23.

Belbin's team roles

Probably the most popular team roles categorisation was developed by Belbin (1981, 1993). He initially identified eight team roles which upon further development were expanded to nine. He argues that it is these nine roles that team members need to fulfil if the team is to be effective and successful. Clearly not all teams are composed of nine people, each of whom takes one of the different roles. Usually each person will find it quite natural to fill two or three preferred roles (and it is to be hoped that team members' preferred roles differ from the preferred roles of the other team members). Belbin's team roles are illustrated in Figure 4.5.

Belbin's team roles have proven popular in team development and teambuilding, so popular that he has incorporated them into a computer-scored questionnaire. One of Belbin's key principles is that 'no one's perfect but a team can be'. He preaches the gospel of balance and diversity within teams, stressing that his team roles questionnaire is purely an initial starting point for team composition and subsequent development. Some naive followers of his prescriptions have taken the 'scores' of individuals as the ultimate truth about what that person contributes to a team. This is a misguided practice, particularly when used to recruit and select new people into a team. Belbin's team roles are not to be taken as black or white, yes or no, true or false. The questionnaire itself is not a fully scientifically valid or reliable tool, particularly for measuring stable aspects of personality. However, this should not be read as a criticism of Belbin's work. He would argue that team role scores are a useful guide in forming a profile of a team and a standpoint from which one can start to identify the weaknesses of a team. Further, because the process involves assessing the preferred roles of each team member and encouraging all members to appreciate the characteristics and strengths of the others, his model provides an accessible and shared language to enable this. When using it we are not swamped with data generated from the questionnaire. It is simply a starting point to provide a common understanding with which to pursue team issues further. If Belbin's questionnaire simply raises the awareness levels in a team about their collective strengths and weaknesses, then it has been a success.

In summary, we can say that it is simply not enough for groups or teams who are working towards a common goal to have a ragbag collection of individual skills. The various behaviours (and routines) of the team members must mesh together in order to achieve their group's goals and objectives (*see* Figure 4.6).

Building and maintaining effective teams

Some managers may 'play' at human engineering by trying to select exactly the right combination of people but more often than not they end up in a state of confusion. Effective teams can come about spontaneously, as a result of a particular set of circumstances. The key to success does not always appear to lie in the selection of team members, as many sports teams are comprised of talented individuals who work

Issues are the future

The increasing pace with which technology is changing and progressing is fuelling an inevitable march towards globalisation. Nowhere is this pace of change more noticeable than in the industry that is responsible for some of the technology which helps to make growth and globalisation more possible, namely the telecommunications industry. Legislation and regulation are also factors driving and affecting the changes in the industry. In the midst of this maelstrom it is easy to forget that there exists the parallel need for cultural change to operate alongside the more concrete aspects of change, such as structural reorganisations. With deregulation of the industry came the inevitable increase in competition and the need for companies like BT to start to think more meaningfully about factors such as customer service. The launching of BT's first dedicated customer service teams has marked a new milestone in their endeavour to stay ahead of the competition.

Traditionally, the manager was seen as the central point for dealing with all 'issues' problems. It was recognised that within the customer service teams it was important to create and facilitate a culture which was more open to discussion and involvement, which was more geared towards teamworking and trust. One of the ways to do this was to develop the role of issues team member because it was recognised that many fruitful and important issues were not being built upon, with the result that they were 'lost' forever. Within the customer service teams the person who held this role was seen as someone who:

- identified issues at team meetings or from colleagues;
- prioritised the issues with the team;
- recorded those issues in an issues log;
- worked with other issue team members to resolve them;
- circulated the issues and solutions to other teams;
- reviewed the log on a monthly basis;
- progressed issues with colleagues and outside groups.

All in all, this new team role was seen as a way of formalising some of the more informal aspects of teams. Some of the skills required to be an effective issues team member were identified – skills such as good communication and interpersonal skills. Further, presentation, time management, planning and organising skills were recognised as important, as was the ability to co-ordinate data and compile brief reports, to gather information and identify issues.

In order to make this new culture change within the teams more tangible it was important for the teams to discuss how they were going to launch this change. They needed to brainstorm and identify what constituted an issue that could be resolved by the issues team member, how the process was to be run (by whom, where and how), what involvement management should have in decisions and how the issues should be made visible.

In the long term, the issues team members will become as much a focal point for the team as the customer service manager leading each team. Issues team members will be there to help develop solutions in order to overcome problems. Empowering members to contribute will reduce dependency on the manager. By taking more responsibility and ownership of the issues, through the issues team member, the whole team will develop. This, in turn, will free the manager to focus on supporting and coaching, delegating and directing.

Discussion questions

1. What problems might be encountered with the creation of these new teams and team roles?
2. What are the advantages and disadvantages of the newly created 'issues' team role?

Fig 4.6 'Issues' team members

poorly as a team, for example Brazil in the 1998 World Cup Final. Likewise, there are many examples of groups of less talented individuals who perform well in a team scenario – Wimbledon FC, for instance.

In his classic work, *The Human Side of Enterprise*, Douglas McGregor (1960) provides an account of the differences between effective and ineffective groups.

- A belief in shared aims and objectives
- A sense of commitment to the group
- Acceptance of group values and norms
- A feeling of mutual trust and dependency
- Full participation by all members and decision making by consensus
- Free flow of information and communications
- The open expression of feelings and disagreements
- The resolution of conflict by the members themselves; and
- A lower level of staff turnover, absenteeism, accidents, errors and complaints.

Fig 4.7 Characteristics of effective work groups

Source: Mullins, L. J. (1999) *Management and Organisational Behaviour*, 5th edn, Financial Times Pitman Publishing, p. 467. Reprinted with permission.

According to McGregor the effective group is cohesive, relaxed and friendly. Their discussion is open, hence disagreement is always possible. Effectiveness is a function of group members' orientation and attitude, not simply the behaviour of the leader. McGregor's views of effective groups corresponds to Tuckman's norming and performing stages of group development mentioned earlier. However, the features of ineffective groups are closer to Tuckman's storming stage. A significant difference between these two writers is that McGregor sees some groups as fixed and trapped in their own poor behaviour, whereas Tuckman implies that groups tend to move out of the ineffective stages into more effective behaviour (or at the very least they fluctuate between the two).

Mullins (1999: 467) views the characteristics of an effective work group as being more holistic and humanistic. He sees the underlying feature of these groups is *'a spirit of co-operation in which members work well together as a united team, and with harmonious and supportive relationships'*. According to Mullins, this may be particularly evidenced when members of a group exhibit the characteristics presented in Figure 4.7.

A mild criticism of these ideas is that the list in Figure 4.7 reflects effective *work teams* rather more than work groups and that this is how it should be – these are teams not groups. Teams operate at the higher order of group dynamics that the list reflects.

Finally, it must be recognised that for a team to be effective it should contain diversity, it should have people with differing outlooks and strengths. To some extent this need for diversity is satisfied (and forced upon us) by the growing inevitability of globalisation and cross-cultural fertilisation. Whereas diversity in terms of occupational or organisational role is an expectation of a team, diversity in terms of nationality, age, ethnicity, personality or even gender is often less readily accepted. It is hard to manage a truly diverse team. Team members invariably have very different values, norms and beliefs about how to behave and even different perceptions of what is going on around them. Kandola (1995) identified that although diverse teams have the potential to be highly effective because of the variety of outlooks they possess, they may often fail to achieve that high potential. Teams need and require integration; this is something that Maznevski (1994) has argued for. This requirement for integration involves a paradox: integration is more difficult to achieve as teams become more diverse (and yet with globalisation, teams will inevitably become more diverse). According to Arnold *et al.* (1998) integration relies on:

- a social reality shared by group members;
- the ability to empathise and see things from others' points of view;
- the motivation to communicate;
- the ability to negotiate and agree norms within the team;
- the ability to identify the true causes of any difficulties which arise;
- self-confidence of all group members.

If one combines Mullins's list with that of Arnold *et al.*, the result is a comprehensive range of characteristics for an effective work team.

Group cohesiveness and performance

Group cohesiveness is related to group effectiveness, and factors which constitute cohesion can be seen to parallel some of the aspects which determine a group's effectiveness. Group cohesion can be thought of as the 'pulling power' of the group, its magnetism, its ability to retain its members. Piper *et al.* (1983: 94) defined it as *'the attractiveness of the group to its members, together with their motivation to remain as part of the group and resist leaving it'*. In a cohesive group, group identity is clear, interpersonal relations are good and people place value upon being a member of the group. Members of such groups experience fewer work-related anxieties and are better adjusted in the organisation than are members of less cohesive groups. They have higher rates of job satisfaction, and lower rates of tension, absenteeism and labour turnover. Cohesive groups develop greater levels of co-operation among their members and membership in itself can be a very rewarding and enlightening experience. All in all, a cohesive group is likely to be an effective one.

On the question of relatedness, Handy (1993) identified the size of a group as an important moderating factor in its ability to be effective. For best participation and involvement, between five and eight members appears to be the optimum. In work groups, size can be related to cohesiveness and member satisfaction too, with larger work groups tending to have lower morale and more absenteeism. Members start to feel less involved and committed in large groups of over 15 members, interaction with all members becomes more difficult and the ability to maintain a common goal becomes harder. The incidence of clique formation also increases, thus decreasing overall cohesiveness.

Mullins (1999: 463) lists a comprehensive number of factors affecting cohesiveness, as set out in Table 4.1.

What we have said about cohesive groups so far amounts to an impressive list of

Table 4.1 Group performance and cohesiveness

Membership	Work environment	Organisational cohesiveness	Group development and maturity
Size of the group	Nature of the task	Management and leadership style	Forming
Compatibility of members	Physical setting		Storming
	Communications	Personnel policies	Norming
Permanence	Technology	Success	Performing
		External threat	Adjourning

Source: Adapted from Mullins, L. J. (1999). *Management and Organisational Behaviour*, 5th edn, Financial Times Pitman Publishing, p. 463. Reprinted with permission.

advantages. They demonstrate greater co-operation, with easier and more flowing communication and an increased resistance to frustration, as well as reduced labour turnover and absenteeism. If a manager aims to develop and lead effective work groups then he or she simply must pay attention to the factors which influence the creation of a group's identity and cohesiveness. However, the tightrope of tension the manager must negotiate in order to develop strong and cohesive groups is a very tricky balancing act, for very strongly cohesive groups also present problems. They start to look in on themselves too much and can become very defensive and protective of their 'territory' and jealous of, or even aggressive towards, other groups. Life may be difficult for new entrants into the group, thereby restricting the introduction of new practices and suggestions. Linked to this last point, and of great relevance in today's increasingly flexible business environment, is the fact that strongly cohesive groups resist change and the 'invasion' of these new ideas. The status quo is comfortable and satisfying and the cohesive group feels it is invulnerable and strong. This results in a powerful set of forces equipped to resist any proposed changes. It must come as no surprise, either, that these over-cohesive groups are viewed as awkward, overbearing and bombastic by others.

Conformity and groupthink

The 'energy' of very cohesive groups is not just directed at people who fall outside the boundaries of the group. Even in a strongly cohesive group, pressure is placed on members to fall into line and conform to the group norms. The potency of this group pressure to conform was illustrated in a classic laboratory study by Solomon Asch (1951). A group of seven subjects were shown a line and asked to say which of three other lines matched it in length. In fact only one of the subjects was a true volunteer, the other six being stooges. The subjects gave their responses with the real volunteer responding sixth. At the first session, all of the group correctly identified the lines. At the second session, the stooges consistently gave incorrect answers. They would say, within earshot of the true volunteer, that a line clearly shorter than the test line was equal to it. In 32 per cent of cases, the volunteer went along with this opinion despite some initial hesitancy. Asch's study demonstrated the power of a group to elicit conformity of opinion and judgement amongst its members. More importantly, it also revealed how difficult it can be to resist other people's opinions, even when one knows that their opinions are wrong.

Asch's work was anchored in the laboratory, where life, and research findings, are not necessarily the same as one might find in the reality of a business organisation. In the light of more recent trends within the business environment towards flatter organisational structures, which empower and entrust individuals to make decisions for themselves, we have to question the validity of Asch's findings. More and more, managers are being encouraged to challenge the status quo and to think more laterally, to be more creative and innovative in a shorter space of time. Organisations are busy developing learning cultures, cultures where everyone has the right to question and where diversity of thinking (not just diversity of people) is positively encouraged and rewarded. Many management consultants, and the tools they use (such as Business Process Re-engineering), are geared towards helping the organisation question and challenge its taken-for-granted assumptions about 'the way we do things around here'. What we can say is that there is always a strong social pressure to conform when amongst our peers but, in the context of a business organisation, this pressure is watered down and moderated for the very reasons listed above.

The work of Janis (1972) developed a theme of Asch's work, that the effective decision-making ability of a group is dramatically and drastically impaired by the presence and pressure of others. Janis's work struck a very practical note of reality because it was extracted and developed from famous cases in world history. The term 'groupthink' was coined, which in Janis's (1972: 9) words is *'a mode of thinking in which people engage when they are deeply involved in a cohesive group, in which strivings*

- Group feels invulnerable, excessive optimism and risk taking pervade the air.
- Warnings that things might be going awry are discounted and rationalised away.
- There is an unquestioned belief in the group's morality.
- Those who oppose the group are ridiculed and stereotyped as stupid, corrupt and weak.
- Pressure is applied to anyone who opposes the prevailing mood of the group.
- An illusion of unanimity develops, silence is taken as consent.
- Members of the group censor themselves if they feel they are deviating from the group norms.
- Self-appointed 'mindguards' are established who protect the group from information and individuals which would disrupt consensus.

Source: Based on Janis (1972).

Fig 4.8 Symptoms of groupthink

for unanimity override motivations to realistically appraise alternative courses of action'. When making decisions, groups do not have either perfect knowledge or perfect rationality and yet groups suffering from 'groupthink' believe that they possess both of these and a variety of other 'symptoms' highlighted in Figure 4.8.

Janis concluded that the historical decisions he looked at were all characterised by a process which involved the group just 'drifting along', which gave rise to the sense of false consensus. Another common factor among the cases was the tendency to curtail discussion and to consider only a very limited range of alternatives. Again we must ask ourselves how applicable these findings about strongly cohesive groups are for today's business organisations. In thinking about this question, one should bear in mind the earlier points noted and the fact that Janis was primarily looking at very significant and important foreign policy decisions.

Communication and conflict

Teams rely on communication; it's their lifeblood. The global and virtual teams of tomorrow will need it more than ever (Coles, 1998a). Intuitively one can see this dependence on communication, albeit in the form of telecommunications, growing. Safe in the knowledge that the main types of communication networks illustrated in Figure 4.9 will still be of some value in the future, we should ponder on communication for a moment. Many management commentators preach individual power and autonomy, self-responsibility, trust, empowerment and the ability to make decisions and act rapidly. This is part of a dominant contemporary philosophy, and if we accept this philosophy, we have to ask the question, 'How relevant are communication networks, when employees are being encouraged to think and act independently?' It is because we are being empowered to be more autonomous and to take responsibility that we must address this issue.

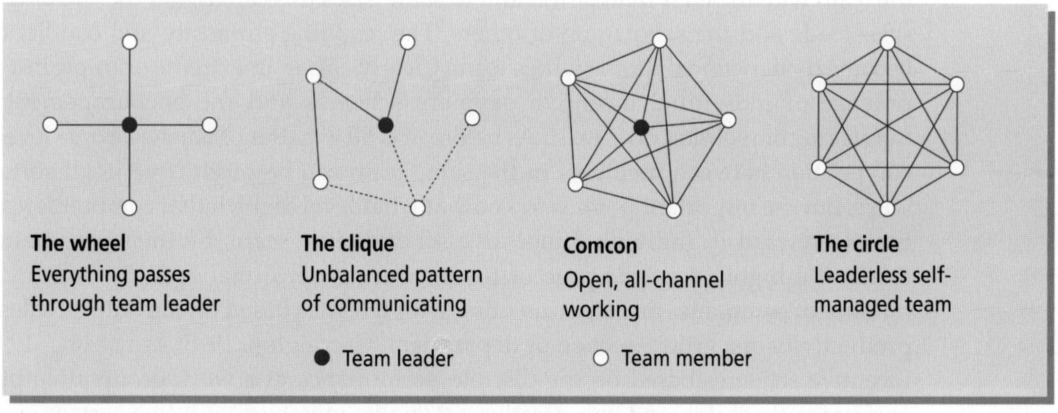

Fig 4.9 The main communication network patterns in teams

E-mail, and other similar forms of communication, tend to 'open up' and democratise communication. Sproull and Kiesler (1991) compared how small groups make decisions through computer conferences, e-mail and face-to-face discussion. The use of an electronic medium caused participants to talk more frankly and more equally, and to make more suggestions for action. In the face-to-face discussions only a few people dominated. However, they also found that the increased democracy of the electronic media interfered with decision making and raised the levels of conflict. Decisions via e-mail were made more slowly and participants expressed more extreme opinions and vented their anger more openly.

Intragroup behaviour and conflict

Organisations are encouraging higher levels of diversity in teams. Diversity is a gateway to being more effective and yet the more homogeneous a team is in terms of shared interests, attitudes and backgrounds, the easier it might be for that team to be a cohesive force. Individuals in the team can empathise and relate to each other more readily. Some variety and variation in individual differences, such as personality or skills, may, on the other hand, act as a positive force for cohesion. However, if these personality differences are particularly accentuated, extreme or acute, personality clashes can occur and this can be a source of conflict and disruption for the team. Belbin (1981) talks about balance in teams and people complementing each other. More sophisticated recruitment and selection processes may be one way of achieving the right levels of balance in a team, ensuring that a whole range of individual differences in areas such as skills, attitudes, attributes and personality is taken into account. In this way we can predict, and moderate against, potential conflict situations.

Another source of conflict for teams can arise where members of the team are in competition with each other for finite resources. Typically, where a sales team operates in a limited geographical area there may be sales people in that team competing with each other for revenue, individual incentives and bonuses. Some members of the team will do better than others and in some cases this can trigger the 'stealing' of sales leads and the sabotaging of others. The resulting animosity and conflict can become dysfunctional for the whole team. Clearly, this is an extreme example but the practice of individual incentive payment schemes and the encouragement of intrateam competition does exist. As before, it is all a matter of balance. Some level of competition between members of the same team can be productive in all sorts of ways, but the important point is to know at what level to pitch that competition and how to reward it. Individual incentive schemes in a team, by their very nature, demand a highly accurate process for measuring performance fairly. A growing number of companies are experimenting with schemes based on the output, sales or productivity of a group, section or department (Carrington, 1995; Armstrong, 1996). Incentive schemes based on the discrete performance of a work group attempt to encourage flexibility and co-operation among its members, and to a certain extent provide opportunities for the employees to decide for themselves how to divide up the resulting rewards and incentives. Armstrong (1996) points out that such schemes appear to be more effective when the work groups:

- stand alone as performing units, with clear targets and standards;
- have a meaningful degree of autonomy;
- consist of people whose work is interdependent;
- contain members who are multiskilled, flexible and good team players;
- perform in a directly measurable way.

Although team-based payment schemes can lead to higher levels of motivation, productivity, co-operation and 'teamness' among team members, there can be problems. The team can end up 'carrying' someone, who ultimately reaps the same rewards as the other members but for less effort. However, what we have learned from the Hawthorne studies indicates that it is likely that the other members of the team doing the 'carrying' would address the situation. In this way, it can be argued that team-based schemes encourage the team to take a more proactive role in managing itself and each other. Alternatively, pressure to conform and the requirement for consideration of others can lead to the reduction of effort to the lowest common denominator and the demotivation of high performers. Another disadvantage with these schemes is that they can help to develop an imbalanced, and skewed, pattern of labour movement around the organisation. Individuals will resist transfer out of high-performing teams for the fear of a potential drop in individual earnings. Likewise, employees may resist being moved into teams that perform poorly. Probably the most important issue in the development, implementation and success of these schemes is the requirement for there to be a change in the culture of the organisation. There needs to be a move away from an individually orientated work environment, which the scheme itself would facilitate, towards the realisation that the individual's pay will not be totally related to his or her own efforts. Indeed, an individual's pay may well be more closely related to the performance of a colleague than to his or her own. This, in turn, will develop a very real interdependence within teams.

Intergroup behaviour and conflict

Groups in organisations are not sealed off from each other; they do not exist and operate within a vacuum. In fact, the situation can be quite the opposite. They can become highly dependent upon each other and the effectiveness of an organisation often relies upon smooth relationships between its different teams (Ancona, 1987). However, since each group is primarily judged on how well it performs its tasks, there will be tension between the need to focus on its own concerns and the requirement to co-operate with other groups, in order that they might perform effectively. As noted earlier, cohesiveness can be of great benefit to a group but it can also result in tension and conflict between groups. The problem is clear: some degree of conflict or competition between groups is both good and inevitable but the mix of 'friendly' rivalry and competition must be balanced with the need for co-operation. This is where many organisations go wrong when structuring, for instance, their sales teams. They view competition between teams as a way of motivating people and as something that is healthy for the workplace. Teams that consistently perform well might receive large bonuses, or other incentives, at the end of the year. But not everyone can be top; the system may well develop a destructive climate of 'winners' and 'losers'. In extreme cases, this intergroup conflict can operate to the detriment of organisational productivity. However, groups that co-operate can co-ordinate their activities better, have a fuller exchange of ideas and information and share both expenses and rewards.

Groups and change

The impact of technology

Technology clearly has a considerable influence on the pattern of group operations and behaviour. One of the most striking issues arising from the work of Trist *et al.* (1963) was that the technological changes being implemented in a coal-mine under observation had brought about changes in the traditional social groupings of the miners. Technological change created a lack of co-operation between different shifts and a disruption to the integration of small groups (*see* Chapter 5).

The type, level, amount and use of technology available to an organisation can often determine how particular tasks or work packages are carried out. In some circumstances, the technology can strongly influence and change the very essence of a job and the way it is performed. For example, the way the work is organised around the technology may limit the opportunities for social interaction and the extent to which it is possible to identify oneself as a member of a cohesive work group. Consequently, this can have adverse, or positive, effects on attitudes to work and the level of job satisfaction. During the past few decades manufacturing organisations have been striving to eliminate some of the more alienating aspects of mass production by increasing the range and type of tasks and responsibilities allocated to small groups. These attempts include the greater use of group technology approaches, autonomous work groups and self-directed teams, as discussed above.

The influence of information technology also demands new patterns of work organisation and impacts on the structure and formation of groups. The downsizing of large-scale centralised organisations into smaller working units can help to develop an environment in which workers may relate more easily to each other.

Global teamworking

With more companies extending their operations across and around the world, the management and leadership of global teams is becoming a new challenge (*see* Chapter 10). That global teams exist cannot be denied. At Hewlett-Packard, the

European export administration manager has a team of 35 people in several countries, including 15 in Britain. In the Ford Motor Company, some senior project managers have direct managerial responsibility for 25 people, of whom the most senior might comprise five project managers, based in Europe, South America, Australia, Japan and China.

There are a number of all-consuming and inextricably linked trends which are encouraging this situation. Heading the list is the revolution in technology, particularly telecommunications. E-mail, voice mail, laptops, hand-held organisers, videoconferencing, internet telephones, interactive pagers – all of these tools make teamwork, mobility and working at a distance a more satisfactory option. The only problem is that technology is changing faster than our attitudes and beliefs about work. Another paradox is that all this wizardry is supposed to help businesses to communicate and manage remote teams. The reality is that few multinationals have started to tackle the challenge. They often have no clear information technology strategy; alternatively, one part of the organisation, due to some technological mismatch, may be unable to 'talk' to another part. Often, few have been trained in the use of new technology and many are unfamiliar with it. Within the same global team the technology can create a two-tier hierarchy of those who can and those who cannot use it.

Cross-cultural teamworking

Much of the research into formulating ideas and models around groups and teams – how they form, how they develop, how they thrive and grow – could be accused of being ethnocentric. Many of the ideas have evolved out of a Western mode of thought. The greatest barrier to intercultural communication occurs when a person believes that 'only my culture makes sense, espouses the right values, and represents the right and logical way to behave'. If we look at the work of Geert Hofstede (1980), we can identify some key differences between the United States and Japan, for example. The USA is one of the most individualistic cultures, Japan is among the countries where collectivism is strong. Further, the USA is a culture with a low orientation towards authority which can tolerate uncertainty. The Japanese, on the other hand, have a national culture with a strong orientation towards authority and are highly motivated to avoid uncertainty in their work lives. Armed with this information we can hypothesise that Japanese business people would not be at ease taking part in some energetic storming, rather, they would be more willing to (over-) conform when in teams. Whatever we might conclude, it is an inescapable fact that the national cultures of the USA and Japan are very different and therefore people from those cultures will go about the process of forming and working in teams in different ways.

It is vitally important to be aware of the business and cultural protocols of the people with whom you are sharing a global teamworking experience. As an example, imagine the scenario of having a face-to-face meeting of the global design/sales team. The Japanese partners are sat opposite the large windows looking out and the most senior of the Japanese visitors is near the door. The seating arrangements may upset your team partners on two counts. First, they will assume that you consider that they are not interested in the meeting, because you have placed them in front of the windows, thus giving them a view to look out on and occupy them. Second, and more traditionally, in Japan, the most senior people are placed furthest from the door, facing it. This dates back to a time in Japan's history of warring Samurai factions when the first people to 'get the chop' were the people nearest the door.

Networks and virtual teams

With the increasing propensity for organisations to downsize and outsource or subcontract a growing number of tasks and functions, some work teams may have a membership consisting of full-time employees, part-time and temporary (fixed-term) people, two-days-per-week associate partners and outsourced workers (*see* Chapter 7). In *The Age of Unreason* Charles Handy (1989) describes a flexible organisational structure design which he calls the 'shamrock' organisation. This structure is made up of three distinct groups of people:

- the professional core;
- the contractual fringe;
- the flexible labour force.

Each of these three elements of the workforce has a different kind of commitment to the organisation and a varying set of expectations; each group needs to be managed in a different way. When they are put together in mixed teams, what might you expect some of the outcomes to be? Many organisations are now undertaking joint projects with other organisations, forming strategic partnerships and alliances or creating loosely coupled teams across several organisations, even with their competitors. Learning and developing in groups and teams is starting to cut across the organisation's traditional boundaries. (*See* the works listed in the Further reading section – Hamel, Doz and Prahalad (1989) or Coles (1998).)

Virtual organisations, workplaces and teams are becoming increasingly commonplace. In a virtual team, the members' primary interaction is through some combination of electronic communication systems, and members may never 'meet' in the traditional sense. Young (1998: 46) makes the distinction between *virtual teams – working together as one across distances simultaneously, with people from the same function* and *cross-functional virtual teams – people working in different functions, business units or across time zones.* Young stresses that virtual teams free the organisation to run 24 hours a day, helping the organisation to break away from the constraints of traditional working time and staff availability. Cascio (1998) lists a number of advantages of virtual teams, including:

- savings in time, travel expenses and elimination of the lack of access to experts;
- teams can be organised regardless of whether the members are in reasonable proximity of each other;

Teamworking at 212 bhp! (brake horsepower)

The sport and leisure industry is now a multi-billion pound concern which is occupying an increasing proportion of the national psyche – just witness the build-up to the Olympic Games, World Cup or Premier Football Championship. Much of the rhetoric which now goes hand in hand with many business organisations, and which has become part of their everyday language (teamworking, motivation, attention to detail, continuous improvement), can be applied to a growing number of sports organisations which are increasingly becoming businesses in their own right. With that development comes the pressure to get every aspect of running the business, club or team right. The pressure is on for clubs and teams to find the extra ingredient of added value which may make the difference between winning and losing, between profit and loss, between survival and extinction AND then to do it all over again for the next match, the next race, the next season. One can very clearly see this approach of continuous improvement in the world of motor racing. Minute adjustments to the car, changes in working practices or extra insights and perceptions from the driver may only add up to a half-second improvement but this may mean the difference between the front row of the starting grid or the sixth row. Where motor sport differs from many other sports is that it is a highly complex mix of a number of differing disciplines and approaches, a mixture which tends to reflect the reality of teams and teamworking in many business organisations.

In the world of motor sport, Paul Stewart Racing (PSR) are celebrating their tenth year: ten years in what is, literally, a fast-moving industry; ten years as a leader in that industry; ten years in a business which changes constantly, in terms of technology, specifications, rules, procedures and key personnel. In those ten years they have won over 130 races and 13 championship titles – indeed, they have won six of the last seven Formula 3 titles. Within their field they are highly regarded and respected as a professional outfit. That respect has been hard earned, the results given above testify to that. However, the name 'above the door' carries an intangible benefit with it, which adds volumes to that hard-earned respect – Stewart Senior is a three times Formula 1 World Champion and you simply cannot earn respect like that overnight.

Once you scratch below the surface and beneath the paintwork Paul Stewart Racing start to talk about seeing their 'sport as a business' where they strive to create and maintain a strong team ethos within which people can fulfil personal career development aspirations. They openly talk about leadership and teamwork, trust, communication, attention to detail and quality, motivation and, of course, winning! They too have 'customers', in the guise of sponsors and suppliers (some 15 in all) and five Key Partners.

Where a sport like Formula 3 differs from other sports is in the mix of the ingredients that go to make up the team. It's not all down to the team, it's often down to one person's performance (the driver) and yet that performance is so often inextricably tied to the technical aspects and preparation and that goes full circle back to the team.

Another important difference in the mix is the ratio of team members to actual performers. Football teams have squads of 20 players and as many again supporting that squad. Formula 3 only ever has one 'player' per car and dozens supporting that one 'player'. This will inevitably thrust a lot of responsibility and pressure on to the shoulders of one person. I am forever being told that the people inside the pit garage are a team and that has to include the driver. How does the team cope with, and live with, the idea that their three weeks (and more) of hard work, engineering, testing, re-engineering and preparation can be 'destroyed' in a moment's lapse of concentration on the first lap of a race? How does the driver cope with the humiliation of that, with the guilt of letting the rest of the team down?

Managing and leading a Formula 3 team has so many parameters and so many conflicting priorities to balance. The team may lose the most significant, important and valuable member of the team – the driver – at the end of a season. A team may even have to handle at least one new driver each and every season or a new driver halfway through the season. The drivers are clearly part of the team but they are not embedded in it. They are, and they are not, part of the team.

PSR attempt to overcome some of these teamworking issues through continual and consistent leadership and personal motivation initiated by the Chairman. Indeed, success both on and off the track is only seen as possible through strong teamwork. The drivers trust their mechanics in the preparation of their cars and the mechanics likewise trust the drivers to do as good a job as possible, rewarding their hard work. Integrity in all the actions of employees is a key aspect. Other important aspects include all employees working

▶

towards the same goals and knowing these goals, as well as the successful two-way flow of information and ideas across the company.

To add further to this teamworking melting pot, the two Formula 3 drivers are not Paul Stewart Racing employees. They come with independent sponsorship and are 'free agents', which might add fuel to the feeling that they are, and they are not, part of the team. But success is as important to them as it is to any of the team, maybe more so. After all, the British Formula 3 Championship is a fertile breeding ground and stepping stone for the Formula 1 champions of tomorrow – but only if you are successful! Further, the two PSR drivers are both Brazilian, a factor which brings some interesting cross-cultural complications to communication with, and management of, them.

In order to deal with some of the above, PSR endeavour to create a team spirit through the development and nurturing of a caring, family attitude to the whole team. This is reinforced by all employees sharing in the rewards of winning and further strengthened by employees wearing the team clothing. With these small but significantly symbolic gestures, a strong bond between all individuals throughout the company is formed. Further, formal driver training, combined with a commercial and social education, is given to the drivers to ensure that they achieve their maximum potential. An atmosphere exists where all employees are encouraged to grow and develop their individual careers. This goes some way to ensuring motivated, ambitious and competent people at all levels in the company. Add to this the potential overlapping synergies provided by the Stewart Grand Prix team and you really do have the beginnings of a global motor racing concern.

Business organisations have much to learn from sporting organisations about teamworking. After all, sporting organisations have been talking about, and 'working' in, teams for a long time. Maybe it's not that business organisations think they have nothing to learn from sport, just that they haven't started looking yet!

Discussion questions

1 Identify some fruitful areas where motor sport, or other sports, can add knowledge and value for organisations interested in looking at, and improving, their teamworking skills.
2 What aspects from this chapter do you see as mapping on to areas discussed in this case?

Note: With acknowledgement to Paul Stewart Racing for their help.

Fig 4.10 Mini-case: Teamworking

- allowing organisations to expand their potential labour market, and to hire and retain people regardless of their physical location;
- dynamic team membership enables people to move from one project to another;
- employees can be assigned to multiple, concurrent teams.

There are, of course, corresponding disadvantages. The very lack of physical interaction, with its corresponding verbal and non-verbal cues, will be detrimental to the quality of communication. Up to 70 per cent of the meaning of a message is derived from non-verbal cues. The synergies that often accompany face-to-face communication will also be lost. Another disadvantage may well be the increased reliance on technology and telecommunications. Technology will become an all too powerful determinant for the way we communicate and how we organise and manage teams and ultimately organisations. Already technology is moving faster than other organisational activities. Virtual teams add another layer of complexity to any teamwork structure. They are built around the latest advances in technological communication, so how do team leaders learn not to over-rely on these advances, such as e-mail, newsgroups and interactive groupware? Some people are just not built for remote teamworking, which virtual teams are bound to encourage; how do we manage the people who get left behind by the whole process? To develop and manage virtual teams requires expertise in both team development and virtual team technologies. Figure 4.10 presents an example of teamworking in the world of motor sports.

Managerial implications

Collaborative work is often viewed as one of the centrepieces of contemporary management and teamworking is firmly at the middle of that centrepiece. A manager's ability is often weighted against his or her skills as a leader of groups and ability at evolving, developing and encouraging teamwork. This chapter has covered some of the key aspects of groups and teams, both for now and in the future, and has attempted to raise a number of issues. To consolidate on these issues, the following implications are of some importance.

1 Some of the aspects which allow groups to be cohesive are being moderated and this must be recognised. Physical proximity helps cohesiveness and yet, with new technology and global teams, proximity is no longer vital. In another way, though, the new technology of telecommunications makes us even more closer than before.

2 Group norms cannot be completely controlled but they can be influenced. Managers need to learn the art of shaping these norms through clear statements about preferred behaviours, by reinforcing these desired behaviours through their own actions and by linking them to rewards.

3 Leading a team is a balancing act between cohesiveness and diversity, between individual and team incentives, between conformity and individualism, between face-to-face team meetings and distant communications, between different but complementary roles.

4 The power of the informal group to effect change and influence the organisation is sometimes overlooked. Networking, be it on the golf course or at a conference or somewhere in cyberspace, can lead to significant business decisions. Managers need to recognise and use the informal, 'shadow side', of the organisation.

5 The growth in teamworking should lead to a significant and meaningful growth in the incidence of group performance reviews and team incentives. Thus, the equitable and fair measurement of a team's productivity or performance will become of paramount importance.

6 In most cases effective teams do not just occur. They need to be consciously built, created and selected for. Roles need to be established and developed, diversity needs to be encouraged and an open culture of trust sought. The negative aspects of cohesiveness and groupthink should be guarded against.

7 Although many textbooks define formal groups as permanent, many organisations are seeking to implement adaptable structures and develop more flexible and proactive patterns of working. In this sense the permanence of a formal group may be no more than the duration of the project in a matrix structure. Less permanence will be more common.

8 Although making group decisions can be time consuming, trigger conflict and involve inappropriate pressures to conform, the decisions are often more accurate, creative and

acceptable solutions. This is because of the innate capacity for groups to demonstrate synergy – 'the whole is greater than the sum of its parts'. But synergy does not just happen, it has to be nurtured and managed.

9 In relation to global and virtual teams, a great many training initiatives and needs must be considered. Issues faced by the manager of such teams include how to manage the anonymous team and what to do about performance management. 'If I can't see them, how do I know they are working?' What is the new social protocol for virtual teams and how do we manage that? Can any of the traditional views of team development still be applied?

10 It is important to understand that teams, and teamworking, may not be the magical panacea for all organisations. Teambuilding has its pitfalls and some groups just do not work well together.

Summary of main points

This chapter has examined the rapidly changing nature of groups and teams. The main points made are:

- humans have an innate 'craving' to be in a variety of groups and organisational life helps to satisfy this need;
- there are clear differences and similarities between informal and formal groups;
- there are significant distinctions between groups, psychological groups and teams;
- groups occur, grow, develop and are maintained in a number of different but complementary ways;
- there is a fine balance between effective and dysfunctional teams;
- technological communication is playing an increasingly important role in the life and functioning of teams.

Conclusions

Globalisation and technology are having a profound effect on the ways in which organisations structure themselves and their work. Technology has taken on an increasingly significant role in the way we organise, structure and manage teams. It has the potential to change the very nature of groups and teams as we understand them. Although technology can assist groups in overcoming the constraints of space and time, it also demands that groups learn and understand it, so that they may fruitfully appropriate its structures and realise its intended benefits and undoubted shortcomings. How computer-facilitated interaction will affect such critical group and team variables as pressure for uniformity, status and power is as yet largely unknown.

Can all, or any, of the traditional models for group development still be applied? What will become of team roles, group norms and cultural values? How do formal and informal groups fit into virtual organisations and workplaces? The scope for further discussion, exploration and research around this growing area is enormous, for it involves all that you have read up to now about groups and teams.

QUESTIONS

1. 'What teams need more than ever in today's business environment is leaders, not managers!' Discuss the rationale for this statement.
2. In the forming stage of Tuckman's model, is the set of individuals involved a group or not? Explain your reasoning.
3. What will be the key issues for work teams over the next ten years?
4. You work as a manager for a large global footwear company and have been asked to join a working party looking at guidelines for the company's newly developed virtual sales teams. As there is no existing 'advice' for managing, or working in, a virtual team, the guidelines will be viewed as a way of working and a set of rules for the virtual sales teams to follow.

   What might the guidelines contain and why?
5. 'Group problem solving and decision making simply creates more issues and problems than it solves!' Discuss the validity of this statement with reference to your experiences of working in groups.

REFERENCES

Adair, J. (1986) *Effective Teambuilding*. Aldershot: Gower.

Ancona, D. G. (1987) 'Groups in organizations: Extending laboratory models' in Hendrick, C. (ed.) *Group Processes and Intergroup Relations*. Beverly Hills: Sage.

Armstrong, M. (1996) 'How group efforts can pay dividends', *People Management*, 25 January, pp 22–7.

Arnold, J., Cooper, C. L. and Robertson, I. T. (1998) *Work Psychology*, 3rd edn. London: Financial Times Pitman Publishing.

Aronson, E. (1992) *The Social Animal*, 6th edn. New York and Oxford: Freeman.

Asch, S. E. (1951) 'Effects of group pressure upon the modification and distortion of judgements' in Guetzkow, H. (ed.) *Groups, Leadership and Men*. New York: Carnegie Press.

Bass, B. M. and Ryterband, E. C. (1979) *Organizational Psychology*, 2nd edn. London: Allyn and Bacon.

Belbin, R. M. (1981) *Management Teams: Why They Succeed or Fail.* Oxford: Butterworth-Heinemann.

Belbin, R. M. (1993) *Team Roles at Work.* Oxford: Butterworth-Heinemann.

Benne, K. D. and Sheats, P. (1948) 'Functional roles of group members', *Journal of Social Issues*, Vol. 4, pp 41–9.

Brown, H. (1971) 'Stability and Change in Social Groups' in Open University Course D100, 'Understanding Society: a Foundation Course', Units 29–31, 'Stability, Change and Conflict', Buckingham: Open University Press.

Buchanan, D. (1987) 'Job enrichment is dead: long live high-performance work design', *Personnel Management*, May, pp 40–3.

Carrington, L. (1995) 'Rewards for all', *Personnel Today*, 17 January.

Cascio, W. F. (1998) 'On Managing a Virtual Workplace', *Occupational Psychologist*, August, pp 5–11.

Coles, M. (1998a) 'Managers tackle worldwide teams', *Sunday Times*, 8 March, p 24.

Coles, M. (1998b) 'Managers learn value of sharing', *Sunday Times*, 19 July, p 24.

Glass, N. (1996) *Management Masterclass: A Practical Guide to the New Realities of Business.* London: Nicholas Brealey.

Gray, J. L. and Starke, F. A. (1984) *Organizational Behaviour: Concepts and Applications*, 3rd edn. Columbus, OH: Charles Merrill.

Handy, C. (1989) *The Age of Unreason.* London: Business Books.

Handy, C. (1993) *Understanding Organisations.* Harmondsworth: Penguin Books.

Hofstede, G. (1980) *Culture's Consequences: International Differences in Work-Related Values.* Beverly Hills: Sage.

Huczynski, A. and Buchanan, D. (1991) *Organizational Behaviour: An Introductory Text.* Hemel Hempstead: Prentice-Hall.

Industrial Society (1995) *Self-Managed Teams.* London: The Industrial Society.

Janis, J. L. (1972) *Victims of Groupthink.* Boston: Houghton Mifflin.

Kandola, R. (1995) 'Managing diversity: new broom or old hat?' in Cooper, C. L. and Robertson, I. T. (eds) *International Review of Industrial and Organizational Psychology*, Vol. 10. Chichester: John Wiley, pp 131–67.

Katzenbach, J. R. and Smith, D. K. (1993) *The Wisdom of Teams: Creating the High Performance Organisation.* Cambridge, MA: Harvard Business School Press.

Maznevski, M. L. (1994) 'Understanding our differences: performance in decision-making groups with diverse members', *Human Relations*, 47(5), pp 531–52.

McGregor, D. (1960) *The Human Side of Enterprise.* New York: McGraw-Hill.

Mullins, L .J. (1999) *Management and Organisational Behaviour*, 5th edn. London: Financial Times Pitman Publishing.

Norstedt, J. P. and Aguren, S. (1973) *Saab-Scania Report.* Stockholm: Swedish Employers' Confederation.

Obeng, E. D. A. (1994) *All Change!* London: Pitman Publishing.

Parker, G. M. (1990). *Team Players and Teamwork.* San Francisco: Jossey-Bass.

Perry, B. (1984) *Enfield: A High-Performance System*. Bedford, MA: Educational Services Development and Publishing.

Piper, W. E., Marrache, M., Lacroix, R., Richardson, A. M. and Jones, B. D. (1983) 'Cohesion as a basic bond in groups', *Human Relations*, 26(2), pp 93–108.

Salem, M., Lazarus, H. and Cullen, J. (1994) 'Developing self-managing teams: Structure and performance', *Journal of Management Development*, 11(3), pp 24–32.

Schein, E. H. (1988) *Organisational Psychology*, 3rd edn. Hemel Hempstead: Prentice-Hall.

Sproull, L. and Kiesler, S. (1991) 'Computers, networks and work', *Scientific American*, 265, pp 116–32.

Thomas, H. (1974) 'Finding a better way', *Guardian*, 17 Jan.

Trist, E. L. *et al.* (1963) *Organizational Choice*. London: Tavistock Publications.

Tuckman, B. W. (1965) 'Development sequence in small groups', *Psychological Bulletin*, Vol. 63, pp 384–99.

Tuckman, B. W. and Jensen, M. A. C. (1977) 'Stages of Small Group Development Revisited', *Group and Organizational Studies*, Vol. 2, pp 419–27.

Valery, N. (1974) 'Importing the lessons of Swedish workers', *New Scientist*, 62 (892), pp 27–8.

Woodcock, M. (1979) *Team Development Manual*. Aldershot: Gower.

Young, R. (1998) 'The Wide-awake Club', *People Management*, 5 Feb., pp 46–9.

FURTHER READING

Adair, J. (1986) *Effective Teambuilding*. Aldershot: Gower.

Belbin, R. M. (1993) *Team Roles at Work*. Oxford: Butterworth-Heinemann.

Coles, M. (1998) 'Managers learn value of sharing', *Sunday Times*, 19 July, p 24.

Hamel, G., Doz, Y, and Prahalad, C .K. (1989) 'Collaborate with Your Competitors – and Win', *Harvard Business Review*, Jan/Feb.

Mullins, L. J. (1999) *Management and Organisational Behaviour*, 5th edn. London: Financial Times Pitman Publishing.

Pringle, D. (1996) 'Is team-working faith misplaced?', *Personnel Today*, 12 March.

Robbins, H. and Finley, M. (1998) *Why Teams don't Work: What went wrong and how to put it right*. London: Orion Books.

Senge, P. (1991) *The Fifth Discipline*. London: Random Century.

5

Organisational theory

LEARNING OUTCOMES

On completion of this chapter you should be able to:

- understand the main developments in organisational theory;
- appreciate some of the contemporary insights into organisational theory informing our understanding of modern organisations;
- understand how organisational theory underpins both the principles and practices of organising and of management;
- begin to appreciate the value of organisational theory as a tool for understanding behaviour in organisations, for diagnosing likely causes of organisational problems and for working towards potential solutions to those problems;
- recognise the close relationship between developments in organisational theory and organisational behaviour.

KEY CONCEPTS

- *classical theory*
- *scientific management/Taylorism*
- *human relations*
- *contingency theory*
- *sociotechnical systems*
- *organisational/ environmental behaviour*
- *enactment*
- *frames, perspective and paradigms*
- *organisations as machines, as cultures and as political entities*
- *learning organisation*

Organisational theory

This is the first of five chapters which deal with behaviour at the level of the organisation. It is vital to understand the origins of, and influences upon, the study of Organisational Behaviour (OB): with that aim in mind, the remainder of this book complements earlier chapters, which discussed behaviour *in* organisations, by exploring the behaviour *of* organisations. In order to appreciate why organisations, and people in them, behave as they do it is important to explore the influences on them and the theoretical and empirical work conducted, largely within the twentieth century, in this regard. To enhance our understanding of modern organisations it is essential to appreciate what has gone before, for this has a profound and lasting influence on today's organisations.

Introduction

This chapter explores classical organisational and management theory (*see* Chapter 6 for greater coverage of leadership and management). You will appreciate that much of the theoretical work conducted in the first half of the twentieth century in this field has a significant bearing on current thought and practice in organisations. The text continues by exploring the main arguments of the human relations school: work conducted, largely since the 1930s, which enhances our understanding of organisations not as mechanical structures and relationships but as human communities. This crucial underpinning will inform the exploration of systems theory and contingency theory, both of which provide useful explanatory frameworks and add rigour to our understanding of OB. The chapter then briefly explores the behaviour of organisations in their environmental context, before, finally, discussing some contemporary views of organisations and behaviour by taking a look at organisations as if through a series of lenses or from a variety of perspectives. This will give added insight and enable you to recognise that, to put it simply, 'what you see is what you look for'. Figure 5.1 illustrates the content of this chapter and, albeit rather simplistically, links the various contributions.

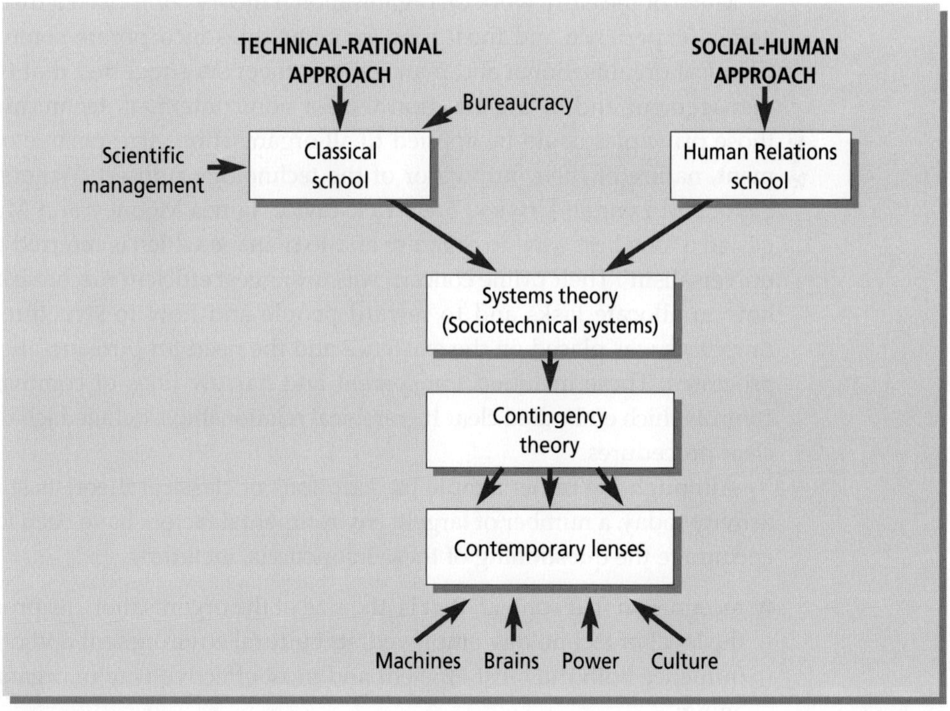

Fig 5.1 Organisation theory

A knowledge of organisational and managerial theory will improve your ability to diagnose and resolve organisational problems. It will underpin and inform your understanding of the rest of this book, of management and leadership, organisational structure, change, politics and power and of organisational culture.

The classical school

Contributions to organisational theory in the early twentieth century were dominated by efforts to identify principles which, advocates suggested, would, if followed, ensure success. The assumption was that these simple laws or principles represented the single best way to manage and organise. Inspiration came from the armed forces which had organised large numbers of personnel, often in dynamic and difficult situations. Even today considerable military language infiltrates common organisational discourse; for example, groups of employees are often referred to as 'the troops' and bureaucratic organisations have 'lines of command'. Organisational members who question approaches are often advised not to 'put their heads above the parapet', and the conventional distinction between line and staff remains in many traditional organisations. In addition to military discourse, mechanistic analogies dominate. Organisations are often viewed as machines, hence the belief that a 'well-oiled machine' is analogous to a sound, efficient operation.

Much of the early work on organisational theory comprised a distillation of managerial experience and most modern companies incorporate some of these ideas. Classical organisational and management theorists suggested that the principles of management and of organisation were a non-contextual, technical, issue. That is, those principles could be applied to all organisations irrespective of size, environment, nature of their outputs or of the technology utilised. Writers such as Henri Fayol and Lyndall Urwick, Frederick Taylor, James Mooney and Mary Follett suggested a 'one best way' to organise and to manage which is referred to as 'structural universalism'. Their prime concern was to suggest efficient mechanisms of control, of how to allocate tasks and to reward people and how to structure organisations. Emphasis was placed on the existence and the need for bureaucratic structures and processes. These included transparent and narrow lines of command or spans of control which embodied clear hierarchical relationships, detailed job descriptions and clear procedures.

Although the rather simple prescriptions of classical theorists still inform much activity today, a number of largely environmental factors have been identified which encourage the questioning of these injunctions, including:

- recognition that context, that is, the size of the organisation, its products/services, the level of technology employed, its cultural environment and other factors, can influence both the most efficient and most effective way of organising and managing;
- recognition that the workforce has, arguably, become a more critical factor in

determining organisational success; the need to attract, retain and motivate a skilled workforce is paramount in most organisations;

- the dynamism of the business environment and the complexity of the marketplace, particularly in the global economy of post-World War II years (since 1945), require organisations to be flexible and innovative; it is widely believed that bureaucratic organisations, built on the principles of the classical school, are ill equipped to embrace change and are more suited to repetitive activities and known territory;
- changes in social expectations and the political and legal environment have ensured that many of the excesses of the late nineteenth and early twentieth century organisations have become unacceptable, unethical and/or illegal;
- recognition that, partly due to dynamism in the business environment, organisations have increasingly sought people with leadership qualities as opposed to mere mechanical management or administrative skills.

Scientific management

The emphasis on rationality, and lack of consideration for human aspects of organisation, led to the application of scientific principles to work management. It can be argued that scientific management comprises a subset of the classical school: the latter is mainly concerned with the wider organisation and its structure, whereas the former focuses on job design. Scientific principles, it was suggested, should be applied to work organisation in order to seek the 'one best way' of conducting any job. The consequence would be significant efficiency gains, an increase in productivity and, hence, in both wage rates and profitability. The school's most influential exponent was Frederick Taylor (1856–1915), and other valuable contributions were made by Frank Gilbreth (1868–1924) and Henry Gantt (1861–1919).

Frederick Taylor

Taylor argued that efficiency, standardisation and discipline would result from a process of scientific management of work tasks. To be more precise, he suggested that:

- a clear distinction should be made between planning a job, a management role, and conducting the tasks, a worker's role;
- a scientific selection process should identify the correct person to perform the task;
- jobs should be standardised and simplified;
- each worker should conduct a minimum of movements, preferably involving just one set of actions;
- there was 'one best way' of organising any set of tasks to be performed and it was management's responsibility to conduct exhaustive measurements in order to achieve this desired state.

Taylor's work in a steel plant – and McDonald's today

Taylor's work at the Bethlehem Steel works in the USA, involving the efforts of a pig iron handler called Schmidt (an alias), is discussed in most OB and organisational theory texts. Taylor sought to alter fundamentally the way in which a simple task, the movement of iron, was conducted. As a result of his detailed time-and-motion observations and measurements, productivity in the process was raised four times, that is, by 400 per cent. In other words, only one-quarter of the workers would be required to move the same quantity of iron; alternatively, the company could move four times the quantity of iron using the same number of workers (although not necessarily the same individuals).

As a result of Taylor's work at the steel works, wages were increased by 60 per cent. The cost of pig iron supplied to all manner of engineering companies declined (Taylor, 1911). Nevertheless, these 'economic' benefits were not often warmly greeted and resulted in almost universal hostility, from workers, management and the US government (Taylor appeared before a House of Representatives committee following investigations into a major strike in 1912).

Taylor's principles were first applied in Britain in 1905 and were criticised by the Iron and Steel Federation. Similarly, in Germany in 1912 they were greeted with considerable hostility, and in France (Renault) they resulted in strike action and violent protest. However, in the USSR, Lenin, shortly after the Bolshevik revolution, established the League for the Scientific Organisation of Work in 1918.

The reader might be forgiven for gaining the impression that such practices are rare, socially unacceptable and no longer considered viable in economic terms. In some industries this is the case. The contemporary need for multiskilling, for workers to be encouraged to show initiative and for them to take responsibility makes the strict application of scientific principles difficult. However, many organisations thrive on scientific management principles and organise accordingly. Perhaps the best examples lie in catering (more specifically in fast food consumer outlets in companies such as McDonald's). In McDonald's outlets, staff have clear and narrowly defined jobs which require limited training, are carefully designed to minimise unproductive movement and scope for human error and are not designed to motivate the employees. There is little or no staff discretion allowed: for example, cooking times are prescribed. The benefits to customers appear to be a standard product, the same every time, delivered rapidly and at a reasonable price and with consistency of service.

Fig 5.2 Mini-case: Experiments with scientific management

Taylor argued that this would raise productivity (his consultancy work invariably bore out this contention) and so give working people the higher wages they sought. He suggested that increases in productivity should be accompanied by the introduction of piece-work, *an incentive payment system which relates bonuses to level of output,* and hence worker satisfaction and motivation would be ensured. He tended to underestimate the strength of worker alienation and rejection of his philosophy, as the mini-case presented in Figure 5.2 illustrates.

It is important to locate developments in scientific management in their historical context. In the early twentieth century, management was a very imprecise activity. Little systematic research had been conducted and practices varied considerably. Workers tended to believe that an increase in productivity on their part would merely result in job losses. Understandably, they took advantage of poor management controls to slow production. This was made possible as workers themselves often designed or organised their own efforts and had little interest in seeking efficiency.

Taylor's thinking preceded the widespread adoption of mass production techniques, possibly best demonstrated by the early (1920s) motor manufacturers; notably by Henry Ford in the USA. As the film, *Modern Times*, starring Charlie Chaplin, satirically portrays, workers performed simple and highly repetitive mechanical tasks. They were no more than 'cogs in the wheel' of a 'well-oiled machine'. It is also important to note that many modern organisations adopt similar principles in order to maintain or increase productivity. This is particularly the case when similar or identical outputs are required on a near-continuous process. Most readers will be familiar with McDonald's, where work processes embody many of the characteristics identified by Taylor (*refer to* Figure 5.2). For example, clear instructions are given concerning the exact time that fries should be immersed in the hot fat or the time required to cook a burger. Very little, if any, discretion is given to employees.

Whereas Taylor's work was novel, even revolutionary, in its time, it is now largely taken for granted. Increasingly, aspects of it have been rejected in favour of more 'human' or social considerations and the whole approach has proven less valuable in many contemporary contexts. Nevertheless, the principles of division between managerial and worker roles, of standardisation and specialisation, of division of labour and efficiency, continue to remain as central precepts in many organisations.

Gilbreth and Gantt

It was not Taylor but Frank Gilbreth who first advocated the use of time and motion methodologies. Like Taylor, he worked at reducing the extent and frequency of 'unnecessary' motions involved in completing a task. He conducted his early works in the building industry. By reducing unnecessary motion, he argued, it would be possible to reduce worker fatigue. It was fatigue, he suggested, that hampered efforts to increase productivity; hence he suggested reductions in the working day and regular brief rest periods at work. By also seeking to influence the work environment by altering lighting conditions, considering permitting music to be played, providing canteen facilities and even chairs for periods of rest, Gilbreth was the first researcher seriously to consider that workers have complex needs.

It was Henry Gantt who introduced detailed instruction cards for workers. 'Desk instructions' are still to be found in many, particularly clerical, tasks today. He also developed new payment systems, combining basic and bonus schemes. Furthermore he recognised the 'human' element in work design considerations. For example, if an employee failed to meet the necessary standard (usually by being unable to work at sufficient speed) the foreman was required to demonstrate that the work could realistically be done at the pace required.

A critique

There is little doubt that the work of Frederick Taylor and others influenced work organisation practices in many organisations, first in the USA and later elsewhere. It could be argued that their efforts stimulated changes which led to significant increases in productivity and facilitated mass production techniques and wage rises which enabled mass consumption. This, in turn, stimulated rapid economic growth in North America and Europe. It would be somewhat naive to argue that such a transformation of the global economy was the result of Taylor's work, but changes he stimulated undoubtedly had some influence on these dramatic events. That said, it is important to evaluate his scientific principles critically and note the drawbacks which have arisen.

Taylor suggested that his fundamental principles could, and should, be applied to any organisation: a claim that they were of universal applicability. This remains a hotly disputed contention. A whole host of intervening factors can and do influence 'the one best way' of managing and organising work. These are further explored later in this chapter (*see* pp 120–4). Practical and effective problems encountered with Taylorism include:

- widespread, often violent, opposition from workers;
- significant resistance in the early twentieth century from management, who saw his work as critical of their efforts, and from the US government which questioned the implications of his approach and its consequences for worker morale and alienation;
- decline in worker morale, not least because of the highly boring and repetitive nature of their work;
- decline in skill requirements for workers, reducing flexibility through lack of multiskilling and enabling management to offer lower wages.

These problems arose due to:

- a failure to recognise the emotional and social needs of workers; they were viewed, by Taylor in particular, as individual units of production, in much the same way as a machine: workers are not machines;
- the assumption that pay was a sufficiently powerful source of motivation to elicit co-operation: although Taylor, rather like classical economists, assumed that workers were rational economic thinkers, who would respond to financial incentives, there are many other variables which influence people's considerations in this regard (*see* Chapter 3);
- the approach clearly represented an overt exercise of management control over working people: it removed any decision-making right from workers.

Subsequent research (*see* the discussion on p 117 on human relations) demonstrated that the social needs of workers are significant and include the need to form relationships, to experience meaningfulness or achievement at work, to have some job satisfaction and task variation, and a sense of responsibility. These aspects were largely ignored by scientific management theorists. Additionally, Taylor, in particular, underplayed the significance of the work group and the breadth of capabilities workers possess. His techniques aimed to reduce difference or individualism: characteristics which, in many situations, are of value.

Human relations

It is possible, although probably not entirely fair, to consider the work and prescriptions of the classical school as characterising the 'forces of dark' and the human relations school as the 'forces of light'. This polarised view emphasises the radical differences between the two schools. It suggests that human relations theorists rejected the view of organisations as mechanistic, rational and impersonal entities which embody strict lines of command and hierarchical positions, specialisation of labour and rules and procedures to cover all activity, in favour of an emphasis on people, involving a consideration of broader issues of motivation, autonomy, trust and openness in managerial and organisational matters.

Chester Barnard (1938) proposed the first new theory of organisations, arguing that they were co-operative social systems, as opposed to machine-like, detached, technical structures. Hence, he noted the existence of the informal organisation, of natural, as opposed to managerially instigated, groups in organisations, of complex information flows, of authority from below; for example, the power to either under- or over-achieve against targets. His work immediately preceded the publication of the now-famous Hawthorne studies (Roethlisberger and Dickson, 1939).

Research was conducted at the Western Electric Company in the USA between 1924 and 1932. Its intent, as with most organisational and management research, was to explore influences on levels of productivity with a view to improving, in true classical style, worker output. However, the research achieved a number of significant and unintended outcomes. The investigators altered certain 'physical' conditions among a control group of workers. Changes to the level of lighting were expected to lead to increases or declines in productivity. However, they found that on almost all occasions when lighting levels were changed productivity increased (even when the light was believed to be insufficient to conduct the task accurately and speedily). Further experiments involved planned changes to hours of work and rest and to other interventions, such as refreshments and consultation with supervisors. Again, invariably, productivity increased as a result of *any* form of intervention.

The research suggested that it was the attention that the control group of workers received which contributed to productivity improvements. Clearly, more complex human needs were involved than had been considered previously by classical theorists. Traditionally, the quality and nature of supervision was viewed as a central determinant of productivity. The experiments also discovered that workers in groups were able to influence the level of their output and exerted social pressures, via informal group mechanisms, to control that output. In contrast to rational economic understanding, which prevailed at the time, workers did not necessarily seek to maximise production in order to receive enhanced bonuses. In other words, social pressures on individuals were often stronger than managerial concerns for enhanced work rates.

These experiments, although methodologically imperfect, generated new insights into motivation, group work, leadership/management and the informal organisation which have, subsequently, inspired considerable research and the blossoming of a significant branch of social study. It should be noted, however, that the human relations approach does not represent a 'getting soft' orientation. The school sought to discover ways of improving output or productivity and, ultimately, profitability. However, the approach moves away from the overt managerial perspective, adopted by the classical school, to consideration of the vital importance of human/social activity as a determinant of productivity and organisational well-being. It became increasingly recognised that people have a complex set of needs and that they seek to satisfy many of these needs in the workplace.

The work of this school has been continued by many researchers, including some referred to in Chapter 3, for example Herzberg, who stressed the importance of intrinsic needs in the motivation equation, and McClelland, who argued that style of management reflects an individual's attitude to his subordinates. McGregor (1960), whose Theory X and Theory Y are now renowned, is discussed in Chapter 6.

Systems theory

The systems approach to the study of organisations combines the often contrasting positions and considerations of the classical and human relations schools and embraces both the technical and social aspects of organisation. It also recognises the presence of contingent, environmental factors which, even though they may lie outside the organisational boundaries, nevertheless influence organisational activity. Attention is focused on the whole organisation, the relationships between its technical, mechanical or structural parameters and its behavioural, social or human elements and its relationship with the business environment. It is, therefore, appropriate at this stage to discuss this contribution to organisational theory.

An organisation is considered to be an open system: *open, suggesting that it interacts with other, broader, systems outside the organisation* (*see* Figure 5.3). These external systems are part of the organisational environment. When viewed as a system, the organisation is an integrated and complex web of relationships between structures, technology, employees and all manner of technical and social processes.

Research conducted at the Tavistock Institute of Human Relations in the UK suggested that the interaction between coal-miners and the technology they used was a critical factor in determining productivity. 'Improvements' in technology did not always lead to productivity gains as they altered the delicate psychological and sociological conditions. Old ways of working were changed by technological advance, resulting in damage to the social fabric of the work team and consequent, lower

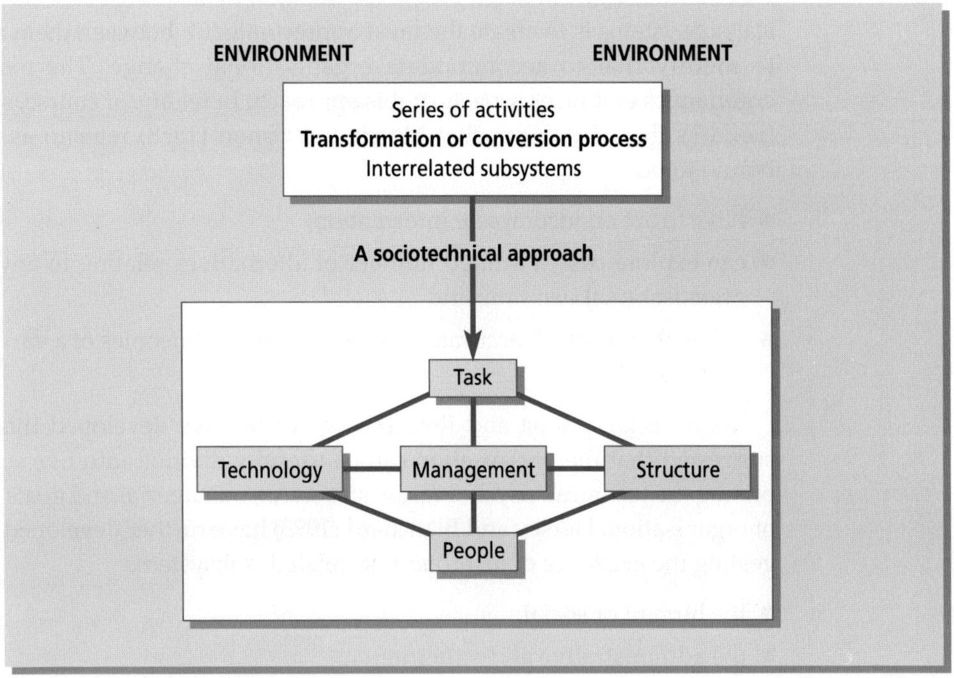

Fig 5.3 An open organisational system

Source: Mullins, L. J. (1999). *Management and Organisational Behaviour*, 5th edn, Financial Times Pitman Publishing, p. 106. Reprinted with permission.

than expected, productivity. The relationship between the technical and social aspects of organisations was highlighted by this research. Table 5.1 illustrates some of the two sets of components.

Table 5.1 Illustration of technical and social subsystems

Technical subsystems	Social subsystems
Physical location	Social needs
Stages in operational process	Psychological needs
Use of materials	Human relationships
Technical equipment	Formal/informal communications
Maintenance	Skills and learning
Logistics/material flows	Meaningfulness of work

The challenge or design problem presented by the range of social and technological subsystems is to create the most appropriate 'fit' between them and continually to modify that to accommodate organisational change. The modern study of ergonomics embraces aspects of this approach. In reality, of course, suboptimisation (i.e., less than 'best', or what March and Simon (1958) refer to as 'satisficing'), is bound to occur as people:

- have to act on incomplete information;
- can explore only a limited number of alternatives relating to any managerial or organisational decision; and
- are unable to attach accurate values to inputs or outcomes of a variety of processes or decisions.

More recently Kast and Rosenzweig (1985) have developed this approach and suggested that the organisation can be usefully divided into five subsystems comprising the technical, psychological, structural, managerial and goals/values aspects of organisation. Hersey and Blanchard (1993) have further developed this work, suggesting the existence of just four, interrelated, subsystems:

- the human or social;
- the administrative and structure;
- the informational and decision making; and
- the economic and technological.

The value of this approach has, perhaps understandably, been questioned by many organisational theorists, who argue that it gives very little practical insight into organisational activity. However, Hirschhorn (1984) suggested that, because of the changing nature of manufacturing, involving semi-autonomous groups and greater delegation of decision making and problem solving, work based on sociotechnical principles warrants careful consideration. Of particular significance is the finding of the Tavistock studies which suggested that work in groups is more meaningful for its participants and that technology need not, if applied appropriately, unduly influence this form of work organisation. It is not therefore surprising that many recent changes in organisational structures place emphasis on the team or group as one of the best ways of managing difficult problem-solving tasks and coping with the needs for organisational flexibility and change.

Contingency theory

The work of theorists from the classical school in particular, and to an extent the human relations school, offered all-embracing, 'one best way' prescriptions on how best to organise and to manage. These panaceas were proposed to be universally applicable.

Research conducted from the early 1960s questioned many of these organisational

Fig 5.4 Contingency factors: the organisational context

prescriptions. For example, Woodward (1965) found that the level and type of technology, being central to the organisation's activity, influenced the structure of the unit. Similarly, others provided empirical evidence to suggest that organisational size, the nature of its output and, more significantly, the characteristics of the business environment in which it operated (e.g. the nature of competition), had a significant, measurable effect on the organisational structure, work organisation or job design, and upon management. The plethora of research in the 1960s, and since, on many aspects of organisational activity largely rejected the 'one best way' philosophy, arguing instead that organisations in many ways reflect the situation in which they find themselves and the strategy they pursue, and that there is a great variety of ways of organising and managing with each, potentially, leading to organisational success (or indeed failure). In other words, organisational structure, job design, management practices and most other aspects of organisations are dependent or contingent on a variety of internal and external tangible and non-tangible variables (*see* Figure 5.4). Implicit is the understanding that organisations are social communities and hence, organisational behaviour can be considered as both a response to and a determinant of many of the complex variables which comprise organisations and their environments. As the word 'behaviour' implies, the human element in organisational activity is emphasised and recognised by contingency theorists as a vital influencing factor on organisations and one that was largely ignored by earlier classical management theorists.

We will now briefly explore three key factors, alluded to above, which have been found to influence organisational structure and activities.

Contingent factor: the business environment

A study of electronics companies in the United Kingdom by Burns and Stalker (1961) attempted to establish why some companies were able to cope with changes in their environment, specifically dynamism in their product markets, whereas others were inept in this regard. They argued that successful innovators had developed an 'organic' structure whereas those with 'mechanistic' structures were less able to adapt. Lawrence and Lorsch (1967) found a similar relationship between the business environment and the internal structure of firms in the United States. Where they differed from earlier researchers was that they did not believe that organisations or their environments were uniform or unchanging. They postulated that the more turbulent and complex the environment, the greater the degree of difference between subparts of the organisation. Hence they argued that successful companies were those that developed appropriate degrees of differentiation between specialist departments while simultaneously promoting integration calling on common goals.

In environments that are certain and stable, organisations will tend to develop a form and structure which is most efficient in relation to that environment, probably one with a high degree of managerial control and mechanistic structures and systems. If an organisation's environment is uncertain and complex, managers design structures with greater inbuilt flexibility. However, perception may play a part in this process, that is, managers in organisations which have an organic structure may perceive the environment as being dynamic and uncertain whereas those in more mechanistic structures may perceive their environment as being more certain; the reality may be quite different. Nevertheless, many firms have failed because managers 'perceived' their environments as being stable and certain when in fact they harboured destructive dynamic forces.

Contingent factor: technology

Woodward's contention was that companies which design their organisational structure to fit the type of production technology they employ are likely to be successful (Woodward, 1965). She found clear variations in organisational structure between companies and argued that much of the variation was linked to differences in manufacturing techniques. For example, structures differed between organisations engaged in specialised or small batch production and those adopting mass production techniques and technologies. She noted, particularly, that certain factors varied considerably according to the production techniques adopted (*see* Chapter 7 for further details). These included:

- typical spans of control;
- levels in the hierarchy;
- the ratio of managers to other personnel and of the total salary bill to total costs.

In other words, and in contrast to the generalisations made by classical management exponents, considerable variability in structure and management activity occurred between organisations, although this appeared to have little significant or discernible influence on commercial success.

Perhaps not surprisingly, Perrow (1970) found that in organisations where routine technology predominates (i.e., there is considerable repetition of tasks and problem solving and flexibility is less in demand) there tends to be little requirement for decision making at the lower levels of the organisation. Middle managers are powerful and the organisations are characterised by careful planning and little co-operation between groups/departments. Bureaucratic principles dominate and the structure is mechanistic. Conversely, in non-routine environments, there is a high level of discretion at lower levels, greater feedback and dialogue between groups and levels in the hierarchy and significant interdependence between groups. This model approximates to the organic structure outlined above.

Contingent factor: organisational size

The Aston studies (empirical research conducted in the University of Aston largely in the 1960s–70s by, among others, D. S. Pugh, J. Child, D. J. Hickson, C. R. Hinings and C. Turner) suggested that organisational size has important implications for organisational design. Despite the fact that organisational size is often problematic to determine and that its influence is difficult to distinguish from the effects of other variables, the Aston studies and the work of Porter *et al.* (1975) and Child (1988) found that:

- size of organisational unit was negatively correlated with job satisfaction, staff turnover and absenteeism from work;
- larger organisations are more likely to be standardised by rules and procedures;
- internal communications and co-ordination are more difficult in larger organisations and are addressed via structural and procedural mechanisms, that is, line managers have a responsibility to communicate with employees and follow accepted procedures when doing so;
- the relationship between organisational size and productivity was unclear and variable;
- increased organisational size is associated with increased bureaucracy.

Contingency: criticisms and conclusions

There has been some criticism of the contingency approach. First, although extensive research has been conducted which is clearly of theoretical and academic value, the outcome of the work is more difficult to apply to the workplace. By its very nature, it is not significantly prescriptive: the answer to the question 'How should we organise?' is, 'It depends'! It depends on a whole host of only partly understood internal and external variables. It is no wonder that the simple, although highly questionable, panaceas offered by the classical theorists had, and to an extent still have, considerable appeal among some managers. Many of the best-selling management books of recent decades tend to offer 'one best way', simplistic prescriptions.

Second, contingency theory can only ever give a partial picture. There are so many variables and combinations of factors which influence organisational activity and company success, and the environment is so dynamic, that complete knowledge is unobtainable. Third, the contingency theorists underplay the significance of intensely 'human' aspects of organisation, such as power, the role of multiple stakeholders and organisational culture. Finally, it should be remembered that organisations and their environments are in constant flux. Change is often rapid and discontinuous. The factors influencing the 'correct fit' between structure and environment, for example, at one time may become less relevant at another time.

With the rejection of 'the best way' of organising, the crucial task of management, and hence the concern of academics and researchers, is to find an appropriate, satisficing 'fit' between the human, task and business environment. Emphasis has subsequently been placed on establishing which variable or variables most influence organisational structure and other organisational variables. The deterministic position suggests that certain key variables will have a significant and measurable influence on organisational structure, job design, the degree of specialisation or standardisation and so forth. However, an alternative position suggests that these organisational variables are themselves strongly and decisively influenced by strategic choice: they are the product of the political power of key stakeholder groups, such as senior management. Others argue that a collective social concept, organisational culture, explains much of the variability found in organisations. Chapter 8 explores this position and the interplay of power and politics within organisations. Clearly, the complex interplay between tangible and non-tangible aspects of organisation and environment provide rich veins for academic and managerial exploration in search of *the*, or *a*, 'truth' or, perhaps more realistically, greater insight into organisations and their behaviour.

Organisational behaviour: beyond the organisation

All organisations exist in a complex and usually dynamic environment. The 'business' environment comprises an array of forces which both act on an organisation and are framed by the organisation. These forces may be categorised. One such typology is the PEST model, where the environment is thought to comprise political, economic, social and technological forces. If we add legal, ecological and competitive processes to this we have included most aspects of the external environment. It can be argued that organisations behave in response to environmental forces and, in turn, their behaviour, or strategy, influences their environment. Wilson (1992) suggests three broad ways of viewing the business environment, namely as:

- an objective fact – a clear, measurable and definable reality;

- a subjective fact, its particular characteristics being dependent on each individual's or group's interpretation and perception;
- enacted (Weick, 1979), where the division between organisation and environment is unclear and, more significantly, where the environment is created and defined by the organisation itself, or rather, by the individuals and groups that comprise an organisation (an illustration is given in Figure 5.5).

The latter two definitions suggest that behavioural elements at the individual, group and/or organisational level influence the nature of the relationship between an organisation and its environment: hence, the relevance of this to the study of organisational behaviour. It is quite possible that two companies in the same sector might view aspects of their environment differently. One may identify certain features, such as a technological change, as an opportunity for growth and development whereas the other might see it as a constraint or threat. There is considerable evidence to suggest that this sort of variable response occurs. What is clear is that the direction of influence between environment and organisation is not unidirectional, simple or static but multidirectional, each influencing the other. What is more, organisations and people in them can assist in the 'creation' of their own environment.

Decision makers in organisations receive and assimilate incoming data from the environment, information and ideas about new products and services, technologies, competitor action, ways of organising and managing and so forth. The data are, however, incomplete and even the most sophisticated scanning and forecasting activities can only hope to collect a small proportion of all environmental data. Individuals, groups and organisations interpret those data in different ways. This difference in reception, interpretation and assimilation is influenced by the history and development of the organisations, of individual perception, power balances, structural issues and organisational culture. It could be said that our individual and collective 'perception' only enables us to see and interpret information in certain ways (*see* Chapter 2). In turn, operational and strategic decisions are based on these interpretative data and so, as Weick (1979) suggests, actions based on subjective information will in turn influence the environment of the organisation. The organisation 'enacts' or creates the environment in which it operates: the mini-case presented in Figure 5.5 illustrates this phenomenon.

Most early organisational research assumed a largely stable business environment. Proponents of the classical school argued that organisations should be machine-like and feature centralised authority, clear lines of command, specialisation and the division of labour and numerous rules and regulations. However, such mechanised and bureaucratic organisations are poorly suited to adapt to dynamic and complex environments. By the 1940s in North America and, increasingly, in Europe the deficiencies of the 'classical' organisation became apparent. Technological changes, increasingly complex markets and social, political and cultural changes created new demands on organisations which many were ill equipped to manage. Although many of the basic principles identified by classical theorists remain entrenched in many modern organisations, other changes have occurred. The human relations school (late 1930s

Innovate: enacting its environment

In Innovate, a computer software company, there was, a decade ago, a collective perception (or at least the prime decision makers shared a perception) that their competitive environment was changing. These perceived changes encouraged them to develop a technologically superior database product. They also believed that numerous smaller software companies might begin to encroach on their other activities if they did not focus research and development (R&D) activity in specific areas. Faced with having to make a decision, Innovate decided to significantly increase R&D spending in an attempt to develop a new database product. A consequence of this was a reduction in the R&D spend and management attention elsewhere.

After two years Innovate had successfully produced and marketed their database product. They remained the market leaders with almost unassailable strength. Their competitors, knowing that Innovate were devoting their considerable resources to this new product, recognised that market supremacy would belong to Innovate. However, there has been a cost. The neglect of Innovate's other software products has meant that competitors have overtaken them in market share terms, in these other product lines. The competitors recognised that there was an opportunity created by Innovate's decision to develop the database product and seek supremacy in this area. The competitors have focused on the areas which Innovate neglected.

Innovate's original perception of their environment led them to a particular strategic management decision. In making that decision Innovate enacted their environment. That is, their actions ensured that their perceptions became an enforced reality. Their actions allowed their competitors to adjust their strategic policy to take advantage of the opportunity. Innovate's perceptions and subsequent actions have become a self-fulfilling prophecy. It could be said therefore that the original erroneous perception held by Innovate of the nature of their competitive business environment has created their strategy and the resultant competitive conditions in the sector. Had their original perception been different, their strategy, and those of their competitors might have been different, and resulted in quite different competitive conditions.

Fig 5.5 Mini-case: Innovate and enactment

onwards) typified by the work of Chester Barnard and landmark studies by the Tavistock Institute, together with the Hawthorne studies, signalled transformation. In the search for greater effectiveness and flexibility in organisations, emphasis has shifted towards the consideration of 'people' issues such as motivation and leadership. A better motivated and well-led workforce will prove to be more flexible and capable of coping with environmental change and complexity.

It is often suggested that the success of commercial firms depends on their ability to foresee and subsequently act on environmental information. Miles and Snow (1978) have identified various types of organisations which possess quite different capabilities, motivations and behaviours in this respect. Their typology of organisations refers to the 'style' in which they operate strategically. This style influences their relationship with the environment and is, in turn, influenced by that environment. 'Defender' organisations, they argue, attempt to create a stable environment which suits their non-dynamic structure and strategy, whereas 'prospectors' view their environment as ever changing and seek continual strategic and structural adjustments to cope with those changes. 'Prospectors' are continually searching for new opportunities and in the process they may create change and uncertainty for others in their competitive environment. Miles and Snow also identify two other categories

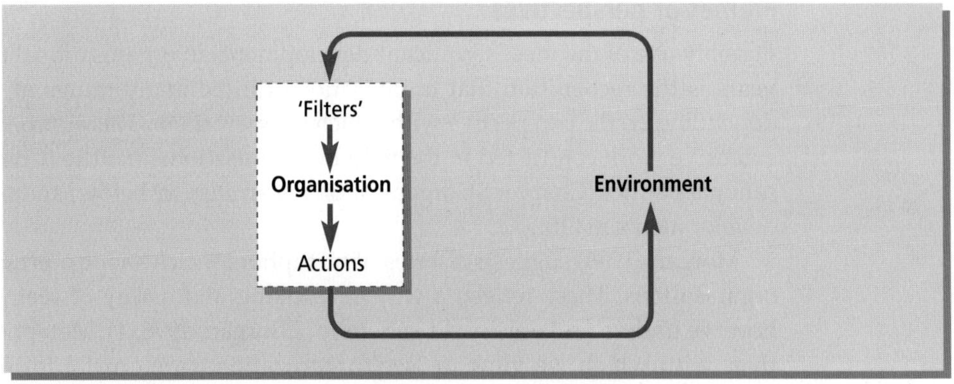

Fig 5.6 Organisation and environment: two-way influence

Source: Reprinted with permission, from Brooks and Weatherston (1997) *The Business Environment: Challenges and Changes*, published by Prentice-Hall.

of organisation, 'analysers' and 'reactors'. The former are capable of acting in both stable and unstable environments; a quality of considerable value. 'Reactors' act only when environmental change 'forces' them to do so. They are not 'proactive' organisations. Boyd *et al.* (1993) state that 'given these differences in internal versus external focus, one would expect a greater potential for environmental misperception among defenders or reactors, relative to analyzers'.

All four types of organisation, it is argued, 'enact' or create their environment. What they choose to see and how they choose to interpret that environment is unique to each organisation. Hence, a defender and a prospector may ostensibly view the identical environment, yet the defender sees stability and continuity all around, whereas the prospector sees only change and opportunity.

Figure 5.6 illustrates the two-way relationship that exists between an organisation and its environment. Clearly each organisation filters data to suit its own capabilities and concerns. Executives can selectively misinterpret aspects of their environment. These filters include an individual manager's cognitive processes; organisational culture and politics; other group or team factors and the strategic orientation of the organisation. Therefore, as stated above, it is quite possible for two organisations to view the same environmental change as either a glorious opportunity for growth and prosperity or a catastrophe threatening organisational survival.

Contemporary lenses

As illustrated above, organisational theory has moved on from an idea of the organisation as a rational decision-making entity. Chapter 8, which discusses power, politics and conflict, indicates that organisations embrace pluralist interests and are perhaps better considered as non-rational. The following section further explores the non-rational view of organisations.

Frames or perspectives

Possibly one of the most significant developments in organisational theory in recent years is the recognition that organisations can be many things at the same time, depending on the perspective with which we view them. This approach builds on the extensive work conducted in the field of organisational culture (Chapter 9), organisational politics (Chapter 8), organisational learning (*see* below) and other theoretical developments in OB.

Morgan (1996) suggests a series of metaphors which shape our understanding of organisations. These reflect 'a way of thinking and a way of seeing that pervade how we understand our world generally' (Morgan, 1996: 4). Metaphors, or perspectives with which we view or 'see' organizations, are crucial for understanding, managing and designing organisations. For example, when managers think of organisations as machines, 'they tend to manage and design them as machines' (Morgan, 1986: 13). As a consequence, thinking in metaphorical terms can influence the organisational structure, systems and ways of organising. For example, the mechanical way of thinking, common to many Western organisations, is so engrained in everyday perception that it proves difficult to organise in any other way.

An alternative perspective or frame with which to analyse organisations is as an 'organism'. Considerable literature is devoted to the study of organizations being categorised into types or 'species', which have 'evolved' via interaction with their environment. This perspective enables us to analyse how organisations are 'born', how they 'develop', 'decline' and 'die' and has led to the development of many 'life-cycle' models. Another popular perspective, the 'structural' frame, is particularly commonplace in Western organisations. So pervasive is this that, as we shall see, it even influences the study of organisational culture. When the structural perspective is adopted, organisational problems are thought to be attributable to deficiencies in structure and, consequently, change initiatives often focus on structural issues, the popular belief being that, if you get the structure right, all else will fall into place. The 'political' perspective is also a commonly used diagnostic and analytical tool. It is argued by proponents of this school of thought that patterns of power and control fundamentally influence organisational activity and ways of organising. There are very many perspectives or paradigms which can be adopted when managing, analysing or researching organisational form and activity. If used as a problem-recognition and problem-solving tool each perspective might identify different problems and generate alternative solutions. Figure 5.7 indicates just some of the alternative perspectives or ways of seeing organisations.

The cultural perspective

The cultural or symbolic metaphor is one very powerful way of viewing organisations. The organisation can be viewed as a culture, in which case even the more mechanical characteristics, such as the structure, rules, policies and systems, can be considered to be products of the culture, or cultural artefacts, which help shape the ongoing reality for people in an organisation. Adopting this perspective ensures that every aspect of organisation is rich in symbolic meaning so that the familiar appears

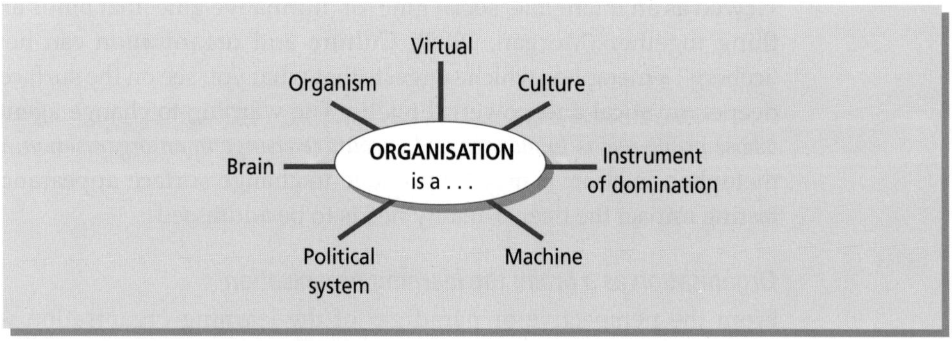

Fig 5.7 Ways of seeing organisations

in a new light. Meetings, other routines and ceremonies, such as selection and promotion boards, become rituals which serve an important cultural purpose. Morgan (1986, 1996) identifies the strengths of the cultural metaphor. It directs attention to the symbolic significance of even the most rational aspects of organisational activity and focuses attention on the human side of organisation. Additionally, culture focuses on shared systems of meaning and hence provides a new focus for the creation of 'organised' action. Hence, if the symbolic elements of organisations can be influenced, such as language, norms, rituals and other practices which communicate key values and beliefs, managing, or at least influencing, culture may become possible. Culture also influences the way organisational members interpret the nature of their business environment, as knowledge of the relationship between the organisation and its environment is an extension of the organisational culture; the environment is viewed through 'cultural lenses'. For example, firms in an industry often develop a language for making sense of their market: they might argue that it is a 'dog eat dog' culture, or suggest that 'he who dares wins'. This language tells us something about the culture of the organisation, not merely about the competitive environment in which it operates.

Weick (1979) and Morgan (1986) argue that organisations 'enact' the realities with which they have to deal. For example, a competitive ethos within firms is likely to produce a competitive business environment. That is, if all or many firms in a business sector believe that they operate in a highly competitive arena, their subsequent action might ensure that competition is rife; they might engage in competitive pricing, special offers, improvements to delivery times and so forth. This has important implications for the analysis of organisational strategy, as strategy itself derives from organisational culture and is influenced by its enacted business environment. Finally, the cultural perspective sheds invaluable light on the process and success, or otherwise, of organisational change. It can be argued that effective organisational change must imply cultural change. This issue is developed further in Chapter 9.

Metaphors have been used to characterise how the culture of an organisation serves as an integrating force. These often portray a graphic, subjective and meaningful interpretation of the concept of organisation. For example, culture can be viewed as an intangible 'social glue' or 'normative glue' that binds and holds everything together (Morgan, 1989). Culture and organisation can be viewed as an 'iceberg', a metaphor which suggests that what you see on the surface masks a much deeper, mystical and powerful reality. The warning to change agents, that is, *those whose prime role is to manage and encourage change in an organisation*, implied by this metaphor, is clear: it may be possible to change surface appearances but to have lasting impact the deeper reality needs to be addressed.

Organisation as a brain: the learning organisation

From the perspective or paradigm of the learning organisation we can analyse organisations as systems of complex information, communication, decision making and learning. Considerable work in Management Information Systems (MIS), Operations Research (OR) and Management Decision Systems (MDS) has attempted to develop decision-making tools and data management principles and practices, in some ways reminiscent of the human brain. The resultant complex systems of data management, in the fields of logistics, production, finance and marketing and the implementation of teams that can 'think' for the rest of the organisation and control activities, is reminiscent of a centralised brain that regulates activity (Morgan, 1996).

An area of particular interest to modern organisational behaviour is the learning capability of an organisation (as opposed to the learning capability and capacity of a series of individuals within an organisation). A contemporary question inviting considerable debate and interest is whether organisations can learn. If they can, it is argued, they are better able to embrace organisational change because they can learn to manage and cope with circumstances which have not previously been experienced.

Argyris and Schon (1974, 1978) suggest that most organisations (and individuals) engage in, and are proficient at, single-loop learning. That is, *learning within accepted limits where an organisation is able to scan its environment, set objectives and monitor its performance to keep it on course, usually resulting in 'same again', single-frame solutions.* In bureaucracies, for example, the fundamental organising principles, based on precedent, rules, procedures and regulations, often obstruct the learning of different ways of working, organising or managing. The same, or similar solutions are generated as a response to perceived organisational problems, with the result that the organisation is locked into single-loop learning and defensive routines. Double-loop learning can only occur when *organisations and individuals reflect on practice, challenge accepted practices and norms, recognise that solutions do not lie in previous experiences and allow alternatives to emerge*. For these actions to occur requires an organisation to be able to break free from the paradigm into which it is locked.

Managerial implications

Organisational theory has a fundamental impact on organisational activity. It can inform our understanding of how organisations are structured and managed, grow and decline, and even help us to understand what organisations actually are. The managerial implications that arise from gaining some knowledge and understanding of this theoretical base are significant and include the following.

1. A recognition that most attempts to develop theories about organisations are aimed at improving our understanding of organisations and of how they operate, thrive or survive. This pursuit for understanding will continue, but that is not the same as believing that 'old' theory is of little value. On the contrary, classical organisational theory continues to play a crucial role in influencing organisational design and the behaviours and attitudes of individuals and groups. Managers need to recognise that their 'taken for granted' assumptions about how to organise and manage are profoundly influenced by classical theory and traditional practice.

2. The principles outlined by Taylor and others have transformed organisational and socio-economic conditions in the twentieth century. These principles are still applied, and will continue to be applied in many, if not most organisations. Managers might examine the benefits of managing scientifically and consider, in the light of the human relations approach, the human implications of the way we organise and manage.

3. Managers might benefit from an understanding that organisations are complex sociotechnical systems and that there exists a complex interrelationship between all human and technical aspects of organisation. This knowledge, together with the development of skills to manage such interrelationships, might enable managers to cope with and manage successful organisational change. It should enable managers to better assess the likely impact of their activities on colleagues.

4. Organisational behaviour is not confined to traditional organisational boundaries. Managers need to be aware that the environment in which they, as individuals, and their organisation operate is likely to be subjectively defined and, in part at least, enacted. The testing of assumptions about the internal and external environment may yield positive results.

5. Recognition that 'what we look for we tend to find' or 'when we wear certain lenses we will only "see" specific things' might enable managers to experiment with alternative 'lenses' or ways of seeing in order to improve their insight into organisational activity. In turn, that improved insight can inform action and enable managers to cope with and manage conflict, communications and change more effectively.

Summary of main points

This chapter has examined many of the prime developments in organisational theory in the twentieth century. The main points are:

- classical theorists aimed to design organisations and develop management principles which were universally applicable, and based on rational, ordered technical arrangements;
- scientific management, a subset of the classical school, focused on job design and work organisation: the human or social element of the work was largely overlooked;
- the classical and scientific traditions remain influential, particularly in Western organisations, although many fundamental criticisms can be levelled at these principles;
- situational or contingent factors were shown to influence organisational and management activity, with the result that the search for a 'one best way' approach was considered hackneyed and inappropriate;
- organisational size, levels and types of technology, the business environment and all manner of internal social aspects act as contingent factors and, consequently, affect organisational activity;
- organisations can be viewed as open systems which embrace complex interrelationships between technical and social subsystems;
- organisational behaviour influences the perception of and, arguably, the 'reality' of an organisation's environment;
- organisations can be viewed through different 'lenses', for example as cultures, brains or machines. Whichever perspective or paradigm is employed will fundamentally influence our reading of organisational practice.

Conclusions

Probably the most significant lesson to be learned from the study of organisational theory is the recognition that our understanding of organisations today, as individuals or collectively, is strongly influenced by historical context, by past and current organisational practice and by the writings of a relatively small number of key researchers in the field. As suggested above by Morgan (1996), when, as is often the case, we are locked into a particular way of seeing and thinking (a paradigm) it is difficult to imagine or devise feasible alternatives to what we take for granted. The early classical theorists did not so much ignore or rule out the possibility that social factors might influence productivity and ways of organising: as early researchers they were largely unaware of the significance of these factors. The frames of reference into which they were 'locked' prevented them from 'seeing'. Similarly, if we consider the social needs of people in the workplace, in isolation from technical, structural, managerial or environmental matters, then we may become locked in an equally unsatisfying paradigm. The final section of this chapter raises our awareness of the value of 'paradigm-hopping', a skill which can be well worth exploring.

QUESTIONS

1 Why do you think Frederick Taylor was so resented by many working people and by many managers? Did his methods bring any benefit to society?

2 If you have experience of working, or observing work, in an organisation where jobs are designed along 'scientific' principles, what effects did you notice on levels of job motivation, satisfaction or morale?

3 The human relations school may be thought to represent 'the forces of light'. What do you understand by this label?

4 Give a hypothetical or real example of enactment in an organisation's environment.

5 Attempt to describe the characteristics of an organisation with which you are familiar from (a) a cultural perspective and (b) a political perspective.

REFERENCES

Argyris, C. and Schon, D. A. (1974) *Theory in Practice*. San Francisco: Jossey-Bass.

Argyris, C. and Schon, D. A. (1978) *Organizational Learning: Theory of Action Perspective*. Reading, MA: Addison-Wesley.

Barnard, C. (1938) *The Functions of the Executive*. Cambridge, MA: Harvard University Press.

Boyd, B. K., Dess, G. and Rasheed, A. M. A. (1993) 'Divergence between archival and perceptual measures of the environment: Causes and consequences', *Academy of Management Review*, 18(2), pp 204–26.

Brooks, I. and Weatherston, J. (1997) *The Business Environment: Challenges and Changes*. Hemel Hempstead: Prentice-Hall.

Burns, T. and Stalker, G. M. (1961) *The Management of Innovation*. London: Tavistock.

Child, J. (1988) *Organization: A Guide to Problems and Practice*, 2nd edn. London: Paul Chapman.

Hersey, P. and Blanchard, K. (1993) *Management of Organizational Behaviour*. Englewood Cliffs, NJ: Prentice-Hall.

Hirschhorn, L. (1984) *Beyond Mechanization*. Cambridge, MA: MIT Press.

Kast, F. E. and Rosenzweig, J. E. (1985) *Organisation and Management*. New York: McGraw-Hill.

Lawrence, P. R. and Lorsch, J. W. (1967) *Organisation and Environment*. Cambridge, MA: Harvard Graduate School of Business Administration.

McGregor, D. (1960) *The Human Side of Enterprise*. New York: McGraw-Hill.

March, J. G. and Simon, H. A. (1958) *Organizations*. New York: John Wiley.

Miles, R. E. and Snow, C. C. (1978) *Organisational Strategy, Structure and Process*. New York: McGraw-Hill.

Morgan, G. (1986) *Images of Organization*. Newbury Park, CA: Sage.

Morgan, G. (1989) *Creative Organization Theory*. Newbury Park, CA: Sage.

Morgan, G. (1996) *Images of Organization*, 2nd edn. Newbury Park, CA: Sage.

Perrow, C. (1970) *Organizational Analysis. A Sociological View*. London: Tavistock Publications.

Porter, L. W., Lawler, E. E. and Hackman, J. R. (1975) *Behaviour in Organizations*. Maidenhead: McGraw-Hill.

Pugh, D. S., Hickson, D. J., Hinings, C. R. and Turner, C. (1969) 'The context of organization structure', *Administrative Science Quarterly*, 14 March, pp 91–103.

Roethlisberger, F. J. and Dickson, W. (1939) *Management and the Worker*. Cambridge, MA: Harvard University Press.

Taylor, F. W. (1911) *The Principles of Scientific Management*. New York: Harper & Brothers.

Weick, K. (1979) *The Social Psychology of Organising*. Reading, MA: Addison-Wesley.

Wilson, D. C. (1992) *A Strategy of Change*. London: Routledge.

Woodward, J. (1965) *Industrial Organization: Theory and Practice*. Oxford: OUP.

FURTHER READING

There are a host of good texts in the field of organisational and management theory and organisational design. For synthesised versions you might consider:

Daft, R. L. (1992) *Organizational Theory and Design*. St Paul, MN: West Publishing.

Alternatively, if you require a more focused approach, most good OB textbooks cover much of the material presented in this chapter. Examples include:

Huczynski, A. and Buchanan, D. (1991) *Organisational Behaviour: An Introductory Text*, 2nd edn. Hemel Hempstead: Prentice-Hall, Chapters 12, 13 and 16.

Mullins, L. J. (1999) *Management and Organisational Behaviour*, 5th edn. London: Financial Times Pitman Publishing.

This high-quality OB text covers much of the ground reviewed by this chapter in further detail (with the exception of the contemporary lenses material). In particular refer to Chapters 3, 4, 15 and 16.

Morgan, G (1996) *Images of Organization*, 2nd edn. Newbury Park, CA: Sage.

This international best seller investigates with insight and skill, as the name suggests, a variety of 'images' or perspectives of organisations.

6

Management and leadership

LEARNING OUTCOMES

On completion of this chapter you should be able to:

- understand the difference between leadership and management;
- know and understand the prime developments in management theory, including the work of Taylor, Fayol and Mintzberg;
- know and understand the main developments in leadership theories encompassed by the trait, behavioural and situational schools;
- appreciate different perspectives on, or approaches to, leadership and management;
- recognise that individuals may operate in limited frames of reference which set limits to their leadership and management capability;
- understand that leadership may be best viewed as a pluralistic concept involving many capabilities which might be shared between a number of leaders;
- understand and analyse the activities of some leaders who have successfully managed change.

KEY CONCEPTS

- *management*
- *leadership*
- *traits*
- *leadership behaviour*
- *leadership style*
- *situational theory*
- *contingency theory*
- *path-goal theory*
- *intrapreneurship and entrepreneurship*
- *leadership frames*
- *pluralistic leadership*
- *transactional and transformational leadership*
- *leadership and change*

Management and leadership

A vital and, some argue, increasingly dominant, aspect of organisation is the role of management and leadership. Research and academic and practitioner interest in management and in leadership has blossomed during the latter part of the twentieth century. As interest in and concern about organisational change have grown, the role of leadership has been emphasised. Similarly, the definition of management and management competencies and the concept of managerialism have stimulated considerable debate in political, academic and organisational spheres.

Introduction

This chapter follows on conceptually from Chapter 5 which examines organisational theory. That theoretical base sheds light on the nature and practice of management and leadership, with the result that it is now appropriate to explore the development of management theory, from the early works of Frederick Taylor to contemporary understandings offered by Henry Mintzberg and others. The chapter explores the difference between leadership and management before going on to examine the development of leadership theory. This body of knowledge has evolved separately from management theory, although many leadership theories appear as relevant to managers and management as they do to leaders and leadership. In keeping with the overall objectives of this book, this chapter also looks at some contemporary issues and provides two fresh insights into leadership, that is, re-framing and pluralism. It concludes by building on the theme of change, examining both theoretical and case study material.

Management from Taylor to Mintzberg

This section examines four writers who consider the functions performed by management, enabling us to define management and explore how thinking has changed through time.

Frederick Taylor

As discussed in Chapter 5, Taylor's work in the early twentieth century focused on the management of the work task. His emphasis on rationality led to the application of scientific principles to work management in order to establish the most efficient way of working. He argued that efficiency, standardisation and discipline would result from a process of scientific management of work tasks. Taylor suggested that it was a prime managerial function to undertake such analysis.

It is important to locate developments in scientific management in their historical context. In the early twentieth century, management was a little researched and very imprecise activity. (Many would argue that little has changed in this regard!) Taylor's work largely preceded the widespread adoption of mass production techniques. Little systematic research had been conducted and practices varied considerably. Workers tended to believe that an increase in productivity on their part would merely result in job losses. Understandably, they took advantage of poor management controls to slow production. They were able to do so as workers themselves often designed or organised their own efforts and had little interest in seeking efficiency.

It is important to note that many modern organisations adopt Taylor-like principles in order to maintain or increase productivity. This is particularly the case when similar or identical outputs are required on a near-continuous process. Whereas

Taylor's work was novel, even revolutionary, in its time, it is now largely taken for granted. Increasingly, aspects of it have been rejected in favour of more 'human' or social considerations and the whole approach has proven less valuable in many modern contexts. Nevertheless, the principles of division between managerial and worker roles, of standardisation and specialisation, of division of labour and efficiency, remain central in many organisations.

Henri Fayol

Although Henri Fayol did not invent the concept of management, he did distinguish it from other organisational activity and outlined, in some detail, what he considered to be the prime functions of a manager. His is a normative and prescriptive model: it indicates how, he considered, managers *should* conduct their activity in order to achieve efficiency. Some readers may be familiar with Fayol's suggested functions of management: they are frequently referred to in numerous definitions of management. Fayol suggested that managers have an obligation to:

- *plan and forecast* – prepare a series of actions to enable the organisation to meet its objectives in the future;
- *organise* – to fulfil the administrative principles embraced by Fayol;
- *co-ordinate* – to ensure that resources, actions and outputs are co-ordinated to achieve desired outcomes;
- *command* – to give direction to employees;
- *control* – ensuring that activities are in accordance with the plan, that orders are followed and principles of management applied.

He also established 14 principles of management, many of which still profoundly influence and significantly reflect the way many 'modern' organisations are managed. This could be considered to be seminal work, an important influence on management theory, and, consequently, is worthy of some consideration here. Table 6.1 lists these principles and attempts to divide them between those which primarily relate to organisational structure and those concerning broader management functions (*see also* Chapter 7).

Although many of these principles were commonplace in organisations before Fayol's work, it was not until 1949 that they were set out in this systematic manner. Some of the principles have been challenged by modern developments in organisations. For example, the principle of unity of command, where each person has one superior to whom they report, although still the norm, is contravened in many matrix organisations. Additionally, the rather rigid principles do not sit well with contemporary developments, such as teamworking, flatter hierarchies, professional control and flexible working.

Table 6.1 Fayol: the principles of management

Primarily structural principles	Other principles
Division of work	Discipline
Authority and responsibility	Subordination of individual interest to general interest
Unity of command	Remuneration of personnel
Unity of direction	Equity
Centralisation	Stability of tenure of personnel
Scalar chain	Initiative
Order	*Esprit de corps*

Source: Adapted from Fayol, H. (1949). *General and Industrial Management*. Copyright Lake Publishing Company, Belmont, Ca.

Peter Drucker

Two more recent writers, Peter Drucker and Henry Mintzberg, have attempted to describe and comment upon what managers *do* (rather than what they should do). This functional approach has a long tradition in management writing. Whereas Drucker gives a prescriptive analysis of the managerial role, rather in the manner of Taylor and Fayol, Mintzberg seeks empirically to comment upon the reality of managers' role.

Drucker (1977) identifies three broad tasks:

- satisfying the goals or mission of the organisation;
- enabling the worker to achieve and focus on productivity;
- managing social responsibilities.

In order to fulfil these fundamental roles, Drucker suggests, managers are required to: set objectives; organise; motivate and communicate; measure and develop people. The prime difference between this later work, and that conducted previously, is the consideration of human and interpersonal issues, including recognition of the importance of communications and wider social concerns. It was, largely, the work of the human relations school (*see* Chapter 5 for details) which placed such concerns on the practitioner and academic agendas.

Henry Mintzberg

In 1973 Henry Mintzberg published his influential work on management, following detailed observations of what managers actually did, whereas Fayol and others presented prescriptive analyses which became 'myths of modern management'. In contrast to what had previously been understood, managers were not found to spend most of their time planning, organising, co-ordinating, commanding and controlling. Instead, Mintzberg identified ten roles which managers fulfil in the conduct of their jobs: these are categorised into three groups, as shown in Table 6.2. Mintzberg (1973) suggested that managers often attempt, and frequently fail, to sequence their roles logically in the pursuit of their objectives. Figure 6.1 indicates a simple temporal sequence of activity, that is, first, the manager builds relationships with employees and networks internally with other departments. Doing so enables the manager to collect information and to begin to act as spokesperson for the group. As stable relationships develop, they yield quality information (the second stage) which finally leads to the third stage: decision making, objective setting and resource allocation decisions.

Table 6.2 Mintzberg: managerial roles

Managerial roles	Managerial activities
Interpersonal roles	All managerial behaviours which establish relationships
Figurehead	Performs ceremonial duties – testifies at hearing, opening of new offices
Leader	Motivates employees – encourages new employees, recognises achievements, recruits and dismisses
Liaison	Networking – joins professional societies, answers external post
Informational roles	Allowing managers to collect and disseminate information
Monitor	Scans for information – reads sector press
Disseminator	Shares information with employees – holds meetings, writes memos, forwards mail
Spokesperson	Shares information with outsiders – makes speeches, keeps superiors informed
Decisional roles	Managerial behaviours which set, implement and monitor progress towards objectives
Entrepreneur	Seeks to change – looks for new ideas
Disturbance handler	Responds to pressures and crises – acts quickly in crisis, faces problems
Resource allocator	Allocates resources to others – manages the budget, constructs schedules
Negotiator	Reaches agreements – solves work disputes, resolves arguments

Source: Based on Mintzberg (1973).

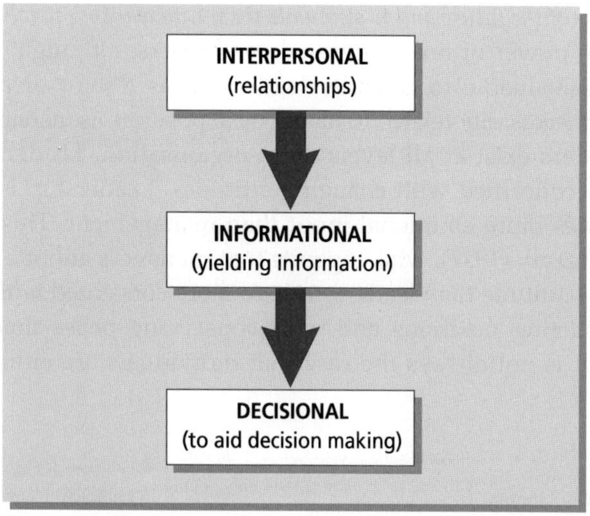

Fig 6.1 Sequence of roles

Kotter (1982), broadly supporting Mintzberg's findings, found that managers appear to spend very little time in isolation on solitary tasks. They prefer, instead, according to Mintzberg (1973), to work or consult with subordinates (48 per cent of their time), with superiors (7 per cent of their time) and with peers and outsiders (44 per cent). A 'typical' manager's day comprises frequent interruptions for brief conversations, by phone, in person, or increasingly, via e-mail and other electronic forms of communication, which serve not only to punctuate activity but also to keep the manager informed. Dailey (1988) suggests that managers should not balk at such interruptions as the resultant impetus given to relationship building and information dissemination proves invaluable in informing decision making.

Differentiating leadership from management

We are now in a position to define management and leadership and to attempt to differentiate the two. *Managers perform functions in organisations and hold a particular, formal, title and/or fulfil a role.* A typical example is a divisional marketing manager, responsible for the marketing of a product range in a geographical territory, or a personnel manager responsible, for example, for the recruitment and selection of staff for a single site organisation. These managers have a title, a role and a series of functions to perform, including the management of subordinates and of physical and financial resources. They are responsible for the performance and the productivity of their subordinates. Fayol stated that management is often concerned with planning, organising, co-ordination, commanding and controlling the activities of staff.

Leaders, on the other hand, aim to influence and guide others into pursuing particular objectives or visions of the future and to stimulate them into wanting to follow. Leadership demonstrates the power of one individual over others, although, as we will see below, it is often valuable to consider leadership as a joint or plural concept. Leadership is not necessarily related to hierarchical position, as management tends to be. Informal leaders exist at all levels of an organisation. Leadership is often a dynamic activity concerned with changing attitudes. Leadership is more inspirational and involves more emotional input than management. This latter point is supported by Zaleznik (1977), who suggests that managers adopt a less emotional and more passive attitude than leaders and are more concerned with seeking compromise in conflicting positions and with conserving order than in initiating transformation. It is not always the case that individuals are either managers *or*

	Management	Leadership
Creating an agenda	Planning and Budgeting – the manager establishes detailed steps and timetables for achieving results, and then allocates the resources	Establishing Direction – the leader develops a vision of the future, and outlines strategies for producing the changes needed to achieve that vision
Developing a human network for achieving the agenda	Organising and Staffing – establishes some structure for accomplishing the plan, staffing that with individuals, delegating responsibility and authority, providing policies and procedures to help guide people, and creating methods or systems to monitor implementation	Aligning People – communicating the direction by words and deeds to all those whose co-operation may be needed so as to influence the creation of teams and coalitions that understand the vision and strategies, and accept their validity
Execution or implementation	Controlling and Problem Solving – monitoring results in some detail, identifying deviations, and then planning and organising to solve these problems	Motivating and Inspiring – energising people to overcome major political, bureaucratic, and resource barriers to change by satisfying very basic, but often unfulfilled, human needs
Outcomes	Produces a degree of predictability and order, and has the potential of consistently producing key results expected by various stakeholders (e.g. for customers, always being on time; for shareholders, being on budget)	Produces change, often to a dramatic degree, and has the potential of producing extremely useful change (e.g. new products that customers want, new approaches to make a firm more competitive)

Fig 6.2 Comparing management and leadership

Source: Adapted and reprinted with the permission of The Free Press, a division of Simon and Schuster, from *A Force for Change: How Leadership differs from Management* by J. P. Kotter. Copyright © 1990 by The Free Press

leaders. It is likely, for example, that a manager may show lead particular occasions. Indeed, Mintzberg refers to leader roles as one o management. Others, such as Handy (1993), Watson (1983) and Kotter (that leadership is merely part of the broader role of management: it is pri cerned with interpersonal aspects of the role. Similarly, a leader, focu attitudinal and organisational change, employing all the political, emotiona symbolic tools of leadership, might also conduct 'normal' managerial responsibiliti Nevertheless, individuals may have a tendency towards either a managerial or a leadership disposition. Many academics have attempted to differentiate leadership from management. One such model, by Kotter (1990), is shown in Figure 6.2.

Kotter clearly differentiates between management and leadership at four stages of activity, that is, when creating the agenda, developing the necessary human networks for progressing the agenda, during its execution and when dealing with the outcomes of this activity. Throughout, Kotter suggests that leadership is more concerned with the human, visionary, inspirational, motivational and dynamic aspects of the total management/leadership role whereas management focuses on the tasks identified by Fayol, that is, planning, organising and controlling, together with problem solving and maintaining a degree of predictability and stability.

Leadership: schools of thought

There has been considerable interest in leadership for centuries. People have been fascinated with the personality or character of exceptional leaders, whether they brought social good or ill to their followers. It is possible to divide leadership research into three broad schools (*see* Figure 6.3).

A concern to discover the personal characteristics, or traits, of good leaders was a particularly salient idea around the middle of the twentieth century. Trait theories can only give a partial and often superficial perspective on the issue of leadership. Later the behavioural theories were themselves criticised, primarily as being non-context specific, a criticism which has led to a focus on the context or situation in which leaders operate. Third, situational theories deal with the leader in an organisational, or other, context and add richness to the study of leadership. The following section synthesises some of the prime findings of each of these three schools.

Trait theories	Behavioural theories	Situational theories
Emphasis on the personal characteristics of leaders	Emphasis on the behaviours of leaders including their style of leadership	Emphasis on the leader in the context or situation in which he or she leads

Fig 6.3 Leadership research: three phases of development

re, and on occasions still are, thought to have a bearing on an indi- lead. These traits included physical characteristics, such as height, ckground, intelligence and a range of personality features. rch attempted, without great success, to establish relationships t variables and leadership success (Stodgill, 1948; Mann, 1959). akly related to leadership. However, Bennis and Nanus (1985) lationship between the effectiveness of leadership and the traits persistence, empowerment and self-control, where logical think-

- the ability to translate ideas into simple forms;
- persuasive abilities;
- explaining phenomena in unique ways.

Persistence traits were thought to be:

- considering setbacks as minor mistakes;
- working long hours;
- attempting to succeed against the odds.

Empowerment traits included:

- enthusing people about their goals;
- being enthusiastic and energetic oneself;
- increasing confidence in employees' own abilities.

Self-control traits included:

- working under pressure;
- remaining calm and even-tempered;
- resisting intimidation.

Numerous other academics and researchers have attempted to establish a link between traits and leadership effectiveness, including some meta-analytical work which brings together the findings of dozens of separate research projects (Lord *et al.*, 1986; Kirkpatrick and Locke, 1991). Each produces its own list of leadership qualities: most appear intuitively sound. Unfortunately, there is only limited agreement between all of these studies. For example, a degree of intelligence appears to be necessary to improve leadership effectiveness. The varied interpretations by the researchers, together with the range and complexity of materials with which they are dealing, have ensured that the findings offer little fresh insight. They are, after all, like much research, attempts to relate two or more variables which might be quite unrelated.

Although this work is of some value there are significant problems with trait theories. Very few traits appear to correlate strongly with leadership effectiveness. Some assume that leadership ability can be measured simply. In many studies leadership effectiveness, success or ability are assumed to be products of position in the organisation or, alternatively, subjective assessment is used to categorise good or effective leaders. The saying that leaders are born and not made cannot be substantiated; it simply is not supported by research evidence. Additionally, trait theories omit any situational or contextual considerations. Surely, some leaders become effective because the situation is 'right' for them (and vice versa). It may well be that appropriate situations 'make' great leaders. Finally, trait theories can lead to unhelpful stereotyping. They can lead to the assumption that once one has, or has not, the required traits, leadership effectiveness is, somehow, decided. If those traits are physical, or otherwise of a nature which makes it impossible for them to be developed or acquired, the implication is that leaders are born, not made, and that management development or experience becomes meaningless.

Behavioural theories

Rather than focus on the traits or characteristics of the leader, the behavioural approach examines leadership behaviour, particularly that which influences the performance and motivation of subordinates. As a result, emphasis is placed on leadership style.

The Ohio State University studies, in the 1940s and 1950s, examined leadership style, and concluded that there were two fundamental types of leader behaviours: 'initiating structure' and 'consideration'. Initiating structure refers to *behaviour which focuses on the achievement of objectives and includes clear supervision and role clarification, planning of work and a results orientation*. Consideration includes *behaviours which encourage collaboration and focus on supportive networks, group welfare and the maintenance of job satisfaction*.

At the same time as the Ohio studies, researchers at the University of Michigan made similar findings. Leaders and managers exhibited characteristics which were employee centred and/or production centred. More recently, these broad descriptions have been labelled 'task' and 'people' orientations. As a result of this work, commentators suggested that it was possible to identify the 'one best' style of leadership, that is, a leader who exhibits high initiating structure and high consideration behaviours: a strong orientation to both task and people issues.

Leadership style

Leadership style refers to *the behaviour of leaders towards subordinates, the manner in which tasks and functions of leadership are conducted*. Tannenbaum and Schmidt (1973) suggested a continuum in leadership styles from a so-called, boss-centred approach to a subordinate-centred approach. Figure 6.4 illustrates a simple style continuum. The suggestion is that managers' or leaders' style can be 'mapped' along a continuum

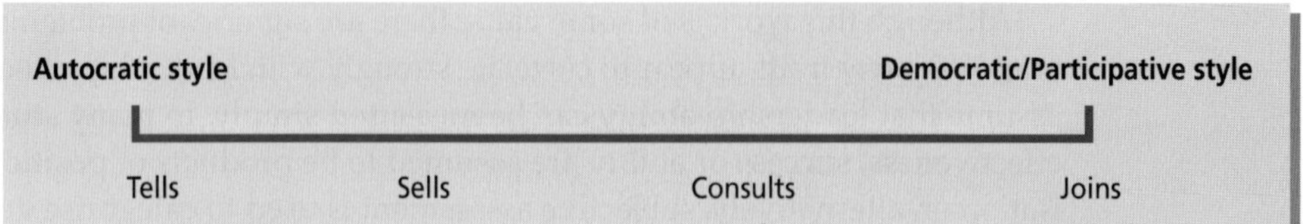

Source: After Tannenbaum and Schmidt (1973) and others.

Fig 6.4 Style continuum

between the authoritarian and democratic extremes. It is likely, however, that a leader's decisions will always be influenced by the situation in which they find themselves. Hence, even if a leader is able to adjust his or her style according to the particular situations there will be a need to consider a host of contextual factors, such as group effectiveness, the nature of the task environment, pressures of time. Tannenbaum and Schmidt recognised that situational factors were important. They argued that forces in subordinates, for example their level of experience and the style to which they are accustomed, and forces in the leader, including knowledge and preferred style, combine to determine the most appropriate leadership style to adopt. In choosing an appropriate style, managers consider their own value system and leadership inclination, the level of confidence they have in their subordinates and their ability to cope with the uncertainties of the situation. They will evaluate the nature and experience of their subordinates, their readiness to assume responsibility, their knowledge and interest. This refinement to the basic model, places their work in the situational school of leadership (*see* below).

A problem with the simple style continuum model is that there is only one dimension. However, other styles, not encompassed in the autocratic–democratic continuum, may be applicable. For example, leaders may consider re-framing a situation, thinking of it differently – in a unique manner or from a different, atypical, perspective (*see* the discussion on pp 153–5 on reframing leadership, where reference is made to the work of Fisher and Torbert). This model also implies that leaders make rational decisions based on a wealth of knowledge about the context, themselves and their subordinates – an assumption that is not necessarily proven by experience. Nevertheless, the model can prove a useful management development tool and raises the value of self-awareness of one's style of leadership.

A simpler version of the work of Tannenbaum and Schmidt suggests that the continuum may involve four distinct styles of leadership, namely:

- *joins* – manager defines the problem, but leaves it open for alternative problem-definitions to arise, and for the scope of the endeavour to expand; then becomes a member of the problem-solving group and hands over decision-making power to the group;
- *consults* – manager both identifies the problem and makes the decision, but only after listening and possibly adopting solutions that have been suggested;

- *sells* – manager decides on the solution to problems and then persuades staff that this decision is most valid;
- *tells* – manager identifies the problems and decides on the solutions, as above, and also expects staff to implement such decisions without questioning.

John Adair

Action-centred leadership, developed by John Adair (1979), prescribes three areas of need which leaders must satisfy, that is:

- task needs;
- individual needs;
- team maintenance needs.

This work builds on that of theorists working in the behavioural tradition and argues that successful leaders need to accommodate both task and people considerations. Figure 6.5 indicates the functions involved in attempting to satisfy each need.

As indicated in Figure 6.5, action taken to meet one need may have an impact on another area. A leader who can ensure the successful conduct of tasks while satisfying individual need and maintaining teamwork, is likely to be highly effective. Adair has embraced the two prime dimensions, task and people, and added a third, team maintenance. The latter further emphasises the human and interpersonal nature of leadership and accommodates contemporary recognition of the importance of teamwork for organisational and therefore leadership effectiveness.

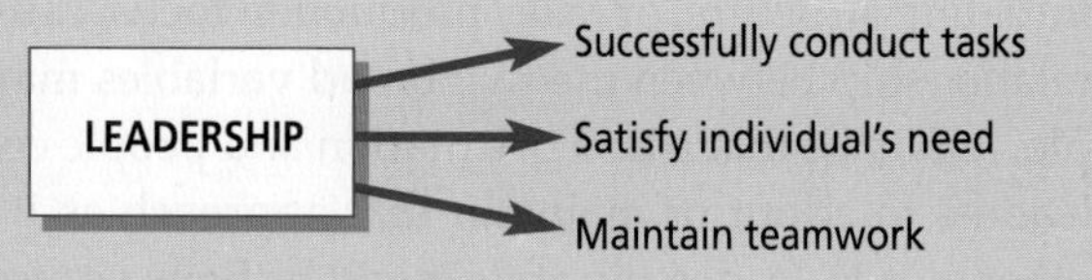

Source: Based on Adair (1979).

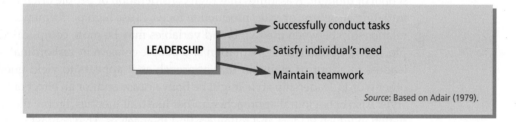

Fig 6.5 Leadership: the fulfilment of three needs

Behavioural school: conclusions

From a simple analysis of the material presented above, it is possible to identify four broad leadership styles:

1. Task/structure orientation.
2. People/interpersonal orientation.
3. Directive/autocratic leadership.
4. Participative/democratic leadership.

Styles 1 and 3 are often associated, as are 2 and 4; hence, these four approaches can be further reduced to just two, as is illustrated by the Ohio State University and University of Michigan research and later work by McGregor (1960) and Blake and Mouton (1964). McGregor's now popular contention, his Theory X and Theory Y, was that leaders and managers could be differentiated from one another according to their attitudes and assumptions about human nature. Theory X leaders consider people, notably subordinates, to be lazy, reluctant to assume responsibility and lacking in ambition and so, they require to be controlled, directed and, if necessary, coerced and punished. In Maslow's terms (*see* Chapter 3) they are motivated only by physiological and security needs. Theory Y represents a direct contrast. It assumes that individuals align themselves with organisational goals and, as a consequence, people require little control or direction, seek rewards consistent with their performance, may accept and relish responsibility, possess initiative and creative skills and are potentially motivated by the higher-order needs for affiliation, esteem and self-actualisation.

Blake and Mouton (1964) suggest that a manager's style can be identified and mapped according to the 'people' and 'task', or 'production', orientation. The mapping exercise allows for degrees of people or production orientation, so that it is possible, for example, to have a high people and a high production tendency (a highly desirable state), a high production and a medium people orientation, a low orientation in both dimensions (a rather precarious state) or numerous other combinations.

The work of the behavioural school represents an improvement over the trait approach. Behaviour is observable and can be learned and the focus is on what a leader does, not on what he or she is. Nevertheless, there are problems with this school of thought. It assumes that high consideration or people orientation, and high initiating structure, or task/production focus, cause high performance. In reality the relationship between the two broad variables may be more complicated. For example, it may be that a task orientation and people concern in surbordinates might lead leaders to adopt or maintain that approach as it appears to yield good results. In other words, leadership style might be both a cause and/or an effect of the followers' style. Also behavioural approaches, rather like trait theories, ignore the context or situation in which leaders and followers find themselves. That context is likely to partly determine the most appropriate style to adopt. For example, an organisation might have a long-engrained norm which necessitates or encourages the adoption of a task orientation. This cultural characteristic may prevent a leader from significantly deviating from that approach. Leadership is context-specific, or at least this is what the situational theories suggest.

Situational theories

When certain aspects of the behavioural and trait approach are combined with consideration of context, or the situation in which leaders find themselves, a complex but more promising explanation of leadership is apparent. We saw in Chapter 3 that consideration of situational or contingent factors improved our understanding of motivation in the workplace. Similarly, our insight into leadership is enhanced by a consideration of these contingent factors. Once again, contingency theory adds complexity, but richness, to our understanding of organisational behaviour.

Fiedler's contingency theory

The contingency hypothesis is that leadership behaviour interacts with the favourableness of a situation to determine effectiveness. It argues that some situations are more favourable than others and, as a consequence, require different behaviours. This theory requires the assessment of both the leader's style and three broad characteristics of the situation or context. Leadership style is said to be relationship centred, where the leader is motivated to maintain good interpersonal relations, or task orientated, in which case the leader is motivated to get on with the job, and is ascertained by requiring leaders to indicate their orientation towards their least preferred co-worker (LPC). Those who describe their LPC in 'accepting' terms are relationship orientated whereas task orientated leaders believe their LPC has few redeeming qualities. This, Fiedler argues, demonstrates a personality trait referred to as the leader's motivational pattern. This relates well to Theory X and Theory Y (McGregor, 1960, above).

The three situational variables are:

- *leader–group member relations* – the nature of work group atmosphere and subsequent loyalty, trust and so forth;
- *task structure* – clarity of the group's work and understanding of the group's goals;
- *position power* – a leader's legitimate power to tell others what to do.

A highly favourable situation would be one where relations were sound and reliable, tasks were clearly structured and goals widely understood and where position power was strong.

Figure 6.6 indicates in which circumstances each leadership orientation is likely to be most effective. A task orientation is considered more suited to highly favourable or highly unfavourable situations. To take a military example, if there is a potentially dangerous task to perform, perhaps an encounter with an enemy in unfamiliar territory, the commander may, recognising the unstructured nature of the task and relying on position power (*see* Chapter 8), adopt a highly task-orientated approach, giving clear orders and demanding compliance. Alternatively, where a manager enjoys good relations with workers and if the tasks to be performed are clearly structured, that is, not much debate or decision-making ability is required in order to perform them satisfactorily, a task orientation may be best employed to ensure high productivity. The 'simplicity' of the task might not warrant a more participative or people-orientated approach and the good relations that exist could survive the adoption of a task approach.

A relationship orientation is best suited to average situational favourability. Fiedler suggests that an organisation should not focus on attempts to change a leader's personality but should select leaders to match the situation's favourability. Although this approach might be of some value in recognising that both situation

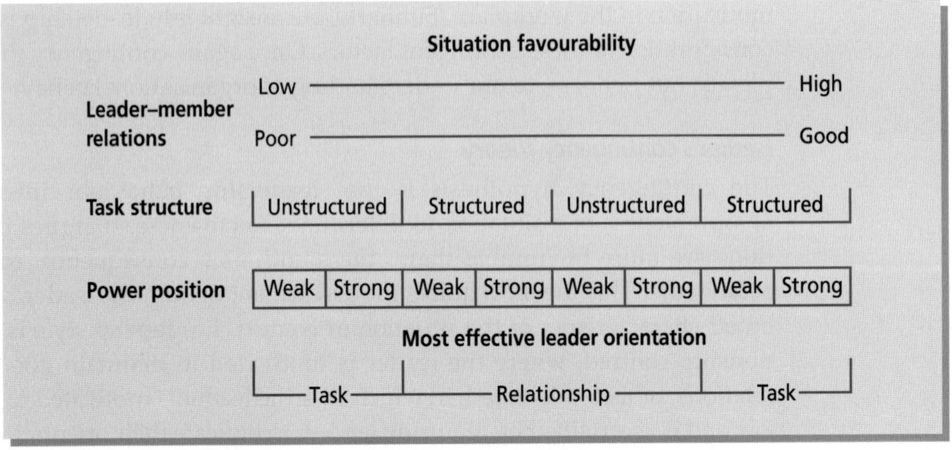

Fig 6.6 Fiedler's contingency model

Source: Adapted with permission from F. E. Fiedler, *A Theory of Leadership Effectiveness*, McGraw-Hill (1967) p. 146.

and a leader's orientation can determine the appropriate choice of leader, it is of less value as a selection technique or a tool of 'social engineering' within organisations.

House's Path–Goal theory

Path–Goal theory was briefly addressed in Chapter 3 (in the discussion of expectancy theory) and is referred to here as it has implications for leadership. It is a situational and transactional model of leadership, in addition to being a motivation theory. House (1971) suggests that it is a leader's function to clarify pathways for subordinates to achieve their desired rewards. When a subordinate recognises that a desired reward is achievable by adopting a particular course of action, then motivation to achieve that reward should follow. The leader provides the rewards and clarifies the pathways between employee effort and performance and between performance and reward. The leader engages in a transaction giving rewards for performance. This requires leaders to exercise flexibility and to develop abilities to engage in:

- *directive behaviours* – including planning, setting expectations and clarifying instructions;
- *supportive behaviours* – offering friendly consideration;
- *participative behaviours* – involving subordinates in decision making;
- *achievement-orientated behaviours* – setting objectives and expecting them to be achieved.

The leader is required to consider environmental factors and subordinate characteristics and then adopt a flexible approach. The prescriptive model suggests an appropriate style for a variety of combinations of situations, for example:

- Directive leadership best ensures high performance for subordinates who require a high degree of work structuring.
- Achievement-orientated leadership behaviours are best suited to subordinates with a strong achievement drive.
- If tasks are clear and routine dominates, then any leadership behaviour may be redundant.

Vroom and Yetton contingency model

Vroom and Yetton (1973) and Vroom and Jago (1988) have developed a decision-making leadership contingency model. Taking into account the quality, level of acceptance and time taken to make each leadership decision, Vroom and Yetton suggested five leadership styles. These are not too dissimilar from points along a style continuum (*see* Figure 6.4). They are:

- *autocratic*
  - decision or problem solving, using information available to leader at the time;
  - leader collects information and then makes the decision/solves the problem;
- *consultative*
  - leader shares the problem with subordinates individually or as a group and then leader makes the decision;
- *group*
  - leader shares the problem with the group and together they attempt a solution or consensus.

The choice of a particular style to achieve quality decisions is informed by three decision rules, which involve an assessment of the degree of structuring of the problem, the amount of information available and the quality of decision required. Similarly, decision rules exist in order to ensure that the outcome is acceptable. This approach can involve the construction of decision trees involving many decision points, or 'branches', to assist the leader in the decision-making process. This is a normative or prescriptive model, providing a series of rules which are intended to inform action.

Research to test this model is largely inconclusive, but it does confirm that various styles tend to be used in particular circumstances. For example, more participative styles tend to occur when it is considered essential that a quality decision is vital, when it is important that the decision is accepted and when subordinates are trusted to consider the group or organisational goals not merely their own.

Vroom and Jago (1988) took this approach further and added 12 contingency factors which inform decision making. These include issues such as leader and subordinate information, time constraints, geographical dispersion and motivation. A series of decision trees can now be used to inform decision making, each offering a rational, prescribed outcome.

Hersey and Blanchard (1988) incorporated the readiness of followers as an additional situational variable, considering four levels from 'low follower readiness' to 'high follower readiness'. Readiness of followers, when combined with a leader's orientation, that is task or relationship behaviour, helps, they argue, to determine the appropriate style to adopt. This model focuses attention on the need to build the morale and commitment of subordinates and the need for a leader to adjust his or her style to the particular qualities of employees.

The situational approach to leadership embraces both style or behavioural issues and context or situation. It is, therefore, more complex but better reflects reality than other, earlier approaches. Nevertheless, not even the models presented above can fully explain the characteristics of effective leadership. They do not adequately embrace the complexities of interpersonal behaviours and relationships nor do they accommodate the rapidity of change which characterises modern organisations. For example, if organisations follow Fiedler's advice and appoint leaders to match the situation, then organisational dynamism might so alter 'the situation' as to make the appointed leader ineffective. Additionally, there remains considerable subjectivity concerning the assessment of an individual leader's style and personality. Someone might appear to have the necessary qualities to match the perceived nature of the situation, yet not prove an effective leader (and vice versa).

Although many of the contingency or situational theories take cognisance of many organisational and environmental variables little attention is paid to organisational culture (*see* Chapter 9) or organisational politics (*see* Chapter 8), both of which may have a profound influence over leadership styles and approaches.

Most of the research presented above implies that leadership is an individualistic concept; that is, it considers the role of the leader as an individual. We explore joint or multiple leadership (pluralism) below.

Intrapreneurs and entrepreneurs

It is unusual in organisational behaviour to consider the nature and activity of intrapreneurs and entrepreneurs. *Entrepreneurship* is the *creation of economic wealth by adding value and involves risking capital, time and energy*. When this activity takes place in an organisation it is referred to as *intrapreneurship*. The intrapreneur often has to succeed in a bureaucratic environment which tends to stifle innovation and dynamism. Both entrepreneurs and intrapreneurs can be considered, in a broad sense, to be leaders. They lead the value-adding capabilities of an organisation, the development of new ideas and ways of solving old problems. They often lead people in accepting novel solutions and new ways of operating. For these reasons, it is worth paying attention, albeit brief, to the concept of intra- and entrepreneurship at this stage.

Rather like the early trait theorists' attempts to explain leadership as a result of physical or other personal characteristics, much work on entrepreneurship considers entrepreneurs to possess exceptional inherent personal qualities. Peter Drucker (1985) has dispelled this myth and suggested that entrepreneurship is, like many managerial and leadership qualities, something which can be learned, whereas success owes more to hard work than to some romantic notion of sheer entrepreneurial talent. Aldag and Stearns (1987) have attempted to explode some of the conventional wisdom or myths of entrepreneurship (Table 6.3). The study of entrepreneurship is developing rapidly, going well beyond this rather simple search for the entrepreneurial profile.

Table 6.3 Myths of entrepreneurship

Myth	'Reality'
Entrepreneurs are doers, not thinkers	Entrepreneurs do engage in careful planning and forethought
Entrepreneurs are born, not made	Evidence suggests that characteristics are acquired and not inherited (McClelland, 1976)
All you need is money	Commitment and single-mindedness are more vital
All you need is luck	This suggests that entrepreneurial skills are irrelevant

Source: Based on Aldag and Stearns (1987).

Reframing leadership

Not surprisingly, and despite the wealth of research in the field, there is no one accepted, explanatory theory or model of leadership. In more recent times, theorists have explored alternative explanatory frames for leadership. In Chapter 5 we suggested that it is possible and valuable to view organisations as if through different lenses, to analyse them from a variety of different perspectives. Similarly, we can categorise different 'types' of leaders by analysing and evaluating the frames of reference or paradigms into which they are 'locked'.

Leadership frames

Some of the more interesting work in this area has been conducted by Fisher and Torbert (1995). They argue that managers fall into one of six frames which represent stages of managerial development. They are:

- opportunist
- diplomat
- technician
- achiever
- strategist
- magician

Table 6.4 outlines the characteristics of managers in each frame. People in these frames view many aspects of organisation, the environment, their subordinates, management and leadership, differently from one another. For example, Achievers, it is argued, see leadership as a process of moulding others to their own way of thinking, whereas a Strategist is likely to attempt to encompass a variety of points of view and ways of thinking.

Table 6.4 Managerial style characteristics

Development stage	Frame	Style characteristics
1	*Opportunist*	■ short-term focus on concrete things ■ manipulative, deceptive, hostile, distrustful, flouts power ■ rejects feedback and externalises blame ■ dubious ethical standards: stereotypes, punishes on 'eye for an eye' basis
2	*Diplomat*	■ conflict avoidance, face saving ■ conformist, works to standards ■ belonging, status, gives loyalty to group
3	*Technician*	■ problem solving, logic, cause and effect ■ self-critical, dogmatic, meritocratic ■ seeks efficiency/perfection
4	*Achiever*	■ long-term goals, feels like initiator ■ welcomes feedback, seeks mutuality ■ appreciates complexity but blind to subjectivity behind objectivity ■ guilt if falls short of own standards
5	*Strategist*	■ creative conflict resolution ■ principle, theory, judgement can usefully inform decision making ■ process and goal oriented ■ aware of paradox, contradiction ■ relativist, individuality, existential humour ■ aware of frame/world view
6	*Magician*	■ seeks participation in historical/spiritual transformations, creator of mythical events ■ reframes situations, blends opposite ■ action researches, interplay of intuition, thought, action and effect ■ sees time as symbolic, metaphorical

Source: Adapted from D. Fisher and W. R. Torbert (1995) *Personal and Organisations Transformations*. © Copyright the McGraw-Hill Companies, Inc 1995.

Whereas managers in the first four frames can recognise themselves as working in that constructed frame and do not fully recognise that others operate from alternative frames, persons in the fifth frame, the Strategist, show awareness of the ever-present interplay of people operating in different frames. They are, therefore, concerned with the testing and framing of assumptions encountered in social interplay. It could be argued that when moving from Achiever to Strategist managers might be able and willing to embrace double-loop learning (*see* Chapter 5) and, as Fisher and Torbert suggest, to make more effort to understand subordinates and push the limits of perceived organisational constraints. Fisher and Torbert (1995) suggest that when moving from Achiever to Strategist the leader makes a significant step forward in terms of effectiveness.

As might be expected, research indicates that the proportion of managers in each of the six categories varies. Table 6.5 reports on a sizeable research exercise, involving almost 500 managers in the USA, from first-line supervisors to senior managers and executives. Of course this and similar work is not without its critics. We can all recognise characteristics of ourselves and others which cut across the positions identified. Few people appear to correspond clearly to one frame alone, and this could prove to be a major criticism of the whole concept which suggests that people are, albeit often not permanently, 'locked' into just one frame. Additionally, research in this area is notoriously difficult and fraught with problems which question its reliability and validity. There is also an assumption that competence in leadership, especially the leadership of major transformational change, is better performed by Strategists and, if they exist, Magicians. There is no real hard evidence to suggest that this is the case. Nevertheless, thinking about frames of reference, reflecting upon one's experiences and attempting to explore alternative approaches, is of considerable value, particularly in developing managerial and leadership understanding and capability.

Table 6.5 Distribution of managers by developmental position

Position or frame	%
Opportunist	2
Diplomat	8
Technician	45
Achiever	36
Strategist	9
Magician	0
	100%

Source: D. Fisher and W. R. Torbert (1995) *Personal and Organisations Transformations.*

Pluralistic leadership

As a theme throughout this book, organisational change is particularly worthy of consideration in any discussion of leadership. In fact leadership of change has stimulated considerable academic and practitioner interest in recent decades.

Traditionally, leadership has been considered an individual or singular activity. That is, one person leads and the rest follow. Hence, each country or each organisation is often considered to have *a* leader. In reality, leadership and leaders are found in all aspects of our lives. Leadership qualities are exhibited by many people much of the time. Leaders, both formal and informal, are found at all levels of most organisations. Yet, it is usually individual leaders who spring to mind when we think of leadership: rarely do we consider outstanding leadership teams. Bate (1994) argues that, particularly in the management of change, leadership is best considered as a collective or plural concept. His contention is that it is networks of leadership which prove effective in change, not necessarily individual leaders. He suggests that leadership comprises five main dimensions and each individual leader is unlikely to be able to offer all these qualities. A leadership team, on the other hand, might embrace the plethora of characteristics required to successfully manage transformational change. The five dimensions of leadership, identified by Bate (1994) are shown in Table 6.6.

Table 6.6 The five dimensions of the leadership of organisational change

Dimension	Leadership role
Aesthetic	Leadership of the creation, expression and communication of new ideas
Political	Leadership of political processes involved in gaining acceptance of new ideas in an evolving culture
Ethical	Leadership in the creation and imparting of a framework of moral standards related to these meanings and ideas
Action	Leadership in transmuting agreed cultural meanings into concrete practices
Formative	Leadership in structuring new ideas, meaning and practices into a framework – a new source of legitimacy within the organisation

If each of these five dimensions is placed at the corner of a pentagon, as in Figure 6.7, it may prove possible to 'map' the leadership capacities of any particular organisation. That is, the pentagon can become elastic, with certain dimensions – the organisation's strengths – being illustrated by an extended 'arm' and under-developed dimensions by a restricted extension. This can prove to be a useful team leadership development activity. The illustration in Figure 6.7 depicts, (1) the elastic pentagon model showing the five dimensions of leadership, and (2) an organisation with strong creative and political leadership skills, but one which is weak on action and the subsequent ability to embed change into its structures.

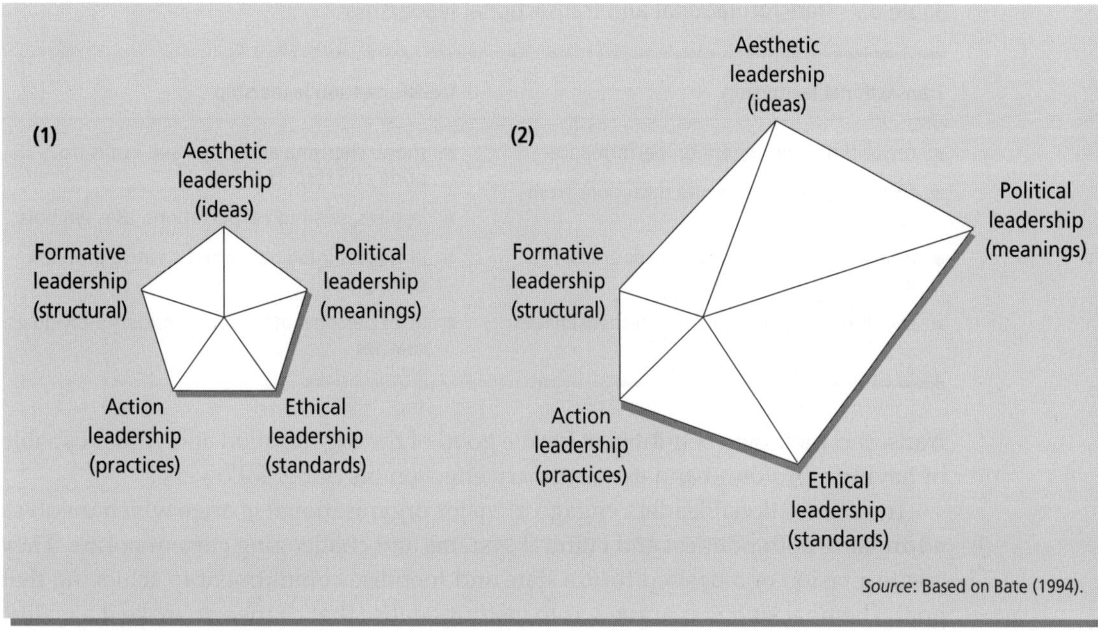

Fig 6.7 The elastic pentagon

Organisational change is best accommodated, Bate (1994) argues, by an appropriate blend and balance of leaders who may have differential inputs at various stages in the change process. As a result a network of leaders, with different strengths and at a range of hierarchical levels, will make the change happen.

Transactional and transformational leadership

We will briefly look at a useful distinction often made between two categories of leader and examine research which attempts to relate leadership style to types of change. Table 6.7 draws on the work of Bass (1990) and others to illustrate two leadership behaviours, that is, transactional and transformational. It appears that transactional leadership is concerned with managing in relative stability whereas transformational leadership implies dynamism and flux.

The activities of certain so-called transformational leaders, for example Nelson Mandela and Mother Teresa, or of Lee Iacocca, Richard Branson, Jan Carlzon, Bill Gates and Steven Jobs from the organisational world, attract considerable media and academic interest. Anecdotal knowledge suggests these leaders possess the trait often referred to as charisma. This trait is difficult to define and virtually impossible to measure, yet, arguably, simpler to observe. The charisma of a transformational leader is thought to inspire and energise followers who, as a result, are more amenable to change, are highly motivated and unquestioning followers. Robbins (1984: 151) suggests that a transformational leader is one who 'inspires followers to

Table 6.7 Transformational and transactional leadership

Transactional leadership	Transformation leadership
■ rewards are contingent on performance	■ shows charisma and vision and instils trust, pride and respect
■ focuses on exceptions and deviations from rules	■ inspires, sets high expectations, uses symbols
■ intervenes only when standards are not achieved	■ promotes intelligence and creative problem solving
■ avoids difficult decisions and responsibilities	■ gives personal attention, considers individuals, coaches

transcend their own self-interest for the good of the organisation and who is capable of having a profound and extraordinary effect on his or her followers'.

Transformational leaders engage in major organisational change which involves addressing both political and cultural systems and challenging current norms. They create a vision of a desired future state and mobilise commitment to achieving that goal. The final step, it is argued, is to institutionalise that change, to make it a reality. In order to achieve transformational change leaders require a deep understanding of organisations and the social interaction which they embrace. They need to master political dialogue and understand the nature of power, equity, the dynamics of decision making and when to push and when to back off (Morgan, 1989).

Dunphy and Stace's change matrix relates four types of leadership style to four types or scales of change (Figure 6.8). This model, based primarily on intuitive

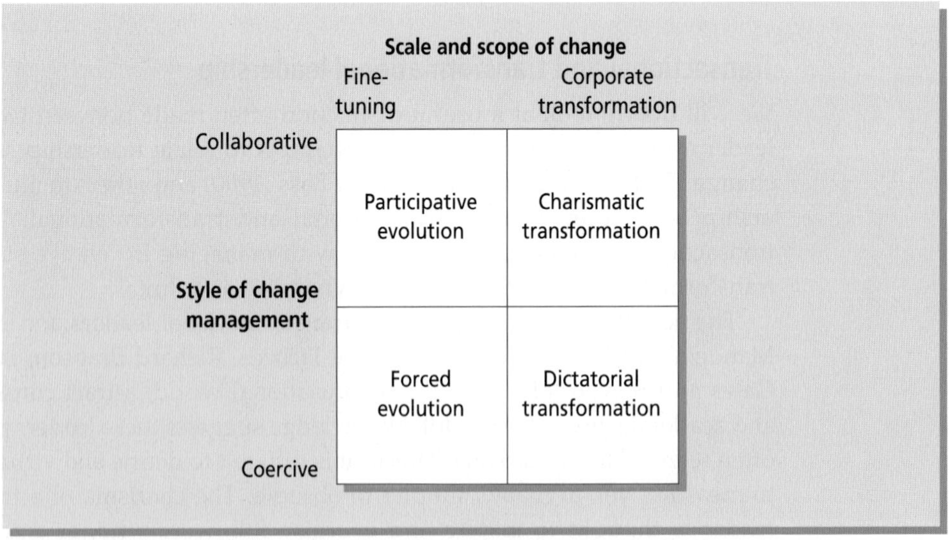

Fig 6.8 Relating leadership style to type of change

Source: Adapted from D. Dunphy and D. Stace (1993) 'The strategic management of corporate change' in *Human Relations*, 46(8), pp. 905–20. Reproduced with permission from Plenum Publishing Corporation.

understandings, suggests that corporate transformation or other major change, when achieved by application of a collaborative or consultative style of leadership, may result in 'charismatic transformation'. Alternatively, transformation may be achieved by adopting a more directive or dictatorial approach. In fact their research, conducted in a range of service sector organisations, indicated that transformational change was more likely to have occurred as a result of adoption of a directive or coercive style. Nevertheless, Dunphy and Stace (1993) suggest that once change is in process, a more consultative approach is required, particularly at subunit level, in order to gain the support of employees. Considerable change management research has commented on the relationship between style and the effectiveness of change initiatives. It is also worthy of consideration that the context of change is a vitally important determining variable in the success, or otherwise, of change management.

Leadership and change

This section primarily comprises two mini-case studies which seek to illustrate, first, the activities of a transformational leader (*see* Figure 6.9 on p 160) and, second, a case of pluralistic leadership (*see* Figure 6.10 on p 161). The mini-case presented in Figure 6.9 explores the leadership of a great man, Nelson Mandela. You are advised also to refer to the work of Fisher and Torbert (1995), above, and the concept of the transformational leader.

The leadership of change mini-case study presented in Figure 6.10 illustrates certain aspects of pluralism in leadership and addresses one of the important themes of this book, that is, the management of change. It acts as a useful prelude to chapters 8 and 9 on power and politics and organisational culture, respectively, and provides a contrast to the approach of the transformational leader (singular), presented in Figure 6.9.

It is of value to briefly consider a simple model useful for analysing organisational change. All change can be considered to have four prime parameters, that is, the content, context, process and timing of change. Content refers to the nature of what is changing, whether it is transitional or incremental or transformational and revolutionary. The context is the internal and external environment in which the change is occurring. An analyst or change agent would need to consider all manner of internal contextual characteristics, such as the predominant management style, the qualities of leadership, the organisation's structure and systems, and attempt to assess the receptiveness of that context. The external environment may not only indicate but also influence both the direction and speed of organisational change.

The process of change encompasses the series of mechanisms and activities that are employed during the change. Change takes place over a period of time: it is not an event, although certain 'events' often punctuate the change process. The content, contextual variables and processes employed in most significant organisational changes also alter over time. Internal and external environments may become more or less hostile to change, whereas the desired nature of change might evolve to fit environmental considerations. The work of Pettigrew and others builds on these concepts and considerations. A knowledge of this model can help us to understand the nature and complexity of organisational change.

Nelson Mandela: the Magician

It could be argued that Nelson Mandela, the first black president of South Africa, approximates to the characteristics of Fisher and Torbert's Magician. Not only has he had a tremendous influence over two or three generations of South Africans, he has also symbolised an image of great value to many millions of people throughout the world. Incarcerated in jail for decades because of his stringent opposition to apartheid in South Africa, he symbolised hope, justice and courage to most black and many white South Africans. In jail he was penniless, confined, abused, denied fundamental liberties and marginalised, yet with unimaginable courage and magical skill he rose, within just a few years of his release, to lead a nation (black, coloured and white) in seeking greater justice and further hope.

Upon release, due to strong Western and internal pressure, he brought a most remarkably diverse nation together, gaining overwhelming popular support in free, democratic elections. Diversity, mutual distrust and, often, undisguised hatred were, and, to an extent, still are based on colour, race and tribal difference. Mandela recognised, examined and confronted such differences while simultaneously standing above them. He embraced, literally and metaphorically, leaders of tribes antagonistic to his African National Conference (ANC) and whites who had sought to remove him (and who would probably have murdered him had such an action not been likely to arouse considerable external and internal opposition), overseas leaders who helped to facilitate his freedom and his people whose support he could count upon.

Acute awareness of the human condition, an apparently total lack of personal vice or any desire for vengeance and a fundamental appreciation of the 'real' and the symbolic as one, make Mandela a great leader. After becoming president, he attended a rugby international in 1995. South Africa were playing and the match was being televised in the country and in most rugby playing countries. Rugby, as a sport, goes to the heart of the division in South Africa between black and white. It is a game beloved by the white minority and was, and largely still is, the preserve of whites. Mandela's presence at the game represented a symbolic (and real) attempt to integrate the two communities, to bring black acceptance of rugby and its importance to white South Africans to the fore. But Mandela did not just attend the game, he wore a Springbok rugby shirt (not a shirt and tie or his flamboyant tribal dress). Few, if any, black Africans had ever had the privilege of wearing it: few if any had earned the right. What is more he wore a 'Number 6' shirt, that of the captain of the team, Pinaar. He also sang along with the country's new national anthem (as opposed to the old Afrikaans anthem, 'De Stem'). A highly symbolic moment.

This simultaneous challenge and acceptance, being part of many groups of people and different from them and honouring a tradition that had incarcerated him for the prime years of his life, endeared people throughout the world to his sheer magical and inspirational qualities.

Fig 6.9 Mini-case: Nelson Mandela

The leadership of change

This mini-case explores the leadership of change in a medium-sized NHS Trust hospital in the Midlands of England. The organisation was successful in achieving significant and measurable quality improvements, surpassing its broad array of objectives and coping with considerable environmental flux in the 1990s.

Rapidly impending, centrally imposed, change in the NHS created a trigger for action. The internal process of change management conceived of and undertaken by the Chief Executive (CEO) and the senior management team was based on a cognitive model of change which was not articulated, but served to delimit and guide their leadership activities. That model (*see* Figure 6.11) is analysed below.

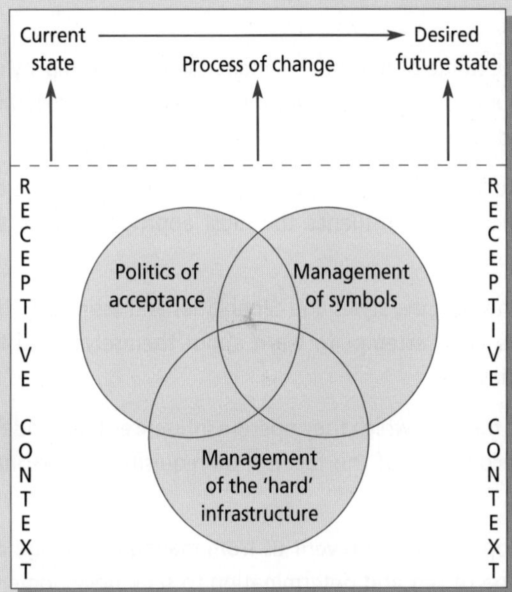

Fig 6.11 A cognitive change model

Source: Brooks (1996).

The three processes, shown in the interlocking circles in Figure 6.11, took place in a context which was made receptive to change, in part, through leadership efforts. Leadership held a vision of a desired future state, an ambition or ideal to aim for. This contrasted with the tired and increasingly unsatisfactory current state of affairs and informed the direction, scale and scope of the change. It could be argued that the 'hard' changes, referred to below, together with a genuine attempt to change the culture of the organisation to make it more receptive to innovation, represent the 'content' of the change. The process of change embraced an ongoing time frame, punctuated by symbolic and tangible actions centred around the politics of acceptance and cultural interventions, all led by a leadership team, an example of pluralistic leadership.

A three-pronged approach to change management was employed:

- the conscious and active management of symbols, including 'talking up the crisis', changing dress and behaviour codes, degradation of some dysfunctional rituals and development of new rituals symbolising change (*see* Chapter 9, Figure 9.7);
- a focus on the politics of acceptance; and
- concurrent attention to 'hard' systems and structures.

Although external change provided a trigger for action, the leadership team consciously heightened the existing sense of impending crisis, partly by using 'crisis' language, while instilling confidence in staff that they were competent to cope with the consequences.

The leadership team oversaw the restructuring of the organisation. Business managers were introduced to each clinical directorate, and systems – including new financial procedures – were developed to facilitate the achievement of operational and strategic objectives. These 'hard' changes enabled the organisation to cope with externally imposed change: the rigours of the internal market. However, these changes were not managed in isolation from the political and symbolic leadership processes.

The leadership team paid particular attention to the politics of acceptance, adopting a collaborative, not coercive, style. They engaged in a great deal of discussion at an early stage and involved individuals and groups who held both formal and informal power. Gaining a common understanding of the realities of the environment and subsequent collective action were emphasised. Instilling in others a sense of ownership of both the problem and the solution was viewed as crucial by leadership. Hence, leaders were created and encouraged, at all levels, to champion the change.

Fig 6.10 Mini-case: Leadership of change

Managerial implications

To an extent, the management implications of the material covered in this chapter are at least implicit but are, nevertheless, emphasised here:

1. Given an understanding of the differences between management and leadership, individuals need to develop self-awareness of their behaviour and attitudes while attempting to identify their leadership *and* management credentials.
2. Individuals need to appreciate when leadership qualities, such as developing and disseminating a sense of vision, are appropriate and, alternatively, when managerial skills, such as negotiation and transaction, are required.
3. Managers need to recognise that the early theorists, such as Taylor and Fayol, together with the conditions they reported, remain partially embedded in our collective understanding of management and, hence, remain influential in many respects.
4. Although certain cerebral and cognitive skills are valuable for successful management, physical and other traits, including most personality characteristics, may not determine or ensure managerial success or failure.
5. Managers should recognise that a wide range of potential managerial or leadership styles exist, possibly along a single continuum, and that they might seek to develop flexibility and self-awareness to both utilise and recognise different styles.
6. Managers might develop the ability to 'read' a situation, that is, to consider the range of situational or contextual factors which might influence the most appropriate style to adopt.
7. Managers need to reflect on their own strengths, styles and capabilities and assimilate the responses of others to their activities in an attempt to learn about themselves and to explore self-development opportunities.
8. Individuals need to recognise that the frame in which they operate influences their understanding, attitudes and behaviour; recognition of this fact is a prerequisite for personal development and growth.
9. Similarly, as the frames in which we operate may prevent us from managing change or transformation successfully, knowledge of self and determination to seek development appear to be vital.
10. Managers might consider that leadership can be viewed as a pluralistic concept, in which case organisational change may be considered to be best led by a network of people operating at different levels and possessing different, but complementary, capabilities.
11. Successful management of major change may involve the adoption of transformational leadership capabilities (as opposed to transactional skills and behaviour) and recognition and accommodation of the complex interplay between the symbolic, cultural, political and contextual factors.

Summary of main points

This chapter provides a synthesis of considerable management and leadership theory and other academic work. The main points made are:

- Frederick Taylor and Henri Fayol made a significant contribution to management theory, with the result that their ideas and principles still influence managerial thinking today;
- many eminent academics, such as Peter Drucker and Henry Mintzberg, have attempted to address the questions, 'What should managers do?' and 'What do managers do?';
- Mintzberg found that managers tend to spend little time on the basic functions identified by Fayol;
- it is possible, but not always helpful, to differentiate between management and leadership, but less straightforward to label individuals as leaders or managers;
- considerable research has attempted to explore the meaning and nature of leadership and can, broadly, be categorised into three schools of thought: trait theories, behavioural theories and situational theories;
- emphasis is now also placed on other 'types' of 'leaders' in modern organisations, that is, entrepreneurs and intrapreneurs;
- contemporary research on leadership has explored a range of leadership frames of reference, or paradigms, which define the scope of thinking and action available to leaders;
- further contemporary writing has suggested that leadership is best viewed as a group or pluralistic phenomenon, as opposed to an individual endeavour;
- two mini-cases are presented, one illustrating the characteristics and efforts of a household name leader and the other providing an example of pluralistic leadership of organisational change.

Conclusions

Despite the extensive research carried out in this field it is still not certain what comprises effective leadership and how we can develop leadership effectiveness. Nevertheless, the material presented in this chapter sheds some light on a number of vital questions. It is important to note the more recent developments in thinking in this regard, while not losing sight of the vital significance that the fundamental principles of management, as outlined by Fayol in the mid-twentieth century, have on modern organisations.

QUESTIONS

1 How might we differentiate between leadership and management? Is there any value in such an exercise?

2 Which of Fayol's 14 principles can be found to apply in modern organisations? What changes in the business environment and in organisations mean that some of the principles are less valid at the end of the twentieth century than they may have been fifty years ago?

3 What is the value of considering frames of reference when discussing leadership? Can we improve our understanding of a great twentieth-century leader, such as Nelson Mandela, by reference to frames?

4 What is the value of considering leadership as a pluralistic phenomenon as opposed to an individual orientation?

REFERENCES

Adair, J. (1979) *Action-Centred Leadership*. Aldershot: Gower.

Aldag, R. and Stearns, T. (1987) *Management*. Chicago, IL: Southwestern.

Bass, B. M. (1990) 'From transactional to transformational leadership: learning to share the vision', *Organizational Dynamics*, Winter, pp 19–31.

Bate, S. P (1994) *Strategies for Cultural Change*. Oxford: Butterworth-Heinemann.

Bennis, W. and Nanus, B. (1985) *Leaders: The Strategies for Taking Charge*. New York: Harper & Row.

Blake, R. R. and Mouton, J. S. (1964) *The Management Grid*. Houston: Gulf Publishing.

Brooks, I. (1996) 'Leadership of a cultural change process', *Leadership and Organisational Development*, 17(5), pp 31–7.

Dailey, R. (1988) *Understanding People in Organisations*. St Paul, MN: West.

Drucker, P. (1977) *People and Performance*. London: Heinemann.

Drucker, P. (1985) *The Entrepreneurial Mystiques*, Inc., Oct, pp 34–44.

Dunphy, D. and Stace, D. (1993) 'The strategic management of corporate change', *Human Relations*, 46(8), pp 905–20.

Fayol, H. (1949) *General and Industrial Management*. London: Pitman Publishing.

Fiedler, F. E. (1967) *A Theory of Leadership Effectiveness*. New York: McGraw-Hill.

Fisher, D. and Torbert, W. R. (1995) *Personal and Organisational Transformations*. New York: McGraw-Hill.

Handy, C. (1993) *Understanding Organisations*. London: Penguin.

Hersey, P. and Blanchard, K. H. (1988) *Management of Organisational Behaviour: Utilizing Human Resources*. Englewood Cliffs, NJ: Prentice-Hall.

House, R. (1971) 'A path–goal theory of leader effectiveness', *Administrative Science Quarterly*, Vol. 16, pp 321–39.

Kirkpatrick, S. A. and Locke, E A. (1991) 'Leadership: do traits matter?', *Academy of Management Executive*, May, pp 48–60.

Kotter, J. (1982) 'What effective general managers really do', *Harvard Business Review*, Jan–Feb, pp 156–62.

Kotter, J. P. (1990) *A Force for Change: How Leadership differs from Management*. New York: Free Press.

Lord, R. G., De Vader, C. L. and Alliger, G. M. (1986) 'A meta-analysis of the relation between personality traits and leadership perceptions: an application of validity generalisation procedures', *Journal of Applied Psychology*, Vol. 71, pp 402–10.

Mann, R. D. (1959) 'A review of the relationship between personality and performance in small groups', *Psychological Bulletin*, 56(4), pp 241–70.

McClelland, D. (1976) *The Achieving Society*. New York: Irvington.

McGregor, D. (1960) *The Human Side of Enterprise*. New York: McGraw-Hill.

Mintzberg, H. (1973) *The Nature of Managerial Work*. New York: Harper & Row.

Morgan, G. (1989) *Creative Organization Theory*. Newbury Park: Sage.

Robbins, S. P. (1984) *Essentials of Organisational Behaviour*, 3rd edn. Englewood Cliffs, NJ: Prentice-Hall.

Stodgill, R. M. (1948) 'Personal factors associated with leadership: a study of the literature', *Journal of Psychology*, Vol. 25, pp 35–71.

Tannenbaum, R. and Schmidt, W. H. (1973) 'How to choose a leadership pattern', *Harvard Business Review*, May–June, pp 162–75.

Vroom, V. H. and Jago, A. G. (1988) *The New Leadership: Managing Participation in Organisations*. Englewood Cliffs, NJ: Prentice-Hall.

Vroom, V. H. and Yetton, P. (1973) *Leadership and Decision Making*. Pittsburgh, PA: University of Pittsburgh Press.

Watson, C. M. (1983) 'Leadership, management and the seven keys', *Business Horizons*, March–April, pp 8–13.

Wright, P. (1996) *Managerial Leadership*. London: Routledge.

Zaleznik, A. (1977) 'Managers and leaders: Are they different?', *Harvard Business Review*, May–June, pp 67–78.

FURTHER READING

Adair, J. (1979) *Action-Centred Leadership*. Aldershot: Gower.

Bate, S. P. (1994) *Strategies for Cultural Change*. Oxford: Butterworth-Heinemann.

Fisher, D. and Torbert, W. R. (1995) *Personal and Organisational Transformations*. New York: McGraw-Hill.

Huczynski, A. and Buchanan, D. (1991) *Organizational Behaviour*. Hemel Hempstead: Prentice-Hall, Chapter 19.

Moorhead, G. and Griffin, R. W. (1995) *Organizational Behaviour*, 4th edn. Boston: Houghton Mifflin, Chapter 12.

Mullins, L. J. (1999) *Management and Organisational Behaviour*, 5th edn. London: Financial Times Pitman Publishing, Chapters 6 and 8.

7

Structure in organisations

STEPHEN SWAILES

LEARNING OUTCOMES

On completion of this chapter you should be able to:

- appreciate the vocabulary of organisational structure;
- explain the main influences on structure in organisations;
- explain the different structural forms that commonly exist in organisations;
- explain the main influences that organisational structure can have on organisations;
- understand how a single organisation is located in a network of interorganisational linkages;
- understand some of the recent developments regarding flexible working.

KEY CONCEPTS

- *bureaucracy*
- *hierarchy*
- *centralisation and decentralisation*
- *multifunctional and multidivisional structures*
- *matrix structures and network structures*
- *organisation size*
- *organisation technology*
- *organisation environment*
- *organisation strategy*
- *organic forms*
- *mechanistic forms*
- *knowledge management*
- *flexible working*

Structure in organisations

Organisational structure has a central and dominant position among the many variables that can influence the performance of an organisation and the attitudes and behaviours of its employees. Early writers on structure tended to emphasise the logic of different structures and to underplay the effects of structure on workplace behaviour. These views have been overtaken by recent work which focuses on organisational flexibility and the pivotal role of individuals and teams in achieving corporate objectives. We will see in this chapter how theory and ideas about organisational structure have evolved and explore current ideas about structuring organisations.

Introduction

Senior management face ever-present challenges to maintain a competitive organisation. Managers are constantly having to review the markets in which their organisation operates, the product and service they offer and the behaviour of competitors. Attention to these problems and challenges calls for an external focus but, at the same time, senior management must keep a close watch on internal structuring to ensure that organisational objectives can be met.

The internal issues can be summarised under the broad heading of organisational structure and can have a critical influence on the ability of an organisation to sustain high levels of individual achievement and performance. The idea that an organisation's structure and processes should *fit* or match its environment has been around for a long time – and there is evidence that firms with good structure/environmental fit perform better than those without good fit (Habib and Victor, 1991; Ghoshal and Nohria, 1993). This chapter examines the idea of organisation structure and elucidates the uniqueness of this particular management concern. The management of internal structure presents problems that are unique to the organisation because they involve the problems of organising a particular set of employees to 'manage-out' inefficiencies and conflicts so that the workforce can provide maximum value to the organisation's customers. Organisational structure has a fundamental bearing on Organisational Behaviour (OB).

A definition of organisation structure

There is no accepted definition of organisation structure yet we can identify some recurring themes in the literature. Anyone who has worked in a commercial organisation will be familiar with the lines of authority used to ensure that people are aware of who they take instruction and objectives from and to whom they are accountable. Lines of authority combine to create a hierarchical (scalar) structure in which, as one ascends the hierarchy, managerial positions become fewer but are associated with higher levels of responsibility. At the top of the hierarchy sits the person with ultimate responsibility for the whole organisation, a President or Chief Executive, perhaps.

Even in small organisations there is a tendency for people to work in groups, often called sections or departments. A small clothing company of, say, 200 people might comprise a design and fashion department, a purchasing department, a production department (for cutting of fabrics and assembly) and a marketing department to handle distribution and sales. This type of organisation is built around functional areas, for example, production and marketing. As the size of organisation increases the attraction of organising into divisions and departments appears to be very strong, for reasons that we will examine later. (In structural terms, divisions are usually much larger than departments.)

Thus, a traditional view of organisation structure is that it describes *the way an organisation is configured into work groups and the reporting and authority relationships that connect individuals and groups together*. Structure acts to create separate identities for different work groups and has a major bearing on the effectiveness with which individuals and groups are able to communicate with each other.

The vocabulary of structure

As in all subjects, the study of organisational structure has created its own vocabulary of terms used to describe the concepts and variables that we associate with it. The most important of these are discussed below.

Centralisation

Centralisation is *the extent to which authority for decision making in the organisation is centralised so that it rests with top management*. In a heavily centralised organisation a head office typically keeps tight control over all important decisions. Divisional managers may well be consulted over decisions affecting them but the balance of decision-making autonomy lies with the centre. In a heavily decentralised organisation, top management give substantial decision-making autonomy to employees. Such autonomy, when given, commonly extends to ways of working and scope to innovate with products and services and to liaise with suppliers and customers. However, it is still unusual for much financial responsibility to be delegated to front-line employees.

Differentiation

Vertical differentiation is *the extent to which an organisation structure comprises different levels of authority*. *Horizontal differentiation* is *the extent to which the organisation is divided into specialisms* (Wilson and Rosenfeld, 1990). Thus an organisation with many reporting levels in its hierarchy and which is organised into many different product or service areas would be highly differentiated. An organisation with a small number of employees and which is engaged in a single product area might have three levels of vertical differentiation (directors, middle managers and supervisors) but little horizontal differentiation.

Integration

Integration refers to *the extent to which different levels in the hierarchy are co-ordinated* (*vertical integration*) and *the extent to which co-ordination occurs across functional areas* (*horizontal integration*) (Wilson and Rosenfeld, 1990). The terms differentiation and integration were also used by Lawrence and Lorsch (1967), who employed a similar definition of integration but who saw differentiation as the extent to which individuals in different departments vary in their orientations to the organisation's goals and values (Robbins, 1993).

Specialisation

Specialisation is *the extent to which there are different specialist roles in an organisation*: the higher the number of specialist roles the higher the degree of specialisation. Specialisation also refers to *the extent to which employees engaged in similar or closely related tasks are grouped together*.

Formalisation

Formalisation is *the tendency of an organisation to create and impose written rules and procedures for working*. Traditionally, this would have included job descriptions and staff manuals detailing the procedures for staff to follow in given situations, many of them trivial in the minds of employees.

Span of control

Span of control refers to *the number of employees that a manager has reporting to him or her*. The number can range from one to 100. As the span of control increases so does the problem of control and co-ordination. The number of subordinates reporting directly to a manager is commonly around 10–12. Above this, some other level of management is usually introduced.

Early thinkers on structure

Business history is a subject that extends back at least 250 years to the origins of the industrial revolution around 1740 in the United Kingdom. The industrial revolution and the subsequent economy it created were characterised by a move from domestic production of goods to a system of production in factories. Such a move required the organisation of employees and the design of structures to co-ordinate materials, production and supply.

An early writer on work processes and structures was the American, Frederick Taylor (*see* Chapter 5). He was intrigued by his belief that workers would tend towards 'loafing or soldiering' (Taylor, 1911: 19) and, therefore, would not achieve the maximum output possible. He believed that the prosperity of the worker was tied to the prosperity of the firm and that workers should respond favourably to efforts to structure their work to achieve maximum output. We now know that workers seek far more from work than to maximise their output and income, yet such theories of work did not emerge until long after Taylor's studies.

Max Weber

Management scholars usually trace the beginning of thinking about structure in organisations to the ideas of the German philosopher and sociologist Max Weber (1864–1920). Weber introduced the term 'bureaucracy' to organisation studies to capture the ideas that:

- people in organisations have their own well-defined tasks and responsibilities;
- organisations contain hierarchical reporting structures which mean that most employees report to another person and may have management responsibilities for others;
- organisations develop their own rules and procedures for completing tasks;
- employees occupy positions in the organisational hierarchy on the basis of merit as judged by others in the organisation;
- employees act in an impartial and unemotional manner, being motivated by a sense of duty towards achieving organisational goals.

It is important to realise that the term bureaucracy has taken on a negative meaning in recent years, with organisations or processes seen as bureaucratic being regarded as self-serving, slow and uncaring. This negative meaning was not part of Weber's ideas and should not be confused with his thinking. Weber held that organisations were bureaucracies to different extents and that increasing bureaucracy would lead to increasingly efficient operations.

With the growth of large organisations in the early twentieth century, bureaucratic forms of organisation increased. There was an increase in the specialisation of jobs and sophisticated rules and procedures for working were created. As we will see, there are some disadvantages associated with bureaucracy: for example, employees can be disaffected if they perceive rules and procedures to be unhelpful or unreasonable, suppressing individual initiative and creativity. Primarily, when business environments were thought to be more stable and predictable it was, arguably, far more straightforward for top management to make good business decisions about products and markets. Now that most organisations exist in intensely competitive environments and many rely on complex technology, they are highly dependent on supportive attitudes and behaviours from the workforce in order to be successful. Far more than was the case previously, managers have to harness the particular knowledge that employees have about customers, products and markets.

Thus, Weber's writing on bureaucracy remains an influential element of organisation theory but the idea that increasing bureaucracy leads to increasing effectiveness is less fashionable. Indeed, current thinkers often argue that bureaucracy should be reduced to give organisations the room to think and manoeuvre in order to sustain high performance.

Structural types

Multifunctional structures

Large corporations appeared earlier in the USA than in Europe (Hannah, 1976: 2) and were common by the end of the nineteenth century. One of the reasons for their success is thought to be related to the structure they employed. This commonly involved centralised control and the existence of separate functional departments, for example, for purchasing, production, marketing (*see* Figure 7.1). Another aspect of their structure was what we now call vertical integration, that is, *the bringing together of operations such as buying materials, production and assembly, distribution and retailing under the control of one enterprise* (Hannah, 1976: 3). General Motors, still a large US car manufacturer, built itself on centralised control over a functionally divisionalised structure and had become a benchmark for other large corporations in the 1940s (Drucker, 1975). The multifunctional form separates and organises according to the various inputs to a firm's business. It is viable where products share common production methods and technologies and it allows employees to become highly specialised in their work.

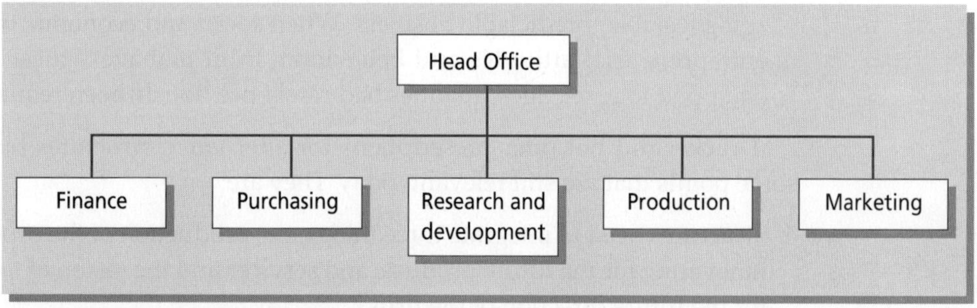

Fig 7.1 Centralised, functionally departmentalised structure in a manufacturing organisation

Writing in 1975, Peter Drucker described how large US organisations like General Motors and AT&T (rather like Britain's BT) had kept basically the same structure for decades. But market changes emanating from the 1960s caused many large organisations to adopt a more restless attitude towards their structures. Drucker pointed to six reasons why the organisational structures that had supported General Motors, and firms like it, for so long had become inappropriate.

1 Pre-war economic growth was mostly based on production and manufacturing whereas the post-war era saw the growth of a strong service sector, particularly in health care, banking and insurance, transportation and retailing. What was good for organising manufacturing was, and is, not necessarily appropriate for organising services.

2 Many of these old, large organisations produced mostly single products with single technologies for single markets. By the 1970s organisations were increasingly becoming multiproduct and multimarket and were using different technologies to produce and deliver.

3 Firms had existed to supply their domestic market and some exported a proportion of their output. Structurally, these organisations had not configured themselves for international business, styling themselves as domestic with some international operations. This contrasts with other companies which became truly multinational in their operations and culture.

4 The new breed of multiproduct, multinational firms were used to managing information, that is, to capturing relevant information, analysing it and making decisions. The old-style firms were not geared for this, simply because there had not been an information problem in the demand-led markets which they had served.

5 The employees of old-style organisations were mostly manual or clerical workers, in contrast to the knowledge workers who dominated other sectors, particularly services. New forms of organising were needed to get the best out of the new breed of employee.

6 Centralised control over functional divisions had been a good structure for managing a stable, predictable business. When social and economic trends called for entrepreneurial attitudes and behaviours from managers these forms were ill equipped to react. Such qualities had rarely previously been required.

Drucker did not offer prescriptions for alternative structures but he did make some points that are still relevant today. They are:

1 Structures need to integrate three things; the production of the product or service, innovating for the future products and services and the vision of top management for the future direction of the firm.

2 Structures do not evolve by themselves, they require careful thought and analysis.

3 Structure should follow a carefully articulated vision of what the organisation is trying to achieve.

4 Work is objective and depersonalised yet it is done by people, thus jobs have to be task focused yet also designed to fit the needs of the job holder.

5 Apart from a few unusual organisations, the hierarchical organisation structure of bosses and staff (super-ordinate and subordinates) is virtually inescapable. Scalar structures give protection to employees, combined with the freedom to innovate.

Figure 7.2 presents a case study that illustrates the relevance of Drucker's points today.

Those darned accountants!

This case shows how structure can be changed in response to environmental pressures. The company concerned makes feedstuffs for cattle, pigs and poultry. It employs around 1500 staff in several locations. The feeds are delivered directly to farms and there are no sales to other sectors. Thus changes that affect farmers' livestock levels will be passed on directly to the company.

Until recently, the company operated decentralised businesses with regional managers having substantial power to make their own decisions (high decision autonomy). Adverse conditions affecting farmers forced them to seek cost savings in animal feeds. The company reacted to falling demand and pressure on prices by switching back to a centralised, multifunctional form on the grounds that this would hand back tight control over costs to top management.

A consequence of the switch, which involved taking away some of the responsibilities from regional managers, was that staff morale diminished. A classic outcome from multifunctional structures also arose, that is, the sales teams sought a wide range of speciality feeds and the manufacturing division wanted to reduce the number of product lines and make longer production runs of the remaining products.

This case is intriguing because it emphasises the practical dilemmas that can face top management. On the one hand, they have to react in the face of falling demand for their product. On the other hand, the classic solution of taking control can lead to low morale and a high risk of quashing the innovation and spirit that the company needs to manage its way out of the crisis.

Discussion question

What are the advantages and disadvantages of reverting to tight managerial control in this case? In the long run, how do you think the switch back to centralisation will affect the firm?

Fig 7.2 Mini-case: Changing from a decentralised to centralised structure

Multidivisional structures

Although functional structures (centralised and integrated) are thought to have been influential in early twentieth century economic growth, their effectiveness was questioned in the 1970s (Chandler, 1976: 2). This is largely because such structures became costly and slow moving when faced with rising competition from new product markets and lower-cost producers. A more efficient structure, called the multidivisional form, began to replace the centralised form (Figure 7.3). In this, *divisions were created to look after all aspects of the production of a particular product, that is, from purchasing materials through manufacturing and distribution.*

In this sense, multidivisional structures focus on a firm's outputs rather than its inputs. They overcome the dangers of weak communication and co-ordination

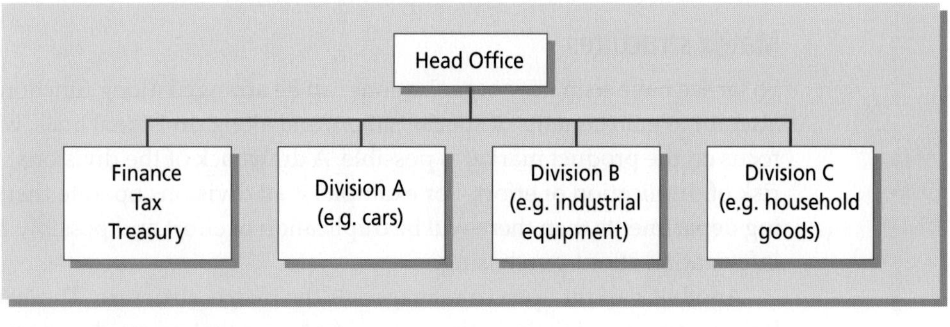

Fig 7.3 Multidivisional structure

Structural transformation at Nestlé

During the 1980s, the Swiss food giant Nestlé operated a 1600-person head office controlling operations in over 100 countries. By the start of the 1990s, Nestlé undertook to reorganise to make it slimmer, faster and more innovative.

Its head office and some of its national companies were originally organised on the basis of strong functional departments. Such specialists previously held tight control over decisions in these areas in the operating companies. Seven new strategic business units (SBUs) were formed to cover Nestlé's main product markets. One SBU covered coffee and beverages, for instance. Each SBU had a worldwide strategic, as opposed to operational, responsibility for product-management decisions in the main functional areas like production and finance. Two hundred head office jobs were cut. Regional management units were given more control over the companies in the regions than they previously had and the principle of 'business asymmetry' was employed, meaning that SBUs can be organised differently depending upon their particular needs as dictated by market conditions and production technologies.

Nestlé's changes were not new to the business world and had been adopted by their competitors long before. This short illustration does highlight some useful propositions, that is:

1 Structures can persist in organisations because of simple resistance to change and/or lack of management acceptance that structure needs to change.
2 Achieving the 'right' balance between decentralisation and centralisation depends on the position of the organisation at a particular time.
3 Effective top management may be able to produce good performance in spite of a sub-optimum structure, but structure can drift to be so far away from market needs that it begins to impede organisational performance.
4 In large multinational organisations, there are four logical lines of organisation: by functional area, by product division, by broad geographic division (e.g. Europe, North America), and by country.

Source: Based on Lorenz (1992).

Fig 7.4 Mini-case: Transition from a functional to a divisional structure

inherent in multifunctional structures and should allow faster response to market changes. Faster reaction is possible as each division has access to, and control over, the key resources it needs, for example, market forecasting and production facilities.

Although such structures are better in these respects, senior management has to ensure that these advantages are not eroded by duplication and diseconomies of scale. Thus, whereas the organisation is structured according to its outputs, extensive communication across functional areas, such as between manufacturing and logistics, has to take place. The mini-case presented in Figure 7.4 illustrates the transition from a functional to a divisional structure.

Matrix structures

So far we have seen how organisations can be arranged along functional lines, and so attempt to gain benefits of specialisation, and along divisional lines, where a stronger focus on the product market is possible. A drawback of the divisional structure is the risk of duplication of effort. For example, if all divisions operate their own purchasing departments then there will be duplication of effort and possibly a lack of shared information about purchasing.

Another variant open to managers is the matrix structure. These are not particularly common and their distinguishing feature is that an employee will have two and sometimes more lines of authority to report to. One of the lines of authority, usually the functional area, will be used to manage the formal side of the employment contract such as attendance, salary negotiations and performance review. The other line(s) of authority are used to involve employees in ongoing projects and initiatives to which they have to make commitments.

When there is a real need for staff to spread their time across a range of diverse activities the matrix structure has something to offer. It can help to manage progress on a number of fronts simultaneously and allows staff to reap the benefits of working together in functional areas. The main objection to the matrix concerns its ability to create confusion over who reports to whom and about the priorities that should be attached to different tasks. Since the functional line manager will have position power (*see* Chapter 8) over the project manager(s) and since there are unlikely to be formalised rules and procedures for participation in development projects, there is a danger that unproductive power struggles can evolve. The focus of attention, the customer, can become lost in such struggles as priorities shift towards self-interest and political posturing. Although matrix structures have much to offer, we should not forget the writings of St Luke, 'no man can serve two masters'.

Figure 7.5 shows how a matrix structure operates in a faculty of a university college. The Dean of Faculty is responsible for the functioning of over 140 academic and

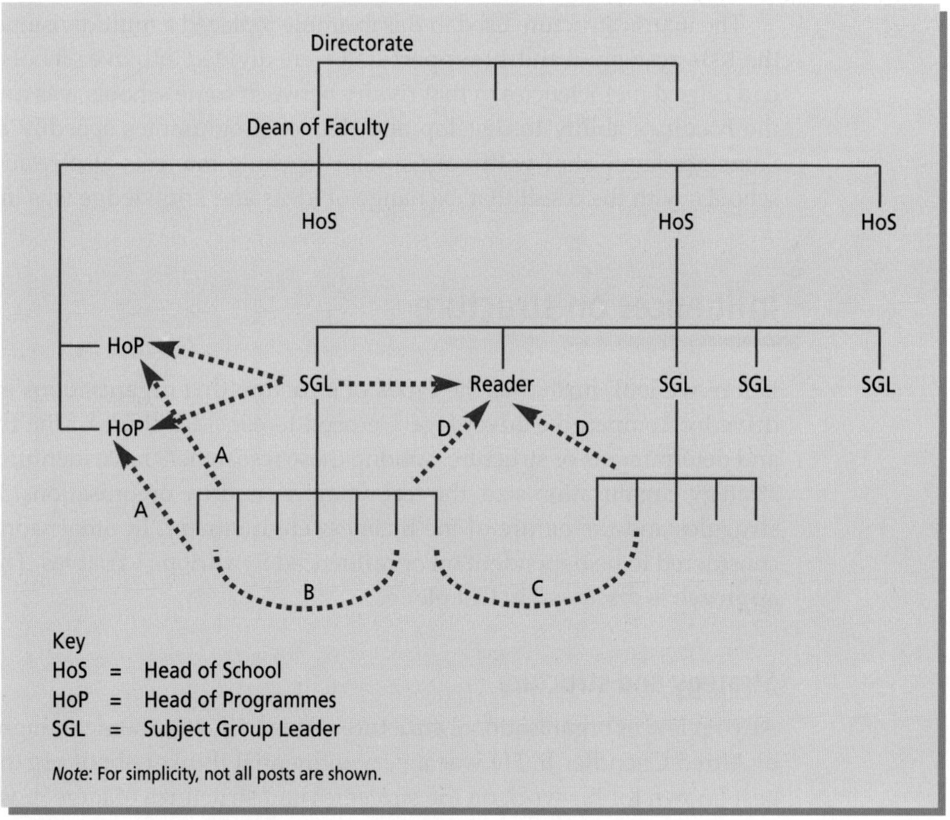

Fig 7.5 A matrix structure in a university college business school

support staff. Academic staff are organised into three schools on the basis of broad subject area. Heads of Programmes are responsible for the development and delivery of courses (programmes) and the two Programme posts cover undergraduate and postgraduate courses.

Within each school are several Subject Group Leaders who are responsible for developing staff in well-defined areas such as Organisational Behaviour. The Readers have special responsibility for helping staff to achieve research objectives. Thus, for mainstream staff management, the line of authority is through the Subject Group Leader to the Head of School and to the Dean of Faculty.

When staff are teaching on a particular course they are responsible to a Head of Programmes as shown by path A in Figure 7.5. This structure, however, also involves a responsibility to colleagues at the same hierarchical level as shown by path B, for example, if a person is teaching on a course for which a colleague is the course director. Path C represents the possibility that a member of one subject group might teach on a programme managed by a member on another group. Path D represents the management of research. Since all staff teach on one course or another, each person has at least two lines of authority, a Head of School (the primary line) and a Head of Programme(s). Additionally, those staff who undertake research will also make commitments to a Reader and thus have three 'masters'.

The matrix structure used in this example replaced a multidivisional one in which the 100+ academics and 40 support staff were divided into five schools. This structure had caused inefficiencies in that rivalry between some schools was causing delays in the Faculty's ability to develop and deliver programmes speedily and effectively. Some academic staff with very similar teaching interests also resided in different schools, with the result that exchange of ideas and knowledge was impeded.

Influences on structure

Before we look further at the types of structure that organisations employ in their drive for competitive advantage we need to consider some of the main influences and determinants of structure. Among these researchers have identified organisation strategy, organisation size, the technologies used by organisations, internal power struggles and the nature of the business environment. In other words, structure is considered to be dependent on or influenced by various variables. This contingency approach is discussed in Chapter 5.

Strategy and structure

Any review of organisational structure needs to include some thoughts on the ideas of Alfred Chandler Jr. He was a very influential thinker about organisations and is best known for his work on the strategies and structures of large, post-war US companies (Chandler, 1962). His definition of structure is '*the design of organization through which the enterprise is administered*'. This includes the lines of authority and communication between the different administrative offices and officers and the information and data that flow through these lines of authority and communication.

One of his main conclusions was that the structure of an organisation follows its strategy. By this he meant that having decided on a strategy to employ, an organisation would need to make decisions about roles and responsibilities and about how resources (capital, buildings, machinery, expertise) would be distributed in the organisation to assist the implementation of strategy. As an organisation made adjustments to its strategy then small and occasionally large adjustments would need to be made to structure. This line of thinking became accepted but it is important to appreciate the differences between the competitive environments that exist now and those that existed when Chandler did his research.

In the 1950s, the demand for manufactured goods often exceeded their supply and organisations were 'pulled' along by consumers anxious to raise their standard of living. In those times, the idea that an organisation could rationally determine its strategy and then put in place a structure to help achieve it was a reasonable one. It was made reasonable because the operating environment was less complex than it is today and the planning and implementation of deliberate strategies (Mintzberg and Waters, 1985) was feasible and widely attempted. Since Chandler wrote about structure, markets have changed, with the result that supply usually exceeds demand and the points made by Peter Drucker, discussed above, have grown in importance. In this more complex world, the idea that managers can rationally plan ahead is weaker because it is much harder to estimate consumer needs and to predict how the organisation's competitors will react to strategic decisions. Strategy is no longer seen as a logical, detached process, and is increasingly seen as something that emerges from the organisation's efforts to stay competitive. The causal relationship of strategy determining structure is, therefore, less convincing. We can now live with the idea that a structure will in some way contribute to the creation of a strategy.

Technology and structure

For the purpose of the present discussion, technology refers to the processes by which an organisation transforms its inputs into outputs. Note that this applies to both products and services and that, according to this definition, all organisations employ a technology. The level or sophistication of technology employed in some organisations may, however, be low.

One pioneering study of the effect of technology on organisations was published by Joan Woodward as early as 1958 (*see* Chapter 5). This extensive study of firms in Essex, England, was carried out in the 1950s. Woodward found that when 92 firms were grouped according to similarities among their production methods and technology, each production system coincided with a particular pattern of organisation. The three production methods she described were:

- small batch or unit production;
- large batch and mass production, for example, car manufacture;
- continuous production, for example of plastics and chemicals.

Woodward's main findings were:

1 The number of levels of authority increased with technical complexity from three to six.
2 The span of control of the first-line supervisor was higher in mass production (41–50) than in unit production (21–30), and in the latter was higher than in process production (11–20).
3 The ratio of managers and supervisors to employees was higher in process production than in mass production, and in the latter was higher than in unit production.

The importance of Woodward's study is that it was one of the first large-scale studies of British companies and, more importantly, it stimulated a continuing interest in the relationship between technology and organisations. Shortly after the Essex study, Charles Perrow (1967) published work on US organisations. He was concerned not to limit technology to production and manufacturing organisations, as Woodward had done, and so he took a broader view of technology. His view embodied:

- the level of routine and variation present in a job; and
- the ease with which breaks in the routine can be analysed and solved.

Thus, the lowest level of technology would involve low levels of variation (high routine) and easily found solutions to any problems that did occur. The highest level of technology would occur when the job was non-routine and when problems required individual analysis before solutions to them could be found. Using this, and other ways of categorising technologies, researchers have looked at the link between the level of technology and organisational variables. Their results have been consistent with Joan Woodward's earlier findings (Wilson and Rosenfeld, 1990). Some trends emerging from the research are:

1 High levels of repetitive work tend to be associated with increasing vertical and horizontal integration (Hage and Aiken, 1969).
2 High levels of routine work tend to be associated with high levels of formalisation, that is, written rules and procedures (Miller *et al.*, 1991).

Size and structure

In the same way that Woodward studied Essex firms in the 1950s, a group of researchers based at Aston University, England, studied firms in the Birmingham area in the 1960s. The Aston studies, as they are called, are another milestone in understanding organisation structure and are briefly summarised here (*see also* Chapter 5).

The Aston researchers found that the effect of technology on structure diminished in large organisations (Wilson and Rosenfeld, 1990) and that size (determined by the number of employees) seemed to have a strong effect on structure. As the number of employees grows there is a tendency for staff in different specialisations to be grouped together so that management can achieve the levels of control it seeks and so that employees benefit from sharing knowledge and ideas. As organisations grow in size, the problem of managing the various specialist departments increases. One common approach to this problem is to decentralise, that is, to push decision-making authority down the hierarchy to the specialist departments. The appeal of grouping together people with similar tasks, knowledge and expertise, coupled with management's inability to directly manage diverse specialisms, leads to greater formalisation, decentralisation and specialisation.

The business environment

Another influential early study that concerned organisations and their relationship with the environment (Burns and Stalker, 1961) was reported in Chapter 5. The lasting contribution of this study to the structure debate was its proposition of two ideal types of working organisation – one 'mechanistic' and adapted to stable operating conditions, and one 'organic' and much better adapted to unstable conditions and climates for change.

Burns and Stalker saw mechanistic structures as those in which tasks and problems facing the overall organisation are broken down into specialisms, with each employee fulfilling his or her task. Tasks are carried out in isolation and top management is responsible for ensuring that tasks are co-ordinated and meaningful to the organisation. Communication tends to be up and down lines of authority rather than across them. Characterised by structures that look like family trees, interaction flows upwards, is filtered at different levels and responses are transmitted down the line.

Organic structures are far better suited to unstable operating conditions in which new problems are created which cannot efficiently be solved by mechanistic processes. In organic structures less attention is given to describing and defining particular jobs. Demarcation is avoided and people conduct their jobs with knowledge of the organisation's overall purpose and of the contributions made by others. Interaction and communication runs across the organisation as much as it runs up and down it.

Burns and Stalker did not describe a structure itself, but rather, the characteristics of both slow-moving and reactive organisations. Their findings are still very important for organisation theory. Managers need to continually assess whether the structure existing in their organisation is stimulating the right attitudes and behaviours to bring about change. Table 7.1 illustrates the prime differences between organic and mechanistic structures.

The Burns and Stalker hypothesis, that the bureaucracy of mechanistic organisations impedes organisational learning and communication, is widely accepted. The contrasting organic style has become so sought after that as a general model for

Table 7.1 A comparison of mechanistic and organic systems of management

Organic	Mechanistic
Contributive nature of knowledge and experience to common tasks	Specialised differentiation of tasks
Adjustments and redefinition of tasks through interaction and communication	Changes to roles are slow and procedural
A network structure for control, authority and communication	Hierarchic structure of control, authority and communication
Knowledge located anywhere in the network	Knowledge assumed to reside at the top
Lateral outlooks and communication	Vertical outlooks and communication
Information and advice	Instruction and decisions
Commitment to common tasks	Loyalty to organisation, obedience to supervisors
Value contacts with external centres of expertise	Internal focus

Source: Based on Burns and Stalker (1961).

outcomes of a structure it is 'accepted wisdom' (Bierly and Spender, 1995). An interesting twist to this hypothesis, however, was proposed by Perrow (1984), who was interested in analysing high-risk organisations and projects. Perrow argued that mankind's technological progress has overtaken our ability to manage such technologies. He pointed to problems with the organic system thesis, namely that when the consequences of failure affect only the future of an organisation the risk can be taken. But when the risk extends to organisations that could cause nuclear leaks, loss of military weapons or national secrets, potentially catastrophic pollution incidents or to organisations which are absorbing massive public spending, it is inappropriate to look for loose, flexible, management structures. Organisation theorists might dwell on the logic of this argument and consider whether the mechanistic form is better suited when the consequence of failure would be catastrophic.

Summary of influences on structure

So far we have seen four classic influences upon structure: the intended strategy, the levels of technology employed, size of the organisation and business environment. These factors variously affect decisions over centralisation and decentralisation, functionalisation and divisionalisation, the amount of specialisation and spans of control. From an OB viewpoint, pinpointing the influences on structure and the influences that structure has on individuals and the performance of an organisation is highly complex. There are so many interrelated variables that it requires large-scale and highly detailed studies of the kind undertaken by Chandler, Woodward, and the Aston group before managers can have much confidence in their findings. From the work of Burns and Stalker we can see that the effects that different structures can have on a workforce in terms of positive attitudes and behaviours are far more important than the actual structures adopted.

The organisation as a system

So far we have examined how structure is typically described and portrayed. Our focus has been on the tangible side of structure, that is, the structural forms that exist in organisations and what they look like. Although they are necessary, it is dangerous to place too much emphasis on the tangible aspects of structure. This is because organisation charts only describe grouping and reporting relationships; they do not tell us much about how the organisation actually functions at the level of the individual. Such portrayals capture a total picture but do little to explain the microlevel nature of working and structure; they do not reveal the informal organisation. They represent only the legal organisation, the body corporate, and do not show the connections an organisation may have with other organisations in its operating environment. They portray the organisation as a closed system. It is common knowledge that all organisations operate in a network interacting with outside agents (*see* Chapter 5). Indeed, collaboration and ventures with other organisations are being used increasingly as means of achieving strategic goals. These ideas are illustrated by Henry Mintzberg, a North American management professor, who was interested in the component parts of an organisation (Mintzberg, 1989). He proposed six 'basic parts' as shown within the core of Figure 7.6. The largest group is usually an 'operating core' which produces and delivers the product or service. At the top of the organisation is a 'strategic apex' which houses senior management. Connecting the core and the apex is a group of middle managers. When the activities of an organisation become complex a group of technical support staff is needed to assist the core, the middle management and the strategic apex. Mintzberg called this a 'technostructure', which might include production planners and information technology specialists. Organisations add staff to fulfil supporting roles, such as personnel management and secretarial services. Mintzberg called these 'support staff'. The final component of the organisation is not a staff group but the organisation's culture (*see* Chapter 9). This is shown in the diagram as bounded by a dotted line although culture will permeate throughout all staff groups. The dotted line around the whole organisation is intentional and represents the idea that the organisation is not closed to the outside world, rather, it is open to it: it is an open system. The size of each of the five dimensions varies according to the product markets in which the organisation operates.

Figure 7.6 takes Mintzberg's view of the organisation and positions it relative to the organisations that operate in the external environment. This adapted version shows other organisations whose activities influence the structure of the organisation in the centre of the diagram. These other organisations commonly include competitors or, in the not-for-profit sector, equivalent organisations with similar goals. A charity might not have competitors in the normal sense but operates alongside other charities which are competing for donations from the same sources. Special interest groups and pressure groups are increasingly active and vocal; consider the publicity

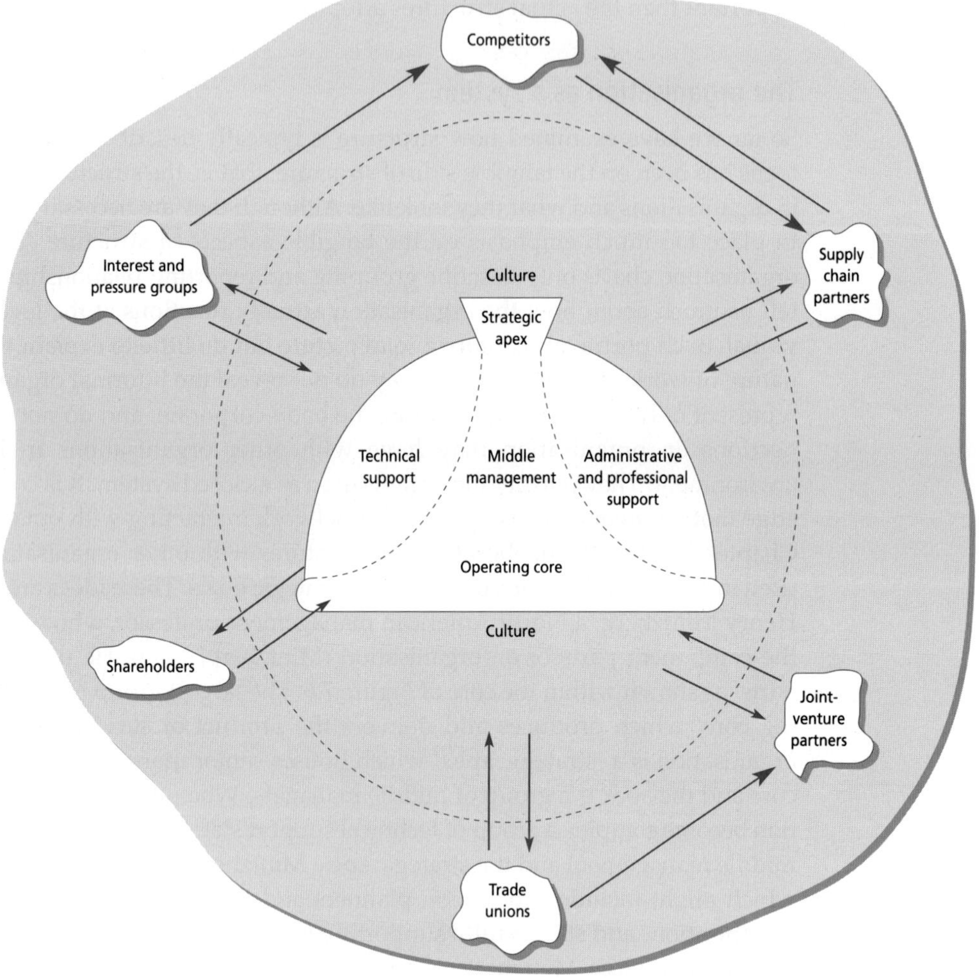

Fig 7.6 External influences on an organisation

Source: Based on Mintzberg (1989).

that Greenpeace created in response to Shell's intention to sink a used oil platform in the North Sea. Many organisations serve the interests of shareholders or, if they are not-for-profit bodies, they have some type of governing council or committee. The arrows in Figure 7.6 link competitors to supply chain partners, and point out that external organisations may well be interconnected. The dotted line around the whole system represents the idea that the organisation's interaction with its operating environment is open, not tightly bounded or closed. The irregular shape of the whole system, and of the external organisations, is intended to represent the changing strength and form of the relationships so created. They are rather like the single-celled amoeba which changes shape and divides continually during its lifetime.

ICI (Imperial Chemical Industries) was formed in 1926 by the coming together of four of Britain's leading chemical producers. Having relied on supplying the British Empire, the company found business becoming increasingly competitive as the Empire collapsed abruptly after the Second World War.

ICI employed around 200 000 in 1980, the number of employees dropping to about 120 000 by 1991 but, in spite of this, its performance had been deteriorating, as evidenced by the falling return on capital. The economic recession in the UK in the early 1990s also depressed ICI's figures. During the 1980s, new technology had brought new product divisions into ICI, namely pharmaceuticals and pesticides, on top of its traditional production of bulk chemicals like chlorine and plastics. In 1991, turnover of the new divisions was £3937 million, turning in an average of 18.3 per cent trading profit, at about £20 000 profit per employee. The core divisions of paints, industrial chemicals and materials had a turnover of £8701 million, averaging 3.6 per cent trading profit, at £3550 profit per employee.

Part of the problem was attributed to a complicated management structure in which financial responsibility was confused. A new structure was introduced to create closer ties between the chief executives of ICI's seven divisions and the nine executives on the main board. Increasing shareholder wealth was a major target.

ICI went through much detailed analysis of the structural options for the company to improve overall performance and chose one that stunned the world chemical industry. The decision was to split ICI into two companies – a demerger. An outcome of this was to make the management of the two new companies more exposed and more accountable. The two companies would not have the constraints of being part of a large group and would be much freer to participate in the restructuring going on in two quite different business sectors.

Demergers were not unknown in the business world but they were uncommon. It was a reversal of the classic approach to managing a large business, that is, that diversification helps to spread risk and offers a safer operating platform. However, modern business philosophy is all about maximising performance and if a particular division is seen to be turning in less than it could then managers will look at ways of 'improving' performance.

Learning points from this and other demergers are:

1 Companies can become too large to be managed optimally.
2 In a reversal of the logic for conglomerate structures, organisations can be seen as being worth less than the sum of their constituent parts.

To date this demerger has proven successful.

Sources: Based on Preston, R. (1991) 'Moving ahead of the pack in global management', *Financial Times*, 23 July, p 18; Urry, M. (1992) 'Corporate theories reversed as demerger trend gathers pace', *Financial Times*, 31 July, p 18; Jackson, T. (1992) 'Parts are greater than the whole', *Financial Times*, 31 July, p 14; Serjeant, G. (1992) 'ICI steals critics' arguments to improve chemistry of profits', *The Times*, 31 July, p 21.

Fig 7.7 The demerging of ICI

In sum, it is better to see an organisation as existing in a network structure that, with the passage of time, will reconfigure itself as new structural linkages are formed and old ones are dismantled. Figure 7.7 illustrates structural changes in ICI.

Structures – present and future

Flexible working

Many organisations have responded to turbulent environmental conditions by attempting to become more 'flexible'. This often involves the adoption of new organisational structures. In most organisations people are both the most vital resource, and the most costly. Traditionally, however, they have been prone to inflexibility and inertia. As a consequence, in recent decades, many organisations have sought to achieve greater flexibility in structure and employment conditions. The implications of flexible working and of the flexible firm on organisational behaviour are significant, not least in terms of employee motivation, team and group work, leadership, organisational structure, communications, culture and change.

The old 'industrialised' scenario of reliable employment, which allowed families shared times for shopping, travel and leisure is metamorphosing into what some have called a 'post-industrial' age. Alvin Toffler (1985), a well-known writer about the future shape of work and of organisations, has termed the present moves towards such a society as a 'super-industrial' age or a 'third wave'. Toffler likens this 'wave' to the agricultural revolution (the first wave) and the industrial revolution (the second wave). Others have referred to it as post-Fordism; that is, *after or following Henry Ford's mass production era*.

The enhanced capabilities of many organisations to customise products and services has been strongly influenced by developments in microprocessor technology and management techniques. Computers enable us to process and communicate data and information extremely rapidly. Advances in telecommunications technology (telephones, faxes, multimedia computers, satellites and the Internet) have brought significant improvements in the quality of data about life and work. These technologies have been harnessed by organisations which wish to operate throughout the world. Quinn (1992) conceives of intelligent enterprises, 'converting intellectual resources into a chain of service outputs and integrating these into a form most useful for certain customers'. Many people in the workplace are often referred to as 'knowledge workers' as their prime role is to collect, use and disseminate knowledge about business opportunities; they manage knowledge.

Flexible working takes many forms. First, 'numerical' flexibility generally affects employees' hours of work. These include longstanding practices such as overtime, homeworking, shift and part-time work and other increasingly common practices, such as flexitime, teleworking, annual hours and zero hours contracts, the use of temporary staff and job sharing.

A few of these terms require some further explanation. Zero hours contracts are similar to temporary work. For example, Burtons, the retail clothes chain, terminated the contracts of 2000 of its staff in the mid-1990s. Some of these people were re-employed on part-time contracts but many others were offered work as and when required by the employer. These 'zero-hours' contracts enable the organisation to adjust staff levels in line with customer shopping patterns. Needless to say, most of the employees concerned were less than satisfied with this arrangement as it introduced considerable uncertainty into their working lives. Another market-driven change has occurred in the electricity-generating business. One company encourages some employees to engage in 'winter/summer stagger', where they work longer hours in the winter to accommodate demand. Hence, people are employed on an 'annual hours' basis.

Homeworking is not new, although the scale of this activity is increasing.

However, teleworking goes a step further by connecting home-based employees by use of computer modem to the organisation and/or other teleworkers. The availability of communications technology has also led to the 'virtual office' where laptop computers, portable faxes and mobile phones enable people to work in any location. Linked with this is the practice of 'hotdesking' where employees 'touch base' at the office and use whatever work space is available, picking up messages on e-mail. Stanworth (1992) found that the most popular working pattern among teleworkers is a combination of home and office working, which helps to overcome the inherent isolation of working from home and increases the feeling of belonging to a team. 'Telecottaging', where a local venue acts as a central point for teleworkers, may be one way of solving this problem.

A second form of flexibility, referred to as 'distancing', describes the situation where employees are replaced by subcontractors, and employment contracts are replaced by contracts for service. Again, this has been commonplace in many industries, such as construction and manufacturing, for many decades. However, the process is increasingly popular in other types of activity including service industries and the public sector. It has a significant effect on an organisation's structure as, increasingly, non-core activities are contracted out. The concept of core and periphery applies where a small number of staff are considered essential, often full-time employees with considerable skill and experience, whereas many others are peripheral and may be employed by satellite or dependent organisations and/or are part-time or temporary staff.

A third form of flexible working is broadly termed 'functional flexibility'. Although in many organisations strict lines of demarcation exist between jobs, these are seen as offering little flexibility and often prove obstacles to effective teamwork and subsequent productivity gains. Multiskilling is becoming more commonplace, where individuals are trained to undertake a broader array of tasks.

Fourth, pay flexibility is increasingly common. This may involve the harmonisation of terms and conditions, including the removal of artificial barriers between white and blue collar workers, such as differences in pension, sick pay and holiday entitlements. This is an approach that the Rover Group, the motor vehicle manufacturer, has used to encourage the development of a teamwork culture. Many organisations have, however, taken a contrasting approach, offering personal non-standard contracts.

Many of these ideas find their ultimate focus in the concept of a 'virtual corporation'. Virtual corporations have been defined by Davidow and Malone (1992) as, *'almost edgeless, with permeable and continuously changing interfaces between company, supplier and customers. From inside the firm, the view will be no less amorphous with traditional offices, departments and operating divisions constantly reforming according to need'*. Such an organisational 'structure' is a clear culmination of a teleworking, information-based, constantly evolving enterprise.

A major study carried out in 1993 into flexible working in Europe concluded that, although there was an overall trend towards greater use of flexible working patterns there was considerable variation in practice between countries, sectors and sizes of organisation. About 15 per cent of the workforce in the European Union works part-time, with growth in this respect being most noticeable in the Netherlands, Germany and the United Kingdom. Non-permanent employment has increased significantly in all European Union countries, as has subcontracting. Watson (1993), using Labour Force Survey data in the United Kingdom, found that 9.7 million people (38 per cent of all employees) were part-time, temporary, self-employed, on a government training scheme or unpaid family workers. This represented an increase of 1 250 000 between 1986 and 1993. Over 80 per cent of all medium and large organisations in the United Kingdom employ some temporary staff. The BBC now offers the majority of new recruits only short or fixed-term contracts. These contracts are becoming increasingly common for researchers and lecturers in higher and further education.

In the United Kingdom there has also been an increase in the number of men working flexibly, from 18 per cent in 1986 to 27 per cent in 1993, whereas the proportion of women in this category remained stable and high at 50 per cent. Men in this category were largely self-employed whereas women were mainly part-time or on temporary contracts. Additionally, over 12 per cent, that is, 2.6 million people, work flexitime, whereas two million, or 9 per cent of the workforce, have annualised hours (most common in the professions, particularly teaching). Over one million employees work school term time only and about 200 000 people share jobs. For example, the Alliance & Leicester Building Society has offered some employees, who are parents (both mothers and fathers) of school-age children, the opportunity to work during term time only. Boots, the chemist, has provided more than 50 job-share 'partnerships' in positions from supervisor to pharmacy manager. These family-friendly measures attempt to motivate employees and help parents balance work and family demands. They also facilitate the retention of competent and well-trained staff.

The mini-case presented in Figure 7.8 on page 190, based on changes in the Metropolitan Board of Works in Melbourne, Australia, illustrates the effects of flexible working and organisational change on structure. Largely as a response to changes in its business environment, such as government directives inspired by wider technological and competitive conditions, the organisation has undergone a major restructuring. The result is a smaller, leaner, delayered and more flexible company. The organisation has moved from a 'mechanistic' to an 'organic' structure (Burns and Stalker, 1961) and from a 'defender' to a 'prospector' (Miles & Snow, 1978). It also demonstrates that the boundary between the organisation and its 'task' environment is not fixed but rather dynamic and flexible.

Melbourne Water

Melbourne Water was formed in 1993 from the long-established Metropolitan Board of Works. It was until recently a typical government bureaucracy which operated in a protected and stable business environment with guaranteed superannuated employment. Impending privatisation encouraged management to structure the organisation along competitive commercial lines as it aimed to become a market leader in the Asia Pacific region in the provision of water storage, purification and distribution capabilities. The new structure is shown on the right of Figure 7.10, the previous hierarchical structure being on the left.

A layer of middle management has disappeared altogether. The executive and senior levels have been combined and supervisors have been reclassed as team leaders. The core workforce is now described as full-time employees and nobody in the organisation is considered to have guaranteed lifelong employment. All maintenance and construction activities are contracted out. Casual semi-skilled workers are employed as required on a daily basis and skilled casual workers are recruited through specialist agencies. Much of the professional work is carried out by consultants. A number of major suppliers are now considered as partners in the organisation as they are required to carry out some of the duties formerly conducted by employees.

Discussion question

What effects are these structural changes likely to have on:

(a) the motivation of different groups in the wider organisational workforce;

(b) management and leadership;

(c) group and teamwork;

(d) power in the wider organisation and its satellites; and

(e) organisational culture?

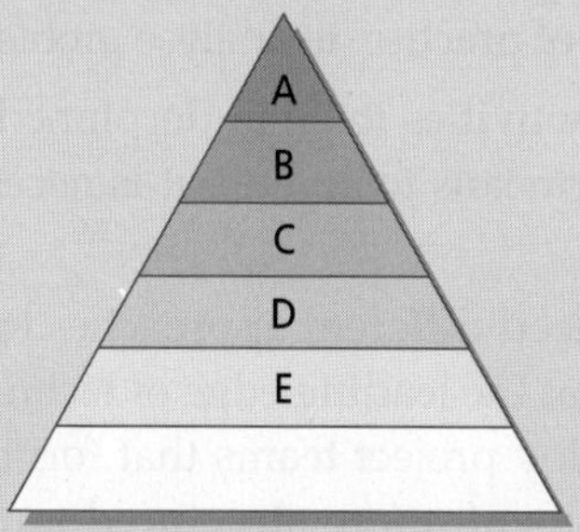

Metropolitan Board of Works

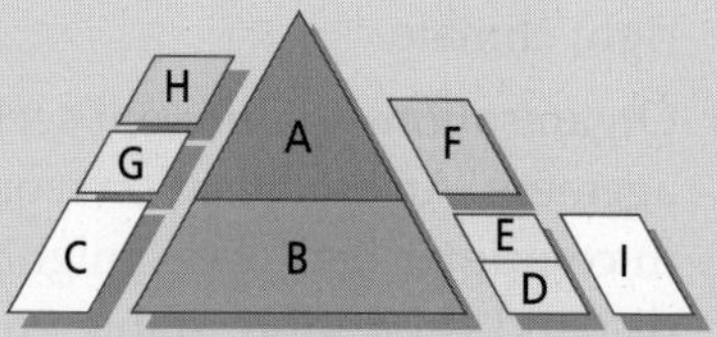

Melbourne Water

ORGANISATIONAL STRUCTURE

A: Executive management
B: Senior management
C: Middle management
D: Supervisors
E: Permanent employees

A: Management
B: Full-time employees
C: Full-time contractors
D: Casual contractors – semi-skilled
E: Casual contractors – skilled
F: Consultants
G: Suppliers
H: Clients
I: Emergency services

Fig 7.9 Flexible organisational structure

Knowledge management

For many small organisations, the market value of their tangible assets (land, building, machinery) approximates to the value of the company if it were to be sold. Historically, structures have reflected how the tangible value of a company was configured. There is, however, an increasing trend for the value of companies to be far greater than the value of their tangible assets. Microsoft's tangible assets accounted for less than 10 per cent of the company's stock-market valuation in 1998. Brands owned by a company are intangible but can have enormous value. Imagine the value of the Coca-Cola brand name!

For some organisations, the knowledge 'owned' has become recognised as its most valuable asset and the term 'knowledge management' has entered the manager's vocabulary. A consortium of seven large companies including Unilever (foods) and ICI (chemicals) was created a few years ago to look into knowledge management and how it could be used to raise shareholder value (the current 'holy grail' of top managers). Several interesting points came out of the study (Jackson, 1998):

1 It is critical to create a culture of sharing what an organisation knows and what it does not know.
2 The more an organisation is connected the more it can meld knowledge and ideas to create breakthroughs. In Unilever, groups in a particular product area meet three or four times a year as 'communities of practice' to analyse problems and set targets.
3 Knowledge management requires activities to be underpinned with information technology, although that is only a means to an end; it is necessary to create the right climate.
4 Organisations in different sectors need different approaches to knowledge management. An organisation working at the leading edge of technology, for example in computer hardware, might employ project teams that form, act fast and then disband. In a more stable environment, more structured approaches could be sufficient.

For companies which use knowledge as a primary competitive weapon, there are implications for structure. Research continually suggests that increasing rigidity in structure tends to be associated with decreasing innovation and so, as a general rule, inflexibility should be minimised. A structure needs to allow people to share and apply knowledge and also to foster a climate in which they can air their voice and take risks. How this is achieved is less important than whether it is achieved. Managers need to look at their business, see it as unique, and impose as little rigidity of structure as is needed to make these things happen.

Network structures

All of the main structural forms described earlier in this chapter exist today with some variation, the multidivisional form being perhaps the commonest. However, it is important to recall that what really matters is the way an organisation operates, not the structure itself. With this in mind, many organisations are now tending towards a structure based on networks rather than formal divisions of inputs (multifunctional) or outputs (multidivisional) (Sullivan, 1996). Network structures reflect the way employees tend to want to manage themselves and be managed and they are, in one sense, structures catching up with the way people want to function (*see* Figure 7.9).

Main characteristics of networks

- Decentralisation of authority and responsibility
- Defined by horizontal connections between groups of equals rather than vertical connections to super-ordinates
- Tasks are broadly defined and spans of control can be large
- Boundaries between specialised departments are removed, for example, the boundaries of a marketing department would be diffuse and blurred
- Networks embody the notion of just-in-time (or real-time) decision making
- Trust and support are needed between people in different roles
- Middle management is needed only sparingly
- Networks need people who are flexible, team oriented, task focused and who are good decision makers.

Fig 7.9 Characteristics of networks

If the rhetoric is to be believed, the advantages of networks are many. They maximise the potential and freedom to react quickly to local market needs while retaining large, sometimes global, scale operations (*see* Figure 7.10). Groups (cells) of people with devolved responsibility can leverage their local skills and knowledge. Disagreement and conflict can be tackled in a more constructive, task-oriented climate, in contrast to the often territorial climate present in multidivisional or multifunctional structures.

External networks which include partnerships and alliances with customers, suppliers and technology collaborators maximise the potential for creating value added. Finally, networks tend to minimise the number of people required for management.

Tubes and tension

This case describes tensions in the structure of one part of a multi-billion pound chemicals company. The company operates three divisions producing: pharmaceuticals, agrochemicals and high value added speciality chemicals. Each division contains several discrete businesses, such as that making colours for paints or dyeing. The Specialities division makes chemicals and includes a business area called Life Science Molecules which make intermediate molecules that are bought and processed by end-users such as agrochemical producers.

Until a few years ago a separate Process Technology Department (PTD) comprising about 200 scientists and engineers supported the business areas, for example by designing a new production facility to a deadline. In the past, PTD would have delivered the facility and had little or no part in the commercial decisions behind their work. Staff in PTD were responsible to a Head of Department but that post has now been eliminated.

The way PTD now works is that its staff are clustered so that project teams work far more closely with people in the business areas. They are far more involved in decisions about the products being made and market forecasting than they were before, and this involvement influences their decisions about the support to give. In the jargon of the company, PTD is 'tubed'. This phrase describes the use of small groups who maintain very close links to their client's businesses.

Counterbalancing this is the fact that the strong identity with a client that staff in a particular 'tube' create can inhibit their interest in what PTD people are doing in other 'tubes'. There is a danger that co-operation and cross-fertilisation of ideas in process technology are neglected in favour of strong identities with clients. Thus there is a challenge for management to create an operating structure that provides for a strong client focus and which simultaneously allows PTD to develop as a scientific and engineering community.

Fig 7.10 Mini-case: Tubes and tension

Managerial implications

The past decade has seen massive restructuring of organisations under the various banners of downsizing, delayering and re-engineering. The decisions which have resulted in sometimes large-scale cutbacks in employee numbers have, arguably, denuded many organisations of knowledge and trimmed the workforce to levels that cannot always sustain the momentum of improvement needed to meet fresh environmental challenges. With this background, we can identify some current implications for management:

1. To maximise organisational performance, management must strive to match structure to the contingencies thrown up by the business environment.
2. Structural change may start a programme of corporate renewal but, by itself, will not sustain it. To sustain change and renewal, fresh attitudes and behaviours (cultural change – refer to Chapter 9) are likely to be needed.
3. Such cultural change calls for managers to identify and utilise each employee's distinctive knowledge and capabilities and to embed this knowledge in the evolving structure.
4. The drives for greater shareholder value (or 'value for money' in the public sector) create strong temptations for managers to control and closely monitor their workforce. Such control and monitoring could, however, depress innovation at the individual level, and managers must look for ways of balancing these two contrasting needs.

5 Managers need to find the appropriate balance between designing an organisational structure which appears to respond to environmental conditions and one which motivates people.

The complexity of the forces affecting structure are shown in Figure 7.11. Persistent pressure to raise performance can manifest itself in many forms. An organisation may seek to become more flexible and responsive in its operations. If performance is considered to be unsatisfactory an organisation can become a target for take-over bids by antagonistic predator companies. Improved performance may lead to growth whereas, in response to weakening profits, a company may seek to cut back some of its activities. Particular responses have implications for the skills required in the organisation, but the mix of skills and activities can influence how these specialisms need organising. From within the organisation latent forces emanating from the technologies employed may influence structural choices alongside the more explicit posturing of managers engaged in power struggles. The level of stability in the organisation's operating environment also influences structural parameters.

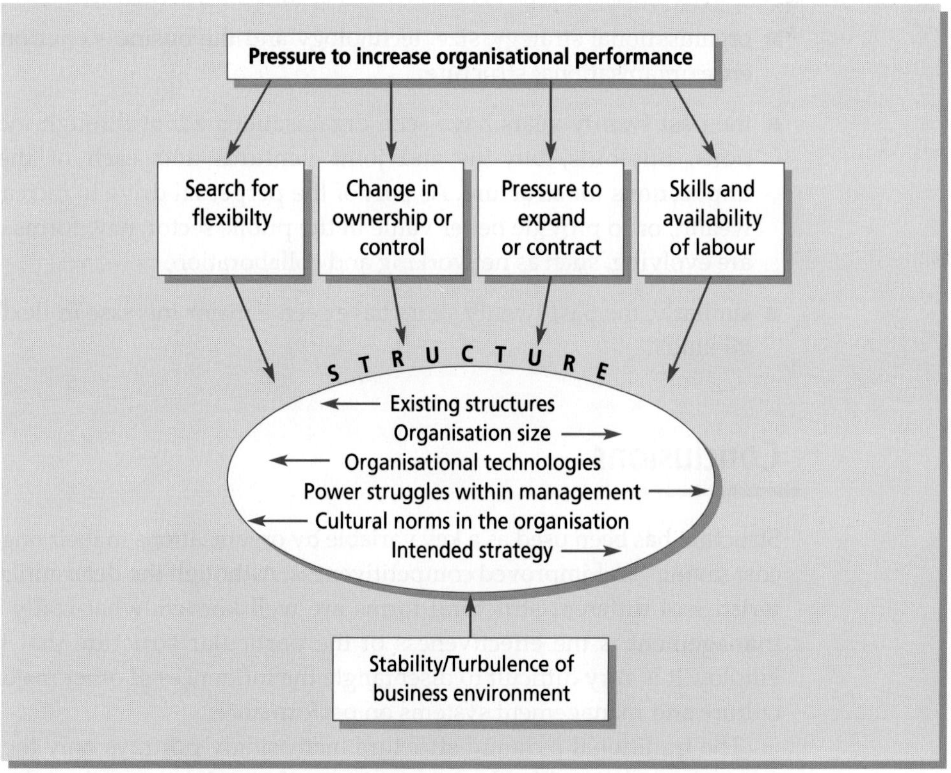

Fig 7.11 Forces influencing organisational structure

Summary of main points

The main points made are:

- most workers are employed in small and medium-sized organisations that may well produce single products for single markets with single technologies with relatively simple organisation structures;
- the prime structural forms are functional structures, multidivisional structures and matrix structures;
- recent managerial 'wisdom' encourages organisations to reduce structural bureaucracy;
- the current management buzz-words, such as re-engineering the organisation, flexibility or empowerment, do not mean that organisations no longer require or enforce strong management. Given current pressures on cost control, much energy is devoted to setting objectives, allocating resources and monitoring progress;
- organisational strategy, size, technology and the business environment all influence organisational structure;
- the past twenty years have seen organisations adapt through mergers, acquisitions, buy-outs, buy-ins and joint ventures and each of these has major implications for structure. As part of the perpetual drive to increase shareholder wealth, or to provide better value in the public sector, new forms of organisation are evolving, such as networking and collaboration;
- similarly, the past twenty years have seen a major increase in flexible working of all kinds.

Conclusions

Structure has been used as a key variable by organisations in their ongoing search for cost savings and improved competitiveness. Although the determinants and characteristics of different structural forms are well known, what really matters to top management is the effectiveness of the particular structure that they choose to employ. It is very difficult to disentangle the influences of other major variables like culture and management systems on performance.

The traditional pyramid structure increasingly portrays only the reporting and governing relationships between groups of people, rather than the way in which groups in an organisation are linked to each other and to external groups. Although we can visualise a formal structure for any organisation, an informal structure also exists but is harder to define and draw. The formal structure can influence the way an organisation implements change and the way it innovates, yet the informal structure, perhaps, has a much bigger influence. It is at this micro-level that aspects of structure can influence many important attitudes like job satisfaction, commitment and enthusiasm and positive behaviours like sharing information.

Traditionally, management has felt it has an upper hand in deciding when and how structure should be modified but, too often, managers have changed structure only in response to some crisis. The prudent manager should keep a watchful eye on structure so that structural changes are made in advance of potential crises and before too much damage is caused to the health and prosperity of an organisation.

QUESTIONS

1 From an examination of organisations in different countries, identify what forces are pulling for organisation structures to converge and what forces are acting to keep structures distinct.

2 To what extent is achieving tight control over costs and incomes compatible with achieving high levels of innovation and creativity from employees?

3 Which of the following do you think is the more likely and why?

   a That an organisation's structure influences its performance in the marketplace.
   b That an organisation's performance influences its structure.

4 What factors, originating inside and outside the organisation, will push structures towards being loose and flexible, and what factors will push structures towards being tight and rigid?

5 How might an employee's job satisfaction be influenced by:

   a his or her position in a hierarchy;
   b the span of control this person has (assuming he or she is a manager);
   c the amount of teamworking this person is involved in;
   d the size of the department in which this person works?

REFERENCES

Bierly, P. E. and Spender, J.-C. (1995) 'Culture and high reliability organizations: The case of the nuclear submarine', *Journal of Management*, 21(4), pp 639–56.

Burns, T. and Stalker, G. M. (1961) *The Management of Innovation*. London: Tavistock.

Burton, J. (1998) 'Seoul to draw up company "death list"', *Financial Times*, 18 June, p 8.

Chandler, A. (1962) *Strategy and Structure*. Cambridge, MA: MIT Press.

Chandler, A. D. (1976) 'The development of modern management structure in the US and UK' in Hannah, L. (ed.) *Management Strategy and Business Development*. London: Macmillan.

Davidow, W. H. and Malone, M. S. (1992) *The Virtual Corporation, Structuring and Revitalizing the Corporation for the 21st Century*. London: Harper Business.

Drucker, P. F. (1975) 'New templates for today's organisations' in *Harvard Business Review on Management*. New York: Harper and Row.

Ghoshal, S. and Nohria, N. (1993) 'Horses for courses: Organization forms for multinational corporations', *Sloan Management Review*, Winter, pp 23–35.

Habib, M. M. and Victor, B. (1991) 'Strategy, structure and performance of US manufacturing and service MNCs: A comparative analysis', *Strategic Management Journal*, 12(8), pp 589–606.

Hage, J. and Aiken, M. (1969) 'Routine technology, social structure and organizational goals', *Administrative Science Quarterly*, Vol. 14, pp 366–77.

Hannah, L. (1976) *Management Strategy & Business Development: An Historical and Comparative Study*. London: Macmillan.

Jackson, T. (1998) 'Melding the minds to master the intangibles', *Financial Times*, 15 June, p 15.

Lawrence, P. R. and Lorsch, J. W. (1967) *Organization and Environment*. Cambridge, MA: Harvard University Press.

Lorenz, C. (1992) 'Lean regime for a fitter future', *Financial Times*, 6 May, p 16.

Miles, R. E. and Snow, C. C. (1978) *Organisational Strategy, Structure and Process*. New York: McGraw-Hill.

Miller, C. C., Glick, W. H., Wang, Y. and Hube, G. P. (1991) 'Understanding technology structure relationships: theory development and meta analytic theory testing', *Academy of Management Journal*, June, pp 370–99.

Mintzberg, H. (1989) *Mintzberg on Management: Inside our Strange World of Organizations*. New York: Free Press.

Mintzberg, H. and Waters, J. (1985) 'Of strategies, deliberate and emergent', *Strategic Management Journal*, July/September.

Perrow, C. (1984) *Normal Accidents: Living with High Risk Technologies*. New York: Basic Books.

Perrow, C. (1967) *Organizational Analysis: A Sociological View*. London: Tavistock.

Quinn, J. B. (1992) *Intelligent Enterprise*. New York: The Free Press.

Robbins, S. R. (1993) *Organizational Behaviour*, 6th edn. Englewood Cliffs, NJ: Prentice-Hall International.

Stanworth, J. and Stanworth, C. (1992) *Telework: The Human Resource Implications*. London: IPD.

Sullivan, D. (1996) 'Multinational corporations, organization structure in' in Warner, M. (ed.) *International Encyclopedia of Business and Management*. London: Routledge.

Taylor, F. W. (1911) *The Principles of Scientific Management*. New York: Harper & Brothers.

Toffler, A. (1985) *The Adaptive Corporation*. London: Pan.

Watson, G. (1994) 'The flexible workforce and patterns of working hours in the United Kingdom', *Employment Gazette*.

Wilson, D. C. and Rosenfeld, R. H. (1990) *Managing Organisations: Text, Readings and Cases*. New York: McGraw-Hill.

Woodward, J. (1958) *Management and Technology*. London: HMSO.

FURTHER READING

Drucker, P. (1988) 'The coming of the new organization', *Harvard Business Review*, Jan–Feb, pp 45–53.

Hatch, M. J. (1997) *Organization Theory: Modern, Symbolic and Postmodern Perspectives*. Oxford: OUP, Chapter 6, 'Organizational Social Structure'.

Morgan, G. (1989) *Creative Organization Theory – a Resource Book*. Newbury Park, CA: Sage, Section 27, 'From Bureaucracies to Networks, The Emergence of New Organizational Forms'.

Sparrow, P. and Hiltrop, J. M. (1994) *European HRM in Transition*. Hemel Hempstead: Prentice-Hall International, Chapter 8, 'Structuring the Organization'.

8

Organisational power, politics and conflict

LEARNING OUTCOMES

On completion of this chapter you should be able to:

- examine the unitary, pluralist and radical perspectives and understand the rational and political models of organisation;
- appreciate the nature of organisations as conflictual political entities;
- explain the meaning of organisational power, politics and conflict;
- identify the different sources and bases of power;
- discuss the links between power, conflict and politics;
- define and understand the concept of powerlessness;
- recognise the power of symbol manipulation and of cultural unity and disunity;
- understand the influence of power and powerlessness in organisational change;
- understand the effect of power and politics on organisational conflict.

KEY CONCEPTS

- *organisation as a political system*
- *organisation as a rational system*
- *unitary, pluralist and radical frames*
- *power bases*
- *covert power*
- *powerlessness*
- *empowerment*
- *organisational politics*
- *interdepartmental conflict*
- *intercultural conflict*
- *symbolism and power*
- *resistance/negative power*

Organisational power, politics and conflict

Power, politics and conflict are often considered as part of the less desirable, more covert, aspects of organisation, yet all are 'real' and endemic to organisations. They fundamentally influence the behaviour of individuals and groups and play an important role in the decision making and problem-solving activities of organisations. As organisational realities they have stimulated considerable research and debate – which this chapter will explore. We will also relate power and politics to the themes of this book, most notably to conflict and to organisational change.

Introduction

There are few aspects of organisational behaviour which, for the inexperienced, appear more mystifying, difficult to appreciate and impossible to manage than power and organisational politics. This chapter explores the political perspective, defines and examines power, politics and conflict in an organisational context and discusses the implications of power and politics for change.

The political perspective

It is possible, and potentially fruitful, to view organisations as if they were political systems, that is, from a political perspective. We explored, in Chapter 5, the use of perspectives or frames with which to analyse organisations. From this perspective concepts such as power, politics, conflict and control are viewed as natural commonplace aspects of organisational reality. Nevertheless, there are alternative frames or perspectives which provide a useful insight. We now examine two contrasting models of organisation, the rational and the political, together with three frames for analysing conflict, the unitary, pluralist and radical perspectives.

If we view organisations as rational bodies, we would consider human behaviour to be based on logic and directed by clear objectives and informed by access to, and assimilation of, perfect information. Nothing is irrational or non-rational, little is random or accidental. The decision process creates and supports clear goals. Decision making is rational: the problem is clearly articulated, alternative solutions are generated, decision parameters which enable choice to be made are known, and alternatives are fully evaluated before the best decision is made. There is an absence of power, politics, conflict and other sources of potential non-rationality or, if present, they do not influence decision making. Decisions always result in optimisation (the best solution is chosen and implemented), organisational members share common values and goals and efficiency is stressed.

An alternative view is that organisations are political entities comprising coalitions that have divergent interests and disagree about goals. Information is not perfect but is, instead, partial and unevenly accessible. What is more, it is open to manipulation and multiple interpretation. Disagreement, tension and conflict are inevitable, with the result that power is required to resolve conflict. Decision making, influenced by differential power, is often non-rational.

It could be considered that in their extremes these two models represent two ends of a continuum and that 'reality' may reside somewhere in between. Organisations that are characterised by complete rationality cannot, in the author's opinion, exist – as human attributes deny this possibility. Similarly, organisations that fully embrace political activity, individual values and differences in goals will prove so dysfunctional as to find survival difficult.

An alternative, although in some ways similar, approach, is to consider organisations from three perspectives or frames: the unitary, the pluralist and the radical frame. This derives from the work of Robbins (1974) and Fox (1975). Each represents a frame of analysis, a way of examining and interpreting organisational activity and, more specifically, for exploring organisational conflict. The *unitary view* suggests that organisations have goals to which all subscribe and that there is a collective understanding of appropriate ways of pursuing those goals. This traditional view was reinforced as a result of the work of the human relations school (*see* Chapter 5). Academics contributing to this view (in the period from the 1930s to the 1960s although much current management writing implies much the same) argued that conflict and instability in organisations were the result of lack of trust and openness and could be resolved by adoption of a people orientation and by communicating freely. Establishing and embedding shared goals would deny conflict its inspiration.

The *pluralist view*, on the other hand, recognises differences in goals, interests and ambitions and concedes that multiple realities exist. Attempts to forge a coalition of these divergent interests becomes a management priority. Conflict is inevitable and endemic. It is a natural phenomenon which cannot be eliminated. This state mirrors the political perspective noted above. As a consequence, conflict cannot be viewed as wholly undesirable, as it would be under the unitary frame, especially as it provides a mechanism for evolutionary change and keeps the organisation responsive to internal and external changes. Within this frame, the manager's role is to manage these divergent interest groups and to achieve compromise and collaboration between stakeholders. There remains an underlying belief that conflict can be resolved and managed.

The *radical view*, influenced by Marxism, suggests that there are fundamental and powerful social/structural and political divisions in society which make coalition impossible and conflict inevitable. Figure 8.1 illustrates the differences between the three frames. These three frames provide a useful basis for analysing organisational conflict. In some organisations, many employees appear to pursue similar objectives whereas in others considerable and ongoing tension exists between different parties. Other things being equal, when an organisation has limited and clear goals, a stable and predictable environment, an empowered staff and a teamworking ethos, conflict may be less apparent than in one where hierarchy and other structural divisions are entrenched, power is fought over, there are multiple and unclear goals and the environment is complex and dynamic.

Morgan (1996: 201) suggests that each frame leads to a different approach to management. He argues, for example, that 'if one believes that one is managing a team, one tends to expect and demand that people rally around common objectives'. Unitary managers cannot sanction conflict and political activity, only legitimate power sources. Pluralist managers, on the other hand, accept the inevitability of conflicts in interest and complex power sources. Their role is to balance this diversity and to work, wherever possible, within the constraints set by organisational goals. Having established these frameworks we will now examine organisational power.

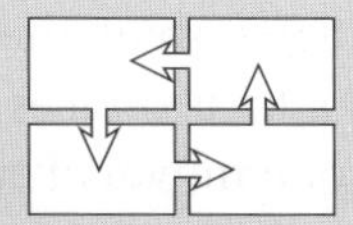

Unitarist
Each organisation has its own single common objective.

This requires acceptance of organisational structures and authority.

Conflict shouldn't be an issue.

Pluralist
Many different stakeholders, with different objectives.

Agreements reached to achieve compromises with the aim of maintaining a balance.

Conflicts are temporary breakdowns.

Radicalism/Class conflict
A constant struggle between owners of the means of production and the labour supply.

Each side attempts to maximise its position and strength in the economy.

Conflict is inevitable.

Fig 8.1 Unitarist, pluralist and radical frames

Organisational power

Robbins (1984: 155) defines power as '*a capacity that A has to influence the behaviour of B, so that B does something he or she would not otherwise do*'. The key word here is 'influence', although it is merely a potential that need not be acted upon. If we assume that conflicts of interest exist in organisations, as in any human community, then power, as Morgan (1996) suggests, is the medium through which such conflicts are resolved. In organisations power is thought to derive from numerous sources. The early work of French and Raven (1959) shed light on this and established that it is neither possessed nor used equally by different individuals and groups.

Sources of power

French and Raven

French and Raven (1959) identified five sources of power:

1 *Coercive power* depends on fear and, in 'carrot and stick' terms, it represents the stick, or sanction and in its extreme it might involve physical abuse. It is unequivocal and the receiver is unlikely to be pleased if this form of power is applied. Compliance may be an immediate response but longer-term commitment is highly unlikely to result.

2 *Reward power* represents the 'carrot', the incentive to behave in a particular manner. It is the power that is derived from an individual's or group's possession and control over organisational resources. People may comply if they consider the

resultant benefit to be of value. Hence, in the workplace rewards are often 'used' to exert power over subordinates. In a positive fashion these include the prospect of salary increases, bonuses, certain perks or promises of promotion or, in a negative sense, they can involve the threat of removal of current or expected benefits. It is scarcity of resources which creates potential for them to be used as a power source. In turn, their use may create dependence.

3. *Expert power* refers to influence that is acquired by possessing special skills or knowledge. This may, for example, apply to individuals with superior technical skills and may not necessarily relate to their position in a formal hierarchy. A useful example is that provided by the internal IT technician whose rapid response to 'call-out' is highly cherished. The relative ignorance of the user, often a far more senior employee, provides the technician with an ongoing source of power which can be exercised by altering the speed of response and quality of service given.
4. *Legitimate or position power* refers to that derived from holding a formal position in an organisation. In bureaucracies, or in the military services, position power is particularly important, as rank is considered of significance. Weber (1947) referred to a similar concept as 'rational-legal authority'. Its legitimacy derives from social approval, and it provides a mechanism for order and the stabilisation of power relations. The trade union movement has traditionally acted as a counter-force to position power. Power at the top of the hierarchy is countered by collective action among those who individually lack power at the lower end. Morgan (1996: 173) notes that 'to the extent that trade union power is legitimized by the rule of law and the right to unionise, it too represents a type of formal authority'.
5. *Referent power* is derived from one's admiration or respect for an individual. Charisma, meaning 'gift of grace', can inspire followers, thus enabling leaders to exert power over subordinates, a fact recognised by Weber (1947) who referred to this as 'charismatic authority' (*see* Chapter 6).

This early work has been further developed. Robbins (1984) distinguishes between the sources of power and the means to exert influence, which he refers to as the 'bases of power'. For example, both position in the hierarchy and an individual's expertise are sources of power, whereas persuasion, knowledge and reward are tools or bases of power. The bureaucrat, holding position power, will have recourse to an array of rules and procedures to enforce or maintain position power. A bully relies on physical presence, the threat of violence or actual physical force. The manager holding reward power will use the principle of exchange in order to exert influence. These are the bases or tools used to exert power. Figure 8.2 illustrates the difference between the sources of power and the tools or mechanisms used to exert that power.

Morgan (1996) noted further sources of power (*see* Figure 8.3) although the items listed include both sources and bases of power. Many of these are consistent with those identified by French and Raven (1959), although some variation and additional elements are included. We will briefly examine the sources of power gained from: (a) the control of knowledge and information, (b) the control of boundaries and (c) interpersonal alliances and control of the informal organisation.

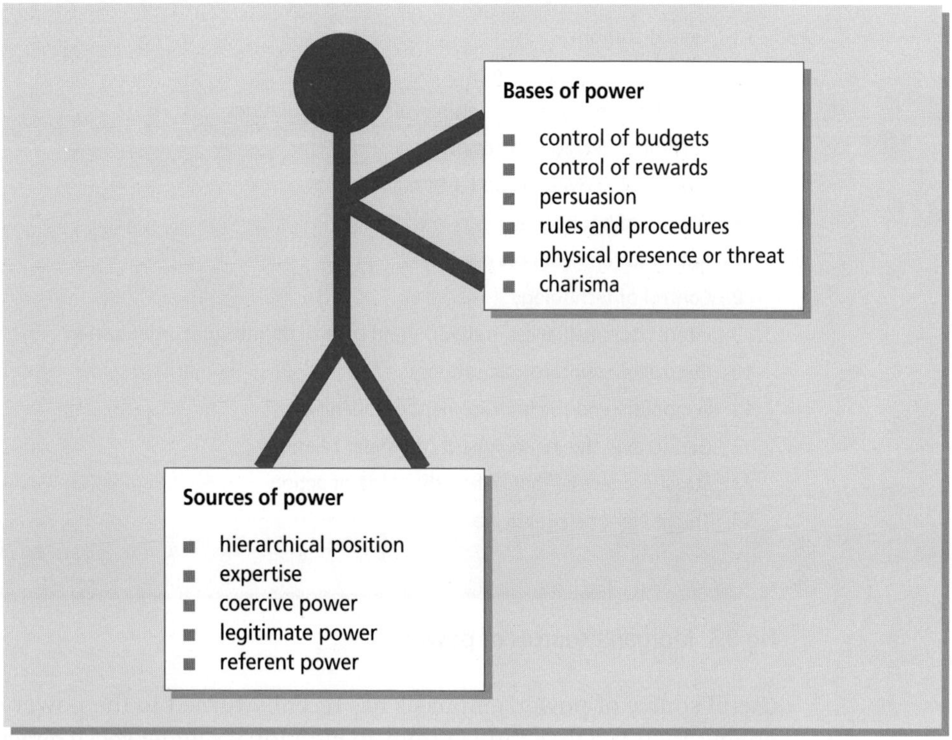

Fig 8.2 The sources and bases of power

The ability to control information and knowledge in an organisation is, in part, related to the position held by an individual or group. By choosing to control the timing, destination and 'quality' of information it is possible to define or influence the organisational agenda and create dependencies. For example, the Labour Government of the late 1990s 'employed' a number of media and information managers, at very high levels (in the cabinet), in order to control and influence government news (to put the government 'spin' on things). The 'gatekeeper' role in organisations is a critical source of power manipulation. Information can be screened to ensure that it complies with or supports the accepted world-view and dissenting and potentially dangerous information can be suppressed or altered. Modern technology has increased the potential for information control and centralisation. Systems now enable managers to monitor and review operations, progress and targets from afar. In national politics it is no wonder that major modern political parties pay a great deal of attention to information management. Technology has radically altered the potential for control and manipulation in this regard.

Modern organisational configurations stress collaboration between functions, units and organisations in the creation of wealth. Control of these boundaries, facilitated by extensive networking, control of information and systems or specialised knowledge, can enable individuals or groups to amass considerable power. Whereas it has long been understood that belonging to the 'old school tie' network proved a

1 Formal authority
2 Control of scarce resources
3 Use of organisational structure, rules and regulations
4 Control of decision processes
5 Control of knowledge and information
6 Control of boundaries
7 Ability to cope with uncertainty
8 Control of technology
9 Interpersonal alliances, networks and control of 'informal organisation'
10 Control of counterorganisations
11 Symbolism and the management of meaning
12 Gender and the management of gender relations
13 Structural factors that define the stage of action
14 The power one already has

Source: Based on Morgan (1986).

Fig 8.3 Morgan's sources of power

useful source of power, emphasis has recently turned to the power of the informal organisation and that derived from an individual's wider social network. The skilled organisational politician constructs a network of informal allies and builds mutually supportive relationships. This can be used just as effectively to pacify potential enemies as to woo collaborators. This network, with the skilled politician at its centre, can be used to inform the manager of events throughout the organisation. By more overt means, such as placing of managers in strategic positions in an organisation, a senior manager can gain power by being well informed, gaining access to numerous sub-networks and creating many dependencies on him or herself. Patronage has long existed, probably having been an endemic characteristic of human organisation since the advent of man.

Three aspects of power are worthy of further discussion. First, negative power is a form of illegitimate influence which can be used to disrupt or to resist. This is of particular significance to the management of organisational change. Second, powerlessness, *a state where an individual or group has, or considers themselves to have, no power to influence a situation,* is further debated below. Third, power can be exerted in a highly covert, or invisible, form. These three are discussed, where appropriate, in this chapter.

Covert power

Power can be either transparent or invisible and covert. For example, as discussed above, many managers are thought to control information, to accelerate or slow down its dissemination. Many staff, especially in traditional organisations, do not have access to certain information. When access is denied, power is being exerted.

Similarly, by exercising control of budgets, managers can exert influence in an 'invisible' manner, with few, if any, colleagues recognising the 'political' decisions that are being taken. Covert power can be used to control decision agendas. Power influences what actually appears on the agenda of a group. Conversely, power can be exerted openly, for example by giving a clear verbal or written order or instruction to a subordinate, or symbolised openly, such as when the Chief Executive parks his or her expensive new car in a named/allocated parking slot.

Covert power can be used negatively or to resist. For example, the Hawthorne experiments (referred to in Chapter 5) recognised that workers can determine the pace at which production occurs; they can increase or slow the rate of work while still giving the impression of being busy. This represents the exercise of power, covertly but by 'agreement'. Often, as we shall see, there is a form of individual and/or collective resistance to attempts to force the pace of organisational change. Subordinates do not often openly refuse to comply but instead pay lip-service to new ideas, sometimes go along with them without being convinced, or concerned, about their merit and, at most, temporarily change their overt behaviour. This represents the exercise of covert power.

Interdepartmental power

The sources and uses of power at the level of the group or organisational department are of value in the study of organisational behaviour. They shed light on organisational activity, structural configuration and power issues, not at the level of the individual but horizontally between departments or functions within organisations. Saunders (1990) and others suggest that power at departmental level derives from five potential sources (*see* Figure 8.4). It is possible that these power sources may overlap. They are as follows:

1 *Dependency* – when Department A depends on Department B for information or other co-operation in order to conduct its own tasks and to be effective, Department B has a source of power *vis-à-vis* Department A. For example, if the Information Technology department in a university largely controls the IT budget, all other departments are reliant upon this department and, rather like a monopoly, it has little incentive to provide a highly responsive service.

2 *Centrality* – this is a measure of the importance of the department's work to the prime goals of the organisation. Alternatively it could be considered as a measure of how dispensable the department is to the organisation. For example, the provision of food and refreshments to employees of a typical service or manufacturing organisation can be, and increasingly is, provided by outside organisations. Catering is not central to a car manufacturer, with the result that the power a catering department holds in that situation is small. Few departments are significantly dependent on this service function.

3 *Financial resources* – clearly departments that generate their own financial resources, particularly if they provide excess income, will (other things being

equal) benefit from this source of power. Conversely, departments which earn a low income may be dependent (*see* above) on other departments. Centralisation of resources can reduce interdepartmental differences, although this clearly makes the centre or HQ the source of power in this regard and, as a consequence, disempowers all departments.

4 *Non-sustainability* – this relates to the issue of centrality. Sustainability is a measure of how easy it would be for the department's function to be performed by others. For example, in the motor manufacturing example given above, whereas the production department of a car manufacturer would not wish to assume catering responsibilities it is straightforward for it to contract out such services, as a highly competitive contract catering market exists in most modern economies. It is less easy, although not impossible, to contemplate a motor manufacturer dispensing with its production capability. A company with a brand name of repute could, conceivably, contract out its production and instead focus on design and brand marketing.
5 *Coping with uncertainty* – departments that have the ability to reduce the uncertainty for others will gain power. For example, the uncertainty created by technological developments can earn the technology or IT department a valuable source of power. It can, if it wishes, cushion other departments from the realities and uncertainties of technological advance.

As a result of this work, it is possible to analyse departmental power sources in any organisation and attempt to assess the relative power each department might

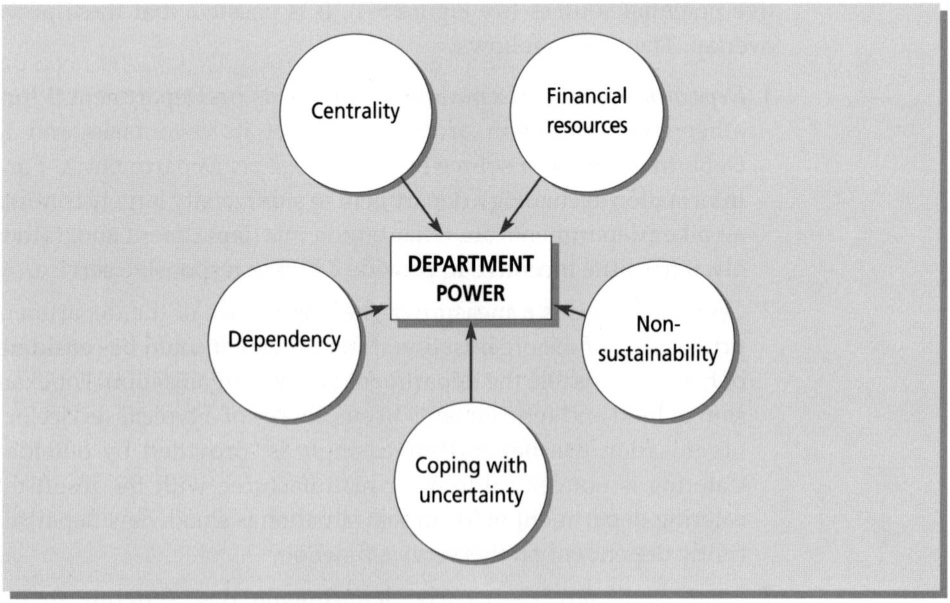

Fig 8.4 Horizontal, interdepartmental power sources

yield. Alternatively this model can be used as a management tool for departmental managers to attempt to increase their power by attempting to build or acquire these power sources.

Culture, symbolism and power

Symbolism

Handy's (1994) four dimensions of power, decision making, non-decision making, power of the system and symbolic power, embrace the cultural or symbolic aspects of organisation. *A symbol, tangible or otherwise, carries meaning which stands for something other than itself.* More obvious organisational symbols include company logos or mottoes, the buildings and works of art that adorn organisations, the use of space in buildings, the type of furnishings and so forth. Less tangible symbols include the tremendous power of language – including the use of imagery and metaphor. All of these, consciously or otherwise, carry meaning, they say something about the organisation. For example hierarchy is, in many organisations, reinforced by symbols. Senior managers often have large offices, are supported by secretaries, have superior quality furnishings and a larger company car than those of their subordinates.

Manipulation of symbols is an expression of power: successful manipulation can create new or reinforce existing power positions and shape the organisational environment in favour of the powerful. It can create meaning – which is a vital ingredient, if not the essential essence, of leadership. Leaders assist in defining situations and in forging new meanings for employees. They use symbols in the process. Chapter 9 explores, in some detail, the use of symbolism in organisations.

Subcultural power and intercultural conflict

In order to maintain collective understanding and unity it is necessary for subcultures to devise initial socialisation processes and ongoing mechanisms which induct and continually forge individuals into the group. Collective behaviours, norms and values are essential qualities of a subculture. Collectiveness better ensures a basis for power. Disparate individuals, whether in the workplace or in wider society, lack power. Collectively, as in a culture or subculture, they, 'speak with one voice', develop a distinctive social identity and, potentially, tap into the sources of power needed to enhance their socioeconomic status.

Rather like the conflicts that exist between departments in any organisation, friction is commonplace between different organisational subcultures. The concept of a subculture is discussed further in Chapter 9. The mini-case presented in Figure 8.5 illustrates the power conflicts that exist between subcultures in the health service. Subcultures in organisations, such as doctors or nurses or managers in a typical hospital, engage in ritual activities in order to enhance their cultural identity and preserve their standing. This is also true of many professional groups, such as accountants, solicitors and teachers. Each has exacting examinations and educational requirements which must be met before individuals are allowed to 'join' and each has a formal or implicit code of practice. Many subcultural groups seek the same, or

Subcultural power: health care

There are few organisations where differences between definable groups are more strongly evidenced than in the National Health Service (NHS) in the UK, Europe's largest employing organisation. Despite the claims that medical personnel work as a care team to ensure quality patient care, numerous subcultures exist and strive for power. A complex 'pecking order' ensures that each group struggles to maintain or enhance its power base.

In a typical hospital ward, for example, there are cleaners or domestics, ward clerks, assistant nurses, staff nurses, sisters, junior doctors, registrars and consultants. Additionally, patients on that ward are often visited by physiotherapists and radiologists, to name just two of the many professions allied to medicine (PAMS), and rely on pharmacists and numerous specialists to ensure recovery and quality treatment. Each of these groups represents a subculture in the broader hospital culture or medical community. Power differentials exist and are often obvious. These differentials are based on many of the sources of power discussed above, such as access to resources, expertise, legitimate power, access to information and to networks and coalition building. Even in one group, such as qualified staff nurses or doctors, microlevel subcultures exist. For example, permanent night nurses do not enjoy the same recognition (of their skills and expertise) as their day colleagues and, hence, are relatively powerless. When attempts are made to introduce annualised contracts and internal day–night rotation on wards, night nurses are relatively powerless to stop this trend.

Of additional interest is the complexity of power interdependencies in NHS hospitals and the role and power position of managers and managerialism. Managerialism has been promoted by government-inspired reforms of the 1980s and 1990s. Management has enhanced its power *vis-à-vis* most other groups, with the result that managerial pay, particularly at senior levels, has increased more rapidly than that of, for example, nurses (a relatively powerless group) and their influence has increased significantly. Nurses have attempted to address this position by union or association action (e.g. by Unison and/or the Royal College of Nursing) although a shortage of nurses in 1998 and beyond may increase the power of this group as their expertise becomes in short supply. Many subcultures gain power by making others dependent on them. In modern hospitals, managers control most of the resources: this better ensures that the dependencies which occur are controlled by management.

Rituals, medical jargon and precedent are all used to hold on to power and to reinforce existing social divisions. Only certain grades of personnel or those holding particular qualifications, are allowed to conduct certain tasks. Demarcation between groups, even when there is little or no rational reason for it, is strong and pervasive. Attempts to remove differences are fraught with difficulties. For example, a recent attempt at a Midlands hospital to issue identical uniforms and to unify pay levels for ward-based domestics, ward clerks and unqualified assistant nurses was greeted with considerable opposition, particularly from ward clerks, who consider the clerical responsibilities they hold to be greater than the domestic responsibilities of cleaners. The uniform symbolised that change and although the staff chose the actual uniform it was almost universally disliked (except by many of the ex-domestics who were net gainers in the change).

Discussion question

How do doctors and consultants preserve their power?

Fig 8.5 Mini-case: Subcultures and power imbalances in the National Health Service

similar, sources of power as identified above. Hence, in the National Health Service in the UK there is a constant, ongoing, struggle for power between managers and medical personnel. Managers draw on considerable position or legitimate power and, notably, usually have control over resource allocation (reward power). The expertise of medical personnel is their prime source of power. The more formal sources, reward and position, appeared to be in the ascendancy during the 1980s and 1990s.

Other subcultural groups preserve their power by creating scarcity and restricted access to their expertise. The Chartered Institute of Accountants, for example, alters the pass mark in its entry examinations in order to protect against an oversupply of accountants in the marketplace. The resultant scarcity increases accountants' power to negotiate favourable terms for their services.

Powerlessness

Powerlessness, a real or perceived state of having little or no power, is an organisational reality for many. A feeling that one has little control over organisational decisions, particularly those that affect one's work life, is commonplace among some people. It may be considered to be a relative concept: if A has less power than B then A may well feel powerless. Ironically, many employees, whatever their rank or role, express feelings of powerlessness from time to time. Even senior managers, who recognise that their organisation is more powerful than any individual within it, or who believe that the environment in which they operate is determined for them, express concern over their perceived lack of power to influence matters.

What distinguishes management from other professions in this regard is dependence. Dependence is a potential trap. Managers direct activities and give orders: these need to be obeyed for power to be exercised. If subordinates do not obey they are withholding compliance and utilising their power to resist and to reinforce mutual dependence. As a result, the credibility of managers is under constant threat. Managers cannot control everything: they do not possess all the information and skills they require to manage successfully and they have many interested parties, or multiple stakeholders, to satisfy. It is not surprising, therefore, that reference has been made to 'the paradox of power' (Calabria, 1982), where the powerful are powerless.

There are, of course, many employees who do not possess the sources of power referred to by French and Raven (1959) or Morgan (1996). Additionally, others feel that they are not supported in what they are trying to do and are isolated and criticised. These employees may be considered to be genuinely powerless. Some, however, harbour little concern about this. Clearly, the salience of an individual's feeling of powerlessness is, in part, a product of the strength of that person's need to be empowered. 'Perceived' powerlessness is, therefore, a function of:

- the strength of an individual's desire or need to hold power (Np); and
- the perceived power of players within the individual's working environment *vis-à-vis* their own power, that is, perceived relative power (Rp).

'Real' powerlessness is a function of:

- the relative strength of an individual's sources and bases of power (Sp).

If we were to consider individual need, perception, context and 'genuine' sources and bases of power, then powerlessness might be thought to be a function of Np, Rp and Sp.

Powerlessness can operate at the collective or group level. Some groups of employees, for instance women, first-line supervisors, some ethnic minorities and disabled people, often consider themselves to be relatively powerless. A collective expression of powerlessness can manifest itself in a variety of ways, not least in trade union activity, pressure group lobbying (e.g., for equal opportunity legislation), collective frustration and low morale and even partial exclusion from the workplace.

Powerlessness in the workplace serves little purpose. Individuals often retrench and become frustrated and disenchanted. They may lose confidence and, curiously, shun responsibility. They may create real or artificial boundaries between themselves and others. Concerned with 'turf' issues and resistant to change which they perceive will further erode their limited power, they can detract from an organisation's attempt to become dynamic and flexible. The solution, many argue, is to empower staff.

Empowerment

In Chapters 5 and 7 we noted that vertical hierarchy and centralisation of power were and, to a large extent, still are the norm in organisations. There is, however, a move towards the development and acceptance of flatter hierarchies and greater devolved power. This manifests itself in the development of self-managed teams (*see* Chapter 4), organic structures, reduced layers of hierarchy, and devolved budgetary control and decision making. *Empowerment occurs where authority to make decisions and to resolve organisational problems is delegated to subordinates.* It is believed that giving power to those doing the work of the organisation should improve flexibility, speed of decision making and the motivation of staff.

Conger and Kanungo's (1988) research indicates that an individual's need for *self-efficacy, a desire to produce results or outcomes*, is better satisfied as a result of empowerment. They argue that motivation is boosted as a result of improvements in the individual's effectiveness and the individual's ability to choose how to complete the task using his or her creative skills (*see* the discussion of intrinsic rewards and needs theories in Chapter 3). The reward resulting from personal control and real or perceived effectiveness in turn improves motivation. A virtuous circle of involvement, effectiveness and motivation is apparent.

Tannenbaum and Cooke (1980) argue that empowerment actually increases the total amount of power, presumably power to do good, in an organisation. The implicit suggestion is that power is not a zero-sum game, but that it grows through empowerment. Senior managers gain power because of the resultant increases in morale, flexibility and productivity whereas subordinates gain the power and authority to make decisions and to act autonomously. There is a degree of intuitive logic to this assumption. However, as many managers will note, increased autonomy, expertise and authority at lower levels can and do make some middle and senior managers redundant, metaphorically and literally: positive for the organisation, potentially disastrous for the individual. For this and other reasons, such as a lack of trust or faith in subordinates' ability, many managers are reluctant to empower their employees.

Daft (1992) outlined the management of the empowerment process (*see* Figure 8.6). In his model, the first stage involves the diagnosis of organisational impediments to empowerment. These might include excessive rules, inflexible systems or procedures, too narrowly defined tasks and reward structures that ignore innovation. A clear vision and rationale for change needs to be communicated from senior managers. The stifling aspects of job design and organisational structure need to be changed. Empowering job design features, such as those discussed in Chapters 3 and 5, will need to be considered and implemented, where rules and procedures need to be reviewed, relaxed and often removed. Additionally, structured change, for example to reduce levels of hierarchy and improve communication, may need to be implemented. Both during the process of change and when staff are empowered, regular constructive feedback between managers and employees is essential.

Since empowerment is often viewed as a necessary prerequisite for organisational flexibility, innovation and change, it appears likely that measures to devolve authority further in organisations will continue.

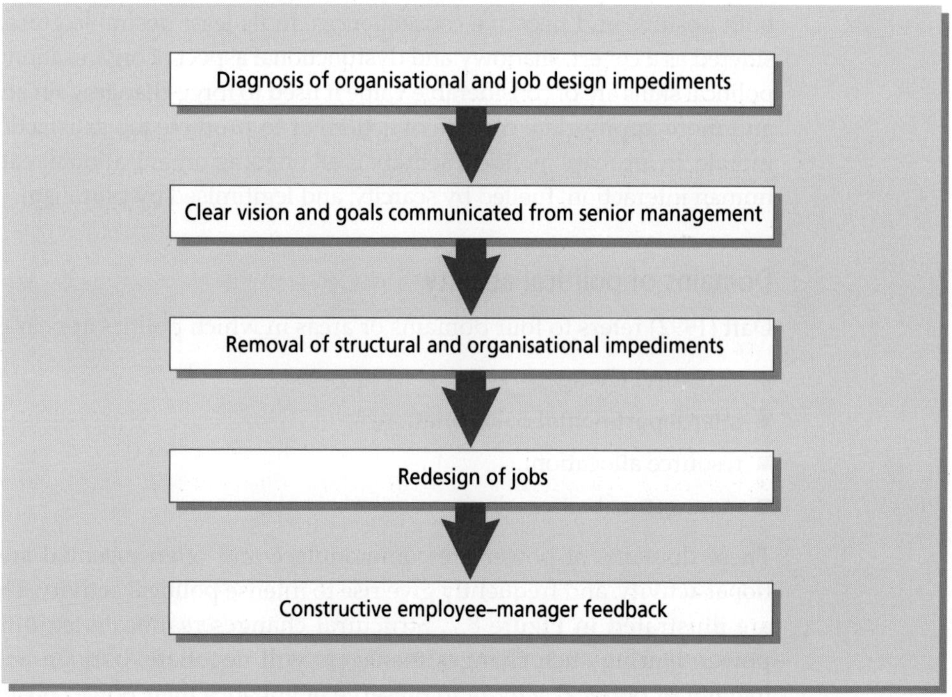

Fig 8.6 Managing the empowerment process

Organisational politics

Conflict, power and politics are closely related organisational realities. Conflict, for example, can arise as a consequence of power differentials and political activity and, in turn, can necessitate the use of power and political skills to help resolve or manage actual or potential conflicts. Hence, *politics can be considered to be a 'process of bargaining and negotiation that is used to overcome conflicts and differences of opinion'* (Daft, 1992: 403). An alternative definition of politics incorporates *the more sinister and self-serving activity that is not sanctioned by the organisation and which can increase the potential for conflict and friction.*

Political activity in organisations results from the conversion of power into action. It is the consequence of the diversity of interests that exists in most human communities and, more directly, from attempts to use power to affect organisational decision making or from activities which are self serving and not organisationally sanctioned. It cannot be assumed that the amount of power held by an individual or group is directly related to their ability to exert influence. Political activity acts as a mediator and is omnipresent and endemic in organisations. It is both the lubricant and the glue which simultaneously frees and binds the organisational machine: it can and does have both positive and negative consequences. In its least desirable guise, politics is considered as a covert, shadowy and dysfunctional aspect of organisation; yet, conversely, political skills are of considerable value if used to forge change, gain acceptance of new and more appropriate courses of action, or to promote job satisfaction and improve morale. In any case, political activity is an ongoing organisational reality, a product of human interaction, fuelled by scarcity, and legitimised by pluralism.

Domains of political activity

Daft (1992) refers to four domains or areas in which politics appear endemic:

- structural change;
- interdepartmental co-ordination;
- resource allocation;
- management succession.

These domains of power are commonplace and often essential areas of organisational activity, and frequently give rise to intense political activity. The four domains are illustrated in Figure 8.7. Structural changes reallocate legitimate or position power. During such changes managers will negotiate, bargain and engage in all manner of political activity to preserve or enhance their power position. As a result, power and political skills are required to manage such change. Interdepartmental co-ordination, Daft (1992) argues, lacks rules and precedents. The resultant conflicts over issues of territory and responsibility require political activities to be resolved. Often, at the level of the individual, succession is a contentious issue. Promotion criteria are often opaque and open to interpretation and misinterpretation. Networks,

Structural change	Interdepartmental co-ordination
Management succession	Resource allocation

Fig 8.7 Domains of political activity

formal and otherwise, alliances and enmities all play a part in creating tension and conflict between parties. Finally, resource-allocation decisions enhance or reduce power bases and the ability of individuals or groups to wield resource power. Budgeting is an intensely political activity, itself requiring sound political skills to manage in order to avoid or suppress dysfunctional conflict.

No human activity is entirely devoid of political activity if we assume that the pluralistic frame, outlined above, approximates reality. The mini-case presented in Figure 8.8 illustrates that point.

Organisational conflict

Conflict is apparent when at least one party perceives that it exists and where an interest or concern of that party is about to be or has been compromised or frustrated. Conflict occurs between individuals, groups and departments: it is, therefore, both an intra- and an inter-group reality. Conflict is common between individuals in the same department or group, between employees at different levels of the organisation, between those with different roles and responsibilities or between otherwise close colleagues. Similarly, conflict can and does occur between workers, often represented by trade unions, and managers, between designers and production managers, between accountants and marketers and so forth. Some conflicts are stimulated by deep-seated fundamental differences, which might be ingrained in the broader society or the context in which the organisation operates. At the other extreme, some conflicts are ephemeral, of immediate concern and often easily and quickly resolved.

Whereas the level of conflict differs between organisations, because of different ways of organising or different cultural norms, some conflict is inevitable (a view consistent with the pluralist perception of organisation). It is a result of interaction in the organisation between individuals and groups: interaction is an organisational necessity (it would not be an 'organisation' without it).

It can be argued that organisations encourage conflict as they both seek collaboration and create internal competition. Organisational hierarchy is a transparent example of this; however, competition between departments for resources, as discussed above, is equally institutionalised.

Politics and sport

It is often suggested that there is no room for politics in sport. However, the two are frequently linked at a variety of levels. At a macro or international level, the political activities of governments frequently influence sporting activity, or inactivity, in their country. For example, in South Africa during the 1970s and 1980s the extreme activities of the apartheid regime ensured that world condemnation of their policies meant that economic, political and social sanctions were enforced. Most sporting links between South Africa and the rest of the world were severed: a bitter blow to the sport-enthusiastic South Africans. Hence, the Springbok rugby team, the South African cricketers and many individual sportsmen and women could not compete at international level. In broad terms the sanctions were successful in bringing pressure to bear on the regime in power. There have also been occasions when national governments have withdrawn or restricted the activities of their own teams in protest against political decisions of others.

However, it is not just at this level that politics impinge on sport. All sports teams, sporting associations and individual clubs are, like organisations, political entities. A football team, for example, has all the ingredients for political activity. Resources are scarce, competition is rife, many individuals and groups have collective and individual representatives, they are in the public domain and the customers often feel passionate about their performance. Football abounds with clichés which symbolise control or the subversion of individualism: they are 'political' clichés. Hence, we are frequently reminded that 'no player is bigger than the team', representing an attempt by management to control staff by bringing collective pressures to bear. Players are 'only as good as their last match', again a political interchange between management and players. Players frequently 'do not fit in with the style of play', often a euphemism for backroom conflict that has occurred. Managerial and boardroom rows figure in the folklore of many teams. Doug Ellis at Aston Villa, for example, draws on a variety of power sources and maintains close control over managers and, hence, players. Ken Bates, the Chairman of Chelsea, sacked Rud Hulit as manager and appointed Vialli (who had been omitted from the Chelsea team for much of the year by Hulit). The media announcement was the end of a lengthy political process and a demonstration of the power of the Chairman. It is said that 'the Chairman can pick the team', not usually in a direct sense, but by bringing political pressures to bear on the managers and coaches to better ensure his wishes are upheld.

Finally, the World Cup in France in 1998 was not merely noted for its quality football but also for the manner in which certain officials, most notably Michael Platini, influenced the standards of refereeing by publicly suggesting that they need to be tougher on professional fouls and other infringements. It was suggested that referees who did not 'get tough' would not be invited to officiate at further games. The result was an escalation in the number of players booked and sent off.

Fig 8.8 Politics of sport

The causes of conflict are many and varied (*see* Figure 8.9). They include the following:

1 Differences in status, often created by legitimate or hierarchical power differentials, create barriers to communications, foster feelings of inequity and cause consequent friction which can lead to ambiguity and confusion over responsibilities.

2 Scarcity of resources, such as promotion prospects, bonus payments and departmental budgets, creates competition which often escalates into conflict.

3 Complex organisational structures or configurations frequently make one group, or individual, dependent on another: in this case conflict may occur between the parties, if only as a result of different priorities.

4 Quite often the objectives and tasks of individuals and groups can directly conflict with one another in the same organisation: a zero-sum game might apply where A's gain is B's loss.

5 Differences of opinion and of influence create friction and win–lose situations.

6 Cultural differences were discussed above: conflicts occur between cultures or subcultures within organisations, largely as a result of a combination of the factors outlined above. Such conflicts in the NHS have been referred to as 'tribalism'.

7 Dynamism in the environment, and consequent organisational responses, can create friction between individuals and groups. Change disrupts existing patterns of resource allocation and stable structural relationships. It often creates scope for 'winners' and 'losers': opportunities for growth and development for some and loss of scope, esteem and power for others.

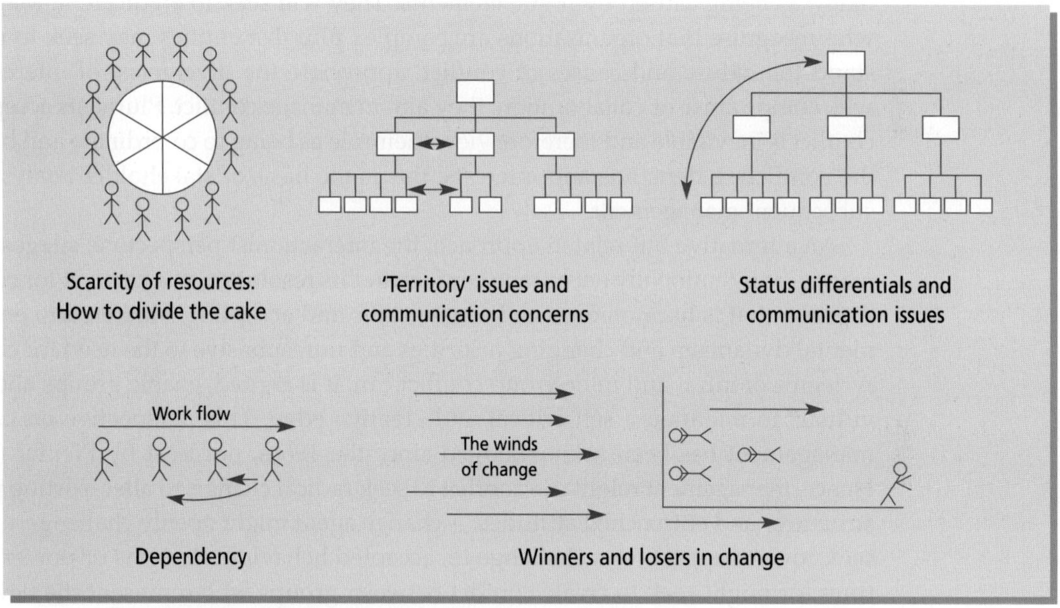

Fig 8.9 Some causes of conflict in the workplace

Sociologists have explored industrial conflict and its many forms. For example, Reed (1989) distinguishes between collective and individual conflict, the former exemplified by actions such as strikes, working to rule and restrictive practices. A number of people act collectively and live out a rational plan in pursuit of a given objective. Individual conflict, on the other hand, is more random, varied and, often, short lived. Taylor and Walton (1971) note that acts of sabotage are a barometer for underlying conflict in an organisation. They represent attempts by employees to assert control over their work situation and reflect an underlying sense of powerlessness. Theft by employees can be motivated by similar causes.

In each of these cases the positive use of power and political skills can help to reduce conflict, to make it manageable and reduce the potentially dysfunctional outcome of friction. However, the existence of power differentials and/or the negative or overt use of power can stimulate further conflict. Clearly, an ambiguity exists. Power is both a cause of, and a mechanism to help resolve, conflict in the workplace.

Management of conflict

Whereas organisational theory has developed to accept that conflict is inevitable, management theory and practitioner concerns demand that conflict is managed and resolved in the workplace. We discussed above the unitary, pluralist and radical frames of organisation. Each of these frames, or rather managerial acceptance of each, would lead to a different approach being adopted to the management of conflict. Managers who believe that the unitary organisation is a desirable and realisable state will view conflict as marginal, the outcome of ineffective management or, more likely, as being caused by rogue elements. They will seek to eradicate it. Managers who recognise that organisations are complex pluralist entities may seek to understand the nature and causes of conflict, appreciate the divergence of interest and seek compromise or collaboration: they aim to manage conflict. Pluralists accept that conflict is inevitable and therefore view their role as being to co-ordinate and balance the conflicting demands and interests: this is the basis of stakeholder analysis and subsequent management.

An alternative but related approach, the interactionist perspective, suggests that managers intentionally encourage conflict and its resolution as a catalyst for change. A group that is harmonious can become static and accepting, blinkered to environmental dynamism and changing priorities and unresponsive to the need for change. A degree of intra- and inter-group conflict can, it is argued, enable groups and individuals to maintain a self-critical and creative edge. This perspective on conflict management has been acknowledged since the 1960s, not least by Pfeiffer (1981). Hence, management might use conflict to seek radical change, to alter existing power structures and entrenched attitudes. A change agent might openly challenge, and/or seek covert support for a challenge to, accepted behavioural norms or power structures, or might seek to create conflict between groups who represent the new way forward and those that embrace the status quo. Similarly, creating a manageable level of intergroup conflict might create greater intra-group cohesion, a desire to pull together to compete with other, hostile groups. This might lead to improvement in effectiveness.

Clearly, a balance needs to be struck between the creation and the control of conflict. Whereas it is probably not possible to suggest what is an appropriate level of conflict, it has been argued that both too much or too little is dysfunctional. Performance, particularly of a group, is maximised when conflict is neither too high nor too low: this is illustrated in Figure 8.10. When conflict is very low, apathy and stagnation may breed. The individual, group, department or organisation may be unresponsive to change and may lack creativity. Work life becomes just too predictable and it becomes difficult to inspire staff to think and act differently and to take the organisation forward. Conversely, too much conflict is disruptive, is time consuming to deal with and leads to a lack of co-operation and collaboration in pursuit of organisational goals. The middle ground might provide for sufficient conflict to promote self-criticism and innovative attitudes and behaviours.

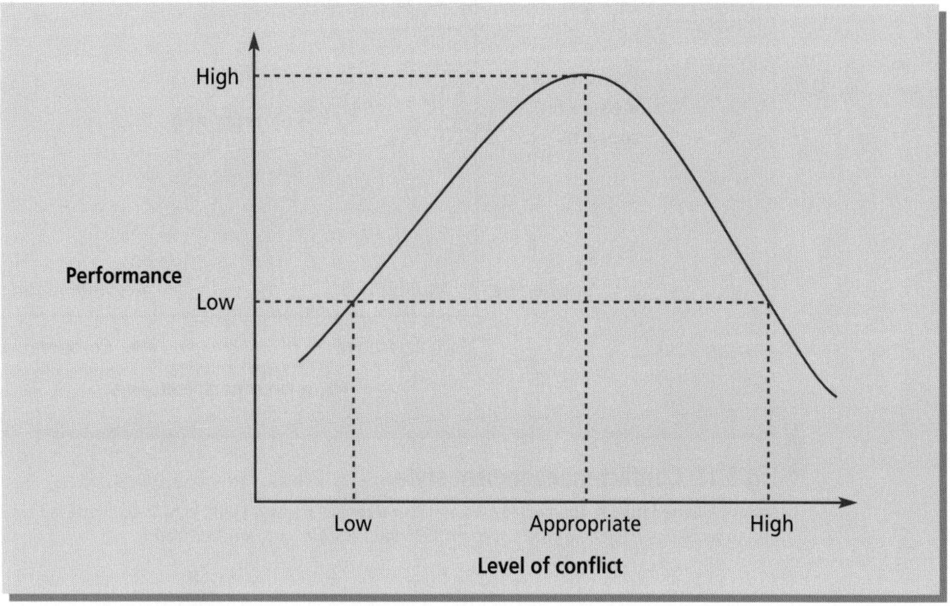

Fig 8.10 Functional and dysfunctional levels of conflict

Conflict-handling model

Thomas (1976) has produced a normative or prescriptive model for managing conflict resolution. It is based on two conflict-management dimensions, themselves reflecting different styles of management. The two dimensions, the degree of assertiveness in pursuit of one's interests and the level of co-operativeness in attempting to satisfy others' concerns, are places along two continuums and are illustrated in Figure 8.11. Five conflict-handling strategies emerge which are of relevance and interest to the individual and the manager.

The five conflict-handling styles are:

1 *Avoidance* – one or more parties in conflict may seek to avoid, to suppress or to ignore the conflict. They may take recourse in bureaucratic procedures or otherwise stall the conflict. This approach may not lead to conflict resolution and if the root causes are endemic and/or likely to become apparent again, avoidance will achieve little or will make matters worse.

2 *Accommodation* – this involves one party putting the other's interests first and suppressing their own concerns in order to preserve some form of stability and to suppress the conflict. Again, if the causes of conflict are endemic or lasting, accommodation may never resolve these root issues. The accommodating party may underperform as a consequence.

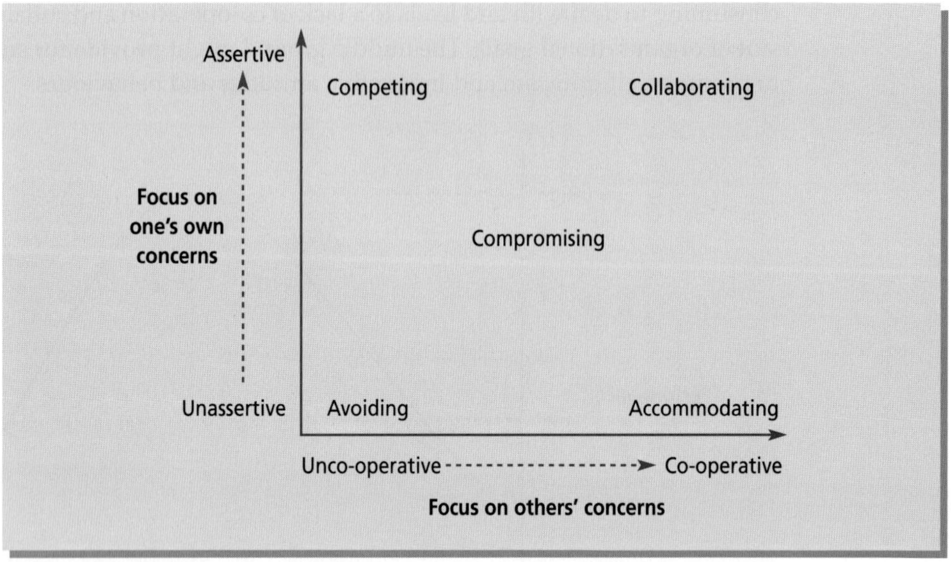

Fig 8.11 Conflict-management style

Source: Adapted from K. Thomas (1976) 'Conflict and conflict management', in M.D. Dunnette (ed.) *Handbook of Industrial and Organisational Psychology*. © Copyright 1976 John Wiley & Sons, Inc, New York.

3 *Compromise* – often seen as the optimum solution: the word compromise in the English language is viewed as positive and constructive. Each party gives something up and a midpoint is often accepted after negotiation and debate. However, in compromise, both parties lose something: there may be a better alternative.

4 *Competition* – this is a state where both or all parties do not co-operate, instead they seek to maximise their own interests and goals. It creates winners and losers. The resultant power plays, dysfunctional behaviours and uncooperative activities might prove damaging to the organisation as well as to at least one of the parties. Even the 'winner' may be damaged in the process.

5 *Collaboration* – from both the individual party's and the organisational point of view this is likely to be the optimum solution. Differences are confronted and jointly resolved, novel solutions are sought and added value ensues: a win–win outcome is achieved.

Thomas (1977) has identified the situational or contextual factors which inform the use of each style of conflict management. The main contingent factors, that is, those which influence the choice of style, include:

- the time available to resolve the conflict;
- the level of importance of the issue(s) stimulating the conflict;
- the preferred style(s) of the participants in the conflict;

- whether one style (or more) is unacceptable in the particular circumstances, for example, where compromise proves vitally dysfunctional for the organisation;
- where issues of commitment, motivation, precedent and lack of information are important.

Implicit in this model is the likelihood that individuals and groups choose a particular style after consideration of the contextual variables. Whereas organisational experience can undoubtedly enable individuals to 'read' a conflict situation better and to respond appropriately, many individuals do have a preferred style. For example some people, both in the workplace and in their home and social lives, thrive on competition and even conflict. This model has inspired the development of tests for personality type which assess an individual's 'natural' degrees of assertiveness and co-operativeness. Such tests attempt to identify a preferred style or styles of conflict handling.

Power and organisational change

The relevance of change, conflict and communications, the themes of this book, are central to the study of power and politics. Conflict, as we have demonstrated, is inextricably linked to political activity and to power in organisations. Change, as has been suggested, threatens existing power structures and both encourages and necessitates political activity. Communications in organisations are frequently 'statements' of power or examples of political activity. The use, manipulation and withholding of information has been seen to be a commonly utilised political activity. We will now explore, briefly, one particular aspect of change management which has a particular relevance to the study of power; more specifically, to perceived powerlessness and to negative power: that is, resistance to organisational change.

Resistance to change

Much has been written about resistance to change. It is viewed as an inevitable aspect of the change process, one which counterbalances the pressures or forces encouraging change. Resistance itself can take many forms, from overt, often aggressive behaviour to covert sophisticated non-compliance. Bedeian (1980) identified four causes of resistance to change: parochial self-interest, misunderstanding and lack of trust in management, contradictory assessments of the implications of change and a low tolerance for change. Organisational change alters the status quo and frequently entails a loss of power for some individuals and groups and a gain for others. Shifting power sources and bases create friction and conflict between real or perceived winners and losers. Organisational change frequently reduces a group's access to resources; structural change can lead to diminishing legitimate or position power, whereas reorganisation can disrupt previously useful relationships and networks. It is hardly surprising that people who perceive or know that their power source(s) may be eroded by change are likely to resist or, alternatively, seek to participate in the process with the intention of altering the nature and consequences of change.

When people exercise power, either individually or collectively, to resist change they are said to be exploiting negative power. The use of the word 'negative' may imply that such resistance is always dysfunctional. That may not always be the case. Successful resistance could be highly desirable and functional for departments or groups. Resistance to a change which is ill informed may prove beneficial to the organisation.

Managerial implications

A number of managerial implications become apparent when one has a basic knowledge and understanding of power, politics and conflict in organisations. Many of these suggest tactics for building or securing power and could be used to abuse power as well as to use power to pursue organisational objectives. Managers may benefit from the following:

1 Recognising the political aspect of their work and making attempts to hone their political skills in order to be more effective. It is unlikely that organisations are rational or adopt a unitary frame; rather, they are political, pluralist, human groupings. Relationships are important. Therefore, it is important to recognise the sources of power and the causes and domains of conflict and political activity.

2 Enhancing their legitimacy through developing expertise in important areas. This often applies to particular skills, for example in IT or process technology, which are in short supply at the level at which managers operate.

3 An awareness of sources and flows of information and from attempting to widen access to information. A Machiavellian extension to this point is the ability to restrict others' access to information and to select favourable information for others' consumption (*see* the mini-case in Chapter 10 on practice in Russia – Figure 10.5). For example, decisions can be influenced by the items that are put on agendas and even on the sequence in which they are placed (Pfeiffer, 1981).

4 Building coalitions which might involve communicating freely, warmly and frequently with individuals and groups in the organisation whose support enhances power. Merrell (1979) suggested that effective managers huddle in small groups to resolve issues, thus stressing the power of the informal, social network. The aim should be to build positive relationships involving interpersonal liking, trust and respect. This may involve reaching out to dissenters and old enemies.

5 An expansion of their networks. Related to coalition building is the need to build similar relationships outside, for example among suppliers and customers, as well as internally.

6 Recognising that successful and effective empowerment creates a win–win situation but that this may necessitate managing fundamental organisational change.

7 A recognition and understanding of other employees' feelings of powerlessness and their consequent behaviours and attitudes.

8 A recognition that the successful management of change involves the use of sophisticated political skills and an emphasis on balancing, co-ordinating and managing the many and varied interest groups that hold power.

9 An awareness of the power of symbols and, in particular, of the unintended symbolic significance of words and deeds.

10 Avoiding making their power open and explicit. There is a general dislike of the open demonstration or abuse of power as most people recognise that self-serving behaviour damages the organisation and its employees. Instead, managers should make their goals and aspirations explicit and leave power implicit. People know who holds power; Kanter (1979) argues that explicit claims to power are only made by the powerless.

Summary of main points

This chapter has explored power, politics and conflict within organisations. The main points made are:

- the chapter has offered a definition of the key terms power, politics, powerlessness, empowerment and conflict;
- there are many sources of power in organisations and mechanisms of power execution: similarly, there are many causes and domains of conflict;
- power, politics and conflict are closely related;
- organisations can be viewed as unitary entities, pursuing common goals; or pluralist, embracing different interests and goals;
- conflict can be viewed as endemic and normal (even desirable), or as exceptional and entirely dysfunctional;
- the use of power and sophisticated political skills is essential in the management of change;
- power can be used to resist change and manipulate its nature and outcomes, just as power is used to manipulate the understanding and interpretation of organisational and environmental events.

Conclusions

This chapter has stressed the intensely human nature of power, political activity and conflict in organisations. Despite the covert nature of much of this activity it is a very 'real' and important aspect of all organisations. The exercise of power, engagement in political activity and involvement in conflict can inspire all manner of human responses, from extreme satisfaction and the resultant dynamism, joy and energy to dire frustration, low morale and withdrawal. Power is an organisational reality and knowledge of its causes, forms and consequences is invaluable both to those who seek to analyse, interpret and understand organisations and to those who wish to work and thrive in the workplace.

QUESTIONS

1 In an organisation with which you are familiar identify the sources and bases of power of each of the main players. What are some of the sources of conflict in that organisation?

2 Identify some of the problems associated with empowerment.

3 Identify the sources of power or influence that you have used in the last week in your dealings with others.

4 Identify one dispute or conflict you have experienced in the last week. What styles of conflict management did the parties, including yourself, employ?

REFERENCES

Bedeian, A. G. (1980) *Organisation Theory and Analysis*. Chicago, IL: The Dryden Press.

Burrell, G. and Morgan, G. (1979) *Sociological Paradigms and Organisational Analysis*. London: Heinemann Educational Books.

Calabria, D. C. (1982) 'CEOs and the paradox of power', *Business Horizons*, Jan–Feb, pp 29–31.

Conger, J. A. and Kanungo, R. N. (1988) 'The empower process: Integrating theory and practice', *Academy of Management Review*, Vol. 13, pp 471–82.

Daft, R. L. (1992) *Organisation Theory and Design*, 4th edn. St Paul, MN: West.

Fox, A. (1975) 'Industrial relations: a social critique of pluralist ideology' in Barrett, B., Rhodes, E. and Bishon, J. (eds) *Industrial Relations and the Wider Society: Aspects of Interaction*. London: Collier Macmillian.

French Jr, J. R. P. and Raven, B. (1959) 'The Bases of Social Power' in Cartwright, D. (ed.) *Studies in Social Power*. Ann Arbor, MI: University of Michigan, Institute of Social Research, pp 150–67.

Handy, C. (1994) *Managing Strategic Action, Mobilising Change: Concepts, Readings and Cases*. London: Sage.

Kanter, R. M. (1979) 'Power failure in management circuits', *Harvard Business Review*, July–Aug, pp 65–75.

Merrell, V. D. (1979) *Huddling: The Informal Way to Management Success*. New York: Amacon.

Morgan, G. (1986) *Images of Organization*. Newbury Park, CA: Sage.

Morgan, G. (1996) *Images of Organization*, 2nd edn. Newbury Park, CA: Sage.

Pfeiffer, J. (1981) *Power in Organisations*. Marshfield, MA: Pitman Publishing.

Reed, M. (1989) *The Sociology of Management*. Hemel Hempstead: Harvester Wheatsheaf.

Robbins, S. P. (1974) *Managing Organisational Conflict: A Non-traditional Approach*. Englewood Cliffs, NJ: Prentice-Hall.

Robbins, S. P. (1984) *Essentials of Organisational Behaviour*, 3rd edn. Englewood Cliffs, NJ: Prentice-Hall.

Saunders, C. S. (1990) 'The strategic contingencies theory of power: multiple perspectives', *Journal of Management Studies*, Vol. 27, pp 1–18.

Tannenbaum, A. S. and Cooke, R. S. (1980) 'Organisational control: A review of studies employing the control graph method' in Lamners, C. J. and Hickson, D. J. (eds) *Organisations Alike and Unlike*. Boston: Routledge and Kegan Paul, pp 183–210.

Taylor, L. and Walton, P. (1971) 'Industrial sabotage: Motives and meanings' in Cohen, S. (ed.) *Images of Deviance*. Harmondsworth: Penguin Books.

Thomas, K. (1976) 'Conflict and conflict management' in Dunnette, M. D. (ed.) *Handbook of Industrial and Organisational Psychology*. Chicago: Rand McNally.

Thomas, K. W. (1977) 'Towards multidimensional values in teaching: the example of conflict behaviours', *Academy of Management Review*, July, pp. 484–90.

Weber, M. (1947) *The Theory of Social and Economic Organisation*. London: Oxford University Press.

FURTHER READING

The references below represent a variety of texts and writings on power in organisations. Additionally, reference can be made to the sources referred to in this chapter.

Huczynski, A. and Buchanan, D. (1991) *Organizational Behaviour*. Hemel Hempstead: Prentice-Hall, Chapter 21.

Morgan, G. (1996) *Images of Organization*, 2nd edn. Newbury Park, CA: Sage, Chapter 6.

Mullins, L. J. (1999), *Management and Organisational Behaviour*, 5th edn. London: Financial Times Pitman Publishing, Chapters 21 and 22.

Pfeiffer, J. (1981) *Power in Organisations*. Marshfield, MA: Pitman Publishing.

9

Organisational culture

LEARNING OUTCOMES

On completion of this chapter you should be able to:

- define organisational culture;
- appreciate that organisational culture exists in a broader social context;
- explore the cultural perspective by identifying the various schools of thought and consequent approaches to the study of organisational culture;
- discuss the ways in which cultural knowledge is learned and stored;
- examine the role played by organisational culture in influencing organisational strategy, performance and change.

KEY CONCEPTS

- *organisational culture*
- *national culture*
- *subculture*
- *rituals, symbols and stories*
- *organisation is a culture – organisation has a culture*
- *cognitive knowledge*
- *culture and organisational performance*
- *cultural change*
- *interpretive perspective*

Organisational culture

Organisational culture is frequently cited as being responsible for all manner of organisational ills and, on occasions, credited with creating positive qualities. It is essential, therefore, that we explore this concept more thoroughly to enable us to understand behaviour of organisations and to diagnose and interpret organisational problems and activities. In short, an intimate knowledge and awareness of culture should improve our ability to analyse organisational behaviour and to manage and to lead.

Introduction

This chapter explores the theoretical underpinning and complexity of the cultural metaphor. It opens with a discussion of the concept of organisational culture within a broader societal context. The nature and influence of national culture, business sector and group norms and individual personalities are considered worthy of brief consideration. It is recognised that culture is a metaphor and a 'way of seeing and analysing' organisations and, as such, is one of many potential 'perspectives' or frames used for organisational analysis. We also explore the vastly different approaches taken in the literature to the study of culture, the consequences of which fundamentally influence our understanding of the concept, of its relationship with organisational performance and its impact on management and organisational change. A precise definition of culture is avoided, as will become clear, for such definitions often serve to reduce or constrict our understanding of this complex notion. Rather, we will explore a myriad of definitions and discuss a variety of key issues which have an impact on our understanding of organisational culture; thus preserving the value and insight into organisational life that this concept provides.

The current fascination with organisational culture began in the 1970s and early 1980s with the work of now eminent writers, such as Peters and Waterman (1982), Deal and Kennedy (1982) and Kanter (1983). However, academics had drawn attention to the notion of culture operating at the organisational or unit level much earlier. For example, in the 1960s Blake and Mouton (1969) suggested a link between organisational characteristics that we might now refer to as cultural and organisational performance. In 1952 Jaques referred to the culture of a factory as 'its customary and traditional way of thinking and of doing things which is shared . . . and which new members must learn' (1952: 251). He argued that culture comprised behaviours, attitudes, customs, values, beliefs and 'the less conscious conventions and taboos' (ibid.). Nevertheless, despite the emphasis given to this concept for over 50 years, there remains considerable debate and contention surrounding the nature of, and the value of studying, organisational culture.

Organisational culture in context

Culture is a shared phenomenon and in the case of organisational culture that sharing takes place at the level of the organisation. Individuals in a culture differ and this is, in part at least, a product of personality differences. It is also possible to have a culture which comprises two or more subcultures. For example, in the National Health Service (NHS) in the UK, as in most health-care sectors throughout the world, a series of subcultural groups work alongside one another. Doctors, nurses, professions allied to medicine (PAMs), ancillary workers and managers, each have their own cultural identity. Each group has its own values, beliefs, assumptions and norms which guide their activity, each has its own rituals and ceremonies, its own stories to tell about organisational life and its own interpretive systems which influence its understanding of organisational symbols. These subcultural groups frequently conflict with one another: NHS staff often refer to the inherent 'tribalism' of their service. The mini-case presented in Figure 9.1 illustrates a series of rituals, which are an important aspect of culture, shared by many ward-based nurses in an acute sector NHS Hospital Trust in the UK.

Rituals in nursing

Organisational routines are an effective coping mechanism for people. They anchor and reassure employees in the workplace and are shared by processes of socialisation and interaction. Routines help give order to our working lives. Some of the routines assume ritualistic significance, which helps both to preserve them and to raise their significance in the organisation. Rituals can become enduring aspects of the culture or the professional culture. Practical justification of the behaviour becomes irrelevant. Thus a ritual is a *prescribed activity, often rigidly observed in a solemn or ceremonial fashion, which has symbolic significance*. Rituals are part of an organisation's culture and help to reinforce the prevailing paradigm. The interpretation of ritualistic behaviour gives us an insight into the culture of an organisation.

Rituals

The morning drugs and drinks round: often as early as 6 a.m., patients are woken, administered drugs and given a drink of tea. The ritual serves to enhance the power of the night nurses and to avoid conflict between them and their day shift colleagues. Often additional sleep would serve to speed patient recovery.

Multiple patient records: all professionals and professions allied to medicine keep separate patient records, with the result that some patients – in-patients in particular – are often asked to give personal information as much as five or six times. This ritual serves to enhance or maintain the power and social identity of each professional group (e.g. nurses, doctors, physiotherapists).

Daily changing of the dressing on patients' wounds: although daily changing of dressings is now less common, many nurses still consider it part of their duty of care to replace bandages daily, or even more frequently, in spite of the cost and often adverse affects of this on the healing process. This ritual serves to maintain the social identity of, and the requirement for, nurses.

Fig 9.1 Mini-case: Rituals

The cultural knowledge of individuals is not identical. Individual difference, perhaps arising from different home, educational and microsocial contexts, leads to intracultural variation. Hence within any culture, or even subcultural group, differences exist. Most cultures are tolerant of such difference, in fact it may provide a mechanism for cultural change or dynamism. For example, national subcultures, based on criteria such as, socioeconomic class, ethnic/religious background or occupation, stimulate both debate and conflict, which can provide an opportunity for learning and change.

Although culture is created and sustained in social contexts, such as in an organisation, it is dynamic and constantly evolving. At the organisational level culture is learned by recruits through the process of socialisation, including training and managerial interventions, whereas educational systems, the media, history, political processes and the like, help shape national culture. In a business sector, such as retailing or iron working, Grinyer and Spender (1979) have shown how organisations tend to adopt similar strategic responses when faced with pressures for change. These behaviours are learned by the processes of business-sector interaction, such as through labour movements in the sector, the trade press and formal managerial or worker associations. Hence a 'recipe', which sets limits for action, is broadly agreed by organisations in a business sector. This recipe is a 'taken for granted' set of beliefs and assumptions which is held, relatively uniformly, throughout organisations within a business sector. The recipe, rather like culture at the organisational level, assists managers to make sense of their world.

Hence, values, beliefs, assumptions, norms and ways of interpreting meaning can be shared on numerous levels, from small subcultures which might thrive in parts of larger organisations, through organisational culture, corporate culture, business sector recipes, to regional, national and supranational cultures (*see* Figure 9.2). It is at least intuitively sound to suggest that influence is exerted between these various levels. For example, the patterning of national values, assumptions and beliefs appears to have some influence over organisational activity in countries. Hence the work of researchers at the national level on culture, such as Hofstede, Laurent, Adler and Trompenaars (referred to in Chapter 10), is important for the understanding of culture at micro-levels.

Organisational culture: definition and debate

There is considerable debate concerning the nature of organisational culture, which has far-reaching consequences for management and all manner of organisational activity including change, corporate strategy and financial and other measures of performance. It is, therefore, vital that we explore the different definitions and implications of the concept of culture in order to enhance our understanding of organisations themselves.

One source of divergence of opinion as to the meaning and value of organisational culture derives from the different subject fields which study the concept. Much work in the 1980s, for example, derived from business and management schools. The aims and main contentions of this writing differed significantly from that which adopted a more anthropological or sociological perspective. Many definitions of culture are incompatible with one another along a number of dimensions. For example, if we define culture in an objective manner as an organisational variable then the understanding that culture can and should be actively managed is implicit. If we view culture as interpretative, intangible and indistinguishable from the organisation itself, we tend to accept that it is a much deeper concept which can only be understood in subjective terms. In the latter case, the management and intentional change of culture is viewed as a more haphazard and doubtful experience. These divergent views stem from different methodological convictions.

Subculture	Professional culture	Organisational or corporate culture	Industry culture or recipe knowledge	National culture	Supra-national culture
The shared characteristics of a group, potentially of virtually any size, that comprises a subset of a larger organisational or professional culture. For example, permanent ward-based night nurses in NHS hospitals are a subculture of the wider group of nurses of the hospital or unit culture where they work and of the broad organisational culture of the NHS.	The shared characteristics of members of a profession or trade. For example, we could refer to doctors or engineers as having common, cultural ways of doing and thinking. These groups have experienced similar education and training and 'sign up' to professional norms and obligations. Often, they experience divided loyalties between organisation and profession.	This is, primarily, the focus of this chapter – culture at the level of the organisation or corporate body. Most organisations have a unique culture, even if this has numerous subcultures and/or professional cultures within it. The relative 'influence' of culture at this level will depend, to an extent, on the strength of corporate identity and influence on its constituent units.	Industry-sector norms exist, particularly in long-established and distinct sectors. These norms are not dissimilar to certain cultural characteristics: they influence how organisations in a sector interpret environmental parameters and place limits on strategy.	Possibly the most transparent manifestation of culture lies at this level. For example, there are many significant cultural differences between the British, the French and the Germans. In addition of course, many ethnic groups, who share strong cultures, cross existing national or political boundaries. Chapter 10 explores this in more detail.	Characteristics which peoples from many countries or states share in common (across national boundaries). At a very broad level one might refer to Western and to Chinese cultures: the former broadly based on Christianity and including peoples from most of Europe, North America and Australasia and the latter based on Confucianism.

Fig 9.2 Culture at ascending levels

In the early 1980s the cultural metaphor received considerable attention from academics and managers hoping to discover the answer to many difficult managerial questions. Far from providing *the* answer, the plethora of research and writing about organisational culture stimulated an active, often contentious, debate. One of the early influential works suggested that strong cultures had a positive effect on organisational performance (Deal and Kennedy, 1982). Strong cultures were thought to exist in organisations which exhibited a close fit between themselves and their environment, possessed a rich and complex system of shared values, a well-specified and routine set of behavioural rituals and an articulate cultural network. Deal and Kennedy (1982), inspired by the strength and cohesiveness of Japanese organisational and national culture, urged a return to the ideas of America's early business leaders in achieving strong cultures. Such cultures, it was argued, provided a system of informal rules which gave guidance to employees and which motivated people by making them feel better about what they did. Hence the research suggested a panacea, a prescription to cure the observed organisational ills in the USA. Their work, like much management research and writing, is primarily aimed at the American manager and academic. Its ethnocentrism is often apparent. This work, together with that of Peters and Waterman (1982), in their best-selling book *In Search of Excellence*, proved extremely influential in both determining the managerial and furthering the academic agendas of the 1980s.

Another popular concept of culture was provided by Schein (1985) who suggested that culture was a learned product of group experience. He placed the various elements of culture in a three-level hierarchy. At the deepest level are underlying assumptions which influence people's 'commonsense' view of their organisational world, including their assumptions about the nature of the business environment, about human nature in general and about relationships in the workplace. These fundamental and taken-for-granted assumptions and beliefs inform cultural values which lie at the intermediate level. At the surface, culture manifests itself, Schein (1985) argued, in cultural artefacts, such as visible behaviour patterns, building design features and technology. Although in many ways appealing, this model provides a rather static view of a dynamic concept. It also underplays the role of symbolic activity in organisations and the role that symbols and stories, for example, play in creating and communicating cultural meaning for people in the workplace. However, it does suggest that what many writers refer to as culture, with such definitions as 'the way we do things around here', might merely be an overt, tangible, surface-level artefact of that culture.

Many attempts have been made to classify views on organisational culture. Sachs (1989), in a special issue of the *Anthropology of Work Review*, identified three approaches to the definition and study of organisational culture. First, culture, as an external variable, derives from the field of comparative management and suggests that culture is brought into the organisation by its members. Studies abound which draw comparisons between national managerial cultures (for example, Hofstede, 1980). The implicit suggestion is that organisational culture closely reflects national culture and that many features of that culture are common to all organisations in a national context. In other words, the culture of the national context is replicated in organisations: a deterministic relationship exists between culture at the two levels. This has important implications for the management of change in organisations, and somewhat precludes the possibility of significant cultural management or change at an organisational level (*see* Chapter 10).

Second, culture can be conceptualised as the expressive and non-job-related aspects of informal organisational life. Studies which take this perspective have focused attention on organisational values which are created and transmitted by stories, myths and legends (for example, Tommerup, 1988), jokes, rituals and ceremonies (for example, Deal and Kennedy, 1982; Trice and Beyer, 1984) and symbols, including language.

Third, culture can be viewed as the informal nature of organisations. Hence employees' views on all aspects of organisation become paramount. Many researchers in the field, therefore, make use of 'native view paradigms', suggesting that it is most appropriate to discover how participants make sense of their organisational realities. The concern is with representing cultures as they appear to those in the cultural group being studied (for example, Isabella, 1990).

Risto (1990) identifies three broad approaches to the analysis of culture. Culture as (a) the structure of social action, (b) symbols and codes of meaning, exploring interpretive analysis and the meaning of language (for example, Goffman, 1982), and (c) the structure of social organisation, following Marx and Weber on the sociology of organisation, where culture is thought to be reflected in the division of labour and the structure of roles and social networks. The major distinction lies between the latter two 'schools of thought', that is, the structural and the interpretive views of culture. This is a valid framework in which to explore and analyse further the plethora of research and writing on culture witnessed in the past two decades.

The interpretive view suggests that culture is created and sustained through symbols and ritual. Language is the prime symbolic offering of culture. In broader terms this view falls in the 'ideational' school of thought. The 'structural' view, however, relies more upon how roles are structured in organisation. Such work might be thought of as 'naive' and broadly derived from a functionalist/materialist school of thought.

An example of the latter is the work of Charles Handy (1989), adapted from Harrison (1972), on culture. This work identified four 'types' of culture based on structural design features. The link between organisational structure, design and culture is clear. Handy (1986) suggests that power cultures are found in small entrepreneurial firms, role cultures in larger bureaucratic organisations, task cultures dominate in matrix-type organisations, where power lies at the intersection of roles, and person cultures are common where the individual is the key element. He identifies the factors which influence the type of culture found in an organisation, some of which, such as organisational size, locus of power, types and levels of technology and characteristics of the business environment, will already be familiar to you.

Power cultures, Handy argues, are found in small, entrepreneurial organisations. In these, as illustrated in Figure 9.3, power lies at the centre of a web. The organisation depends on informal communications and people who adopt the attitudes and norms of the central power source (often the owner/senior executive) will be valued and trusted. Power relations are clear. *Role cultures* have high levels of bureaucracy and co-ordination is provided by a small, élite, senior management. An organisation characterised by role culture is departmentalised, often into clear functions and areas of specialisation. Employees have clear roles clarified by job descriptions. Work is rationally allocated and organisational life is impersonal. The organisation is suited to stable environments where efficiency is stressed and required. Role cultures provide security for employees. The *task culture* adopts a project focus and is represented in Figure 9.3 by a net where power lies at the intersections. A task culture is common in matrix organisations (*see* Chapter 7) where a team culture exists alongside autonomy. As a consequence these organisations are more flexible than those characterised by a role culture and they can react to changing markets. Finally, in the *person culture*, the individual is paramount. These cultures are common to professional organisations,

Power culture

Frequently found in small entrepreneurial organisations, power culture relies on central power, informal communication and trust. A unity of purpose negates the need for bureaucracy. The competence, flexibility and dynamism of the central power force, often the owner, is essential. Increased size might 'break' the tight web-like relationships, in which case the organisation might establish a satellite or replicate itself elsewhere. Power cultures place considerable demands on staff.

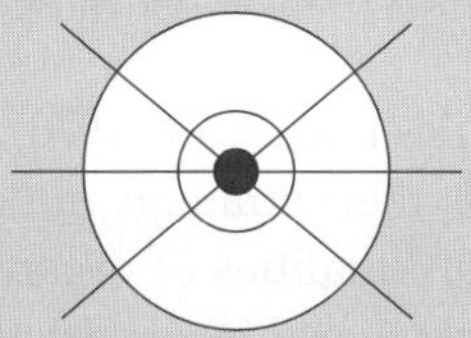

Role culture

In contrast to the smaller power culture, this cultural type is characterised by high levels of bureaucracy and formality. A small group of senior managers control the co-ordination between specialists and functional areas as the diagram below illustrates. Rules, procedures and job descriptions are the norm. Work is thought to be rationally allocated to staff. Suited to stable environments, role cultures find change difficult to cope with. They provide security and predictability for staff.

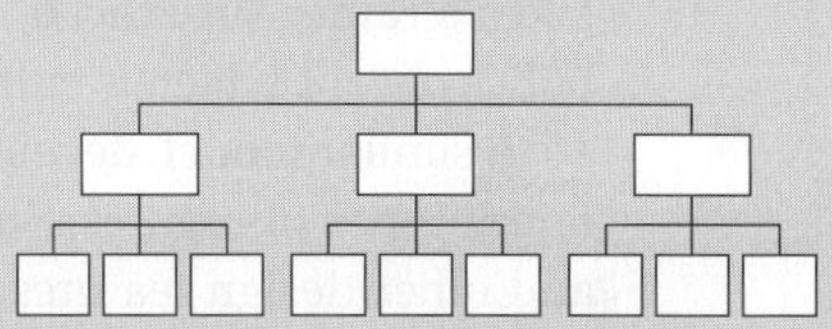

Task culture

Task cultures are often found in matrix organisations where power resides at the intersection of responsibilities. Employees tend to hold joint or multiple responsibilities and work relatively autonomously. Influence is based on expertise as opposed to rank. The need for authority is reduced by the existence of both individual control and teamwork. Operational decisions can be made quickly, making the organisation flexible. These organisations find specialisation, or achieving economies of scale, difficult.

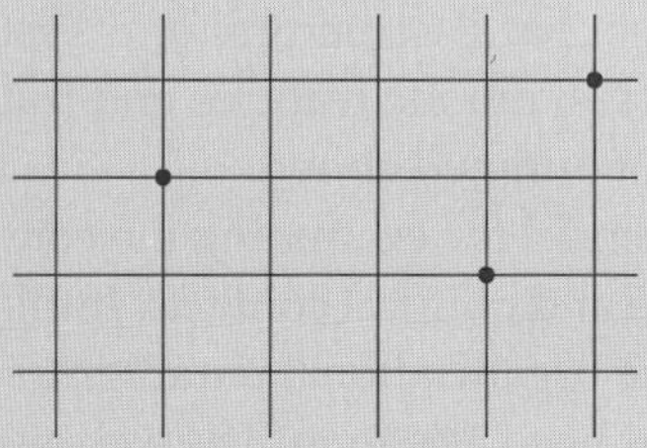

Person culture

The individual is the key feature in this culture, which only exists if individuals come together because they see some mutual benefits ensuing. Teams of professionals, or even 'hippie' communities, illustrate this culture type. There is no formal control and no single or overriding objective: individual objectives predominate in the constraints that 'organisation' involves. Influence is shared and based on expertise and mutual respect. Individuals tend to share common interests. There is little, or no, formal structure, as shown below.

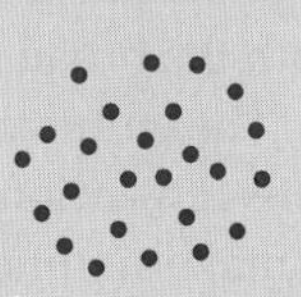

Fig 9.3 Handy's cultural types

Source: Based on Handy (1989) and Harrison (1972).

such as firms of accountants or solicitors. There is limited formal control and communication links are informal.

It is, however, important to place this analysis in a broader context. For example, it derives from a school of thought that links structural factors closely with organisational culture. In fact it does not fully differentiate between structure and culture: it does not recognise them as separate perspectives or frames with which to view organisations (as is illustrated in Chapter 5). It implies that major structural change will lead to cultural change and suggests that the management of culture, like any other organisational variable, is quite possible and likely to yield positive results. It is also a deterministic model, that is, it suggests that a particular type of culture will result from a particular, given, set of structural criteria. All of these assumptions are challenged by other writers and theorists in this field, who argue that Handy's work takes a rather superficial, even trite, view of this complex, all-embracing and symbolic concept which is culture.

A similar model, developed by Miles and Snow (1978), suggests that there are different types of organisations *vis-à-vis* their strategic outlook. The culture, structure and other design features and human qualities of organisations conspire to enable managers in organisations to 'see' their world in a restricted way. For example, Miles and Snow (1978) suggest that there are conservative organisations which adopt low-risk strategies and well-tried solutions. These 'defenders' contrast with the more innovative 'prospector' type organisations. Although this model is of value, its limitations are apparent. It is a simple categorisation of a complex human organisational phenomenon that takes little or no account of the potential uniqueness of culture. However, it does link culture with organisational strategy.

In contrast, the interpretive view of culture embraces the complexity and subjectivity of culture while rejecting any simple causal relationships between culture and organisational structure. It may be too simplistic to view culture from either of the two perspectives identified here, as both interpretive/symbolic and structural aspects work in tandem in organisations. Johnson and Scholes (1994), in attempting to illustrate the complexities of strategic management in a cultural context, suggest that the organisational paradigm, or 'way of seeing', is embraced in a cultural web (*see* Figure 9.4). The cultural web comprises 'hard' structural and systems characteristics of organisations, together with 'soft' symbolic features and thus attempts to embrace both the broad schools of thought outlined above.

The cultural web is a useful model for examining the complex interrelationships between various cultural features and cultural contexts. Implicit also is that, in order to make significant changes to the organisational paradigm, some or all of the 'hard' and 'soft' supporting mechanisms need attention. The web also brings to the reader's attention the potential significance of ritual, of organisational stories and of symbols in both creating and sustaining organisational culture. The routines and rituals (*see* Figure 9.4) represent the taken-for-granted but symbolically significant aspects of organisational life. Some rituals are dysfunctional in as much as they contradict or countermand the organisation's objectives. Yet rituals help to give the culture its identity; they reinforce the 'way things are done around here' and indicate what is

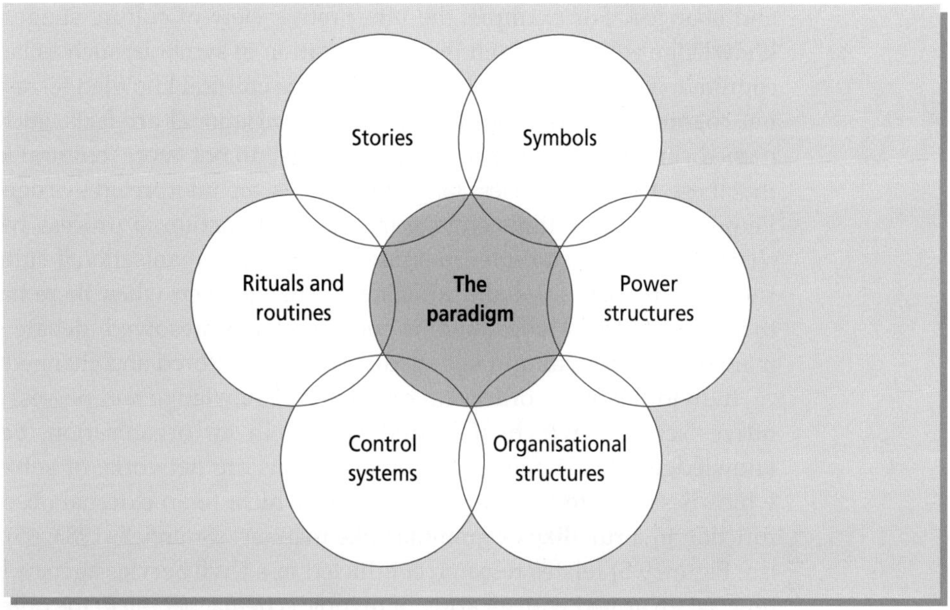

Fig 9.4 The cultural web

Source: Reprinted, with permission, from Johnson and Scholes (1999) *Exploring Corporate Culture: Text and Cases*, 5th edn, published by Prentice-Hall.

important and valued by employees. Organisational stories serve to 'locate' the culture in the history and development of the organisation. They also demonstrate the nature of the culture and the limits of cultural behaviour. Hence they both delineate and reinforce culture. All aspects of organisation and of behaviour by employees and managers can carry symbolic significance. Similarly the systems, tangible artefacts, organisational structure and consequent organigrams (organisational structure diagrams) all convey important information about the organisation. These symbols are interpreted by organisational members. Language itself, notably that of more senior and powerful personnel, carries particular symbolic significance. It helps people to understand what is required and expected, what the norms and values of the organisation are and how to comply with them (as well as the consequences of non-compliance). Some argue that symbols and their interpretation lie at the heart of the concept of culture and this indicates a possible avenue for those who desire to manipulate or change the culture.

This debate continues later in this chapter, in the context of organisational change and performance. First, we briefly explore the mechanisms by which organisational and other levels of cultural knowledge may be learned, shared and stored.

Cultural knowledge

The discussion above suggests that there is disagreement between commentators and academics regarding the nature of organisational culture. An understanding of that debate is essential to inform our understanding of how culture is learned, sustained and changed. For example, the interpretive view of culture suggests that cultural knowledge is derived from the interpretation of symbols, such as language. From a cognitive perspective, knowledge, including cultural knowledge, resides in individual cognitions. This is not to say that organisational artefacts, such as office size, named carparking spaces and organograms, do not 'store' cultural knowledge, just that these artefacts, like less tangible symbols, are interpreted by cognitive processes. People in organisations engage in social interaction, a process which reinforces shared meanings and interpretations. That said, organisational cultures have been shown to be pervasive and resistant to change even when there has been a rapid turnover of staff. Hence there is considerable, unresolved, debate concerning the manner in which cultural knowledge is learned, stored and changed.

Individuals store, order and understand knowledge and possess a series of cognitive 'schema' which, if shared widely in an organisation, become cultural knowledge. This suggests that organisations are networks of subjective meaning which is shared to 'varying degrees and which, to an external observer, appear to function in a rule-like or grammar-like manner' (Smircich, 1983: 65). The mini-case (*see* Figure 9.5) relates research conducted in a Civil Service agency. It demonstrates how, when armed with an array of myopic schema, people in the organisation stifled change.

Myopic schema: Civil Service agency

A series of collectively-held cognitive schema were identified in an organisation. These schema influenced people's views of their organisational world. Each acted as an obstacle to the realisation of radical change. They were:

- Impersonality, unemotionality and rationality: these schema encouraged people to keep their own counsel, not to share information, to be rational at all times and hence to avoid constructive confrontation, heated debate of issues and experimentation. Decision making was thought to be rational and by the book. Individuals were not prepared to object or show dissent.
- Segmentalism, élitism and conservatism: people and systems were reminiscent of Kanter's (1983) segmentalist organisations (*see* the text below). Tasks, responsibilities and problems were all departmentalised and rarely shared. Hierarchy and consequent position power dominated decision making and people were extremely reluctant to try novel methods or to experiment.
- Submissiveness and parochialism: people were highly concerned about 'their patch' and rarely took an overall organisational perspective. They were beholden to their superiors who took away any responsibility they might have had for the well-being of the whole organisation. They merely expected to 'keep their own houses in order'.

These mental maps or schema enabled the organisation to function efficiently but not to embrace change.

Fig 9.5 Mini-case: Civil Service schema

Organisational culture: performance and change

As suggested above, the structural and interpretative views of culture would lead us to adopt very different approaches to the management of major organisational change. In the early 1980s organisational culture became increasingly considered as both an obstacle to change and a vital ingredient of organisational success or failure. The 'excellence' tradition, bolstered by the best-selling book *In Search of Excellence* (Peters and Waterman, 1982), suggested that 'excellent' companies possessed, among other attributes, strong cultures which exhibited particular and unique characteristics. The unidirectional and linear causal link, implicit in this tradition, suggests that culture and performance are inextricably linked. Thus manipulation of the structure of culture to create, for example, decentralised, project-based organisations which place individuals at the centre of attention, are those which will succeed (note that this work largely falls in the structural school of thought identified above). Wilson (1992) argues forcefully that intellectual justification for this approach, despite its widespread acceptance and incorporation into organisational theory, is difficult to find. Even in 'practical' terms evidence is slight. For example, many of the excellent companies identified by Peters and Waterman (1982) and by Kanter (1983), in her book *The Change Masters*, failed to sustain their success throughout the 1980s. Additionally, the sound financial performance of other companies, identified as 'excellent', may be attributable to factors such as their having a monopoly position in their marketplace. For example, IBM's success, according to Peters and Waterman (1982), was attributable to their ability to sustain innovation, to manage culture and to locate potential deviants in teams controlled by strong management. Nevertheless, IBM enjoyed considerable monopoly power during much of the 1960s and 1970s and Delamarter (1988) suggests that its success can be largely attributed to that favourable market position. Similarly, Silver (1987) argues that McDonald's, another 'excellent' company, achieves its success by adopting scientific management principles of deskilling and designing narrow, monotonous jobs largely aimed at young, cheap labour (*see* Chapter 5). It has little, it is argued, to do with the kind of people-centred, innovative cultures identified by Peters and Waterman (1982).

The prescriptive overtone and the mixture of cultural and structural management, implicit in these popular works, typify views expressed by exponents of the structural view of culture. Additionally, these accounts virtually ignore major sectors of business activity, such as financial services, motor manufacture and petro-chemicals. Hence the work is thought to be empirically flawed. Theoretical criticisms are many and include the assumption that there is a 'one best way' of organising and that there is a simple causal relationship between culture and performance. This school of thought tends to adopt a senior management/control perspective and tends to borrow, somewhat selectively, from organisational theory and management research (Wilson, 1992).

The link between organisational culture and economic performance appears inconclusive. Research by Denison (1984, 1990), Schein (1984) and Meyer and Zucker (1989) suggests that causal relationships between culture and performance are far from simple, linear and unidirectional. For example, Denison's work suggests that there is a positive relationship between decentralisation and return on investment. However, he also suggests that cultures based on participative decision making correlate with below-average long-term performance. Calori and Sarnin (1991) found little relationship between company values and profitability.

Kanter (1983) argued that there are, broadly, just two types of culture: segmentalist and integrative. She outlined the characteristic features of each (*see* Figure 9.6 for an illustration of some of these characteristics) and suggested that some organisations which posses all or many of the integrative features will embrace organisational change and will thrive in a dynamic environment. Segmentalist cultures, on the other hand, are, at best, slow to react and struggle when required to change. She outlines the characteristics of each; in many cases the two categories represent polar opposites.

Segmentalist culture

- Views organisational problems narrowly
- Locate problems and hence responsibilities narrowly within department's or individual's remit
- Has segmented structure, divided into departments, and functions often work against one another
- Shuns experimentation
- Avoids confronting problems and conflicts
- Has weak co-ordinating mechanisms
- Emphasises precedent, policies, procedures and systems
- Inward-looking

Integrative culture

- Sees problems as related
- Views problems and responsibilities as shared and connected
- Has matrix or team/project-based structure
- Innovates and tests assumptions: invites experimentation
- Invites confrontation and eventually transcends differences
- Creates mechanisms of co-ordination for sharing information and ideas
- Looks for novel solutions
- Outward-looking

Source: Based on Kanter (1983).

Fig 9.6 Segmentalist and integrative cultures

Organisational culture change

The management of cultural change, which many argue is essential to ensure continuous organisational dynamism, is the subject of considerable debate. Many researchers have suggested models of cultural change. For example, Dobson (1989) identified a four-step approach: (a) change recruitment, promotion and redundancy policies in order to influence the composition of the workforce. This involves an active HRM role in identifying both employees who display the beliefs and values the organisation wishes to promote and those who do not; (b) reorganise or restructure the organisation to ensure that those employees and managers who display desired qualities are given positions of power; (c) effectively communicate the new values; (d) change systems in order to reinforce the new beliefs and values. Such models imply that cultural change can be achieved by a combination of personnel, structural and systems changes. However, the political power required to both initiate and implement such changes led Dobson (1989) to suggest that change is 'top-down' and imposed.

A somewhat broader, yet similarly prescriptive, model of cultural change is suggested by Cummings and Huse (1989). They argue that cultural change may result if the following prerequisites are in place: a clear strategic vision; top management commitment; symbolic leadership; supporting organisational changes and changing organisational membership. In their work, which is similar to but broader than Dobson's work, Cummings and Huse (1989) locate such change in a strategic framework. They also accept the need for symbolic intervention, such as 'visioning', and the use of symbolic behaviours and language.

These models are based on empirical research, although both can be criticised as they tend to underestimate the difficulty involved in changing culture. They have been widely criticised as being too simplistic and putting forward recommendations which are too general to be of use to individual organisations (for example, Gordon, 1985; Hassard and Sharifi, 1989). Figure 9.7, a mini-case, explores the management of organisational cultural change.

Other researchers, while accepting that cultural change occurs, take a more considered view of the ease and pace with which such change takes place. Schein (1985) argued that it is essential to understand how the existing culture is sustained before it can be changed. An analysis of the values, assumptions and beliefs which underlie organisational activities reveals culture, he suggested, as an adaptive learning process. Schein's (1985) approach places emphasis on the way organisations communicate their culture and how assumptions are translated into values. Schein, Barnes (1996: 117) suggests, 'seeks to understand the mechanisms used to propagate culture and how new values and behaviours are learned'. Clearly, once these mechanisms are revealed, such knowledge forms the basis of a strategy of cultural change. However, Schein (1989) was critical of the idea that cultural change can be achieved by a top-down, management-led approach. Others have suggested that the time frame for cultural change is from six to 15 years (Uttal, 1983), though some writing, by the less informed and empirically weak, naively suggests the time frame can be as little as one year.

Pettigrew (1990) recognises the difficulty of managing culture. He identifies seven reasons why culture is difficult to change, an explanation which cuts across some of the definitional divides addressed here. The seven issues are:

1 Levels – culture exists at a series of levels, from beliefs and assumptions to cultural artefacts (*see* Schein, 1985).

The management of organisational cultural change

This mini-case explores a cultural change process in a medium-sized NHS Hospital Trust in the Midlands of England. The organisation was successful in achieving significant and measurable quality improvements, exceeding its broad array of objectives and coping with considerable environmental flux in the mid-1990s. It was widely considered that aspects of the organisation's culture had changed.

Successful leadership of cultural change required the leaders to think culturally, to be guided by a mental map which indicated where they were coming from and what the intended destination was actually like. They employed cultural tools to negotiate this journey. Additionally, they could not ignore the politics of change nor the hard systems and structural changes that were needed to reinforce and symbolise major change. They used the real or perceived crisis caused by the imminence of a change of status (to quasi-independence or Trust status) as a trigger for change. This crisis increased the receptiveness of employees and of the context in general.

Of particular interest was the cultural, symbolic 'tools' which were employed. Whereas many managers ignore or trivialise the concept of culture and, at best, only think about culture, the CEO in this case thought culturally: that is, he considered the situation in cultural terms. He made every effort to utilise the power of symbols. He showed awareness that his actions carried both overt face-values, influence and symbolic significance. This awareness enabled him to calculate the effects of his language, dress, style and actions in symbolic and, therefore, cultural terms.

His insistence on wearing jeans and T-shirts and playing loud pop music at management away-days was a symbolic attempt to reduce barriers and to signal change. The suggestion was that experimentation and change were exciting. He graphically symbolised innovation and enthusiasm by his style of facilitating meetings: darting from flip chart to flip chart, encouraging brainstorming and ideas, publicly embracing employees' concerns and views. Additionally, he frequently gave small gifts to 'islands of progress', sub-units in the hospital which had exceeded targets. This symbolised the rewarding of desired behaviours and attitudes.

Rituals

New rituals were created which symbolised change. Hence, reclassification of hospital porters, cleaners, domestic staff and caterers as ward assistants signalled a new and enhanced social identity for this group which helped to overcome some of the old demarcation issues. Away-days became a ritual of 'sensemaking', attempts to listen and explain and to help people through the ensuing changes.

Stories

Organisational stories symbolise what is important in an organisation and help to shape its culture. The stories of how this CEO held meetings, refusing to sit down, inviting criticism and challenge to existing ways of doing things and engaging in open and frank discussion, signalled that experimentation was welcomed.

Values

Collectively held values underpin organisational culture. It is not surprising that attention to the organisational value system became a top priority for the management team. From the early stages, planned workshops and impromptu discussions with senior and middle managers and clinical consultants worked on developing the organisational mission – perhaps the prime symbolic expression of any organisation. The workshops sought to build gradually a value statement which reflected both individuals' personal values and the fundamental purpose of the hospital. The resulting statement is simple and holds few surprises: but, far more importantly, it is 'owned' by many.

Fig 9.7 Mini-case: A model of change

2 *Pervasiveness* – not only is culture deep, it is broad and embraces all organisational activity.
3 *Implicitness* – much of culture is taken for granted. Therefore, it is difficult to change things which are implicitly part of people's thinking and behaviour.
4 *Imprinting* – culture has deep historical roots.
5 *Political* – culture has connections with the power distribution in an organisation, as certain power groups have a vested interest in the prevailing beliefs and cultural behaviours remaining as they are.
6 *Plurality* – organisations often have plural or more than one culture, that is, a set of subcultures and different group norms and behaviours.
7 *Interdependence* – culture is closely connected with the politics of the organisation, with its structure, systems, people and priorities.

Pettigrew (1990) recognises the role of power and politics in organisations and the interconnectivity of all organisational phenomena and processes. He therefore takes a broad view of culture and cultural change. His paper draws on empirical research in Jaguar Cars and ICI and suggests a list of 13 prescriptions for management to follow to improve the chances of successful change occurring.

Cultural change programmes are often managed by one or more senior managers working with the Human Resource Management (HRM) or Human Resource Development (HRD) department. However, the part played by HRM and training and development in the reproduction and change of organisational culture extends well beyond recruitment, selection, redundancy management and other 'organisational membership' measures. Many management development and training activities are concerned, implicitly or explicitly, with reinforcing or changing culture. For example, if a company wishes to instil a collective value of better customer care, then this is often facilitated through training and development programmes. It is also often built into performance appraisal and reward systems. Hence a coherent and consistent series of direct HRM interventions aim to reshape an aspect of organisational culture. It is quite possible to add to these training interventions and systems changes an element of symbolism. For example, if people who displayed ideal customer orientations were made into heroes or heroines and if a ceremony were held to acknowledge and reward such examples, then that ritual might transmit new or evolving meaning to organisational members.

Brooks and Bate (1994), when commenting on the limitations of many traditional top-down methods of change, suggest that successful cultural change requires:

- an awareness of the present culture;
- an awareness of the desired future culture;
- 'management' of the politics of acceptance; and
- a trigger for change.

Thus an essential rule for any cultural change should be: 'know your own culture, then change it', if necessary. Similarly, the holding of ideals or ambitions, a vision or model of the desired future state, would appear essential to facilitate purposeful change. It is important to recognise that politics and culture enjoy a complex relationship. It all depends on how we view organisations. Certainly, for any new paradigm to take hold in an organisation, it needs legitimisation. Hence, as culture is collectively 'owned', it seems reasonable that some attention needs to be paid to collective, political acceptance of the need for dynamism and of the direction of intended change. Finally, it is often considered that successful cultural change is facilitated by a real or perceived crisis, 'a state of affairs that acts as a trigger or catalyst for second-order change' (Brooks and Bate, 1994: 189).

Wilson (1992: 78) argues that 'following an interpretive view of culture leads us to a very different analytical and methodological perspective on how sense may be made of organizational change'. What becomes important is not the notion of an amenable and malleable culture but the cognitive and interpretive processes by which individuals in the workplace make sense of the change and, as a consequence, either support it, facilitating it for others, or seek to destroy or resist it. Thus the interpretation of symbols, such as language, lies at the heart of this view. Although culture may appear more obscure and less readily analysable from this perspective it need not necessarily be so. Symbols abound in organisations and the importance given to them is significant. Recognition that the way in which change and other management initiatives are interpreted is seen as vital from this perspective. Hence 'reality' becomes a social construction, that is, what is real is influenced by the complex cognitive processes of individuals and the myriad of social interactions between people in the workplace. A collectively held, socially derived interpretation of events then becomes a cultural belief. For example, Isabella (1990) views organisational transition as itself subject to change from an interpretive perspective. Hence, during a change process people will view that change and the 'realities' of the change process and its outcome differently at different stages of the process (*see* Figure 9.8).

It is argued that this interpretation of the change process, especially if it is a collective or cultural interpretation, will influence the eventual acceptance, or otherwise, of the change and the future success of the organisation. In order to answer the question, 'What will the change mean for me?', people make sense of information and piece it together within a rich context of past and present organisational events. In this view of culture, managers are not powerless to change culture but need to pay attention to the symbolic consequences of their actions, while aiming to foster desired

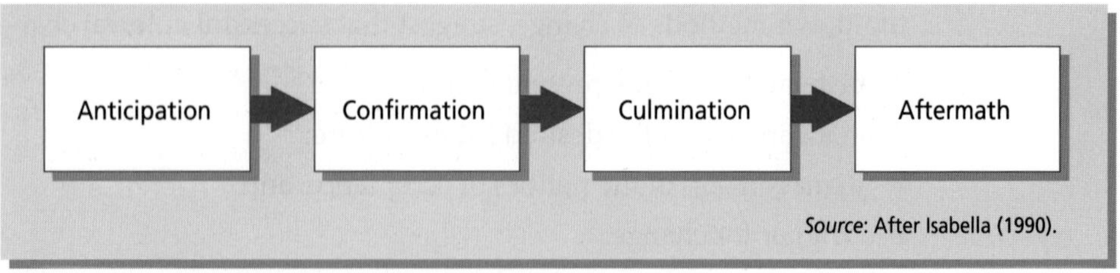

Source: After Isabella (1990).

Fig 9.8 Evolving interpretations of a change process

values. However, they can never control culture – as many management writers suggest is possible.

If we consider organisations themselves as if they are cultures, as Wilson (1992) and Isabella (1990), above, have done, then this fundamentally influences our understanding of management action and of business strategy. For example, if managers as strategists are part of the culture then both the process of strategy making and the resultant strategies will be profoundly influenced by the subjective processes found in that culture. Partly as a consequence of this, some academics argue that culture neither can nor should be consciously changed. Meek (1982: 469) commented that 'culture as a whole cannot be manipulated, turned on or off . . . culture should be regarded as something an organisation "is", not something it "has": it is not an independent variable nor can it be created, discovered or destroyed by the whims of management'.

Finally, the ethics of management's attempts to control culture are worthy of consideration. It has been argued (for example, by Van Maanen and Kunda, 1989) that managerial interest in organisational culture is motivated by a desire to control what employees think, feel, do and say. Any such attempts to intervene and change culture may be viewed as little short of cognitive control. If culture is a collective concept then the 'right' to manipulate it to one group's advantage may be ethically questionable.

Organisational learning and change

Organisational learning is a much debated contemporary issue of particular significance in the study of culture and of change. It was briefly discussed in Chapter 5. The question, 'can organisations learn?' invites often heated and contentious debate. Clearly, individuals in organisations can and do learn, yet we have evidence that organisations as a whole (as well as individuals in them) continue to repeat activities which sometimes lead to dysfunction and lack of success. It appears to many that organisations do not learn, neither do they learn, except slowly, to cope with a dynamic environment. Argyris (1964) and later Argyris and Schon (1978) argued that the important distinction in this debate lies between an organisation's ability to engage in single-loop or double-loop learning. They conclude that most organisations are locked into mere single-loop learning. Single-loop learning occurs where an organisation learns to conduct tasks, as if by rote, or to manage itself in a particular, predictable way. Double-loop learning involves greater questioning of both the organisation's objectives and its methods of achieving them in a continuous and progressive fashion. In double-loop learning an organisation will not automatically attempt to solve a problem or conduct a task in the same way as it has in the past but will possess the ability to reflect on previous experiences, to learn from them and to innovate and experiment with alternatives.

Single-loop learning is likely to be common in segmentalist (Kanter, 1983) organisations, whereas double-loop learning requires individuals and groups to be willing to discuss sensitive issues openly and to confront differences of view and seek ways of clarifying vague and ambiguous ideas and data. They must attempt to engage in collective reflection and problem resolution.

Managerial implications

Knowledge and increasing awareness of organisational culture have significantly influenced managerial thinking and practices in recent decades. Yet, as we have seen above, there remains no clear understanding and/or agreement over the meaning or value of this concept. That said, implications for managers may include:

1. There is a need to be aware that most people view organisations from one, or a limited number, of perspectives and that what we see is strongly influenced by that 'lens'.
2. Managers need an ability to reflect on their perspective(s). To embrace or experiment with others may shed new light on old organisational problems and may lead to the generation of novel solutions.
3. Managers should understand that culture is shared and pervasive, and influences every aspect of organisational life, including strategy, structure, employee relationships, communications, interpretation of the business environment and so forth.
4. A knowledge of and sensitivity to an organisation's culture appears to be an essential prerequisite for successful management of change.
5. An awareness that culture changes and can be changed is necessary, but it is likely that 'cultural tools' will need to be employed to achieve success.
6. Managers need an understanding that everything one does, wears or says carries symbolic significance and sends meaning to employees: understanding how they might interpret that meaning could prove valuable.
7. Managers must accept that many organisational routines become ritualised and carry symbolic significance: they are often dysfunctional and do little in themselves to achieve organisational objectives but serve to bind groups together.

Summary of main points

This chapter has been critical of the often simple and trite way in which culture is discussed and has sought to delve more deeply into this complex concept. The main points are:

- culture is an intensely 'human' and shared phenomenon which exists in a rich international, national and organisational context;
- identifiable subcultures thrive in many, especially large and diverse, organisations;

- there is considerable contention concerning the nature of organisational culture, with many suggesting, or implying, that it is an organisational variable, like structure, and others arguing that organisations *are* cultures;
- there are many typologies of culture, which are attempts to identify a small number of cultural types into which all organisations can be classified;
- cultural 'knowledge' is stored and interpreted by an individual cognitive process and shared and disseminated through interaction and collective interpretation;
- although apparently paradoxical, culture is both enduring and ever changing;
- cultural change processes are the subject of considerable organisational and managerial research and practical concern but all agree that culture is difficult to change;
- culture is related to organisational performance, change and organisational learning.

Conclusions

Organisational culture is a complex field of study stimulating definitional and methodological debate and contention. It can be seen that the concept has been linked to organisational performance, to management behaviour and to organisational change, structure and strategy. Consequently, whatever views carry most salience with the reader, the concept of organisational culture must be recognised as of vital importance to the understanding of organisation and all activities and processes operating within and in connection with organisation.

QUESTIONS

1 What rituals are observable in your organisation?

2 What do the rituals, identified in Question 1 above, 'say' to you about your organisation?

3 How can an understanding of culture enhance our understanding of organisational behaviour?

REFERENCES

Argyris, C. (1964) *Integrating the Individual and the Organization*. New York: Wiley.

Argyris, C. and Schon, D. A. (1978) *Organizational Learning: A Theory of Action Perspective*. Reading, MA: Addison-Wesley.

Barnes, B. (1996) *Managing Change: A Strategic Approach to Organisational Dynamics*. London: Financial Times Pitman Publishing.

Blake, R. R. and Mouton, J. S. (1969) *Building a Dynamic Corporation Through Grid Organization Development*. Reading, MA: Addison-Wesley.

Brooks, I. and Bate, S. P. (1994) 'The problems of effecting change within the British Civil Service: A cultural perspective', *British Journal of Management*, Vol. 5, pp 177–90.

Calori, R. and Sarnin, P. (1991) 'Corporate culture and economic performance: a French study', *Organization Studies*, 12(1), pp 49–74.

Cummings, T. G. and Huse, E. F. (1989) *Organizational Development and Change*. St Paul, MN: West.

Deal, T. and Kennedy, A. (1982) *Corporate Cultures: The Rites and Rituals of Corporate Life*. Reading, MA: Addison-Wesley.

Delamarter, R. T. (1988) *Big Blue: IBM's Use and Abuse of Power*. London: Pan.

Denison, D. R. (1984) 'Bringing corporate culture to the bottom line', *Organizational Dynamics*, Autumn, pp 5–22.

Denison, D. R. (1990) *Corporate Culture and Organizational Effectiveness*. New York: Wiley.

Dobson, P. (1988) 'Changing culture', *Employment Gazette*, December, pp 647–50.

Goffman, E. (1982) *The Presentation of Self in Everyday Life*. London: Pelican.

Gordon, G. (1985) 'The relationship of corporate culture to industry sector and corporate performance' in Kilmann, R., Saxton, M. and Serpa, R. (eds) *Gaining Control of the Corporate Culture*. San Francisco: Jossey-Bass.

Grinyer, P. H. and Spender, J. C. (1979) 'Recipes, crises and adaptation in mature businesses', *International Studies of Management and Organization*, 9(3), pp 113–23.

Handy, C. (1989) *Understanding Organizations*. Harmondsworth: Penguin.

Harrison, R. (1972) 'Understanding your Organization's Character', *Harvard Business Review*, Vol. 50, May–June, pp 119–28.

Hassard, J. and Sharifi, S. (1989) 'Corporate culture and strategic change', *Journal of General Management*, 15(2), pp 4–19.

Hofstede, G. (1980) *Culture's Consequences: International Differences in Work-related Values*. London and Beverly Hills, CA: Sage.

Isabella, L. A. (1990) 'Evolving interpretations as a change unfolds: how managers construe key organizational events', *Academy of Management Journal*, 33(1), pp 7–41.

Jaques, E. (1952) *The Changing Culture of a Factory*. New York: Dryden Press.

Johnson, G. and Scholes, K. (1999) *Exploring Corporate Culture: Text and Cases*, 5th edn. Hemel Hempstead: Prentice-Hall.

Johnson, G. and Scholes, K. (1994) *Exploring Corporate Strategy*. Hemel Hempstead: Prentice-Hall.

Kanter, R. M. (1983) *The Change Masters*. New York: Simon & Schuster.

Meek, V. L. (1982) 'Organizational culture: origins and weaknesses', *Organization Studies*, 4(4), pp 453–73.

Meyer, M. W. and Zucker, L. G. (1989) *Permanently Failing Organizations*. Beverly Hills, CA: Sage.

Miles, R. E. and Snow, C. C. (1978) *Organizational Strategy, Structure and Process*. New York: McGraw-Hill.

Morgan, G. (1986) *Images of Organization*. Newbury Park, CA: Sage.

Morgan, G. (1989) *Creative Organization Theory*. Newbury Park, CA: Sage.

Peters, T. J. and Waterman, R. H. (1982) *In Search of Excellence*. New York: Harper & Row.

Pettigrew, A. M. (1990) 'Is corporate culture manageable?' in Wilson, D. C. and Rosenfeld, R. H. (eds) *Managing Organizations*. New York: McGraw-Hill, pp 266–72.

Risto, H. (1990) 'Sociology as a discursive space – the coming age of a new orthodoxy?', *Acta Sociologica*, 33(4), pp 305–20.

Sachs, P. (ed.) (1989) 'Anthropological approaches to organizational culture', *Anthropology of Work Review*, Washington DC: Society for the Anthropology of Work, Special issue.

Schein, E. H. (1984) 'Coming to a new awareness of organizational culture', *Sloan Management Review*, 25(1), pp 3–16.

Schein, E. H. (1985) *Organizational Culture and Leadership: A Dynamic View*. San Francisco: Jossey-Bass.

Silver, M. (1987) 'The ideology of excellence: management and neo-conservatism', *Studies in Political Economy*, 24(1), pp 105–29.

Smircich, L. (1983) 'Concepts of culture and organizational analysis', *Administrative Science Quarterly*, Vol. 28, pp 339–358.

Steers, R. M., Shin, Y. K., Ungson, G. R. and Nam, S. (1990) 'Korean corporate culture: A comparative analysis', *Research in Personnel and Human Resources Management*, Supplement 2, pp 247–62.

Tommerup, P. (1988) 'From trickster to father figure: Learning from mythologization of top management' in Jones, M. O., Moore, M. D. and Snyder, R. C. (eds) *Inside Organizations*. Newbury Park, CA: Sage, pp 319–31.

Trice, H. M. and Beyer, J. M. (1984) 'Studying organizational cultures through rites and ceremonials', *Academy of Management Review*, Vol. 9, pp 653–69.

Uttal, B. (1983) 'The corporate culture vultures', *Fortune*, 17 October, pp 66–72.

Van Maanen, J. and Kunda, G. (1989) 'Real feelings: Emotion expression and organizational culture' in Staw, B. and Cummings, L. (eds) *Research in Organizational Behaviour*, Vol. 11, pp 43–103.

Wilson, D. C. (1992) *A Strategy of Change: Concepts and Controversies in the Management of Change*. London and New York: Routledge.

FURTHER READING

Books and papers on organisational culture exist which directly confront and contradict one another. Having read this chapter you should be more able to appreciate the value of most works on culture. Any of the references above may be of value but those listed here represent a cross-section.

Kanter, R. M. (1983) *The Change Masters*. New York: Simon & Schuster.

Morgan, G. (1997) *Images of Organization*, 2nd edn. Newbury Park, CA: Sage, Chapter 5.

Peters, T. J. and Waterman, R. H. (1982) *In Search of Excellence*. New York: Harper & Row.

Schein, E. H. (1985) *Organizational Culture and Leadership: A Dynamic View*. San Francisco: Jossey-Bass.

Smircich, L. (1983) 'Concepts of culture and organizational analysis', *Administrative Science Quarterly*, Vol. 28, pp 339–58.

10

The impact of national culture on organisational behaviour

JON STEPHENS

LEARNING OUTCOMES

On completion of this chapter you should be able to:

- understand the differences in national culture;
- appreciate different ways of classifying cultures;
- understand culture shock and culture shift;
- evaluate the ways in which national culture can affect individual and organisational behaviour, including motivation, leadership and management styles and practices;
- understand how the effectiveness of organisational structures may be influenced by culture and how structures vary in different cultures;
- comprehend the main arguments of the convergence/divergence debate;
- consider the crucial role of communication in overcoming crosscultural problems in organisations;
- appreciate the increased managerial significance of crosscultural awareness.

KEY CONCEPTS

- *national culture*
- *cultural determinism*
- *power distance, uncertainty avoidance, individualism/ collectivism, masculinity/femininity, Confucian dynamics*
- *ethnocentrism*
- *cultural differentiation and profiling*
- *culture shock*
- *culture shift*
- *perceptual gaps*
- *management styles*
- *cultural stereotyping*
- *convergence/divergence*

The impact of national culture on organisational behaviour

With the increased move towards internationalisation and globalisation of business activities, the impact of national cultures on organisations is becoming of increasing importance. Differences in national cultures may have a bearing on how organisations deal with each other and also on behaviour within organisations which comprise a mix of nationalities. This chapter therefore explores the concept of national culture and then seeks to examine areas of organisational behaviour where cultural differences may be significant.

Introduction

The environment in which most organisations exist is increasingly dynamic and turbulent. Rapid change affects the workings of the organisation and organisational behaviour. One of the factors that is creating change in the environment is internationalisation and globalisation. The world is becoming a much smaller place as a result of changes in transport and technology. For instance, it is now feasible to commute from London to Paris, Lille and Brussels by means of high-speed rail links (Eurostar), with further routes throughout Europe being opened up as the high-speed train network grows. Air travel is growing at about 7 per cent a year, with increased deregulation creating cheaper prices so that business people and tourists can more easily travel between continents. Information technology has also shrunk the world in that communication across borders has never been easier with e-mail, the Internet and, increasingly, teleconferencing providing swift links between people in organisations in different countries.

At the same time more and more companies are seeking an international presence as a means of diversifying their markets, helped by the development of trade blocs. In the European Union (EU), for example, the single market programme sought to remove a range of barriers that had previously inhibited trading and business across borders. Despite the recent (mid–late 1990s) slump the economies of South-East Asia have attracted massive investment from other countries and have also, in turn, invested heavily in Europe and the Americas.

These developments mean that an increasing number of organisations are operating in several countries and, thus, managers in the organisation's host country are having to deal with nationals from other countries. From a European perspective it is not merely European companies investing and developing overseas; it is also organisations from other countries which have invested in Europe. Again there is a likelihood of increased contact with managers in other countries, even if the organisation operates predominantly in one country. These developments have placed the issue of national culture much higher on the organisational agenda. There is clear evidence that an increasing number of organisations are having to deal with cultural issues and that the success or otherwise of their efforts may have a significant impact on the organisation's overall effectiveness. However, before an organisation can deal with issues arising from national cultural differences, it must first be able to identify what these differences are likely to be and also consider specific issues of significance. Identifying and discussing these is the prime objective of this chapter.

National culture

One of the biggest problems faced when looking at national culture is to find an acceptable definition. Kroeber and Kluckholm (1985) found over 160 definitions of culture in their research. This may be because culture can be viewed from an anthropological or sociological perspective as opposed to a purely organisational one, although the latter is the area on which this chapter focuses. Two useful examples of definitions of culture are as follows. Mead (1951) suggests that culture *'is a body of learned behaviour, a collection of beliefs, habits and traditions, shared by a group of people and successively learned by people who enter society'*. Hofstede (1984) defines culture as *'the collective programming of the mind, which distinguishes the members of one human group from another . . . culture, in this sense, includes systems of values'*. A more thorough definition and discussion of culture, predominantly at the level of the organisation (as opposed to the nation), is given in Chapter 9.

The most deep-rooted element of culture is the set of values and fundamental, taken-for-granted assumptions held by a group of people. Such values and assumptions about all manner of phenomena, including those about what is 'right' and what is 'wrong' and what is 'good' and what is 'bad', manifest themselves in people's attitudes and behaviours. Often surface behaviour is driven by a much deeper value, assumption or belief which is itself a product of cultural conditioning. As will be shown, cultural differences can be substantial and may lead people to view 'similar' phenomena in quite different ways. For example, people in a particular country may cherish their personal right to freedom of speech, whereas another culture may feel that such a right should be subordinate to what is in the best interests of society as a whole.

The discussion above implies that culture comprises some commonly held values among a group of people which have been determined by the environment in which they grew up and which, to some extent, will influence their behaviour both inside and outside the organisation. Because of Hofstede's work on classifying cultures there is a tendency to look at this in purely national terms, although there may be substantial subcultures within a society; for example, the Catalans see themselves as having a different culture from that of the rest of Spain, although there are points of similarity. A country may have several strong subcultures which may not always correspond with national stereotypes, and businesses sometimes need to be aware of this. Culture is shared; however, that is not to say that everyone in a particular culture thinks and acts in the same way (as Chapter 2 makes clear). Individual differences are significant. When describing cultures we look for 'typical' values, beliefs and attitudes and 'norms' of behaviour. Subcultures can also exist, based on other than geographical criteria. In some countries subcultural differences may follow social class, gender, age, ethnic origin, religion or occupational group, for example.

Figure 10.1 illustrates the origins of commonly held values. As can be seen, these are all factors that may influence how our values develop within the society in which we grow up and work. Perhaps one of the most critical factors is that of language. Returning to the example of Catalonia, we may note that the Catalans have a different language than Spanish (Castilian) and this serves to bond the people of the region together and to reinforce their culture. Sometimes the introduction of new languages, for example those which are compulsory in schools, may have an impact on culture. An example here is the marked shift towards Mandarin Chinese in Hong Kong before Hong Kong was returned to China in 1997. People believed that with Hong

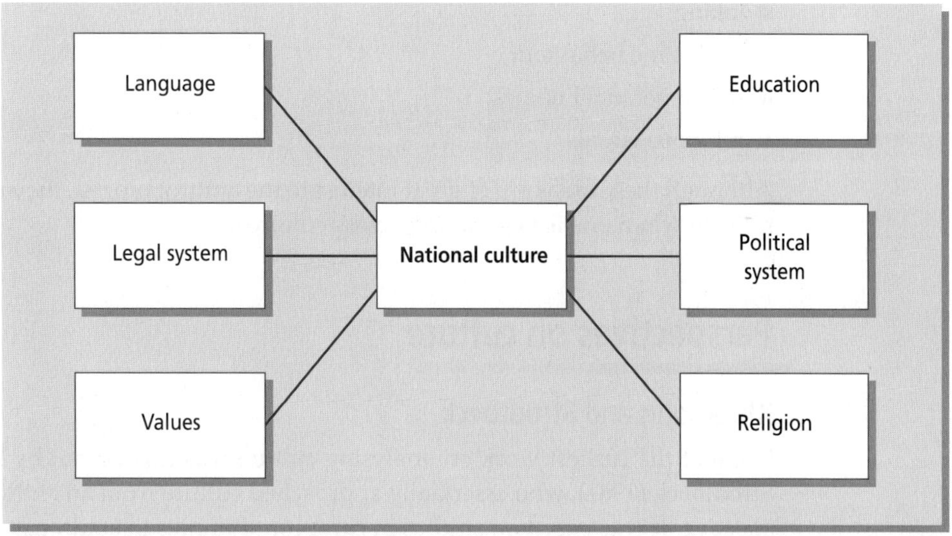

Fig 10.1 Factors affecting national culture

Kong's integration into the People's Republic of China, there would be increased opportunities for those speaking Mandarin Chinese, as opposed to the type of Chinese spoken in Hong Kong (Cantonese). It remains to be seen how this switch in use of language will influence the evolution of culture. Sometimes, changes to language which are influenced by other cultures can be fiercely resisted, as we have seen in France where the Academie Française has been trying to prevent the introduction of 'pop-culture' words which were mainly English.

Religion may also have a significant bearing on culture. The effect may be especially pronounced in countries where the religious and political systems are closely interlinked, such as in Iran or Israel, but it will also be significant in determining the types of values developed. For example, Confucianism has certainly influenced the collectivist views and long-term perspective held throughout Asia. Perhaps the Protestant work ethic has influenced the degree of individualism that is encountered in many Anglo-Saxon countries (*see* the discussion below of Hofstede's analysis).

Numerous factors help to determine the way we look at things in the world, how we see ourselves and how we see others. Murdoch (1945) identified many specific factors in which there may be cultural differences. These include:

- courtship;
- dream interpretation;
- food taboos;
- use of gestures;
- greetings between friends and business contacts;

- joking;
- meal-time behaviour;
- use of personal names;
- religious rituals.

Although these areas are of great interest to the anthropologist, they may also be significant when one is negotiating across cultures.

Perspectives on culture

Kluckhohn and Strodtbeck

Some of the earliest work on analysing culture was carried out by Kluckhohn and Strodtbeck (1961), who essentially approached culture from an anthropological perspective. It was based on studies in rural communities in south-east USA, although it was applied in a much wider cultural context. Kluckhohn and Strodtbeck were able to classify values into six basic orientations to the world from which a cultural profile would emerge. The six orientations of value were:

- the nature of individuals;
- the person's relationship to their environment;
- the person's relationship to other people;
- the nature of the person's activity;
- the time dimension of the person's activity;
- the space dimension of the person's activity.

These orientations were then further subdivided as shown in Table 10.1.

Table 10.1 Kluckhohn and Strodtbeck's Value Orientation Dimensions

Perception of	Possible dimensions		
1 Individuals	Good	Good and evil	Evil
2 Relationship to environment	Dominant	Harmony	Subjugation
3 Relationship with others	Individualistic	Extended groups	Hierarchical groups
4 Nature of activity	Doing	Controlling	Being
5 Relationship to time	Future-looking	Present-looking	Past-looking
6 Relationship to space	Private	Mixed	Public

Source: Adapted from Kluckhohn and Strodtbeck (1961) and Adler (1997).

Nancy Adler

Nancy Adler (1997) looked at these dimensions from an American perspective and suggested that Americans see individuals as a mixture of good and evil who are also capable of changing and improving themselves, hence, the demand for books and programmes which propose to make people better managers or put them more in touch with their inner self. In terms of their relationship to the environment, Adler suggests that Americans see themselves as dominant over nature and their environment rather than feeling a need to live in harmony with their environment, as people with a more Confucian-type perspective would do. When it comes to relationships with other people, the American culture can clearly be seen to be individualistic as opposed to depending more on groups. There is still the belief that anyone can rise to the top with the right combination of skills and drive, sometimes called the 'log cabin to president' philosophy. They believe that your birthright should be no barrier to your development in society. People who achieve are seen as the 'champions' of the country, whether it is Bill Gates with Microsoft or Michael Jordan on the basketball court. Adler suggests that the individual will be expected to make decisions and perform independently whereas, in the more group-orientated or collectivist cultures, there is greater dependence on the group, whether it is the extended family (as in Chinese family businesses) or the company (such as in the giant groups of interlinked companies in Japan called *keiretsu*).

When we consider the nature of people's activity we can see clearly that the Americans are 'doers' or action orientated: if there is a problem you go and sort it out yourself. This may have a significant impact on management style and activity in the organisation in that individuals will be expected to engage in problem-solving activity by themselves rather than rely on others for a solution. A recent (1998) television series called *The Tourist Trap* exposed people of different nationalities to similar experiences in order to evaluate their reactions. One 'event' involved intentionally leaving the breakfast in a deserted kitchen to see how the groups would react. The American group soon found the kitchen and organised the breakfast themselves without any complaint, whereas the Japanese group remained politely waiting in the main room. It took them a long time to go and find the kitchen and even then they were reluctant to take over from the staff who were temporarily absent.

When looking at the time dimension of their activities, Adler found the Americans to be future orientated in that they believed you should look at issues and assess the potential future benefits that could be produced, although they tended to look at these benefits very much in the short term rather than in the long term. Past-orientated cultures are more likely to be found in Europe and Asia. This might partly be a result of a greater sense of history or a belief that actions should fit in with beliefs and traditions. It is also noticeable that many Asian companies adopt a longer-term perspective and this may explain Japanese companies' preference for long-term market growth rather than short-term profits.

The final dimension of Kluckhohn and Strodtbeck's work refers to how individuals address the space dimension of their activities. This is often reflected in office layouts. In some cultures there may be separate offices and access to people may be restricted or guarded by a 'gatekeeper' or secretary. Other cultures have a more open approach and may value the openness of managers in the organisation. Whereas, Adler suggests, Americans prefer considerable private space, there is considerable evidence from Japanese companies that they are happy with smaller offices. This can be seen in the Japanese company Sony, which has a plant in Bridgend, Wales, where it is company policy that managers should spend some time of the day with or near the workers and also mix in their company canteen.

The Kluckhohn–Strodtbeck model is a useful introduction to cultural analysis and many aspects of it were developed by other writers, especially Trompenaars (1993). It must be remembered, though, that it was based on anthropology rather than organisation studies and that the research was not carried out in a wide range of countries.

André Laurent

Laurent (1983) developed our understanding of national culture further and his research built on that of Kluckhohn and Strodtbeck. It was manager focused and was based on about 60 questions to assess managers' work values. Its geographical spread was much greater as it included nine West European countries and the USA and it was also expanded by Laurent, Adler and Campbell (1989) to include Japan, Indonesia and the People's Republic of China (PRC). Laurent was essentially seeking to prove that commonly held beliefs by managers in a country were a result of national cultural factors and, thus, he argued that care should be taken when assuming a universality of management and organisational theories. Such theories, particularly the prescriptive ones, might suggest an approach that would work in one country but prove less effective in another (*see* below and also Chapter 5 on contingency theory).

Mead (1998) and Adler (1997) have identified some key aspects of Laurent's analysis and focus specifically on the issues of:

- managers' attitudes towards hierarchy;
- the willingness to bypass lines of hierarchy in the organisation;
- managers' relationships with subordinates;
- the importance of managers in society.

These four themes were reflected in the following statements:

- 'The main reason for a hierarchical structure is so that everybody knows who has authority over whom' (Statement 1);
- 'In order to have efficient work relationships it is often necessary to bypass the hierarchical line' (Statement 2);
- 'It is important for managers to have at hand precise answers to most of the questions that their subordinates may raise about their work' (Statement 3);

- 'Through their professional activity, managers play an important role in society' (Statement 4).

The responses to these statements can be seen in Table 10.2.

Table 10.2 Laurent's analysis of managers' roles

Country	Statement 1 % Agreeing (1989)	Statement 2 % Disagreeing (1989)	Statement 3 % Agreeing (1989)	Statement 4 % Agreeing (1983)
Spain	—	74	77	—
Denmark	—	37	23	32
UK	34	35	27	40
Netherlands	31	44	17	45
Germany	26	45	46	46
Sweden	30	26	10	54
Switzerland	—	41	38	65
Italy	42	56	66	74
France	43	43	53	76
Belgium	—	42	44	—
USA	17	32	18	52
Japan	50	—	78	—
Indonesia	83	51	73	—
PRC	70	59	74	—

Source: Based on Laurent (1983); (1989).

This evidence clearly supports Laurent's hypothesis that much of management behaviour is culturally determined or influenced. This is especially clear in relation to attitudes to authority in the organisation. Evidence of the Confucian principle of respect for and obedience to elders and superiors is shown by people's preference for clearly defined hierarchical structure and their unwillingness to bypass this structure. We also see the more individualistic American culture, with less respect for hierarchy and the belief that individuals should be willing to undertake their own actions, even if it means bypassing the established hierarchy.

What is more interesting from Laurent's analysis is the massive diversity which he found in Europe. Indeed if you contrast, say, Sweden and the Netherlands with Spain and Italy you see marked differences in practically every area. Thus, although we might predict that the Confucian-influenced Asian countries would expect superiors (managers) to have precise answers for questions (not least because of the fear of losing face), we see very similar responses in Spain and Italy, so in some respects the values of their managers are closer to those found in Indonesia than in Sweden. This finding has implications for situations when managers in Europe come together through acquisitions, joint ventures or strategic alliances. Ronen and Shenkar (1985) have identified nine clusters of countries which, they argue, have similar cultural characteristics. It is interesting to note that member countries of the European Union fall into five separate cultural groups. For example, the United Kingdom and Ireland are in their 'Anglo' cluster (together with Australia, the USA, Canada and New Zealand), the Scandinavian countries of Sweden, Denmark and Finland are considered 'Nordic', France, Belgium, Italy and the Iberian countries are 'Latin-European', Greece is 'Near-Eastern' and Germany and Austria are 'Germanic'. It is not surprising that there are differences in perception and in substance between EU members' national governments.

Geert Hofstede

In many ways Geert Hofstede is seen as the major writer on crosscultural analysis because the model he developed (Hofstede, 1980, 1984, 1991) has survived the test of time, is relatively easy to use and is comprehensive. Hofstede was influenced by Laurent's work but decided to take his analysis further by defining some clear themes for analysis. He extended Laurent's original Western Europe/USA spectrum to a more global one. His data for this were provided by gaining access to the American computer company IBM. Through this he was able to investigate the attitudes of 116 000 employees in 50 countries, clearly a more extensive analysis than that of Laurent. Table 10.3 illustrates his findings.

Four cultural dimensions, discussed below, emerged from his extensive data. They are referred to as:

- power distance;
- individualism/collectivism;
- uncertainty avoidance;
- masculinity/femininity.

Power distance

Power distance represents *the social distance between people of different rank or position*. For example, in a country with a high power distance score (e.g. Malaysia) subordinates would be unwilling to question superiors and would look to them for direction. Thus they may well accept an unequal distribution of power and autocratic leadership styles. Low power distance suggests less dependence between superiors and subordinates. A leader may have to earn respect in a low power-distance country. This is one of the most significant of Hofstede's dimensions and can clearly be seen to concur with Laurent's earlier work. In Table 10.3, the higher the index number for power distance (PDI), the greater will be the gap between managers and subordinates. A low PDI figure suggests that there is a much smaller gap.

Individualism

Individualism reflects *the extent to which an individual relies on a group (a collectivist approach) or takes individual initiative in making decisions, solving problems and engaging*

Table 10.3 Hofstede's cultural criteria

Country	Abbreviation	Individualism Index (IDV)	Rank	Power distance Index (PDI)	Rank	Uncertainty avoidance Index (UAI)	Rank	Masculinity Index (MAS)	Rank
Argentina	ARG	46	28–29	49	18–19	86	36–41	56	30–31
Australia	AUL	90	49	36	13	51	17	61	35
Austria	AUT	55	33	11	1	70	26–27	79	49
Belgium	BEL	75	43	65	33	94	45–46	54	29
Brazil	BRA	38	25	69	39	76	29–30	49	25
Canada	CAN	80	46–47	39	15	48	12–13	52	28
Chile	CHL	23	15	63	29–30	86	36–41	28	8
Colombia	COL	13	5	67	36	80	31	64	39–40
Costa Rica	COS	15	8	35	10–12	86	36–41	21	5–6
Denmark	DEN	74	42	18	3	23	3	16	4
Equador	EQA	8	2	78	43–44	67	24	63	37–38
Finland	FIN	63	34	33	8	59	20–21	26	7
France	FRA	71	40–41	68	37–38	86	36–41	43	17–18
Germany (FR)	GER	67	36	35	10–12	65	23	66	41–42
Great Britain	GBR	89	48	35	10–12	35	6–7	66	41–42
Greece	GRE	35	22	60	26–27	112	50	57	32–33
Guatemala	GUA	6	1	95	48–49	101	48	37	11
Hong Kong	HOK	25	16	68	37–38	29	4–5	57	32–33
Indonesia	IDO	14	6–7	78	43–44	48	12–13	46	22
India	IND	48	30	77	42	40	9	56	30–31
Iran	IRA	41	27	58	24–25	59	20–21	43	17–18
Ireland	IRE	70	39	28	5	35	6–7	68	43–44
Israel	ISR	54	32	13	2	81	32	47	23
Italy	ITA	76	44	50	20	75	28	70	46–47
Jamaica	JAM	39	26	45	17	13	2	68	43–44
Japan	JPN	46	28–29	54	21	92	44	95	50
Korea (S)	KOR	18	11	60	26–27	85	34–35	39	13
Malaysia	MAL	26	17	104	50	36	8	50	26–27
Mexico	MEX	30	20	81	45–46	82	33	69	45
Netherlands	NET	80	46–47	38	14	53	18	14	3
Norway	NOR	69	38	31	6–7	50	16	8	2
New Zealand	NZL	79	45	22	4	49	14–15	58	34
Pakistan	PAK	14	6–7	55	22	70	26–27	50	26–27
Panama	PAN	11	3	95	48–49	86	36–41	44	19
Peru	PER	16	9	64	31–32	87	42	42	15–16
Philippines	PHI	32	21	94	47	44	10	64	39–40
Portugal	POR	27	18–19	63	29–30	104	49	31	9
South Africa	SAF	65	35	49	18–19	49	14–15	63	37–38
Salvador	SAL	19	12	66	34–35	94	45–46	40	14
Singapore	SIN	20	13–14	74	40	8	1	48	24
Spain	SPA	51	31	57	23	86	36–41	42	15–16
Sweden	SWE	71	40–41	31	6–7	29	4–5	5	1
Switzerland	SWI	68	37	34	9	58	19	70	46–47
Taiwan	TAI	17	10	58	24–25	69	25	45	20–21
Thailand	THA	20	13–14	64	31–32	64	22	34	10
Turkey	TUR	37	24	66	34–35	85	34–35	45	20–21
Uruguay	URU	36	23	61	28	100	47	38	12
USA	USA	91	50	40	16	46	11	62	36
Venezuela	VEN	12	4	81	45–46	76	29–30	73	48
Yugoslavia	YUG	27	18–19	76	41	88	43	21	5–6
Regions:									
East Africa (1)	EAF	27	(18–19)	64	(31–32)	52	(17–18)	41	(14–15)
West Africa (2)	WAF	20	(13–14)	77	(42)	54	(18–19)	46	(22)
Arab Ctrs (3)	ARA	38	(25)	80	(44–45)	68	(24–25)	53	(28–29)

Source: G. Hofstede (1984) *Culture's Consequences: International Differences in Work-Related Values*. Copyright © 1984 by Sage Publications, Inc.

in productive activity. We have already noted that the American culture has a tendency to be very individualistic, whereas Asian cultures tend to be much more collective. In some cultures relationships in key groups (whether at work or within the family) may be highly significant. The Chinese have a concept, *guanxi*, which means connection or relationship and much time is spent in cultivating relationships both within and outside the family and building up networks. Thus, rather than rely on themselves individually, they can use these relationships and expect them to be used in return. This collectivism is found in many Asian countries although there have been some changes in Asian countries more exposed to Western influences.

In Table 10.3, the higher index numbers (IDV) for individualism suggest cultures where there is more individualism. Not surprisingly, the USA tops the list, with the UK and other 'Anglo' countries scoring high. This dimension may be significant for managers who are developing an appropriate managerial style when they are operating overseas: they may encounter problems if they try to get their subordinates to act more independently rather than in groups. In Korea, for example, people would not be happy if required to act independently and to justify their independent action; they would fear the loss of face they would suffer if there was any criticism from a superior. Social interaction in China or Korea is carried out with the express purpose of not allowing people to lose face and a Western manager needs to be aware of this.

Uncertainty avoidance

Uncertainty avoidance essentially *reflects people's attitudes to ambiguity* in a society or country. Hofstede found that in some cultures there was unhappiness or uncertainty with ambiguous situations and that people wanted more direction and were less comfortable with change, especially when it was not explained to them. People who are not comfortable with uncertain or ambiguous situations may develop anxiety or stress and, thus, work less effectively in an organisation where there is little direction and considerable uncertainty. They may be happier with written rules to cover every situation (as they might find in a bureaucratic organisation) and with job security.

From Table 10.3 we can identify a country which has a high level of uncertainty avoidance, such as Greece. The description above would apply to Greek people. From the table we can also see that there are a number of countries with low uncertainty avoidance, such as Sweden. Their low score suggests that people in these countries are more willing to take risks and are much less resistant to change than those in high uncertainty-avoidance countries. The managerial implications are obvious. If we imagine a Swedish company with a subsidiary in Greece, where it is seeking to introduce new methods, or perhaps a change in corporate culture, we can see that the process will have to be handled carefully. The risk of resistance and conflict if changes are pushed too quickly, in a culture which is resistant to change and ambiguous situations, is very real.

Masculinity

Masculinity is one of the more complex variables introduced by Hofstede. It reflects *values which are widely considered to be more 'masculine', such as assertiveness, competitiveness and results orientation*, whereas 'feminine' values can be seen to be co-operative and to show greater awareness of feelings and equal opportunities. This value also relates to the degree of discrimination against (usually) women in the organisation.

From Table 10.3 it is not surprising to find that Japan has the highest masculinity (MAS) score and Norway one of the lowest, although you will find considerable variance among Western European countries, which confirms Laurent's findings that it can be misleading to talk of a 'European' culture.

Hofstede's findings indicate four areas of potential difference between cultures, but it is now commonly accepted that a fifth variable exists. This resulted from the Chinese Values Survey carried out by the Chinese Culture Connection (1987) which sought to evaluate the effectiveness of Hofstede's cultural dimensions in a specific Asian context where there would be a significant influence of Confucianism. Their evaluation was further tested by Bond and Hofstede (1988) who showed that three of the four dimensions identified by Hofstede were present, the missing one being uncertainty avoidance. What did emerge from the study by the Chinese Culture Connection Group (1987) was the evidence of a fifth dimension which seemed particularly applicable to Asian cultures and which indicated that most Asian countries had a long-term perspective about work and the organisation. In the study this was labelled 'Confucian dynamics' but Hofstede called it 'long-term orientation' (LTO). This orientation may be useful for explaining the different behaviour of, say, Japanese organisations and Western organisations. The Japanese may be much more influenced by long-term market share than immediate short-term factors, such as dividends. It may also explain why Asian companies are keen to build long-term relationships with Western companies rather than attempt take-overs or other short-term activities.

A further development which stems from Hofstede's work is the clustering of countries with common cultural characteristics. An example of this can be seen in Figure 10.2. Figure 10.2 shows groups of countries that have similarities in the two fields of uncertainty avoidance and power distance. For example, we can see that the cultures of Argentina (ARG) and Spain (SPA) are close on these two criteria, possibly because of their common cultural and linguistic heritage. It would suggest that in both countries managers are comfortable with a large power distance from subordinates and that ambiguity is not popular and thus a more autocratic leadership style might be suitable. It is therefore likely that in these two respects there would be few problems, stemming from cultural differences, in any alliance between a Spanish organisation and an Argentine organisation.

There have been some criticisms of Hofstede's model. One of the most obvious is that although his study included a substantial number of countries, there were none from Eastern Europe and Russia and many Asian countries were ignored. The explanation is, of course, that the survey was explicitly based on IBM and in 1980 and 1984 IBM did not have a significant presence in these countries. This omission has to some extent been corrected by the Chinese Values Survey and more recent work applying the work of Hofstede to Eastern Europe. However, this leads to a second

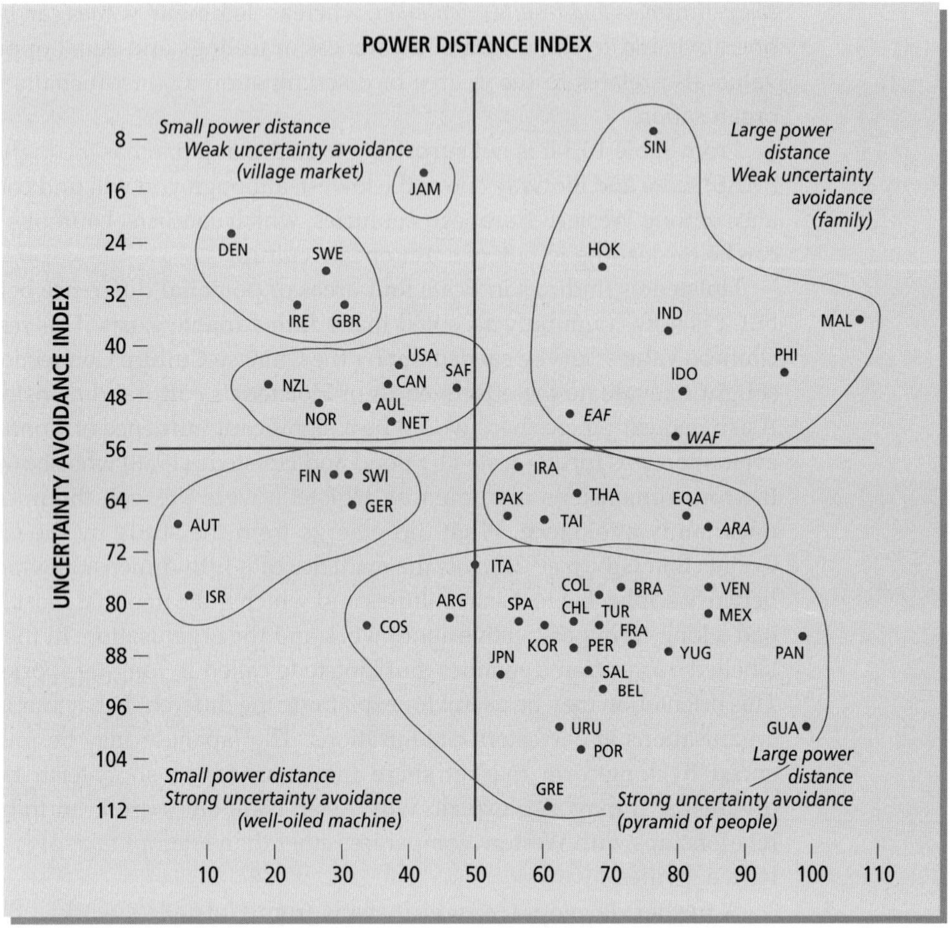

Fig 10.2 Uncertainty avoidance and power distance clusters

Source: G. Hofstede (1984) *Culture's Consequences: International Differences in Work-Related Values*. Copyright © 1984 by Sage Publications, Inc.

Note: The country abbreviations are explained in Table 10.3.

criticism in that the results were based on an organisation with a very strong corporate culture which may have distorted the findings. Despite this, most subsequent research has upheld the validity of his analysis and it remains the most popular model which is used worldwide to evaluate cultural differences between countries and assess their implication for organisational behaviour.

Fons Trompenaars

Fons Trompenaars' (1993) work draws on that of Kluckhohn and Strodtbeck and also that of Hofstede, but seeks to extend the analysis. Whereas Hofstede sought to explain differences in cultures, Trompenaars, coming from a consultancy background, was more concerned with practical problems and solutions for managers dealing with a crosscultural environment. Trompenaars' questionnaire survey directed to 15 000 respondents provided data enabling him to identify seven dimensions of culture, which are:

- universalism v. particularism;
- collectivism v. individualism;
- affective v. neutral cultures;
- specific v. diffuse relationships;
- achieving v. ascribing status;
- time as sequence v. time as synchronisation;
- inner directed v. outer directed.

One of these dimensions, collectivism v. individualism, is familiar to us from Hofstede's work but the others require further explanation.

Universalism v. particularism

The *universalist* approach suggests *a culture that is driven by rules and prefers a rational and logical approach in the belief that there are universal rules which should be respected.* A *particularist* culture is based more on people relationships (e.g. *guanxi*) and may encourage more flexibility in the interpretation of rules. High universalist countries include Canada, the USA and the UK and particularist countries include China and Thailand. This may explain the confusion often experienced by Western managers when negotiating in Asia, especially if they are under the misapprehension that Western rules of business behaviour will apply in the East, particularly in terms of contractual negotiations.

Affective v. neutral cultures

This dimension relates *the extent of emotional behaviour found in a culture*. In affective cultures, such as Italy, emotions are revealed more openly in the organisation than they are in neutral cultures, such as Japan and Germany, where such openness would be frowned upon and where people might find emotions difficult to handle. The implications for international teamworking may be significant if some members exhibit emotional behaviour in the way they communicate and others prefer 'the stiff upper lip' approach. The use of emotion may distort the meaning of communications whereas an individual who displays inhibition may be hiding his true feelings or viewpoints and thus may contribute less effectively to the group.

Specific v. diffuse relationships

In a *specific* culture, Trompenaars argues that *managers separate their work relationships from other relationships*; that is, the manager–subordinate relationship may be observed at work but at the squash club people are on first-name terms and treat each other as equals. This contrasts with behaviour in a *diffuse* culture, where the relationship at work influences all relationships outside work; so a person who is a subordinate at work would be very cautious about approaching his or her superior outside work in a relatively open manner without some prompt from the manager concerned. Diffusion is very strong in cultures where there is high respect for seniority and can be clearly linked to Hofstede's power distance factor.

Achieving v. ascribing status

In an *achieving* culture *status is considered to be achievement based*, whereas in other cultures status is ascribed to an individual because of factors like age or gender. Thus high-ascribing cultures are to be found in Hong Kong, Argentina and Egypt whereas achievement cultures are found in the USA and Scandinavia.

Time as sequence v. time as synchronisation

Time as sequence suggests *a rational, linear approach to issues* ('one step at a time'), whereas *time as synchronisation* suggests that *time is seen as circular* with the possibility of parallel activities, such as might be found in Japan. Trompenaars suggests that this relates to Bond and Hofstede's (1988) dimension of 'long-term orientation' (or 'Confucian dynamics') and that it may be very significant for organisational behaviour. In cultures where time is seen as sequential there may be a tendency towards short-term relationships and timing may be seen as very important. There is potential for conflict with people in cultures where the concept of time is more elastic and where long-term relationships carry more weight.

Inner directed v. outer directed

The dimension of inner or outer direction contrasts countries like the USA and Switzerland, where there is *a belief that the individual should seek to control the natural and human environment*, with nations like China where man aims to be in harmony with nature: this belief is central to both Confucianism and Buddhism. It is this belief which may explain why, in countries like Japan, organisations are seen holistically as operating in harmony with their surroundings and with the people within the organisation, and which could further explain why direct conflict or confrontation is often resisted.

Trompenaars has developed his work with Charles Hampden-Turner (1993, 1997) and they have extended their field of analysis, especially in Asia. They replaced the affective/neutral dimension with an equality/hierarchy one which corresponds more clearly to Hofstede's findings. In many ways they have confirmed and developed the work of Kluckhohn and Strodtbeck, Laurent and Hofstede. The work of analysing culture still goes on (*see* Gatley, Lessem and Altman, 1996) but a common thread that emerges from all of these studies is that organisations operating in a multinational context need to be aware of the cultural differences they are likely to encounter if they are to avoid potential problems. They also suggest that there is no unalterable formula for reconciling cultural differences but that every case should be seen on its own merits. However, the awareness of the likely cultural problems to be encountered could, ultimately, give an organisation competitive advantage over its rivals.

Culture shock and culture shift

Imagine the scenario. You have just moved to start a new job in an exciting new country with a totally different culture to that of your own. The initial reaction to this may well be one of excitement as you read the guide books and start to learn a few words of the language. The first few days of your new job may be exciting as you begin to absorb some of the new sights and sounds; what Torbiorn (1982) calls 'the honeymoon'. Then, with mounting horror, you begin to realise that your command of the language is seriously inadequate. Furthermore, you are finding that relationships with people in your organisation and socially are not going smoothly. You appear to have offended someone without realising it. From a feeling of euphoria you rapidly descend to feeling that you are in an increasingly hostile environment, in which you feel alienated and lost. This experience is referred to as *culture shock*, that is, *the startling experiences and difficulties first encountered when entering an alien culture*. This is increasingly being recognised as a serious issue for companies which send managers overseas. The manager may end up disillusioned and may even leave the company as a result of this bad experience. If this happens, it represents a major loss for both the individual and the organisation.

The ability of the individual to overcome these problems to some extent depends on his or her own personality but there is an increasing recognition that managers overseas need increased support from the organisation. It is also interesting to note that many of the early problems faced by Eurodisney near Paris were cultural in origin and were partly the result of American management coming into contact with French culture.

Another factor of which organisations should be aware is reverse culture shock, which occurs when a manager who has been overseas for some years, and has adapted well to his or her new culture, is faced with returning to the home country, perhaps because of some organisational restructuring. Imagine a British manager who has been in Malaysia for the last twenty years returning to the UK of 1999, having been used to the UK of 1979. Such a move can cause culture shock and may require support for the manager from the organisation. Awareness of the possibility of reverse culture shock might also explain why the long-term posting of managers overseas is becoming less commonplace: there is a trend towards their being replaced by locally employed managers.

Culture shift is *cultural change, more specifically, the extent to which a culture can change and the speed at which such changes occur*. There are many factors that might induce cultural shift in a country. Changing economic conditions, high levels of investment by overseas multinationals and social, political and religious upheaval can all affect culture and in turn, be further influenced by the evolving culture. Mead (1998) highlights the case of the *shinjinrui* in Japan. Traditional Japanese workers were exceptionally loyal to their company and leader and would regard the company's interests as paramount. *Shinjinrui* means 'new human beings' and reflects the influence of a number of predominantly younger workers who are less loyal to the company and who would not, for example, automatically work overtime. In Hofstede's terms, this reflects a move towards more individualism and, therefore, represents some degree of cultural shift, although Mead cautions against overstating the nature of this change, as the extent of the shift is at present quite small.

Another interesting case is that of Hong Kong where the ethnic population is over 90 per cent Chinese and yet there has been significant investment by overseas multinationals, especially American companies. Table 10.4 illustrates Hofstede's and Trompenaars' rankings applied to Hong Kong, China and the United States (in order to see how close the Hong Kong culture is to the Chinese one) in areas where there may have been an element of cultural shift.

It appears that Hong Kong remains close to China in terms of power distance, individualism, achievement, universalism and affectivity, as their common cultural origins might suggest. On the other hand Hong Kong is closer to the United States in terms of uncertainty avoidance, masculinity, internal control and specificity, which suggests there has been a degree of culture shift as a result of Western influence. Hong Kong remains an essentially Chinese culture but one with a much more individualistic, risk-taking and non-deterministic nature than that of mainland China.

Table 10.4 Cultural comparison of the USA, China and Hong Kong

	Mainland China	Hong Kong	United States
Hofstede (1980)			
Power distance	20	15	38
Uncertainty avoidance	1	49	43
Individualism	23	37	1
Masculinity	54	18	15
Trompenaars (1993)			
Achievement	32	20	2
Universalism	39	38	7
Internal control	19	8	7
Specificity	34	16	17
Affectivity	41	38	20

Source: Adapted from Hofstede (1980) and Trompenaars (1993).

Organisational behaviour and national culture

This section briefly explores the interaction of culture with many of the prime areas of interest in organisational behaviour (OB) which have been covered in this text. It examines the cultural-specific nature of many of the theories in OB and criticises their essential ethnocentrism.

Convergence or divergence?

The assumption of cultural convergence dominated business, organisational and management studies up to and including the 1960s. The convergence hypothesis argues that *management is a universal phenomenon and that 'good practice' which usually emanated from the USA or Europe, could and should be applied throughout the world.* Theodore Levitt (1983) argued that national cultures were converging, with the result that culture was becoming an unimportant variable for business to consider. However, in recent decades, and especially since the 1980s as we have seen, considerable attention has been paid to cultural differences between nations. There is a growing acceptance that 'good' managerial practices may be those which best fit and are in keeping with a particular culture. Differences between cultures have been increasingly recognised, with the result that the divergence hypothesis is now given considerable credence. Supranational organisations like the European Union, which were founded on the convergence belief, have had to recognise significant national differences.

Culture and individual behaviour

One of the most challenging issues in OB is the extent to which national culture influences individual behaviour and, as a result of this, whether behaviour needs to be modified when faced with a different culture. National cultures influence most aspects of individual behaviour including the cognitive framework through which we view people of other countries. People who have been predominantly influenced by their own culture, and who have had little or no exposure to cultures of other countries, may tend towards a more ethnocentric or parochial view, whereby all contacts with other cultures are seen through the eyes of an individual's own culture and are judged accordingly. This can lead to a very narrow view of the world, in which other cultures may be considered negatively. This may influence behaviour and lead to a perceptual bias on the part of the individual.

In practice there may be very different cognitive styles in different cultures. For example, a study by Abramson *et al.* (1993) showed clear differences between Canadian and Japanese cognitive styles: the Canadians looked for quick decisions and had little interest in building relationships whereas the Japanese favoured relationship building and did not like being rushed into making a decision; the problems of negotiating in this context are clear. This finding can be related back to Hofstede's work where the individualism index for Canada is much higher than that of Japan (*see* Table 10.3). The Japanese approach to decision making is described by Min Chen (1995), who suggests that they use the processes of *nemawashi* and *ringi seido* for decision making. Nemawashi literally refers to dealing with the roots of trees but reflects *the process of informally sounding out employees' ideas about a proposed policy or action, often under the cloak of anonymity*. Ringi Seido is more formalised, in that *a proposal originating in one part of the organisation is circulated around the organisation for others to make comments; the final decision on the proposal will be taken by senior managers after they have viewed all the feedback.* The purpose of both methods is to eliminate dissension when the proposal is carried out. It reflects the more communal approach that is found in Japanese culture, reflected in the practice of Quality Circles.

With the development of multinational activity involving more crosscultural contact, there is a need for individuals to develop a more 'global' mindset, where issues are considered from a wider perspective than from a traditional ethnocentric position. The challenge in international companies is to move managers from an ethnocentric to a global mindset.

There are many problems inherent in measuring determinants of individual behaviour, such as personality, across cultures. The effectiveness of personality testing may be diminished in cultures where there is no familiarity with such tests (Lonner, 1990). Jackson (1993) and Cronbach (1990) further support the argument that the value of intelligence tests and personality profiles may be limited, according to the cultural context in which they are applied: they can be discriminatory if not designed for that culture.

Another area where culture could influence individual behaviour is in the field of perception. Adler (1997) shows that there is likely to be a high level of selective perception between different cultures and countries, especially if the individual has an ethnocentric view. Selective perception can, in turn, lead to perceptual stereotyping, *the tendency to group or pigeon-hole people according to a single or limited number of apparently dominant characteristics*. All too often the dominant characteristic is nationality. This has the potential to affect relations between managers of different nationalities and cultures when they have to work together. Hoecklin (1995) describes a situation where a group of British and Italian managers were brought together for a joint project in a chemical company. Their mutual perceptions of each other are illustrated in Table 10.5.

In the situation described by Hoecklin, one can see that there is the potential for misunderstanding, confusion and even resentment if the respective managers carry their mutual perceptions into their dealings with one another. However, Hoecklin explains that the company took time to explore these perceptual differences with the combined group in order to establish a clear way of working together. Ultimately their project was successful. This case highlights the critical role of communication when dealing with perceptual bias and stereotyping. It is only through communicating effectively with people from other cultures that these cultural stereotypes can be managed. The mini-case study presented in Figure 10.3 illustrates the need to consider communication in intercultural activities.

Culture and motivation

There has been considerable debate as to the validity in a crosscultural context of some of the motivation theories described in Chapter 3. Adler (1997: 166) argues that 'American motivation theories, although too often assumed to reflect universal values, have failed to provide consistently useful explanations for behaviour outside the United States'.

Table 10.5 Mutual perceptions of British and Italian managers

British of the Italians	Italians of the British
■ excessively flexible	■ obsessed with rules/procedures
■ entrepreneurial	■ inflexible
■ creative	■ good planners
■ people orientated	■ formal
■ emotional	■ avoid confrontation
■ undisciplined	■ disciplined
■ not very time conscious	■ hide emotions
■ unable to meet deadlines	

Source: Based on Hoecklin (1995).

Malaysia is a very pluralistic society, with over half the population being Muslim Malays, over a quarter Chinese and substantial minorities of Indians and other groups. There are distinctive subcultures within the Malaysian culture. It is a collectivist society where social harmony is very important and influences individual behaviour as well as relations in the community and in organisations. Therefore, the organisational approach is very much towards collective decision making and consensus.

The right form of communication is crucial for the visitor to Malaysia. One of the first issues is how to address people. In Hofstede's survey (see Table 10.3), Malaysia ranked highest on power distance so it is important to assess the rank or status of an individual and adjust one's approach. Professional or honorific titles are important to individuals so these must be respected.

King (1998) identifies some situations which a Westerner from a highly individualistic culture might encounter. People in individualistic cultures are quite comfortable engaging in open debate about an issue (possibly a proposed business contract) and might stress their sides of an argument forcibly. This tendency towards openness in discussion may not be greeted with universal acclaim in Malaysia where social harmony is important and where compromise is preferred to confrontation. The Malaysian will go to great lengths in order to save an individual from 'losing face'. A low-key approach which spares the feelings of others would be productive for the Westerner.

In terms of non-verbal communication, the smile can mean many things in Malaysia. A smile and a nod may suggest that the person respects your opinion but does not necessarily mean that the person agrees with it. A smile can also signify embarrassment or even annoyance, especially when a person is being put in a situation where there is the possibility of losing face. Silences are also perfectly acceptable in Malaysia as they are seen as a sign of politeness in that an individual is reflecting on a comment made before answering. Westerners may find problems with this.

It is important for people from one culture to respect another culture in which they find themselves. They should certainly not take the ethnocentric view – expecting the foreigners to respond as people would in their own home country.

Fig 10.3 Mini-case: verbal and non-verbal communication in Malaysia

Hofstede (1980), in his analysis of different cultures, identified the culture of the United States as being one of high individualism, high masculinity and low power distance and having a low need to avoid uncertainty. A more collectivist culture, such as is found in China, would have a very different profile, which makes some of the assumptions around which motivational theories were built less relevant. For example, Maslow's (1943) model of motivational needs has been questioned by many writers such as Onedo (1991) who, when studying motivation in Papua New Guinea, found that security needs were ranked as more important than autonomy needs. Similar inconsistencies were found in countries having a high need for uncertainty avoidance, such as Japan and Greece. Nevis (1983), in his study of the People's Republic of China, found that security needs (linked to loyalty to the nation) were the overriding motivational need and that self-actualisation, which is the highest level of need in Maslow's model, was considered of little significance. As might be expected, the need to belong (to family and/or community) was found to be a more powerful driving force, often more important than seeking to meet basic physiological needs. This reflects the more collectivist view held in China at that time, although it has been pointed out that China has changed considerably since the Cultural Revolution, when the study was carried out, and that there may have been some culture shift in China in the 1990s which could lead to more individualism.

Herzberg's (1968) model of motivation has an equally uncomfortable evaluation when exposed to crosscultural studies. Hines (1973) tested the model in New Zealand and found that some of the concerns that acted as hygiene factors in Herzberg's analysis, such as supervision, were seen as motivators in the sample studied. Adler (1997) suggests that the motivator/hygiene model seems to vary according to the culture in which it is tested and so the universality of the model must be in doubt.

McClelland's needs theory (considering the relative needs for achievement, power and affiliation) (McClellend and Burnham, 1976) does fare a little better in a crosscultural context, although Hofstede (1984) suggests that the concept of achievement is a Western one. The model seems to be especially applicable in countries having low uncertainty avoidance and high masculinity, although the actual need to achieve may be lower in some cultures than others, especially in less individualistic ones.

Vroom's (1964) expectancy theory assumes that individuals are rational decision makers who will choose between alternatives on the basis of which course of action is likely to give them most advantage. The theory seems to work best in cultures where there is an emphasis on 'internal attribution', where the individual feels he or she has the ability to influence the environment. This appears to be most applicable in cultures which exhibit Trompenaars' concept of 'inner direction' and in cultures with high individualism. However, it is likely to be much less effective in collectivist cultures where individuals have an external locus of control and where maintaining harmony between the individual and the organisation is of paramount concern.

Culture and leadership

The issue of leadership and leadership styles are important to international managers when they are operating in a different country. Increasingly, prospective international managers are encouraged to undertake courses of study which seek to improve their cultural awareness. One of the most important factors will be that of power distance. The French manager is used to significant power distance when dealing with employees and so, more autocratic styles of leadership are tolerated in a French cultural context (Barsoux and Lawrence, 1990). There are very clear lines of hierarchy between the leader and subordinates and it is unlikely that these will be circumvented. Contrast this with the American manager who is probably used to low power distance, has easier accessibility to subordinates and probably deals with people at all levels of the hierarchy on first-name terms. Clearly the more democratic leadership style adopted by American managers may cause confusion if applied in a French context where people are used to more formality and authoritarian leadership styles. Effective leaders in an international context need to adapt to the constraints and expectations of the particular culture in which they are operating, otherwise there is always the danger of conflict through misinterpretation. The early years of Eurodisney in Paris were hampered by such conflicts between an American management and an essentially French workforce and it was only when a French chief executive officer was appointed that matters improved.

Culture and structure

With the increase in internationalisation that is taking place in the latter part of the twentieth century, the issue of organisational structure is becoming increasingly important when companies seek to develop by expanding overseas. Some of the most significant work in this regard has been undertaken by Hofstede (1984, 1991) who has looked at bureaucracy from a cultural perspective. Given the nature of bureaucracy, the two elements of Hofstede's model which appear most relevant are power distance and uncertainty avoidance. Hofstede has built his models of bureaucracy around these, as can be seen in Figure 10.4.

The most traditional model of bureaucracy is referred to as 'full bureaucracy', which has its roots in Hofstede's dimensions of high power distance and high uncertainty avoidance. An organisation characterised by this model is dominated by rules and regulations (which remove uncertainty) and has a strong hierarchical system with clear power distances between individuals at different levels. It is characterised by vertical top-down communication, conveyed by formal means. An alternative model is 'marketplace bureaucracy', which relates to cultures with low power distance and low uncertainty avoidance. There is greater flexibility in this model than there is in the full bureaucracy with more willingness to bypass hierarchy and fewer rules. An organisation characterised by this sort of bureaucracy would have little difficulty moving towards a more flexible type of organisation, such as a matrix or flexible firm (*see* Chapter 7). The two hybrid models are 'personal bureaucracy', characterised by high power distance but low uncertainty avoidance (which

Power distance (PD) / Uncertainty avoidance (UA)	Low	High
Low	Low UA, low PD **Marketplace bureaucracy** *e.g. UK, Scandinavia*	High UA, low PD **Workflow bureaucracy** *e.g. Israel, Germany*
High	Low UA, high PD **Personal bureaucracy** *e.g. Hong Kong, India*	High UA, high PD **Full bureaucracy** *e.g. Belgium, France*

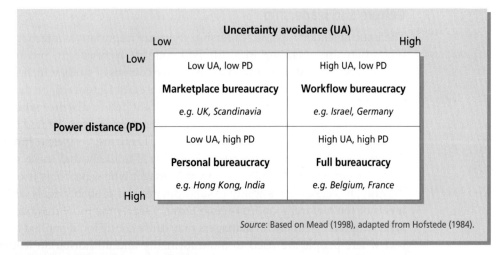

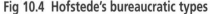

Source: Based on Mead (1998), adapted from Hofstede (1984).

Fig 10.4 Hofstede's bureaucratic types

Hofstede links to the Chinese family model) and 'workflow bureaucracy', which is suited to cultures with high uncertainty avoidance and lower power distance. The latter may resemble a professional organisation in which there are experts who are readily accessible, but which is still driven by tight rules and procedures.

One of the criticisms of bureaucratic models of organisational structure is that they are slow to react to changes in their environment because of rigidity in their communications and the inflexibility of their rules and regulations. Recent shifts have been towards organisational structures that can respond more quickly to their changing environment, such as matrix structures or the modern flexible organisations with their core and periphery workers (*see* Chapter 7). From a cultural perspective, it would appear that the types of cultures most likely to adapt to these changes are those with a low power distance and low uncertainty avoidance. These newer structures are likely to operate more easily in the USA, the UK and Scandinavian countries, for example.

Change in eastern Europe

Each of the eastern European countries has a distinctive economic and social history. Before the Second World War (pre 1939), Hungary maintained close ties with Germany and Romania had close ties with France. Russia, however, had been far more isolated since the revolution of 1917. After the war (post 1945), Russian influence extended across eastern Europe, forming a massive economic trading bloc. Industry was dominated by large, state-controlled conglomerates that produced a vast range of industrial and consumer goods to targets set by the state and which were inefficient by Western standards. There were substantial imports and exports between bloc countries and competition, as we know it, was largely absent. Private enterprise was allowed but only took place on a very small scale and was closely regulated.

After around forty years of existence, the Soviet bloc began to disintegrate in the late 1980s. This was a mostly peaceful transformation and what is interesting about it to organisation theorists is the truly revolutionary nature of the forces for change that had an effect in such a short time. In the new order, organisations, many of which were in monopoly situations before, were faced with sudden falls in revenues as guaranteed markets and government subsidies were dismantled. Managers of the large conglomerates were left to their own devices as state control was rolled back. A further high-impact change was that these organisations had to start competing in capitalist markets which operated according to different 'rules' and values. Organisations that were relatively inefficient, by capitalist standards, had to cope with a profit-driven focus.

Due to the recent nature of events in eastern Europe it is too early to be firm about issues of organisation structure. We can, however, note some issues that were typical of those facing these conglomerates and which would have implications for design of structure. The following points are taken from Pearce and Branyiczki (1993):

1 Because of the dominance of state control, employees and managers looked upwards for instructions and guidance.
2 Faced with such mould-breaking changes it was the people working in them not the organisations themselves that were faced with attitudinal and behavioural change. New roles in areas like marketing or financial management had to be learned.
3 Existing roles like procurement and manufacturing had to be upgraded to approach the sophistication of Western levels.
4 Employees had to cope with unlearning attitudes and behaviours that had sustained them in a state-controlled conglomerate but which would not help a smaller private organisation operating in free markets.
5 New attitudes and behaviours had to be implanted, for example, greater openness to feedback and willingness to contribute to change, from other managers in the organisation and from the marketplace.
6 Organisations needed to implement new control and reporting structures and people unused to managerial positions had to face up to tough decision-making responsibilities.

The implications of these general observations for structure differ between countries. The differences arise as there are wide divergences of approach to management in eastern Europe. For example, on Hofstede's individual–collective dimension of culture, managers from Poland, Hungary and Slovenia would tend towards individualism whereas managers from the Czech Republic would be relatively more collectivist. A study of Czech and British managers revealed some differences in their views of themselves and others (Pavlica and Thorpe, 1998). British managers tended to emphasise the need for continual development of work skills and saw the manager as a communicator among a diverse set of people. In contrast, Czech managers did not put much value on staff development and de-emphasised the needs of others at work. They saw subordinates as incompetent or lazy and held the view that the manager is a dominant male (*see* Table 10.6).

The rough but informative contrast presented in Table 10.6 suggests that different culture-driven managerial 'types' may well invoke different organisation structures, given their contrasting beliefs and assumptions about the people working in those structures. It also serves to remind us that, although structure can impede the progress and performance of an organisation, a good structure will be unable to overcome unhelpful attitudes endemic in an entire, or part of a, workforce.

Table 10.6 Contrasting attitudes of British and Czech managers

British managers	Czech managers
■ See employees as part of a flexible labour force who need communication and interaction	■ See employees as incompetent or lazy
■ Stress personal and interpersonal skills	■ Stress individual personal qualities
■ See manager as social communicator	■ See manager as dominant and superior male
■ Have concern about staff development	■ Underestimate the needs of others, neglect staff development

Source: Based on Pavlica and Thorpe (1998).

South Korean *chaebol*

South Korea had one of the highest economic growth rates in the world during the 1980s and early 1990s, although this success story faltered in the late 1990s. At the centre of the Korean economy lie large conglomerates called *chaebol*. These are groups of large companies that operate in diversified business areas such as car manufacture, shipbuilding, consumer electronics and textile production. Examples include Daewoo, Hyundai and Samsung. It is of value to understand something about the organisations that powered such consistent economic growth and their key characteristics are summarised below (Milliman, Kim and von Glinow, 1993).

Most *chaebol* are tightly controlled by one or two families. This leads to firm control over decision making and promotion to management positions is strictly on family connections. In comparison with other countries like Japan and the USA, there is less professional management at the top of a *chaebol* hierarchy. In part because of close family control, *chaebol* have not exercised as much social responsibility or distributed their earnings (profits) as much as large organisations in other countries have done.

A large majority of South Koreans identify closely with the values of Confucianism. This creates very strong identification with the family unit, and the idea of 'family collectivism' affects all aspects of business organisation. There is a very strong identification with the work group and attempts to sustain group harmony. Employees are expected to show respect to the employer. Confucian values that put women subservient to men affect group operation and working conditions for women. Age and seniority are respected highly and absolute loyalty between subordinates and their boss is endemic. Executives expect to be obeyed without question. These societal values have led to the presence of four main employee groups:

- core employees based around the owners;
- permanent managers and technical staff;
- temporary staff;
- women who usually occupy clerical or assembly-type jobs.

Asian societies such as Korea and Japan embody the concept of face which is achieved when tasks and obligations are met. Losing face is a serious issue for individuals and this means that Koreans are highly motivated by group factors. These characteristics of Korean society combine to bring about highly vertically differentiated organisational structures which rely on top-down decision making (Milliman *et al.*, 1993).

By the late 1990s, a corporate financial crisis in South Korea was blamed partly on the *chaebol*, which had borrowed too heavily to support industrial expansion (Burton, 1998). The South Korean government also accused the *chaebol* of blocking financial reforms by refusing to restructure their way out of the crisis. It is interesting to speculate on the extent to which the extensively hierarchical nature of the *chaebol* had, over a period of years, contributed to the corporate crisis.

Change, conflict and communication

We have already seen in this chapter how the changes brought on by internationalisation and globalisation have led to greater emphasis being given to national cultural issues. The danger with such changes is that if cultural factors are not addressed, there will be the potential for conflict. If one looks back at the case of the Italian and British managers, referred to earlier in the chapter, one can see that there was the potential for conflict in the project they were undertaking if the cultural issues had not been addressed. We have also seen how communication is critical at individual and organisational levels to avoid cultural stereotyping and the negative effects of culture shock. These issues are highlighted in the mini-case presented in Figure 10.5.

A study conducted by Barnes *et al.* (1997) questioned executives from a number of Western firms who had undertaken strategic alliances with Russian partners. Many of these had experienced culture clashes which in some cases had led to the alliances or joint ventures breaking down where incompatible cultures had caused conflict, despite the great potential offered to expand into new markets or to exploit abundant raw materials at low cost. Some of the key cultural problems that arose from the survey were an emphasis on hierarchy, the importance of national pride, *blat* (*see* below), the value of mutual protection and the lack of organisational loyalty.

The emphasis on hierarchy was a leftover from the previous economic and political structures which reinforced the relatively high level of power distance in Russia. There was a need to please people in authority positions. Given the emphasis on hierarchy, knowledge and information were seen as levers of power. Withholding of information was a source of power in the organisation, a situation which contrasted with Western practice where people are more used to sharing information throughout the organisation. This lack of openness was a means of avoiding conflict with superiors but meant that negotiations and discussions were difficult.

The importance of national pride should not be underestimated in Russia. Jones (1998) points out that there is a cultural inheritance in Russia that regards foreign investment and alliances with suspicion and often hostility. Western organisations have to be careful to avoid offending Russian pride, and certainly will not progress far if they imply superiority in one matter or another.

Blat is the process of giving favours to others based on private, often family, links. It is a mixture of nepotism and *guanxi* which is found in China. Many business agreements or activities will only succeed because of *blat*. Although networking also occurs in the West, most business dealings are based on a more open procedure, so the process of *blat* causes confusion and misunderstanding for Western businessmen or women when dealing with Russians.

The value of mutual protection reflects the perceived need to protect each other and reinforces the need for trust to be developed. Trust is developed through personal contacts over a longer time span than may be usual in the West. This reflects the more collective society in Russia, as compared with the individualism of the West. There is a preference for working with groups and connections rather than alone. The mutual protection afforded may relate to business or personal activities but can also be linked to corruption and crime.

The lack of organisational loyalty is difficult for some Western or Asian managers to comprehend. It stems from the old output planning system, in which there were few rewards for commitment and effort. Workers did not see themselves as part of the organisation and certainly did not trust their managers, and these attitudes have persisted.

It can be seen that some of the solutions to cultural problems with Russian strategic alliances or joint ventures lie in the areas of building good personal relations, learning to work with the hierarchical system, avoiding an ethnocentric perspective on Russia and developing organisational loyalty. These may not solve all the business problems, but may help avoid cultural conflict.

Source: Based on Barnes *et al.* (1997).

Fig 10.5 Doing business in Russia

Managerial implications

Many implications for managers involved in working overseas or in other crosscultural contact have been identified throughout this chapter. The prime implications include the following.

1. An awareness of cultural characteristics can help prepare a manager for visits overseas or for working in international management teams. This may reduce cultural shock and improve interpersonal relations with those with whom they deal.
2. Managers should be aware of cultural stereotyping and the effect this may have on relations with overseas partners, customers or suppliers.

3 Managers should be aware of effective verbal and non-verbal communication when working in different cultures.

4 Managers should consider obtaining appropriate training in crosscultural management prior to commencement of an overseas posting or engaging in crossnational negotiation.

5 Caution should be exercised when attempting to apply organisational behaviour theories which originate in one culture (most often Anglo-American) to individuals, groups or organisations in other cultures.

6 Certain management structures, such as bureaucracy, may work better in some cultures than in others, so international managers should take culture into account when planning structural changes to the organisation.

Summary of main points

The main points made in this chapter are:

- national cultures may influence all manner of management activity and leadership styles in different countries;
- a number of key dimensions of culture have been identified by researchers in the field which serve to identify significant and measurable differences between national cultures;
- when first encountering a new culture, foreigners may experience a form of 'shock';
- cultures are always evolving, a process referred to as culture shift;
- national culture impacts on perceptual stereotyping;
- many theories covered in this book and in OB generally are ethnocentric and are often less applicable to non-Western cultures than they are to those from which they derive;
- the need for effective communication when seeking to collaborate with people in different cultures.

Conclusions

This chapter illustrates that there is a danger in looking at organisations from a purely national, or ethnocentric, perspective. This is because organisational behaviours that are thought to be exhibited in one culture may not be commonplace in another. Prescriptions for 'how to manage' developed in the USA or in the UK or

Europe will not be universally applicable. With the trend towards internationalisation and globalisation seeming ever stronger, these issues will become increasingly important for managers and workers in organisations who will have growing contact with people from other cultures and countries.

QUESTIONS

1 Identify the aspects of culture shock which you experienced on your last visit abroad. How would you propose to cope with these on a further visit?

2 Given the perceptions of British and Italian managers identified by Hoecklin (*see* Table 10.5), what problems might have ensued if the two groups had not sought to identify cultural differences before the beginning of the project?

3 Identify some typical cultural stereotypes and explore why they might have arisen and how valid they are.

4 Using Laurent's analysis, examine the differences between managers in France and in the UK.

5 A German company is planning a joint venture with either a Belgian company or a Greek company. You are asked to advise the company on the potential for any cultural differences between these two prospective partners and the German parent. It is suggested that you make use of Hofstede's analysis.

6 What advice would you give to a manager about to work on a joint venture in Russia?

REFERENCES

Abramson, N., Lane, H., Nagai, H. A. and Takagi, H. (1993) 'Comparison of Canadian and Japanese cognitive styles: Implications for management interaction', *Journal of International Business Studies*, No. 3, pp 575–87.

Adler, N. (1997) *Organisational Behaviour*, 3rd edn. Cincinnati, OH: South-Western College Publishing.

Barnes, J, Crook, M., Koyabaeva, T. and Stafford, E. (1997) 'Why our Russian alliances fail', *Long-Range Planning*, 30(4), pp 540–9.

Barsoux, J.-L. and Lawrence, P. (1990) *Management in France*. London: Cassell.

Bond, M. and Hofstede, G. (1988) 'Confucius and economic growth: New trends in culture's consequences', *Organisational Dynamics*, 16(4), pp 4–21.

Chinese Culture Connection Group (1987) 'Culture, contingency and capitalism in the cross-national study of organisations', *Journal of Cross-Cultural Psychology*, 18(2), pp 143–64.

Cronbach, L. (1990) *Essentials of Psychological Testing*. New York: Harper-Collins.

Gatley, S., Lessem, R . and Altman, Y. (1996) *Comparative Management: A Transcultural Odyssey*. Maidenhead: McGraw-Hill.

Hampden-Turner, C. and Trompenaars, F. (1993) *The Seven Cultures of Capitalism: Value Systems For Creating Wealth in the United States, Britain, Japan, Germany, France, Sweden and the Netherlands*. New York: Doubleday.

Hampden-Turner, C. and Trompenaars, F. (1997) *Masking the Infinite Game: How East Asian Values are Transforming Business Practices*. Capstone.

Herzberg, F. (1968) 'One more time: How do you motivate employees?', *Harvard Business Review*, Vol. 46, pp 53–62.

Hines, G. (1973) 'Cross-cultural differences in two-factor theory', *Journal of Applied Psychology*, 58(5), pp 375–7.

Hoecklin, L. (1995) *Managing Cultural Differences: Strategies For Competitive Advantage*. The Economist Intelligence Unit, London: Addison-Wesley.

Hofstede, G. (1980) *Culture's Consequences: International Differences in Work-Related Values*. Beverly Hills, CA: Sage.

Hofstede, G. (1984) *Culture's Consequences: International Differences in Work-Related Values*, abridged edn. Beverly Hills: Sage.

Hofstede, G. (1991) *Cultures and Organisations: Software of the Mind*. Maidenhead: McGraw-Hill.

Jackson, T. (1993) *Organisational Behaviour in International Management*. Oxford: Butterworth-Heinemann.

Jones, A. (1998) 'Assessing the Obstacles to FDI in Russia', Paper presented at CREEB conference, 1998.

King, V. (1998) *A Simple Guide to Malaysia*. Folkestone: Global Books.

Kluckhohn, F. and Strodtbeck, F. (1961) *Variations in Value Orientations*. New York: Peterson.

Kroeber, A. and Kluckhohn, C. (1985) *Culture: A Critical Review of Concepts and Definitions*. New York: Random House.

Laurent, A. (1983) 'The cultural diversity of Western conceptions of management', *International Studies of Management and Organisation*, Vol. 13, pp 75–96.

Laurent, A., Adler, N. and Campbell, N. C. (1989) 'In search of appropriate methodology: From outside the People's Republic of China looking in', *Journal of International Business Studies*, Spring, pp 61–74.

Levitt, T. (1983) 'The globalisation of markets', *Harvard Business Review*, May–June.

Lonner, W. (1990) 'An overview of cross-cultural testing and assessment' in Brislin, R. (ed.) *Applied Cross-Cultural Psychology*. Newbury Park, CA: Sage.

McClelland, D. C. and Burnham, D. H. (1976) 'Power is the great motivation', *Harvard Business Review*, Vol. 4, March–April, pp 99–112.

Maslow, A. H. (1943) 'A theory of human motivation', *Psychological Review*, 50(4), pp 370–96.

Mead, M. (ed.) (1951) *Cultural Patterns and Technical Change*. Paris: UNESCO.

Mead, R. (1998) *International Management*, 2nd edn. Oxford: Blackwell Business.

Milliman J. F., Kim, Y.-M. and von Glinow, M. A. (1993) 'Hierarchical advancement in Korean chaebols: A model and research agenda', *Human Resource Management Review*, 3(4), pp 293–320.

Min Chen (1995) *Asian Management Systems*. London: Thunderbird/Routledge.

Murdoch, G. P. (1945) 'The common denominator of cultures' in Linton, R. (ed.) *The Science of Man in the World Crisis*. New York: Columbia University Press, pp 123–42.

Nevis, E. (1983) 'Cultural assumptions and productivity: the United States and China', *Sloan Management Review*, Spring, pp 17–29.

Onedo, A. (1991) 'The motivation and need satisfaction of Papua New Guinea managers', *Asia-Pacific Journal of Management*, Vol. 8, pp 121–9.

Pavlica, K. and Thorpe, R. (1998) 'Managers' perceptions of the identity: A comparative study between the Czech Republic and Britain', *British Journal of Management*, 9(2), 133–49.

Pearce, J. L. and Branyiczki, I. (1993) 'Revolutionising bureaucracies: Managing change in Hungarian state owned bureaucracies', *Journal of Organisational Change Management*, Vol. 2, pp 53–64.

Ronen, S. and Shenkar, O. (1985) 'Clustering countries on attitudinal dimensions: a review and synthesis', *Academy of Management Review*, July, pp 445–54.

Torbiorn, I. (1982) *Living Abroad: Personal Adjustment and Personnel Policy in an Overseas Setting*. New York: Wiley.

Trompenaars, F. (1993) *Riding the Waves of Culture*. London: Nicholas Brealey.

Vroom, V. H. (1964) *Work and Motivation*. New York: Wiley.

FURTHER READING

Adler, N. (1997) *Organisational Behaviour*, 3rd edn. Cincinnati, OH: South-Western College.

Gatley, S., Lessem, R. and Altem, Y. (1996) *Comparative Management: A Transcultural Odyssey*. Maidenhead: McGraw-Hill.

Jackson, T. (ed.) (1995) *Cross-Cultural Management*. Oxford: Butterworth-Heinemann.

Joynt, P. and Warner, M. (1996) *Managing Across Cultures*. London: International Thomson Business Press.

Mead, R. (1998) *International Management*, 2nd edn. Oxford: Blackwell Business.

CASE STUDIES

This final section of the book contains three case studies, each of which draws upon and reinforces many of the principles, concepts and understandings covered in this book. The reader is invited to analyse critically the scenarios portrayed in an attempt to 'get beneath the surface' of human behaviour in organisations.

The grid below illustrates the applicability of each case to each chapter. Whereas each case can illustrate many aspects of organisational behaviour it might, equally, be used to focus on one area, such as motivation or teamwork.

Chapter:	2: Individual	3: Motivation	4: Groups and teams	5: Organisational theory	6: Leadership	7: Structure	8: Power and politics	9: Organisational culture	10: Global
Case 1 ■ Motivated teams: An intercultural case	*	***	***	**	**	**	*	**	***
Case 2 ■ Organisational change: multiskilling in the health-care sector	**	**	***	**	**	**	***	***	
Case 3 ■ Competition, structure and change: Rank Xerox	*	*	*	**	*	***	**	**	**

Key

*	some relevance
**	significant relevance
***	major relevance/focus

CASE 1

Motivated teams: an intercultural case

This case explores how a simple yet sound belief in people takes shape on the ground. The context is a Swedish-owned heavy truck assembly plant which is located in France. The case outlines the novel processes of work organisation employed in this complex multicultural setting. Although both are European countries, Sweden and France are, in key cultural terms, polar opposites, and this case represents an example of a successful intercultural business activity.

The case looks at the nature of, and differences between, Swedish and French national cultures in an attempt to account for the success of the plant and the skill of its managers in overcoming potential cultural pitfalls and discusses the contributions made by each culture to the success story. It is based on a series of semi-structured interviews with senior management from both France and Sweden and observation of activities on the ground.

Scania, Angers (SAN)

The plant is owned by Scania, a Swedish multinational organisation primarily concerned with the manufacture and marketing of trucks and buses. Trucks for the French, Italian and Iberian markets are assembled in Angers in a converted combine harvester plant covering 50 000 square metres. Since it opened in 1992, output has increased significantly and production plans suggest that a continued rapid increase is likely for some time to come. The plant produced 7 trucks a day in January 1994, increasing to 30 trucks a day in 1995. In 1998 it produced around 40 trucks a day.

There are just four levels of hierarchy in the plant including the managing director and seven senior managers. All but one of the senior managers are Swedish, serving fourteen French cluster managers and their teams.

Management philosophy and the cluster team

A teamwork approach filters through all aspects of organisational life. Involvement in teamwork is not an option. Thorough socialisation and continuous training and coaching is the norm. One of the few French senior managers, Bernard Proux (human resources management), spells out, in a style characteristic of his culture, SAN's philosophy (*see* Figure C1.1). Teamwork is central to this function as a prime mechanism for the development of skills and as an important source of personal motivation.

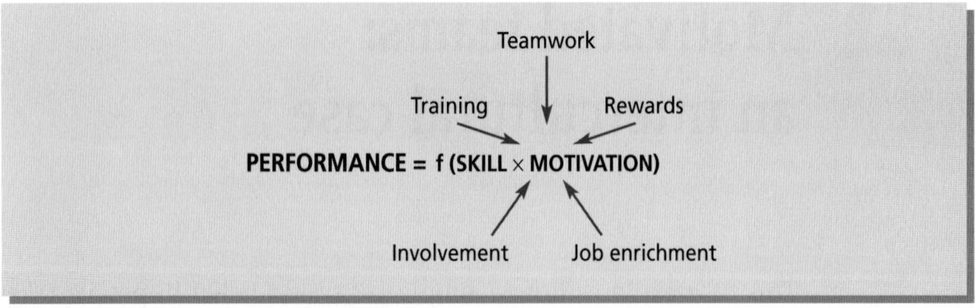

Fig C1.1 Teamwork and the performance equation at Scania, Angers

Teamwork and employee involvement in plant-wide work processes and in the broader aspects of company activity are regarded by management as a vital motivational tool and, therefore, as a performance-enhancing investment. Training is viewed similarly.

The work cluster

The basic form of work organisation focuses on the cluster team. Clusters are described by the managing director as '*a technical unit of production made up of workers who assemble components forming a semi-finished or manufactured product*'. They are a team which is responsible for a discrete element of production. For example, one cluster is responsible for assembling the cab, others for construction of the engines and the brake systems; another manages delivery of the trucks.

The focus in the plant is the cluster organisation. All managers are clear in their determination to insist that all activities have to be justified in terms of their value added to the cluster operation. The cluster manager has overall responsibility for the team of between 20 and 25 employees. No further formal hierarchy exists in each cluster although each comprises people with differing skill levels and experience. In general terms each cluster member is multiskilled (French = polyvalent) and enjoys a long period of initial training and induction, partly in the cluster, before becoming fully operative. This multiskilling allows greater flexibility and frequent job rotation possibilities in a teamwork setting. With a supervisory or managerial ratio of less than 1 : 20, clearly cluster teams are largely self-directed.

Although the precise responsibilities of each team vary depending on the array of tasks they are expected to perform, they are all responsible for:

- budget (including salary negotiations);
- materials handling;
- quality inspection;
- recruitment;
- components subassembly and line assembly;

- daily preventative maintenance;
- cleaning up.

SAN does not employ quality inspectors. Clusters are charged with the goal of achieving continual improvement.

As can be judged from the above list, financial decisions are largely decentralised, giving cluster managers considerable personal responsibility. Costs, the financial manager argues, 'are controlled at the point where they are generated'. Hence the senior finance manager, rather like his quality and human resources colleagues, actively serves the clusters in helping them fulfil their duties and responsibilities.

It is seen as a prime responsibility of management to develop employee motivation by giving the necessary leadership and support to teams. Hence cluster managers will establish the team targets, in conjunction with group members. Teams then enjoy a degree of flexibility in how they achieve these targets.

All new employees undergo a lengthy period of training which has two prime objectives. First, workers learn the skills required to operate effectively in one of the clusters. Second, they are educated in the way of working, the operational philosophies, team ethos and management styles.

Have cluster teams proven successful?

Productivity in the plant has exceeded targets established in Sweden. Quality levels have shown continuous improvements since the plant opened in 1992 and are already comparable to those in Sweden and Holland. Output has increased significantly since 1992 and is set to continue to rise. Absenteeism is very low by any standards, at about 2.5 per cent. This compares favourably with the French norm for manufacturing and assembly plants of over 5 per cent. Safety standards are continually measured and all targets have been met or surpassed. The working environment appears relaxed and relatively stress free. Staff at all levels appear to be well motivated.

Teamwork at all levels and in all relationships

Teamwork is a central tenet of the management philosophy and culture of SAN. Teams operate at all levels, in all departments, at all functions and between each level, department and function. Hence there are small, often temporary, teams in each cluster, such as a small subassembly group. The cluster itself is managed and operates as a team. Workers feel a sense of belonging to the whole cluster and, as quality standards suggest, take a pride in their cluster's output. In this participative environment teams contribute to defining and developing action plans at one level and are actively encouraged to show an interest and become involved in company-wide activities and concerns.

The management at SAN has attempted to identify the requirements for successful corporate teamwork. This is viewed in the context of the customer–supplier or the intergroup relationship. The responsibilities of each are made clear during initial, and often subsequent, training and are also continually reinforced by management and peer group feedback. The receiver or customer is required to:

- define their needs clearly;
- justify those needs in respect to the objectives of SAN;
- ensure that meeting the request will contribute added value;
- give feedback to the sender or supplier.

The sender or supplier is expected to:

- know and, if necessary help define, the customer's requirements;
- manage priorities in the interests of overall SAN objectives;
- seek consensus in the exchange of information;
- keep their clients informed of progress;
- supply a service which meets reliability, quality, time limit and cost standards.

Customer–supplier relationships are encouraged at the interface between cluster teams. Hence the boundary is characterised by co-operation and the adoption of a supportive attitude. This helps to ensure a seamless handover of each cluster's finished product.

All managerial personnel in SAN employ a consultancy-style approach with those colleagues who avail themselves of their service. In fact SAN management argues that the customer–supplier relationship extends to all contact of an interpersonal, interdepartmental and external nature and that customer satisfaction is the prime objective.

Individualism and trust

No one is required to clock in or out of the plant and no formal check is kept of people's timekeeping. Obviously expectations are set and these are, with very few exceptions, met. Yet this individual responsibility is monitored, more often than not, by peers within a team framework.

Each cluster member has an annual review with the cluster manager. This serves two major purposes: to negotiate salary on the basis of experience and skills level and to ascertain training and development needs. During the interview managers establish the record of the worker over the past year from both a quantitative and qualitative perspective. Objectives for the forthcoming year are also set during the review. The assessors are given training to assure fairness, consistency and objectivity in this process. This method of pay negotiation rejects uniformity and aims to ensure that merit awards are based on each individual's results. Collective bargaining does not exist. Hence the cluster manager has a considerably wider brief than the more traditional supervisor in an assembly plant.

The performance interview is also viewed as a management tool to help forge a strong, company-orientated, organisational culture. Bernard Proux (HRM) argues,

'The interview . . . represents a concern for fairness in that everyone who takes part must be aware of any difference between the company's system of values and their own'. It is clear that certain attitudes are required of all employees. As a senior manager suggests, 'No one must be able to say "that is not my concern, I am not responsible for that".'

Consequences of cultural differences and similarities

Scania is a Swedish company and the managing director and the majority of its senior management team are Swedish and exclusively male. Almost the entire workforce, including junior managers and cluster managers in the plant at Angers, are French. Table C1.1 shows the rankings of Sweden and France on Hofstede's (1980) four indices (*see* Chapter 10).

On three of the four indices in Table C1.1 there is a significant difference in score and ranking between French and Swedish cultures. Ironically on the fourth, the individualism index, the two countries are identical. It is this index, individualism–collectivism, which is most successful in predicting the possibility of successful teamwork. The index implies that teamwork, or collective concern and endeavour, does not come easily to either culture. It may account for the degree of individualism still apparent in this teamwork context and, hence, the compromises that exist. For example, salary negotiations, performance payments and training needs analyses are all conducted at the level of the individual. The ranking of other countries on the individualism index includes: USA 1st, Great Britain 3rd, Germany 15th, Japan 22nd.

Table C1.1 Swedish and French rankings on Hofstede's cultural indices

Cultural variable	France*	Sweden*
Power Distance Index (1st = large hierarchial power distance)	15	47
Uncertainty Index (1st = strong containment of uncertainty by creating order)	10	49
Masculinity–Femininity Index (1st = highly masculine culture)	35	53
Individualism Index (1st = individualism is culturally strong and collectivism is weak)	10=	10=

Note: Ranking, out of 53 countries.
Source: Hofstede (1984).

The two most significant differences between the countries are on the power distance and uncertainty avoidance indices. On these two important criteria Sweden and France represent extremes in a European context (*see* Figure C1.2). French culture supports the maintenance of large power distances between different groups, both in the workplace and in society in general. Swedish culture seeks to minimise such differences and embraces a strong commitment to egalitarianism. Just a handful of countries in Hofstede's sample score lower on the power distance index than Sweden. The Swedish belief in people is legendary. A number of historical, social and economic factors conspire to encourage this enviable trait. Associated with the egalitarian norm is the norm of accessibility; Swedish managers tend to be highly approachable and open. In fact it is argued that in Sweden managers have to have a good reason for not seeing an employee!

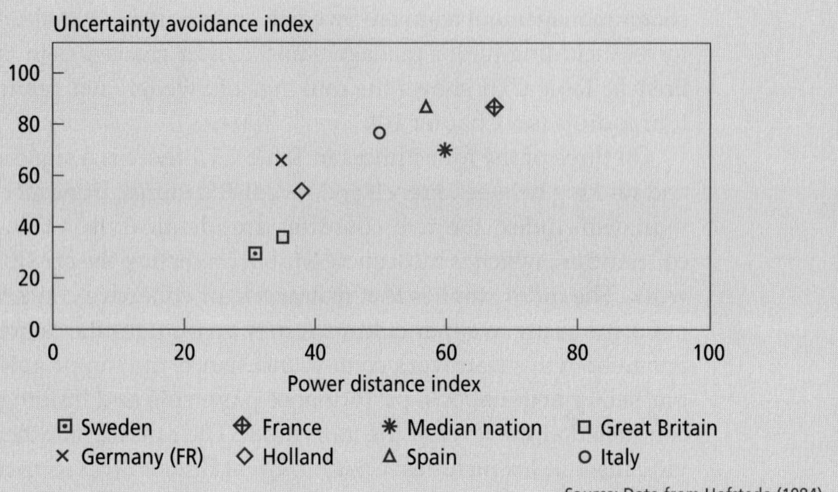

Source: Data from Hofstede (1984).

Fig C1.2 France and Sweden: cultural comparisons on power distance and uncertainty avoidance

The difference between the two cultures is significant in relation to their desire to avoid uncertainty and associated anxiety. The French have a firm desire to avoid uncertainty, which usually means that rules and bureaucratic procedures dominate. This contrasts sharply with the more laid-back Swedish character. The Swedish are very tolerant of uncertainty in the workplace and are less concerned to organise, regiment or tie down everything and everyone.

The work environment in France is likely to be characterised by authoritarian, top-down management styles, hierarchies and formal procedures. Theory and logic are stressed. By contrast the Swedish are likely to be more informal and easy-going. Lateral communications and networks are more important, as is consensus building.

Evidence abounds in SAN that managers not only think about culture, but also think culturally, both at the level of the organisation and on a national level. This is evidenced not least by the choice of the word cluster, which was chosen intentionally as a culturally neutral term in France. The Swedish management team are acutely aware of the potential tensions that exist and the natural tendencies of many employees to revert to traditional attitudes and behaviours.

Some problems, possibly of cultural origin, do occur. These problems highlight some issues with which managers in intercultural settings have to cope. They stress the need for continuous cultural vigilance. Managers take steps to prevent any mass retreat of people to their cultural homeland. The Swedes at this plant are experienced international managers; thinking culturally is second nature.

Conclusion

This case has outlined the prime features of a management philosophy being acted out in a crosscultural setting. Managers at Angers are not complacent; they are fully aware of the continued efforts needed on everyone's part to ensure that the cluster philosophy takes root and grows. They are also aware that teamwork does not come naturally to culture-bound individuals from either France or Sweden. However, their unswerving belief in people transcends all differences and difficulties and promises continued success for this and other plants adopting similar principles.

The management style and methods of work organisation outlined in this case represent a significant compromise with French cultural norms. They have been required to make more sacrifices than their Swedish masters. One may suggest that the Swedish are guilty of cultural imperialism; however, their actions have created a paradoxical scenario, that of imposed empowerment. They have required French workers and management to conform, by and large, to their culture-laden management philosophy. It appears that they have been vindicated by success.

REFERENCES

Barsoux, J. L. and Lawrence, P. (1991) 'In search of intelligence', *Journal of General Management*, 17(2), Winter.

Hofstede, G. (1980) *Culture's Consequences: International Differences in Work-Related Values*. Beverly Hills, CA: Sage.

Hofstede, G. (1994) *Cultures and Organisations*. New York: Harper Collins.

QUESTIONS

These questions should help to relate this case study to the materials presented in the book. This case study covers considerable OB territory and these are but a few potential questions of value.

Motivation and groupwork

1 With reference to Chapter 3 of this book, which covers motivation, attempt to explain why employees at Scania, Angers, are or appear to be well motivated.

2 Why might a group-based work process achieve greater productivity and lower staff turnover than more traditional production line operations?

Organisation and leadership theory

3 How do the management philosophy and practices at SAN differ from those suggested by Henri Fayol (*see* Chapter 6)? How is control achieved in this plant?

4 How would you describe the prevailing leadership style employed in the plant? How have situational variables influenced that style?

National culture

5 What 'contribution' does each culture make to the apparent success of this plant; that is, what are both the Swedish and French qualities which contribute to this success? Do you consider this to be a case of cultural imperialism?

6 A few problems have been encountered at SAN which may, in part at least, be cultural in origin. For each of the problems identified below, attempt to suggest a plausible cultural explanation.

(a) *Problem*: the French, who make up the vast majority of the workforce, are not natural team players. Perhaps the real problem is that neither are the Swedish!

(b) *Problem*: cluster managers oppose a reduction in their 'territory' as new clusters are added.

(c) *Problem*: rapid expansion has led to a reduction in socialisation training: a few workers have experienced problems fitting in.

(d) *Problem*: (i) there is some confusion among employees over hierarchical grade and pay and status differentials; e.g. two specialist engineers are unwilling to work alongside as 'equals' with the half-dozen technicians; and (ii) workers in clusters are not hierarchically graded and have no official title. Many want to be given a title with an associated grade like their colleagues in other French firms.

(e) *Problem*: some French managers tend to put a great deal of effort into paperwork which is of marginal value. As one Swedish manager put it, 'they produce lots of stuff which is done very well but serves little purpose [whereas] we do practical things but don't necessarily do it well'.

CASE 2

Organisational change: multiskilling in the health-care sector

Introduction

This case study looks at an attempt to induce multiskilled, ward-based teams of support workers in a medium-sized NHS Trust hospital in the UK. Although only directly involving about 250 people in an organisation employing over 2700 staff, the change represented part of a wider, strategic transformation in the NHS with its focus on human resource issues. The driving force is an attempt to realise continual improvement in quality and value for money.

This case is relevant to those studying organisational behaviour, human resources management (HRM) and organisational change: analysis is reinforced by an understanding of motivation, group and teamwork, organisational theory, power and politics, leadership, change management, organisational structure and culture and various HRM issues.

The Microcontext: A medium-sized NHS Trust hospital

The case is set in a NHS Trust which provides a full range of acute and midwifery services to a population of about a quarter of a million people. The Trust's income exceeded £55 million a year in 1997–98 and it employed over 2700 personnel (about 1600 full-time equivalents). Of its employees, 62 per cent work part-time; over 80 per cent of all personnel are female. Forty-three per cent of staff have over five years' tenure. The staff turnover rate is rather low compared with that of many urban hospitals and is declining. Absenteeism, for sickness, currently stands at 3.6 per cent which compares favourably with many hospitals and other public and private sector organisations. Absenteeism among ancillary staff, those largely affected by this change, is about double the hospital average.

Much of the change in this and many other hospital Trusts focuses on human resource issues. Of particular interest is the debate concerning junior doctors' hours (resulting from the Calman Report, 1993). Reductions in their hours of work and a demand from management for greater flexibility has demanded the transfer of appropriate duties between various professional and ancillary groups. Furthermore, an intrinsic and stated element of the Trust's business plan is to 'produce a multiskilled workforce'. Although not always conceived as such internally, the attempt to change to 'generic working' at the care assistant/ancillary levels was part of a much larger manpower planning policy, itself part of a wider organisational development process.

The Site Services Directorate was responsible for the implementation of generic working. This directorate broadly comprised two major areas of responsibility, one of which is Hotel Services, in which domestic and portering staff are located, managed by a Deputy Director of Site Services, David Stacey. Hotel Services and, more specifically, its Director, Anita Patel, 'owned' the change and defined and refined it during residential management team meetings and subsequent attempts at implementation.

Change content: The generic worker concept

This section outlines the nature of, and rationale for, the attempted introduction of the generic worker concept. It was one of seven key changes outlined in the Trust's business plan, 1997–98, which included significant reductions in waiting times, compliance with government initiatives and the introduction of major new information systems. The relevant objective states: 'To introduce teams of generic hotel service assistants at ward level so as to improve flexibility and responsiveness to patient needs by combining the role of porters, domestics and catering staff'. The change aimed to devolve all portering and domestic staff to ward level. They would be multiskilled and consequently able to undertake a full range of domestic and portering roles, including cleaning, transporting patients, moving equipment and serving food.

The change involved all porters and domestic staff. In total these roles account for 151 whole time equivalent (WTE) staff, of which porters account for 44 WTE and domestics (cleaners and 'ward hostesses') 107 WTE. As many domestics work part-time the total headcount involved in this change was approximately 250 people. Some of the porters are assigned to specific departments or directorates, such as X-ray, but most are 'located' in a central pool and respond to demand for their services. There are three porter-managers. The domestics are divided into teams under a supervisor and are designated an area of the hospital to clean and in which to conduct other duties, such as serving food and assisting nursing ancillary staff. They can, on occasions, respond to domestic emergencies and alter their normal routines. All these staff are employed in the Site Services Directorate, and report to managers in that unit, a fact which often creates frustration elsewhere in the Trust. This is particularly so in the case of ward managers, who have little control over the activities of the domestics.

The management philosophy underpinning the generic worker concept is a familiar one. A multiskilled, flexible workforce is thought to facilitate operational planning and enhance both the efficiency and effectiveness of service provision. The assumption is that employees benefit from the resultant job enrichment and co-operative teamwork; cost savings are there for the making via enhanced efficiency, and patient care is improved.

The scope and scale of change

It was proposed that all domestic and portering staff were to be based at ward level rather than, as at present, in a central 'pool'. Most would require additional training to undertake food serving, cleaning and portering roles. Staff would then undertake a wider array of tasks and be required to embrace flexibility and teamwork. All existing formal status and pay differentials between members of Hotel Services, with the exception of management, would be removed. As a consequence of generic working, many staff were to be upgraded and all would receive a basic pay rise representing 2 per cent for porters and 8 per cent for domestic staff. Performance pay was to be based upon attendance. Overtime and weekend working would be carefully monitored in an attempt to reduce costs. Some staff would be required to change their shift pattern and the total hours they work in any one week. The change directly involved about 250 people and included taking on an extra 35 000 hours' work a year previously allocated to nursing assistants.

Talk on the ground

It was thought that the successful implementation of generic working would bring many potential benefits from a managerial perspective. Almost without exception, managers stressed its positive features. The Finance Director, Steve Tompson, argued that successful implementation would help to 'provide good value for money' and 'make cost savings'. It would ensure, for the time being at least, competitiveness with external commercial players. The single grade and pay spine, which would apply to all 250 generic workers, would reduce status differentials and simplify the highly complex bonus schemes that had evolved. From an operational point of view it would bring enormous benefits of flexibility and would simplify work scheduling. Managers argued that it would serve to 'even out' the workload for porters and improve efficiency by avoiding 'waiting for action time' and 'wasted journeys' and other 'duplication of effort'. Therefore, not inconsiderable cost savings could be realised. It would formalise control, especially over porters who are 'difficult to track down'. It might, for example, stop porters using their 'pull' over nursing staff. The HRM Director, Phil Davies, felt it would improve worker motivation as porters would 'feel part of a team' and 'be included if chocolates were given out or nights out were planned'. They would 'take a pride in their work' and be 'recognised at ward level'. One manager responsible for its implementation suggested that generic working is 'going to make it very clear what I am providing and to whom', so facilitating the provision of an up-to-date service-level agreement and competitive tendering.

Deborah Lion, the manager responsible for establishing the pilot scheme which ran on one large ward, argued that 'The domestics think it's a great idea', 'Women will go for it to see the men cleaning' and 'They really enjoy the varied workload'. Others attempted to explain why staff were positive about change with comments like, 'Now they don't know what other duties they're going to be doing and they really enjoy that so their job satisfaction has gone up'. However, managers were far less effusive when asked to identify likely reasons for, or sources of, resistance to the implementation of generic working. Issues focused on likely demarcation concerns at the interface between Hotel Services and other groups such as nurses and, within Hotel Services, between porters, cleaners and domestic staff.

Friction

Ms Lion, concerned over the issue of 'ownership' of tasks, commented that 'Basically if anything needs moving we move it, if it needs feeding we feed it, if it needs cleaning we clean it and that's what generic working is about'. Needless to say, tensions arose at the interface between Hotel Services and nursing. The manager responsible for establishing the pilot scheme which ran on one large ward, commented, 'We looked at taking over the service of dispensing food to patients'. Hotel Services believed their staff to be better trained to carry out food dispensing duties. Some ancillary nurses were reported to have 'felt very threatened' and responded with, 'Oh well, that's your job now, I'm not doing it'. Part of the change process involved the reallocation of duties, such as food dispensing to patients, from nursing to domestic staff. This amounted to 37 500 hours' work a year and a movement of resources from clinical directorates to the Site Services Directorate.

Personal involvement in the change process was heightened for those managers at the interface between domestic staff and supervisors, as success in introducing generic working would have eased many of the tensions involved in operating the current system. Scheduling tasks would be simplified as would pay and bonus schemes. A number of managers and staff expressed a strong desire to reduce the level of uncertainty they faced under the current system. One porter commented at the commencement of the project, 'At present the porters are understaffed and suffering from low morale with a poor sickness record. The portering service can best be described as "fire-fighting" – there is no service-level agreement in place against which to measure performance.'

One of the major contentious issues which arose during the pilot scheme was that of work rotas. A Directorate General Manager (DGM), Frank Terry, from a clinical directorate, commented: 'The goalposts have been endlessly moving . . . it changes with the wind. One minute they were going to be doing XYZ and then the next minute it was ABC.' Another argued, 'They were told that all the rotas would be displayed [and] there would be no names attached – they would apply for which rota they wanted. When they saw the rotas they reckoned that they were all fixed for specific people.' Another manager, 'close' to the change, argued, 'The rotas are so difficult to follow [so that] when they went up on the board it was "Where's my job? I haven't got a job" so if they vote no it's because we've changed hours and changed rotas.'

Implementation: structure and process

A small management team comprising the Director of Site Services, her deputy and the managers of domestic and portering staff fine-tuned, 'customised' and planned the implementation of this initiative. The manager specifically responsible for the day-to-day implementation of the concept, the head of the domestic staff, Deborah Lion, was a junior/middle manager, at the fourth tier of management. She played a relatively minor role in the decision to introduce the initiative in the hospital or in its inclusion in the Trust's business plan. A subordinate of hers, a first-line supervisory manager responsible for portering staff, Bert Creaton, managed the daily 'portering' operations in a pilot scheme on the Deelman Ward. The small management team were enthusiastic and dedicated. They articulated the benefits of the scheme with conviction.

A pilot scheme ran for a year, during which time issues were raised and discussed, changes were made and plans were altered. The pilot involved about 12 domestic and portering staff. The original aim was to appoint a team leader who would allocate duties as they arose. This was thought to have created unnecessary sources of uncertainty and a system of management allocation of tasks on a more permanent basis was soon adopted in the pilot. Those managing the change did not gather the whole workforce together to discuss the changes. Such a process, they felt, would prove difficult. Instead they believed that if it could be made to work well on the pilot scheme then the good news would spread and people would come on board. Thus they relied quite heavily on the undoubted power of the informal communication process as opposed to numerous team briefings. They also utilised the staff noticeboard to display rotas and other important developments.

Teething problems

Many of the porters, almost exclusively male, quite openly expressed their unwillingness to undertake cleaning duties, which some thought were 'women's work'. This gender issue raised its head in many consultations between porters and managers and was a frequent topic of conversation between porters. One manager commented, 'Porters believe the girls are going to be running off doing portering duties all the time and they are going to spend all their time cleaning . . . and they've got these views from the union'. Other 'demarcation' issues were also brought to the fore during the pilot scheme. A group of domestics, known as 'ward hostesses', enjoyed a somewhat privileged position among their colleagues whose work focused almost exclusively on cleaning, involving little or no contact with patients or clinical personnel. The subgroups comprising the generic worker role were often referred to as 'tribes' by managers from across the hospital. One Hotel Services manager said, 'We arranged awareness sessions with nursing staff but no one turned up to them'. One manager, expressing a certain powerlessness, summarised the nature of the problems: 'It is about boundaries between groups. We have nurses, PAMs (professionals allied to medicine), physios, doctors – all these groups, and making them work in teams is impossible.'

Deborah Lion suggested domestic staff believe that this is simply 'a cost improvement exercise'. The trade union, UNISON, openly and persistently recorded its disapproval of the extent of the proposed changes. It strongly opposed generic working from the outset and advised all its members not to facilitate its implementation. Such a change would fundamentally alter the terms and conditions of employees and would necessitate contractual changes and facilitate local determination of pay and conditions. This would contravene national union policy and UNISON's clear position regarding local bargaining. Employees had not yet accepted the principle, let alone the practice, of local determination of pay and conditions.

In a series of meetings between managers in Hotel Services and UNISON representatives debate was often hostile and, allegedly, personal. Few minutes were kept of meetings and little signed and agreed documentation exists. A senior manager suggested that, 'If you're going to negotiate with the unions you get your shopping basket and work out what it's going to cost you' and 'There were few minutes [which] were not jointly signed and nobody had worked out the costs beforehand and [as a consequence] they were always arguing about things which one side thought was agreed three meetings ago'.

Tension before the ballot

The pilot scheme ended in December 1998 and was followed by a union ballot aimed at ascertaining the staff's position *vis-à-vis* acceptance or otherwise of generic working. On the eve of the vote, managers in Hotel Services felt it would be a close-run affair. They were unsure of staff collective opinion and nervous about the outcome. A number of managers argued that the union vote was couched in terms that were tantamount to a vote of confidence in the union itself. One suggested that, 'In a way they were being asked to vote "do you support your union?": management one side, union the other.' Emotional investment in the change process was not inconsiderable, as Deborah Lion's comment suggests: 'I'll be very sorry if they do throw it out . . . I'll be quite upset from their point of view. It'll be easier to manage and the main reason we are here is for the patients.'

The vote

Union members in Hotel Services were eligible to vote in the UNISON-organised ballot on the single issue of generic working. Twelve staff voted in favour of change, 150 against, the rest abstained. The scale of rejection left little doubt concerning the level of resistance to the change initiative. In the face of this clear rejection the planned change as proposed by management will not now be implemented in the foreseeable future. This result does not indicate, however, that the change scenario was a failure; judgement of that nature would depend on one's perspective.

It is appropriate to conclude this case with the HRM Director's thought-provoking comment: 'Inside the hospital is a little cottage with roses hanging over the door, where everything is just as it has always been, and it's all quite happy. Nothing is touching that. Nothing is touching the real heart of what is going on.'

QUESTIONS

Motivation

1 How might the motivation of staff have been affected during the change process? Use any theoretical frameworks presented in Chapter 3 to support your answer.

Team/group work

2 What are the merits and drawbacks of the kind of multiskilled teams which this change would have helped to encourage?

Organisational structure

3 What does this case tell us about contemporary management thinking regarding organisational structures and individual roles?

Change, culture and politics

4 What sources of power, or power bases, are threatened by this change?

5 How important is the context of change to the implementation process? How did the context in this case influence the final outcome of the change process?

6 What was the scale of this change for those staff involved in the process; that is, those who were expected to become generic workers?

7 Why was this change initiative, which held so much promise and generated such enthusiasm from management, so emphatically rejected by staff? Drawing on the work of Morgan (1986, 1996) as noted in Chapter 5, together with the materials presented in Chapters 6, 8 and 9, attempt to give (a) a managerial, (b) a cultural, and (c) a political explanation for the 'failure' of this initiative.

CASE 3

Competition, structure and change: Rank Xerox

Introduction

Rank Xerox is a joint venture between Xerox Corporation and Rank Organisation PLC. The dominant parent, Xerox Corporation, manufactures, markets and services a range of products and services worldwide. It is a multinational organisation employing about 90 000 staff in over 130 countries. Its turnover is around $US20 billion.

Rank Xerox employs about 18 000 people in over 80 countries primarily in Europe (including Russia and the ex-Soviet republics), Africa and the Middle East. Its turnover is around £4 billion (about $US6.3 billion). Its pre-tax profits are about 16 per cent of turnover.

Development and decline

During the 1960s Xerox experienced rapid growth, partly from the introduction of the 914, the first plain paper copier. Significant competition did not exist until the early 1970s at which time turnover and profits were soaring. In the early 1970s IBM and Kodak entered the copier business and targeted the same lucrative segments of the market created by Xerox. Xerox, wrongly as it turned out, believed these two multinational giants to be their main competitive threat. During this time a number of Japanese manufacturers entered the market with low-volume machines that delivered reliable, high-quality outputs. Xerox had virtually ignored this 'bottom end of the market'. The Japanese manufacturers' solid performance, however, enabled them to build a stronghold and, later, to move up-market to compete in Xerox's main markets.

Also in the 1970s, Xerox was accused by the Federal Trade Commission in the USA of illegally monopolising the office copier business. As a result of negotiations Xerox opened about 1700 patents, adjusted its pricing policy and patent licensing restrictions and gave technical assistance to organisations which wanted to use its patents.

Over less than a decade in the late 1970s to early 1980s Xerox's market share fell from a peak of about 85 per cent to less than 40 per cent. In the early 1980s Xerox's fortunes dropped most significantly. Its return on assets fell from a healthy 19 per cent in 1980 to below 10 per cent by 1982. Over 20 000 jobs were lost worldwide. Levels of management were removed in micro-restructuring activities. In 1983 wages were frozen. New product development slowed.

Embracing quality

As is often the case when faced with such difficulties the organisation searched for alternative approaches. In 1982 the then CEO explored Total Quality Management (TQM) and confronted his organisation with the stark reality that its Japanese competitors were better on cost and quality. Additionally, the Japanese had greater expectations of their products, their customers and their organisation than Americans appeared to hold. The Xerox Quality Policy was established in 1983. Figure C3.1 illustrates this policy, which still exists today.

Rank Xerox is a Quality Company.

- Quality is the basic business principle for Rank Xerox.
- Quality means providing our external and internal customers with innovative products and services that fully satisfy their requirements.
- Quality improvement is the job of every Rank Xerox employee.

Fig C3.1 Rank Xerox quality policy

The Leadership through Quality strategy, developed in the mid-1980s, suggested that implementation of strategy relied on work process improvements and empowered employees to add value for the customer. Diagrammatically at least, human resources were viewed as the essential feature of successful operations. Figure C3.2 illustrates this.

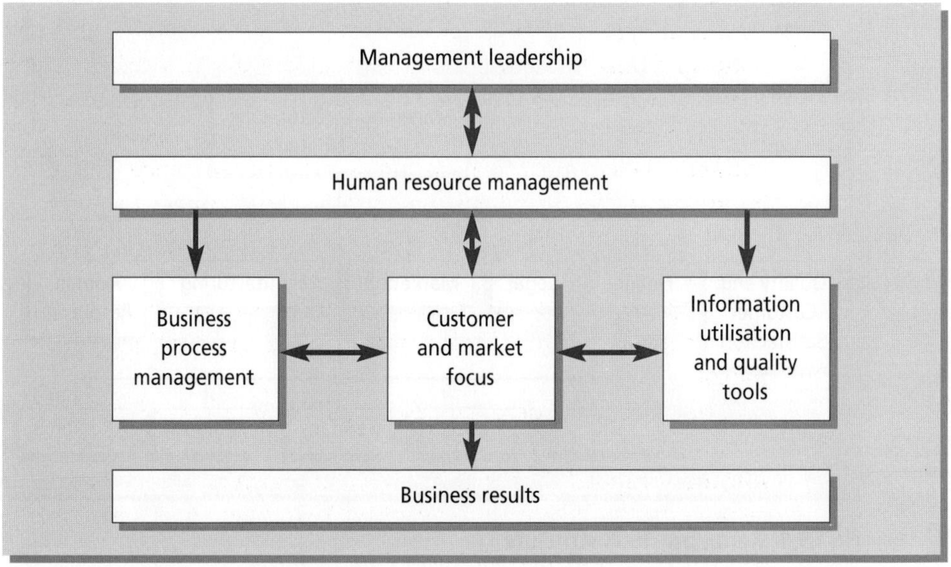

Fig C3.2 The Xerox management model: Xerox 2000 Leadership through Quality

Xerox measures its progress fastidiously. This measurement includes considerable evaluation of HR issues, such as development, reward and recognition, work environment measures, recruitment performance and so forth. It recognises the interconnectivity of all aspects of the business, HR, business processes, customers, service developments and the like.

Structural change

Until the late 1980s Rank Xerox had a hierarchical centralised structure comprising seven functions. Figure C3.3 illustrates this structure. Hence, finance, marketing, manufacturing and human resources, for example, were centralised functions which supported regional activities in five designated areas (namely, UK, France, Germany, Region A – the rest of Western Europe, Region B – Africa, Eastern Europe and ex-Soviet Asia). The regional departments were responsible for customer operations.

In 1988 the Xerox Corporation and with it Rank Xerox restructured in an attempt to become more responsive to its customers. It created worldwide business divisions. Product development and marketing responsibilities were assumed by nine worldwide business divisions. These were:

- Office Document Products (ODP)
- Document Production Systems (DPS)
- Printing Systems Division (PSD)
- Office Document Systems (ODS)
- Personal Document Products (PDP)
- Desktop Document Systems (DDS)
- Xerox Business Services (XBS)
- Xerox Engineering Systems (XES)
- Xerox Software (Xsoft)

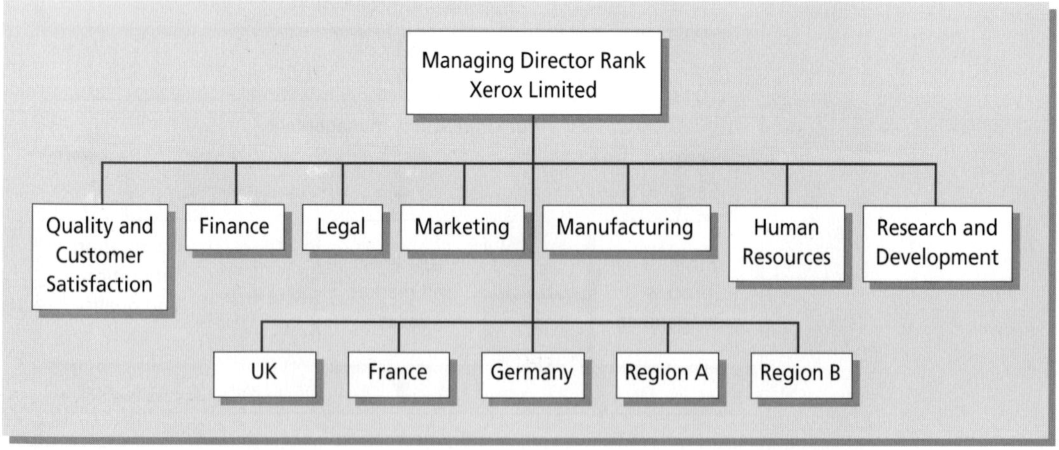

Fig C3.3 Xerox pre-1988 structure

The seven functional areas in Rank Xerox were divided into two groups: HR, finance, legal, and quality and customer satisfaction comprised the Core Enterprise Group (IHQ); and manufacturing, supply chain and R&D responsibilities belonged to the Technology and Business Support Group (TBSG). The head of each business division was to be responsible directly to the Chief Executive Officer (CEO) of the Xerox Corporation. Additionally, each business division would have a representative who would report to the Managing Director (MD) of Rank Xerox.

A matrix was created as Rank Xerox customer operations were divided into what were called Entities. These were UK, France, Germany, Nordic, Central, Southern and International. The Entities were further divided geographically into Customer Business Units (CBUs). In each Entity each business division was represented. These had dual responsibility to the Entity General Manager and to the worldwide business division.

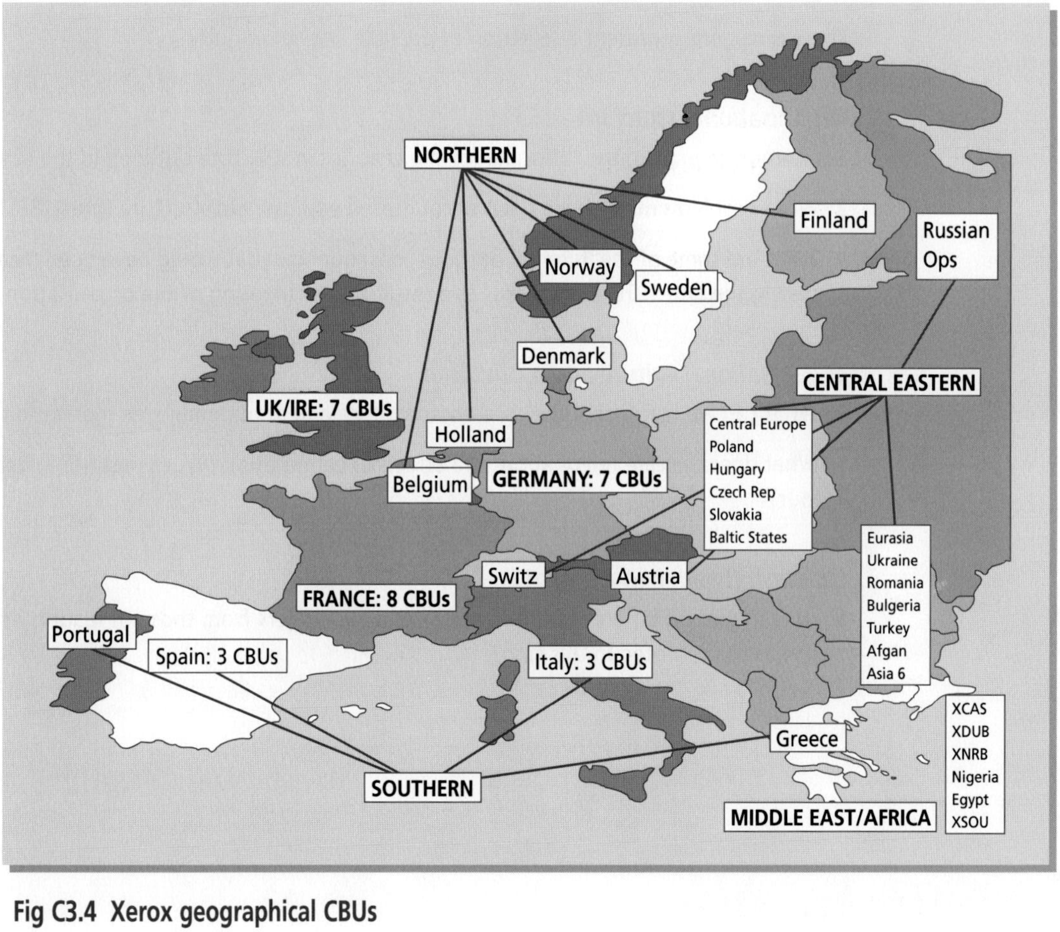

Fig C3.4 Xerox geographical CBUs

A further restructuring took place in 1996. The nine worldwide business divisions were arranged into three worldwide business groups. These are:

- Office Documents Product Group (ODPG)
- Desktop Products Group (DPG)
- Printing Systems Group (PSG)

At the same time the Entities were changed to France, Germany, UK, Northern, Central Eastern, Southern and Middle East and Africa. Figure C3.4 illustrates the geographical territories in Europe.

At the time of writing Rank Xerox is enjoying something of a resurgence in its fortunes.

QUESTIONS

These questions represent a selection of possible lines of enquiry.

Organisational structure

1 Attempt to explain the rationale for the changes in structure outlined in the case.

2 What problems might have been encountered with the old structure (pre 1988)?

3 What are some of the 'human' or social consequences that would have been created during the late 1970s/early 1980s as a result of restructuring of the organisation?

Organisational culture and motivation

4 What can we learn from the case about culture and about employee motivation?

5 What does the case tell us about the effects of competition on organisational behaviour?

Leadership and management

6 How might we differentiate the activities of managers from those of leaders in the scenarios presented in this case?

Index